CURIOSITIES *and* TEXTS

CURIOSITIES
and
TEXTS

The Culture of Collecting
in Early Modern England

MARJORIE SWANN

PENN

UNIVERSITY OF PENNSYLVANIA PRESS

Philadelphia

10 9 8 7 6 5 4 3 2 1

Published by
University of Pennsylvania Press
Philadelphia, Pennsylvania 19104-4011

Library of Congress Cataloging-in-Publication Data
Swann, Marjorie.
    Curiosities and texts : the culture of collecting in early modern England / Marjorie
Swann.
        p.   cm. — (Material texts)
    Includes bibliographical references (p.) and index.
    ISBN 0-8122-3610-6 (acid-free paper)
    1. England—Civilization—17th century. 2. Collectors and collecting—England—
History—17th century. 3. English literature—Early modern, 1500–1700—History and
criticism. 4. Curiosities and wonders—England—History—17th century. 5. Natural
history—England—History—17th century. 6. Antiquarians—England—History—17th
century. I. Title. II. Series.
DA380.S93 2001
942.06—dc21   2001027021

Contents

Introduction

In 1634 the indefatigable traveler Peter Mundy was between voyages, cooling his heels in London. He filled his time at one point by going to Lambeth "to view some rarieties" at the home of the elder John Tradescant. According to Mundy, he spent a "whole day in peruseinge, and that superficially," the enthralling wealth of objects that Tradescant had accumulated, which included

beasts, fowle, fishes, serpents, wormes (reall, although dead and dryed), pretious stones and other Armes, Coines, shells, fethers, etts. of sundrey Nations, Countries, forme, Coullours; also diverse Curiosities in Carvinge, painteinge, etts., as 80 faces carved on a Cherry stone, Pictures to bee seene by a Celinder which otherwise appeare like confused blotts, Medalls of Sondrey sorts, etts. Moreover, a little garden with divers outlandish herbes and flowers, whereof some that I had not seene elswhere but in India, being supplyed by Noblemen, Gentlemen, Sea Commaunders, etts. with such Toyes as they could bringe or procure from other parts.

Mundy concluded his description of Tradescant's collection with the ultimate compliment a seasoned traveler could bestow: "I am almost perswaded a Man might in one daye behold and collecte into one place more Curiosities then hee should see if hee spent all his life in Travell."[1]

Tradescant's "rarieties"—and Mundy's enthusiasm for such a conglomeration of objects—were typical manifestations of the interest in collecting which permeated seventeenth-century English culture. By the 1690s, collecting was an activity of such established social importance that John Evelyn could earnestly suggest that "Diligent and Curious Collectors," including Tradescant, should be commemorated by having medals struck in their honor.[2] The very terms "collection" and "collector" as we now use them were specifically products of late Elizabethan and Stuart England. By 1651 the word "collection," used since the mid-fifteenth century to refer to gathered historical or literary materials, had also come to designate an assemblage of physical things ("scientific specimens, objects of interest, works of art"), while the term "collector," first used in 1582 to refer to a literary compiler, similarly came to refer to an individual "who collects works of art, curiosities, etc."[3]

This expanding range of signification reflected the proliferation of forms of collecting in early modern England. During the Jacobean period, art collecting became a fashionable activity among English aristocrats. Before he died in 1612, Prince Henry had begun to accumulate Italian paintings, statues, and "a cabinet of ten thousand medals, not inferior to most abroad, and far superior to any at home."[4] Likewise, a group of ambitious courtiers—including the earl of Arundel, the duke of Buckingham, the earl of Pembroke, the marquis of Hamilton, and the earl of Somerset—purchased large quantities of foreign art, employing agents on the Continent to procure paintings and statues for their burgeoning collections; Arundel, for example, thus acquired England's first collection of ancient statuary, and by the Civil War he owned 799 paintings. Charles I also avidly followed his brother's lead and collected art. When Rubens visited London in 1629, he stated "that he had never seen so many great paintings in one place as in the galleries of the king and the court nobility"; surveying the same cultural phenomenon in 1651, a more jaundiced observer complained that during Charles's reign, "great summes were squandred away on braveries and vanityes: On old rotten pictures [and] on broken nosed marble[s]."[5]

Lower down the social scale, men in seventeenth-century England assembled "cabinets of curiosities" rather than collections of art. Sir Francis Bacon famously described the scope of such a "cabinet" as "whatsoever the hand of man by exquisite art or engine has made rare in stuff, form or motion; whatsoever singularity, chance, and the shuffle of things hath produced; whatsoever Nature has wrought in things that want life and may be kept."[6] Antique coins, scientific instruments, minerals, medals, rare or unusual zoological specimens, plants, natural and manmade objects from Asia and the Americas, intricate carvings, portraits of important historical figures—the early modern English cabinet of curiosities was an exuberant hodgepodge of "the singular and the anomalous."[7] Whereas initially the word "cabinet" referred to a cupboard with shelves and drawers that held small physical objects, by the seventeenth century the term was used more loosely both to refer to the architectural space that contained the curiosities (whether cupboards, a closet adjoining a bedroom, a summerhouse, or other rooms) and to designate the collection in its entirety; thus in 1671 Evelyn enthusiastically recorded that he had visited the physician Sir Thomas Browne, "whose whole house & Garden [is] a Paradise and Cabinet of rarities."[8]

Browne's home was only one notable example of the "cabinets" that were assembled in early modern England. In 1599 the London house of the politician Walter (later Sir Walter) Cope contained "an apartment, stuffed with queer foreign objects in every corner," including "An African charm made of teeth," a unicorn's tail, a mummified child, a Chinese cap "made out of goosefoots," Queen Elizabeth's seal, "A round horn which had grown on an English woman's forehead," and an "Indian canoe" suspended from the ceiling.[9] John Bargrave, a clergyman who eventually became a canon of Canterbury Cathedral, spent much of the Interregnum traveling on the Continent, during which time he amassed enough curiosities to fill three cabinets. Bargrave's collection included fake antiquities, the mummified finger of a French soldier retrieved from the vaults of a church in Toulouse, a working model of the human eye (which Bargrave tested for accuracy by attending two public dissections at the University of Padua), and a chunk of "jasper stone," subsequently polished, which Bargrave had broken off "the butt end" of an obelisk in Rome.[10] Despite the fact that he himself was not a traveler, the London apothecary James Petiver nevertheless managed to obtain an impressive range of non-European plants, insects, and animals by asking "all *Practitioners* in *Physick, Sea-Surgeons,* or other *Curious Persons* who *Travel* into *Foreign Countries*" to gather specimens for him.[11] Ralph Thoresby, a cloth merchant who lived in Leeds, built a large extension onto his home to accommodate his library and his enormous number of "rarities"; coins and medals were Thoresby's particular specialty, but his collection also contained a wide range of antiquities, zoological and botanical specimens, mathematical instruments, 1,500 portraits, and the hand and arm of the Marquis of Montrose.[12]

Texts also became collectible objects. In sixteenth- and seventeenth-century England, scholars, doctors, lawyers, and clergymen assembled libraries of books related to their work. Such books were tools of an owner's trade, purchased and admired for their use-value: the sixteenth-century mathematician and alchemist John Dee, for example, assembled a famous library in conjunction with his studies in science and the occult.[13] With the ever-increasing interest in collecting which arose during the Renaissance, however, books also became adjuncts of collections of curiosities. Collectors of antiquities and natural history specimens bought books related to their obsession with certain kinds of material objects. This link between books and collections of curiosities meant that the two types of objects were often housed together—the famous library of Sir Robert Cotton, for example, also contained coins, sculptures, medals, precious stones, and a fossilized fish. In such settings, books were still regarded as repositories of knowledge, but as printing made available more and more books, greater attention was paid to the physical qualities of books by the people who accumulated them. During the latter half of the seventeenth century, the appearance of one's books en masse became an integral part of one's image as a virtuoso, that is, a gentleman with cutting-edge interests in natural history and the arts. John Evelyn, who had collected 5,000 books by 1687, helped establish a new English fashion for bindings with paneled sides and gilded spines incorporating a title. After visiting Evelyn and seeing the chic appearance of his library, Samuel Pepys decided he had to make *his* books appear more elegant, too, so in 1666 he sent for the Navy joiner and had him construct the first freestanding glazed bookcases (or "bookpresses") ever seen in England. Pepys then went "to Paul's churchyard to treat with a bookbinder to come and gild the backs of all my books to make them handsome, to stand in my new presses."[14] In all, Pepys collected and displayed about 3,000 volumes in his eleven elegant bookpresses; the entire collection is now preserved at Magdalene College, Cambridge.[15]

Unlike ostensibly private libraries or cabinets of rarities, other seventeenth-century collections served unabashedly commercial or institutional purposes. Like Tradescant's curiosities, which were open to the public for an entry fee of sixpence,[16] Robert Hubert's collection of "Rarities of Nature" became an entrepreneurial venture. The main body of Hubert's rarities, "Collected in thirty years time with a great deal of Pains and Industry," was open to London's paying public "every afternoon." To customers who were "more curious" (and who could afford "some more Charge"), Hubert also offered special exhibits which varied according to the day of the week—on Mondays and Thursdays, for example, one could view additional "things of the Sea," while extra "things of the Land," including "strange Fruits and Excrescents," were displayed on Wednesdays and Saturdays.[17] In 1666 the fledgling Royal Society bought Hubert's collection for the bargain basement price of £100. Although the collection remained open to the public, some members of the Society clearly distinguished between its previous incarnation as private "rarities" and its new status as the "Repository" of the Royal Society. Robert Hooke disdainfully asserted that "the use of such a Collection is not for Divertisement, and Wonder, and Gazing, as 'tis for the most part thought and esteemed, and like Pictures for Children to admire and be pleased with, but for the serious and diligent study of the most able Proficient in Natural Philosophy."[18] For men like Hooke, the collection was a vital tool in the Society's program to reform knowledge: it would serve as the basis of both a complete description of nature rooted in "particulars" and of a new "philosophical language" which would clearly convey the essence of things and concepts.[19] By 1681, swollen with donations from merchants, travelers, and Fellows of the Society, the collection had more than doubled in size. Ironically, as the Repository grew it became more like a typical seventeenth-century cabinet of curiosities: Hubert's original focus on natural objects became diluted in a swirl of manmade items, including weapons, two armored figures fashioned from plants and insects, and "a stone bottle," previously "filled full with Malaga sack, and well stopped, but . . . now empty, though said never to have been opened, and the outside . . . all covered over with a thick mucous coat."[20] From such sticky beginnings would arise the collections of the British Museum in the next century.[21]

*　*　*

The seventeenth-century vogue for collecting—whether the accumulation of art by aristocrats or the acquisition of curiosities by "middling sort" individuals—was one aspect of the brave new world of consumer goods that emerged during the Renaissance. The early modern period in England, historians now recognize, cannot be understood without reference to material culture, "that segment of man's physical environment which is purposely shaped by him according to a culturally dictated plan."[22] Although in 1982 Neil McKendrick, John Brewer, and J. H. Plumb challenged conventional narratives of the development of Western capitalism by locating "the birth of a consumer society" in eighteenth-century England, scholars have increasingly come to find consumer culture originating even earlier.[23] The course of Renaissance history, Lisa Jardine argues, was shaped by acquisitiveness, a new urge to possess desirable commodities that both fueled and was created by an emerging "global mercantilism."[24] Beginning in the fifteenth century, international trade expanded, domestic economies grew and diversified, markets spread, and commodity production increased; as consumer goods thus proliferated in Western Europe, their exchange and possession became "an important source of cultural confusion and innovation."[25] The wealthy sought to acquire spices, textiles, paintings, printed books, tapestries, and jewelry; the humble bought toys, buttons, lace, and knitted stockings. As part of a process that accelerated through the Stuart period, the new patterns of consumption which emerged in early modern England quickly permeated all levels of society: "By the end of the sixteenth century goods that had been deemed rich men's luxuries in 1540 were being made in so many different qualities and at such varied prices that they came within the reach of everyman."[26]

This growing Renaissance preoccupation with physical objects was intertwined with fundamental economic, cultural, social, and psychological changes which culminated in "the seventeenth-century emergence of an ideal self as owner: the individual surrounded by accumulated property and goods."[27] Thus we find in the burgeoning consumer culture of early modern Europe the origins of a recognizably modern form of consciousness. Before the advent of capitalism, C. B. Macpherson has argued, property was understood as a right to revenue based on title to land; by contrast, under the capitalist "possessive market society" that emerged in early modern England, "property comes to be seen as a right in or to material things, or even as the things themselves," and human identity and relationships become dominated by the market.[28] As Richard A. Goldthwaite observes, in the Renaissance, "People entered a realm where possessions become an objectification of self for the first time—a step that was to have enormous implications for the subsequent history of the West."[29]

In acknowledging the importance of physical *things* in shaping early modern history and culture, we thus need to reevaluate the nature of early modern selfhood. Although cultural anthropologists have demonstrated the extent to which individuals and groups construct their identities through the consumption of physical objects,[30] this understanding of objects as a creative medium that can be used to fashion new cultural meanings has had surprisingly little impact on Renaissance studies. New Historicist literary scholarship has catalyzed a rich reconsideration of the processes by which subjectivity was formed in the early modern period, but "in the main we have proceeded as if it were both possible and desirable for subjects to cut themselves off from objects."[31] Recently, however, literary historians have begun to recognize that we cannot adequately assess "Renaissance self-fashioning" without paying attention to the material culture of early modern England, and innovative new scholarship has revealed that physical objects such as clothing, stage props, needlework, and miniature portraits functioned as vital components of the life and literature of sixteenth- and seventeenth-century England.[32] In the chapters that follow, I examine how people in the seventeenth century creatively inhabited their rapidly expanding world of material things. More specifically, I extend our new understanding of the cultural importance of physical objects by analyzing the experiences of *collectors*, individuals who participated in the vogue for collecting which swept early modern England.

Collecting may be defined as a form of consumption characterized by the selection, gathering together, and setting aside of a group of objects.[33] In the past decade, scholarship on early modern collecting practices has undergone a sea change. Previously, historians tended to emphasize the continuities between early modern collections and twentieth-century museums, arguing that "in terms of function, little has changed" in Western collecting practices since the late sixteenth century.[34] Werner Muenster-berger, in analyzing the behavior of collectors from a psychoanalytic per-spective, has likewise argued that Euro-American collecting is fundamen-tally transhistorical in nature, since collectors have always been motivated by the same psychic structure of anxiety: according to Muensterberger, an experience of emotional trauma, usually in childhood, compels an individ-ual to gather objects as surrogates for human love and reassurance, the collection functioning as "a compensatory store of self-assertion."[35] Re-cently, however, scholars in a variety of disciplines have reacted against such evocations of a static tradition of collecting and have instead stressed how collecting practices change over time. Tony Bennett, Carol Duncan, and Alan Wallach have analyzed the collection as a medium for representing and legitimizing different political systems; they examine how the royal art galleries of Renaissance Europe were transformed into public museums in the eighteenth and nineteenth centuries and argue that national museums were intended "to make a new conception of the state visible to the inspec-tion of the citizen by redeploying expropriated royal treasures in a demo-cratic setting."[36] While demonstrating that collections have been used to construct identities in historically variable ways, this teleological narrative of the national museum does little to explain the nonaristocratic forms of collecting which flourished during the sixteenth and seventeenth centuries. Eilean Hooper-Greenhill pays more detailed attention to the variety of collections which arose in the early modern period and at the same time goes even further in positing the historical contingency of collecting. In *Museums and the Shaping of Knowledge*, Hooper-Greenhill presents a series of case studies to argue that the history of the museum cannot be under-stood as a linear trajectory of development. Using Foucault's theory of epistemes (conceptual frameworks that determine structures of knowl-edge), Hooper-Greenhill contends that the collections of different eras are composed according to different epistemological principles. From this van-tage point, she argues, we should recognize that the Medici Palace and early modern curiosity cabinets were informed by the preoccupation with occult correspondences characteristic of the "Renaissance episteme," while the Repository of the Royal Society was, in part, shaped by the "Classical episteme" which aimed to taxonomize reality as a hierarchical series of differentiated objects.[37] Hooper-Greenhill thus helpfully insists upon the historically specific nature of early modern collections; however, her Fou-cauldian emphasis on epistemology and concomitant disregard for the ef-fects of human agency oversimplify the diverse ways in which early modern collections were socially meaningful.

Building upon anthropologist James Clifford's insight that collecting is one of the "crucial processes of Western identity formation,"[38] Susan Pearce's work in museum studies has greatly enhanced our understanding of collecting as a complex material practice. Pearce analyzes collecting as a flexible, dynamic technology of identity which functions "in that obscure zone between cultural ideas of value and the deepest levels of individual personality,"[39] a politically charged cultural form which encompasses both social practice and subjective experience. As Pearce demonstrates, the possessive selfhood fashioned through collecting can be achieved by both individuals and groups. An individual can use a collection as a creative medium through which s/he can construct and project an image of him/herself; similarly, communities can "develop strategies which enable them to bring together the accumulating possibilities of objects and other social structures—like family relationships, notions of surplus and prestige, and religious practices—in order to maintain the social pattern and project it into the future."[40] Although a collection may thus be intended to encode and perpetuate conservative cultural values, collecting can also serve as a practice through which individuals or groups "rethink" themselves and use accumulated objects to "establish alternative ways of seeing themselves that are outside of and contrary to existing definitions."[41] Hence a collection is always steeped in ideology and functions as a site of processes of self-fashioning that may serve either to reinforce or to undermine the dominant categories of the society in which the collection appears.

By analyzing early modern English collectors, I seek to explore how the collection, an ideologically volatile cultural form, was used to construct social selves and modes of subjectivity in seventeenth-century England. Studies of Renaissance collections tend to emphasize continental practices and do not analyze carefully the distinctive features of seventeenth-century English collecting.[42] Although I shall necessarily discuss European collecting in general, I agree with historian Lisa Tiersten that the expressive nature of material culture must be situated "within historically specific political, social, and economic contexts."[43] Collecting in England "took shape lower down the social scale" than elsewhere in Europe, practiced by what Richard Helgerson calls "transitional men," individuals who were "uprooted . . . from familiar associations and local structures" by education, socioeconomic aspirations, and the dislocation of civil war and regicide.[44] Using objects as a creative medium of self-fashioning, collectors like Tradescant and Hubert created distinctive forms of identity because they were both empowered and constrained by the social, political, and cultural conditions peculiar to England in the seventeenth century.[45] My emphasis on the use of material culture by members of "the middling sort" thus allies my project with what Patricia Fumerton calls "new new historicism," an emerging body of scholarship which finds transgressive struggles for social power occurring in "everyday practices and representations."[46]

* * *

What most distinguishes this study from previous scholarship on early modern collecting is its attention to the interrelationships of material and literary culture. I demonstrate that texts—both as physical objects and as vehicles of representation—were vitally important to the negotiation of the meanings of collections and collectors in early modern England, and at the same time, I argue that modes of textuality and authorship were shaped by sixteenth- and seventeenth-century collecting practices. On the surface of a bone spoon from New England, the renowned collector Sir Hans Sloane recorded incidents from the life of the man who had made it:

An Indian spoon made of the breast bone of a pinguin made anno 1702 . . . by Panenau an Indian whose squaw had both her leggs gangreened and rotted of to her knees and was cured by bathing in balsam water made by Winthrop Esq., New England. The method was thus, he ordered two ox bladder to be filled with rare balsamic liquor made warm and the stumps putt into the bladders and tyed above the knees. The bladders with the water was kept constantly bloodwarm and the leggs were perfectly cured in a few days time.[47]

This impulse to textualize collections catalyzed the development of a peculiarly early modern literary genre, the catalogue: indeed, Sloane included the same narrative that he had inscribed on the spoon in the catalogue of his collection. The early modern collection was complexly situated on the emergent border between the private and the public, at once the property of a specific individual or group (and often located within household architectural spaces associated with privacy), yet also requiring a nonproprietary audience to validate the noteworthy status of the collection and its owner. In part to obtain this audience, seventeenth-century collectors tended to display their collections in published catalogues.

Unlike the quantifying enumeration of an inventory, a catalogue offers a self-conscious interpretation of the objects it presents. The entries in Robert Hubert's catalogues, for example, frequently note the exotic provenance of individual items, whether geographical—"A great *Sea Porcupine fish* of the West *India*"—or social—the head of a toucan "did belong to the King of *Spain*."[48] In other entries, Hubert explains how individual objects display his superior skills and knowledge: a "great Sturgeons-head" is "a Rarity hard to be procured, for the bigger the head of the Sturgeon is, the more difficult it is to dry, because it is very fat"; an "extraordinary great Cameleon" prompts Hubert to inform his readers that a chameleon can "change suddenly into divers colours; not according to the colour of the objects that are successively before him (as some affirm) but (as I have often observ'd them while they were sitting on Trees) according to the divers motions of his spirits, in anger, fear, grief, delight, & c."[49] His catalogues thus construct an image of Hubert as a man whose collection embodies, object by object, a monument to his personal mastery of a large and complicated world. Yet apparently that mastery can be augmented and transferred, for Hubert promises that he will further textualize his collection if someone purchases it:

> Besides these above mentioned things, there are Chests and Boxes furnished with many hundreds of Rarities, as several shells, stones, bones, marcasits, mineralls, fruits, Nutts, excrescences, and such like things all different in shapes, and operations, and of divers countries, Their Names and Natures being omitted for to avoid prolixity: But if the owner of this collection of Rarities does sell them to any Noble minded party, he then, God willing, will write at large a more ample declaration to the expressing of each thing in particular, to honour that vertuous person that shall buy them.[50]

For Hubert, the published catalogue stands as the culmination of the process of collecting and secures the identity and status of the owner of the collection, whether he actually creates the collection or simply buys it ready-made.[51]

As a printed book, the catalogue both represents physical objects and yet is also a material artifact itself—an object produced by the collector to demonstrate his proprietary relationship to other objects. Recent studies have pointed out that print as a technology does not have an "ontological status prior to culture," that our apprehension of the "nature" of print is constituted within specific historical contexts.[52] Thus the features of the printed book taken to be intrinsic qualities by scholars like Walter Ong—its "sense of closure," its aura of definitiveness—are now understood as cultural constructs.[53] Seventeenth-century writers were fascinated by the physicality of the printed book and the possible subject positions which one might assume in relation to such a material object. The concept of proprietary authorship—the idea that a writer *owns* the texts he produces—was not firmly established, and as the relationship between texts, identity, and physical objects evolved during the early modern period, there were no clear boundaries between collecting and authorship. As mentioned previously, before the seventeenth century the terms "collection" and "collector" referred to the compilation of texts, and my study demonstrates that the extension of the concept of collecting to the accumulation of other types of artifacts not only encouraged the textualization of collected objects, but also reflexively conferred a new status upon the gathering and display of literary materials. The printed catalogue exemplifies this complicated interplay between identity, textuality, and physical objects. Is the creator of a catalogue an "author" as well as a collector? Is the writer who gathers the texts he has produced within the bounds of a printed book legitimized as an "author" because he is a *collector*?

This productive blurring of categories of material practice also characterizes other textual forms associated with early modern collecting. After providing descriptions of Tradescant's rarities and a "Catalogue" of his plants, the *Musaeum Tradescantianum* concludes with a list of the "Principall Benefactors" to the collection. The 109 names, arranged in order of social rank beginning with "King Charles" and "Queen Mary," include peers, Archbishop Laud, doctors, military officers, merchants, and private citizens.[54] Hubert elaborates upon this model and refers to the rich and famous throughout his descriptions of his "rarities," thus representing his collection as the product of personal exchanges with members of Europe's social, intellectual, and political elites: a grey agate that changes color when submerged in water "was presented to the better adorning of the forementioned curiosities, by worthy Sr. Francis Peters," while a "prickled *Crab* called the *Sea Spyder* . . . was given to the augmenting of these Rarities, by the Learned *Petrus Carefour*, the King of *Denmark*'s Resident in the united *Provinces*."[55] Like the *Musaeum Tradescantianum*, Hubert's catalogue concludes with a hierarchical list of people, "*A Catalogue of the Names of those Great Princes and Persons of Quality, whose love of Virtue, Learning, and of the admirable Works of God in Natural Rarities, has been shewed by their Bountiful adding of something to the encrease of the fore-mentioned Collection*."[56] As he did for the objects presented in the main body of the catalogue, Hubert provides contextualizing accounts of his benefactors: monarchs and nobles are listed with their titles, while individuals who rank below the peerage are briefly described to indicate their social importance. Thus in his published text, Hubert presents himself as a collector of rare men as well as rare physical objects.

The catalogues of Tradescant and Hubert suggest some of the ways in which the collection could be used to create new relationships between material objects, identity, and textuality in early modern England. In their catalogue entries and lists of benefactors, Tradescant and Hubert transform "Great Princes and Persons of Quality" into artifacts they have gathered, assembled, and displayed. Like the visitors' books created by early modern collectors on the Continent,[57] such name-dropping catalogue entries and lists of elite benefactors are designed to exhibit the collector's membership in networks of political, social, and cultural prestige. The published catalogue thus becomes a theater of mastery in which the collector fashions and displays himself as a figure of power who presides over both a group of "rarities" and a community of individuals he has simultaneously assembled; the textualized collection constructs and embodies new social relations, new alignments of people as well as physical objects. It is this representational flexibility of the collection, its capacity to fuse in various ways the identities of objects and people, things and texts, that made it an attractive cultural form in England during a period of great socioeconomic, political, and cultural change.

The chapters which follow analyze in much greater detail how collecting practices were used to imagine—and sometimes to realize—new forms of selfhood and social identity in seventeenth-century England. I first examine the history of the famous collection of rarities assembled by the Tradescant family. John Tradescant the elder exploited the collecting practices of the Stuart elite as both a model and a source of artifacts for his own assemblage of curiosities. Beginning with cast-offs from his aristocratic employers, Tradescant gathered a personal collection of rarities and eventually opened the first public museum in England, accessible to anyone who could pay the admission charge. Tradescant thus combined an elite mode of self-fashioning with middling-sort entrepreneurialism to create a hybrid identity for himself as a collector. John Tradescant the younger's desire to represent the collection in print ironically led not to the preservation of the family's identity as collectors but rather to a hostile take-over of the objects displayed in the "Ark." Elias Ashmole, a lawyer and relentless social climber, helped to catalogue the collection and pay for its incarnation as the printed book *Musaeum Tradescantianum*; upon the death of John Tradescant the younger, however, Ashmole transformed his role as cataloguer of the collection into ownership of the objects he had textualized. As soon as he had gained possession of the Tradescants' rarities through a series of legal maneuvers, Ashmole recast the artifacts as a new type of material display designed to create and perpetuate his own identity: the Ashmolean Museum at Oxford. The history of Ashmole's appropriation of the Tradescant collection thus reveals how the identities of people and things, texts and artifacts, the cataloguer and the collector, could be fused so as to fashion novel forms of social authority in seventeenth-century England.

I next examine the development of early modern English natural history to explore how collections could also be used to construct new social groups. Sir Francis Bacon argued that the study of natural history should be founded upon collections of "particulars," but, Bacon maintained, in order to assemble the immense number of particulars needed for a complete natural history, he would first have to create a collection of men, a new bureaucracy which Bacon envisioned himself administering. After Bacon's death, English virtuosos adopted Baconian natural history as the basis of their own efforts to assemble an elite circle of singular gentlemen; likewise, the Royal Society developed a Baconian collection of rarities, a "Repository," to align its own quest for members with the virtuosos' agenda of individual and corporate self-fashioning. Just as the Royal Society published a catalogue of its Repository to enhance the organization's reputation and increase its membership, so the apothecary James Petiver displayed in printed books both the natural curiosities he had assembled and the collection of assistants, many of them his social superiors, who had given him specimens. The Baconian natural history collection thus became a powerful technology by which diverse new social groups were created in seventeenth-century England.

Analyzing the relationship between texts and practices of collecting also sheds revealing new light on the shifting ideologies of the early modern landscape. My examination of chorography and antiquarianism in Chapter 3 demonstrates that the English countryside was perceived as a space filled with physical objects—objects which, as the seventeenth century wore on, came to represent a new political order of landownership. As they created texts about the landscape and its history, writers like William Camden and Richard Carew became collectors, gathering, arranging, and exhibiting artifacts that symbolized the identity of genteel English landowners. During the Civil War and Interregnum, Sir William Dugdale regarded the chorographic and antiquarian texts he wrote as superior physical objects, repositories of artifacts symbolizing the identities of ancient landholding families that would endure even as funerary monuments were defaced by iconoclasts and grand homes were battered and sequestrated. Although scholars have often ascribed a similarly conservative outlook to Sir Thomas Browne, my analysis of Browne's antiquarian literary works reveals that Browne held a deeply equivocal attitude toward the social authority of the landed elite. Browne thus represents a transition between the ideology of landscape and collecting exemplified by Dugdale and the Restoration portrayal of the landscape as groupings of *owned* objects, a new outlook which characterized both the county natural histories of Robert Plot and late seventeenth-century English country house poems. By the third quarter of

the seventeenth century, the cultural understanding of the English countryside as the site of hereditary landholding had decisively eroded, giving
way to a new landscape of possessive individualism constituted by objects
and their owners.

In Chapter 4, I analyze some of the ways seventeenth-century English
writers combined practices of collecting with the technology of print to
create new modes of authorship for themselves. Conceiving of their writings as physical objects which they owned, Ben Jonson and his literary
"son" Robert Herrick fashioned innovative forms of authorial selfhood as
they transformed their individual texts into collections. Rooted in the humanist "notebook method" of reading and writing, the composition and
circulation of texts in early modern England was often regarded as a process
of collecting. Jonson himself practiced the notebook method, treating classical literature as bundles of fragments which could be appropriated by
readers and writers; I argue that Jonson's construction of proprietary authorship within print culture should be viewed as a revision of this mode of
textual collecting. In his 1616 folio *Workes*, Jonson became the collector of
the literary artifacts he had produced, recontextualizing both manuscript
poems and previously published dramatic works within one monumental
printed book. Although his *Workes* appeared when Jonson was only forty-
three years old, to Jonson's contemporaries—especially to the members of
his literary coterie, the "Tribe of Ben"—the folio implied the end of Jonson's career. Collections and collectors exist reciprocally; a collection is
not simply the product but also the *producer* of its collector, and Jonson's
attempts at self-fashioning after 1616 were thwarted by the continuing
material presence and representational power of his *Workes*. Several years
after Jonson's death, Herrick developed and revised Jonson's practice as
an author/collector. In *Hesperides*, published in 1648, Herrick created an
oeuvre in the form of a printed book containing more than 1,400 poems.
Herrick conceived of the self as an assemblage of discrete objects, and he
accordingly constructed *Hesperides* as a catalogue of his life's experiences, a
textual ark that would preserve the artifacts comprising his identity in the
face of the tumult of the Civil War. My analysis of the diverse strategies of
textual self-fashioning developed by Jonson and Herrick thus reveals how
differing constructions of individual identity rooted in proprietary authorship could emerge from the dynamic culture of collecting in seventeenth-
century England.

The epilogue briefly examines the rise of the national museum by
analyzing the circumstances under which the British Museum was established during the 1750s. Focusing on the career of Sir Hans Sloane and the

process by which his collection became the foundation of the new Museum, I suggest how the potentially subversive characteristics of seventeenth-century collecting were realigned with dominant political ideologies and institutions during the eighteenth century. My analysis of this dynamic relationship between nationalism, the public sphere, and the collection demonstrates that our history of possessive selfhood has been decisively shaped by the culture of collecting which flourished in early modern England.

Chapter 1

Cultures of Collecting
in Early Modern England

Collecting was a vital social practice during the early modern period because it served as a point of convergence for a wide range of cultural forces. Several distinct modes of collecting flourished in Stuart England, variously interacting and merging to create new, hybrid forms of the collection. The early modern English collector could thus inhabit a correspondingly diverse range of subject positions. The history of the collection of John Tradescant the elder affords a case study of the complex and changing web of social meanings which collectors created and negotiated in seventeenth-century England. To analyze the Tradescant collection, however, we first need to consider some of the multifaceted early modern modes of collecting which shaped it.

The Collection as Aristocratic Display

The medieval esteem for "magnificence" as a hallmark of noble virtue continued to underwrite courtly culture during the seventeenth century, entailing the display of aristocratic wealth through extravagant hospitality. At the courts of James I and Charles I, the monarchs' lavish provision of banquets, jewels, precious metals, and rich clothing amidst a throng of similarly ostentatious courtiers demonstrated the Stuarts' princely power and status in this time-honored fashion.[1] However, after James made peace with Spain in 1604, new forms of aristocratic material display began to emerge in England. As they gained more knowledge of princely culture on the Continent from diplomats and travelers, members of the English elite began to emulate the European fashion for art collecting. Charles I literally imported the European model of the princely gallery to England when he bought a significant portion of the famous collection of paintings and sculpture amassed by the Gonzaga court at Mantua. When the Gonzaga collection became available for nearly £16,000 in 1627, wars with Spain and

France had left Charles so strapped for funds that he had mortgaged his jewels, and he was warned that such a costly block purchase of art could prevent him from financing Buckingham's expedition to the Isle of Rhé; but Charles bought the Gonzaga collection nonetheless.[2] Throughout his reign Charles also purchased smaller collections, received gifts from diplomats and courtiers, and commissioned art works such as portraits by Van Dyck and the Rubens ceiling for the Banqueting House. The palace of Whitehall alone came to contain "a substantial proportion of the finest collection of pictures ever assembled" in Britain, including works attributed to Titian, Correggio, Caravaggio, Raphael, and Giulio Romano.[3] Charles thus established himself as one of the great collectors of art in seventeenth-century Europe.

The art collection as an exhibition of elite status was qualitatively different from the traditional material display of "magnificence." In 1610 Lord Roos visited the Continent and approvingly reported that Spanish palaces were full of paintings rather than people: for Lord Roos, such princely collections of art objects replaced the aristocratic entourage as a symbol of political power.[4] To some extent, art works displayed their owner's elite status simply on the basis of the objects' price tags: like jewels or plate, valuable paintings bespoke their owner's wealth, especially if a large collection of art works had been assembled. Compared to objects fashioned from gems or precious metals, however, the pictures gathered by princely collectors were inexpensive.[5] Although paintings were not composed of intrinsically valuable raw materials, they were considered desirable markers of status because they embodied a kind of knowledge that transformed them into high culture: their value was understood in cultural rather than financial terms. Initially, pictures were esteemed strictly for their subject matter rather than their aesthetic quality or attribution, and collectors sought to acquire the painted images of famous historical figures: Charles I, for example, had a series of portraits ostensibly representing the monarchs of England since the time of Edward III, as well as pictures of other members of the British royal family and various ruling houses of Europe.[6] In the latter half of the sixteenth century, this emphasis on the iconography of portraiture was complemented by a new concept of the artist as genius which was promulgated by writers such as Vasari. The ability to understand and appreciate "great" artists came to be considered a sign of erudition and refinement, and by the seventeenth century Europe was being swept by "a veritable picture-mania with huge collections formed by voracious collectors" as "a powerful symbiosis was achieved between the cultural prestige of painting and the social prestige of princes."[7]

The practice of princely art collecting which emerged in Renaissance Europe exemplifies Pierre Bourdieu's argument that taste is not the innocent, "objective" apprehension of aesthetic value, but rather a technology of domination, a means by which social groups can establish and maintain their superiority.[8] In seventeenth-century England, this concept of the art collection as a form of power is starkly apparent in the career of Thomas Howard, Lord Arundel. Because of his accomplishments as a collector, Arundel was lauded for being "as great for his noble Patronage of Arts and ancient learning, as for his birth and place."[9] But politics, rather than a disinterested appreciation for aesthetics, drove Arundel's desire for art works. Queen Elizabeth had deprived Arundel's family of the Dukedom of Norfolk, and Arundel was determined to have the title restored; to this end, his devotion to collecting art "was in effect supporting his family's claim to ducal status by acquiring some of the outward forms of European nobility."[10] Arundel's dynastic preoccupations were especially obvious in his avid pursuit of works by Holbein, who had painted members of the Howard family during their Tudor heyday.[11] The art collections of Charles I and ambitious Stuart courtiers like Buckingham and Hamilton were likewise intended as displays of cultural capital which would increase their owners' prestige among the cosmopolitan elite of early modern Europe—and garner enhanced political power in the process.

The Stuart art gallery was a late offshoot of the elite collecting practices which had become widespread in Europe during the Renaissance. Fifteenth-century Italian humanists, citing classical precedents, suggested that the greatness of a ruler could be displayed through his accumulation of rare and elegant personal possessions; on the Continent, the ownership of such items as bronzes, paintings, books, tapestries, and ceramics came to be understood as a sign of princely splendor, "the logical extension of magnificence into the private world."[12] This new rationale for collecting physical things was readily allied with a traditional cosmology of analogies and correspondences, according to which the order of God's creation—the macrocosm—could be represented in miniature by the arrangement of a group of objects. As a symbolic mirror of the world, the collection-as-microcosm also had to depict God's power to intervene in natural processes and produce miracles, so objects which were rare or "monstrous" were particularly valued because they embodied "a world subject to Divine caprice."[13]

Although it was thus rooted in a medieval, theocentric model of the cosmos, the collection-as-microcosm was easily secularized and transformed into a new symbol of the Renaissance prince's social status and political power. The encyclopedic collections of rare and beautiful objects assembled by members of the ruling dynasties of Europe during the six-teenth century were intended to signify their owners' domination of both nature and culture. Many of the Habsburg rulers created *Kunst- und Wun-derkammern* (chambers of art and marvels), specially built and decorated rooms which contained rare examples of the artifice of both man and nature. In the collections of Archduke Ferdinand II and Emperor Ru-dolph II, for example,

Pieces of gold- and silversmith work, exquisitely wrought and set with an abun-dance of precious stones, were juxtaposed with natural phenomena such as unicorn horns (actually narwhal tusks), exotic sea shells, sinuous pieces of coral (considered to be a kind of divine sculpture) and sometimes dubious freaks of nature. Musical and scientific instruments, coins and medals, books and codices, arms and armor and automata all had a place in this ambitious attempt to recreate the infinite variety of the universe.[14]

The Habsburgs also amassed paintings—Philip II of Spain accumulated more than 1,500, Ferdinand II had approximately 1,000 pictures, while Rudolph II owned about 3,000. Rudolph's enormous collection of inani-mate objects was also supplemented by a menagerie, an aviary, and formal gardens.[15] The microcosmic collection of Francesco I de' Medici included

two chests of Christall guilded over; divers statuas, not of brasse, but of mixt metals, shining here like silver, there like gold; a cup of Amber, a little Mountaine of pearles, wrought together by the hands of Duke Francis; a Pyramis of Pearles as they grow in oyster-shels; two knives set with Jewels, and a third Indian knife; a naile halfe turned into gold by Tomeser an Alchumist, the other part still remaining Iron; a piece of gold unpolished, as it was digged out of the Mines; two pictures of Flemings . . . a clock of Amber; a piece of Amber falling upon a Lizard, and retaining the lively forme thereof; a stone called Vergoara that cureth poyson; the head of a Turke all of pure gold; a most beautifull head of a Turkish woman; a Table of gold, and of Jasper stone, and other Jewells.[16]

In the 1570s Francesco assembled his rarities in a secret chamber adjacent to his bedroom in the Medici Palace in Florence.[17] The walls of Francesco's *studiolo* were lined with two tiers of paintings that served as doors for the cupboards containing the objects of his collection, the significance of indi-vidual objects indicated by the symbolic paintings which were themselves a collection of art works. Each wall of the chamber was dedicated to a dif-ferent element, and the subjects of the paintings correspondingly repre-sented human activities and mythological scenes associated with earth, fire, air, or water.[18] Seated within this microcosmic chamber, Francesco thus constructed himself as the dominating center of nature and culture; more-

over, as Eilean Hooper-Greenhill has commented, the secrecy of the room
"reserved to the prince not only the knowledge of the world constituting his
supremacy, but the possibility of knowing itself."[19]

These encyclopedic groupings of objects were intended to signify their
owners' political and cultural leadership, and the display of a princely collection was thus a calculated exercise in image management. Rudolph II
and Duke Albrecht V showed their *Kunstkammern* to foreign dignitaries
and ambassadors, and allowed favored artists and scholars to have access to
their collections.[20] In 1584 Francesco I de' Medici put many of the objects
he had previously kept in his private *studiolo* on public display in the Uffizi
Gallery: "The need to legitimize the Grand Duke and his dynasty meant
that the glorification of the prince, the celebration of his deeds and the
power of his family had constantly to be exposed to the eyes of all and to be
strongly impressed on the mind of every subject."[21] Symbolism specific to
the individual collector could further emphasize the ideological message
conveyed by a princely assemblage of physical objects. The sheer size of
Rudolph II's collection was to be understood as an index of his political
stature; it was fitting that the greatest ruler in Europe should be the greatest
collector in Europe. The collection of Emperor Maximilian II included a
fountain shaped like an imperial crown which incorporated figures and
iconography representing the entire cosmos: "The universe was thereby
shown to be under the control of the Emperor, whose portrait statue stood
at the fountain's summit."[22] Similarly, the famous portrait heads of the
seasons and elements painted by Arcimboldo for Maximilian and Rudolph
depict human figures formed from amalgamations of physical objects and
decorated with emblems of the Habsburg dynasty: Arcimboldo's paintings
of assembled objects depict the Habsburg emperors as ruling over the forces
of the cosmos, allegorizing both the Habsburgs' imperial power and the
political function of the objects assembled within a *Kunst- und Wunderkammer*.[23] Thus a ruler in Renaissance Europe would attempt to portray
"his claims to mastery of the macrocosm of the greater world, and over the
body politic of which he was sovereign"[24] through his ownership and display of a microcosmic collection of objects.

Humanism and Collecting

Renaissance humanism influenced the ideology and the scope of aristocratic collections.[25] The humanists venerated Greek and Roman antiquity as the source of ideas and values which they believed should underpin
all facets of European society and culture. To this end, they advocated the

development of an educational system rooted in the study of classical texts, maintaining that only such *studia humanitatis* could form an individual with the character and wisdom necessary in political leaders and their teachers and advisors. In England the transformation of the royal household into a comparatively large, centralized bureaucracy under the Tudors created a new demand for government functionaries, and sixteenth-century British humanists "were remarkably successful at establishing their brand of teaching as a necessary credential for upward mobility in service to the state."[26] The ideological nature of humanism was thus ambiguous: on the one hand, northern humanists conceived of their training as a complement to absolutist government and "rarely questioned the legitimacy of royal power or its institutions"; yet by insisting that moral virtue, "honed by appropriate education and placed at the service of the state, was the only justification for claims to status," the humanists simultaneously challenged a traditional emphasis on blood and lineage as the foundation of an individual's social standing.[27]

This Janus-faced allegiance to the elite status quo and to a new concept of social identity unrelated to lineage also marked collecting practices influenced by humanism. Just as the ruling elites of Europe incorporated humanist values into their self-definitions and allied the virtues of lineage with the virtues of a humanist education, so elite collectors during the early modern period sought to exhibit their knowledge of antiquity through the objects they amassed and displayed. As art historian Ronald Lightbown observes, "The history of royal and princely collecting in the sixteenth century is in many ways the history of how the tastes of lettered humanists . . . became the tastes of the great."[28] Henry Peacham asserted that the ownership and display of classical statuary, inscriptions, and coins bespoke a collector's mastery of humanist knowledge and thus his rightful status as a cultural leader within cosmopolitan Europe: in France, Spain, and Italy, Peacham informs the would-be compleat gentleman, "the Gardens and Galleries of great men are beautified and set forth to admiration with these kinds of ornaments." "And indeed," Peacham avers, "the possession of such rarities, by reason of their dead costlinesse, doth properly belong to Princes, or rather to princely minds."[29] Humanism thus came to inform the agendas of elite European art collectors, first on the Continent and then in England. From the fifteenth century onward, "the Greek world simply served as a quarry" for European statue hunters, as "antique marbles were more eagerly pursued than any other kind of work of art, more even than pictures."[30] British collectors followed suit in the seventeenth century. Arundel was the first to "transplant old Greece into *England*," adorning the gardens and galleries of Arundel House with ancient sculpture and inscriptions, and Peacham noted approvingly that Charles I likewise "hath amply testified a Royall liking of ancient statues, by causing a whole army of old forraine Emperours, Captaines, and Senators all at once to land on his coasts, to come and doe him homage, and attend him in his palaces of Saint *Iames*, and Sommerset-house."[31] Ancient coins were also eagerly sought by collectors with humanist pretensions. Coins were valued both as physical embodiments and representations of classical civilization. Peacham extols the virtues of coins as "the very Antiquities themselves," and enthuses,

But would you see a patterne of the *Rogus* or funerall pile burnt at the canonization of the Romane Emperors? would you see how the *Augurs* Hat, and *Lituus* were made? Would you see the true and undoubted modells of the Temples, Alters, Deities, Columnes, Gates, Arches, Aquaeducts, Bridges, Sacrifices, Vessels, *Sellae Curules*, Ensignes and Standards, Navall and murall Crownes, Amphytheaters, Circi, Bathes, Chariots, Trophies, Ancilia, and a thousand things more; Repare to the old coynes, and you shall find them, and all things else that ever they did, made, or used.[32]

Because they were small, numerous, and relatively inexpensive, ancient coins were available not only to elite collectors, but also to men of lesser means who wished to display their educational credentials. As John Evelyn observed pragmatically, "Every one who is a lover of *Antiquities*, especially of *Marbles* and *Inscriptions*, may yet neither have the faculty to be at so vast a Charge, or opportunity of Collecting them so easie and tollerable an Expence as he may of *Medals*."[33] In the late seventeenth century Elias Ashmole, son of a saddler, bragged that he had accumulated "neere 9000 Coynes and Medalls Ancient and Moderne."[34] By the time Ashmole was busily amassing his coins, the values of humanism had been thoroughly appropriated by the landed elite; rather than posing an implicit challenge to aristocratic mores, plebeian coin collectors like Ashmole were self-consciously emulating the collecting practices which had become the elite norm in seventeenth-century England. In the importance accorded coin collecting, like the vogue for gathering classical statues and inscriptions, we see how Renaissance humanism "endowed Roman and Greek antiquities with a certain cachet" that made them fashionable components of aristocratic collections of art and rarities.[35]

Travel, "Wonder," and Collecting

This humanist idealization of the past coexisted with an insatiable thirst for novelty in early modern England. Throughout Renaissance Europe, the desire for new goods had led to commercial contact with Asia, the Middle East, Africa, and the Americas; rather than satiating consumers, however, any influx of foreign objects only whetted the cultural appetite for exotica from distant lands. In a letter to the Earl of Salisbury, the Earl of Southampton recounted a plaintive conversation with James I:

> Talkinge with the King by chance I tould him of the Virginia Squirrills which they say will fly, wherof there are now divers brought into England, and hee presently and very earnestly asked me if none of them was provided for him and whether your Lordship had none for him, sayinge that hee was sure you would gett him one of them. I would not have troubled you with this but that you know so well how hee is affected to these toyes.[36]

Flying squirrels were the tip of the foreign goods iceberg in seventeenth-century England. By 1674, John Evelyn could enthusiastically acknowledge the profound effect of non-European objects on English material culture: "*Asia* Refreshes us with Spices, Recreates us with Perfumes, Cures us with Drougs, and adorns us with Jewels: Africa sends us Ivory and Gold; *America*, Silver, Sugar and Cotton."[37] During this era of burgeoning international trade, collecting was an important way of making sense—and cultural capital—of foreign lands. Assembled and displayed in curiosity cabinets, objects from distant places "substantiated relations of knowledge and power that were distinctive to the period of exploratory voyages."[38] Travel and collecting became mutually sustaining activities: not only was the experience of travel represented by the foreign objects in European collections of "rarities," but travel itself became predicated upon the very existence of such collections. As Lorraine Daston observes, "Travel was the alpha and omega of collecting, being both the source of the bulk of the objects—the voyages of exploration and subsequent trade with newly discovered lands created a steady flow of exotica—and the occasion for inspecting them in Amsterdam, Oxford, Venice, Paris, Augsburg, Uppsala, or wherever the curious and peripatetic tourist might land."[39]

The publication of travel accounts, geographies, atlases, and botanies spread interest in foreign objects, as did displays of items procured on voyages abroad. In the nascent phase of colonialism, indigenous people were brought to Europe and exhibited as living curios: Christopher Columbus returned to Spain with seven Indians whom he displayed; natives from Brazil were showcased in royal pageants in sixteenth-century France, while captives from the Middle East, Africa, and the Americas were put on view at a festival in Bordeaux in 1565; Sebastian Cabot displayed three kidnapped North American natives to Henry VII; and later in the sixteenth century Martin Frobisher exhibited an Eskimo he had captured on Baffin

Island.[40] The tendency for such exotic human specimens to die could be overcome by the resourceful collector: a visitor to the Royal Society's Repository remarked upon "the skin of a moor, tanned, with the beard and hair white," while Samuel Pepys records that when he went to examine Sir Robert Viner's curiosity cabinet in 1665, Sir Robert "showed me a black boy that he had that died of a consumption; and being dead, he caused him to be dried in a Oven, and there lies entire in a box."[41]

The desire to possess the foreign which so literally and brutally governed the capture and display of natives from distant lands likewise underwrote Renaissance collectors' enthusiasm for exotic natural and ethnographic objects. A man of modest means who never visited the New World, John Bargrave amassed only a few North American items, having obtained a "string of Virginian Indian wampum" and three examples of Canadian quillwork as gifts.[42] By contrast, other British collectors actively sought to acquire substantial numbers of objects from the New World, and the relative scarcity of Americana fostered "intense rivalry" among English collectors.[43] The Swiss traveler Thomas Platter was particularly impressed by the foreign artifacts in Sir Walter Cope's collection and concluded that "there are also other people in London interested in curios, but this gentleman is superior to them all for strange objects, because of the Indian voyage he carried out with such zeal."[44] John Tradescant the younger made three trips to North America, while Hans Sloane traveled to the West Indies, where he gathered the objects for what Evelyn approvingly described as "an universal Collection of the natural productions of Jamaica consisting of Plants, fruits, Corralls, Minerals, stones, Earth, shells, animals, Insects & c."[45] Sloane's chief rival as a collector, John Woodward, cultivated a network of North American contacts to furnish him with exotica, including a large shipment containing "Shells, Bones and Teeth of Fishes."[46]

The collection containing objects from foreign lands, like the display of captured Indians, was to some degree an "exhibition of what [was] to be effaced, repressed, or subjected to new and more rigorous mechanisms of control," a representation of "the inclusiveness of the European view of the world and its facile ability to incorporate and domesticate potentially transgressive worlds and customs."[47] Yet such an assessment needs qualification, for it obscures the extent to which foreign objects were esteemed precisely because they could *not* be effaced or domesticated by European categories of meaning. As Paula Findlen argues, rather than the encyclopedism characteristic of earlier Renaissance collections, seventeenth-century collections "were distinguished by their exoticism, which invested such categories as 'wonder' and 'marvel' with new meaning."[48] In the early modern period, the term "wonder" could designate both an object and a viewer's emotional and intellectual response to an astonishing physical thing. "The object that arouses wonder," notes Stephen Greenblatt, "is so new that for a moment at least it is alone, unsystematized, an utterly detached object of rapt attention," and the experience of seeing such an object elicits "an instinctive recognition of difference," an "anamorphic combination of fear and thrill."[49] Thus in early modern England, wonder was aroused by things so strange that they defied rational understanding.

In part, then, the appeal of collections of curiosities to sophisticated seventeenth-century viewers "lay in the refusal of the individual objects to submit docilely to precise categorization,"[50] and foreign physical things were valuable insofar as they were amazingly anomalous. Natural objects were considered "wonderful" if they were rare, exotic, or remarkable in form (unusually large, small, grotesque, or beautiful): its large beak made the Brazilian toucan a "wonder"; the bird of paradise from New Guinea was deemed "marvellous" on account of its plumage; the dodo was "wonderful" because it was a flightless bird.[51] Human artifacts were likewise esteemed as "wonders" if they were particularly rare, ingenious, or fashioned from natural objects in unusual ways: featherwork, tobacco pipes, kayaks, and snowshoes from the New World were much prized, as were examples of Chinese porcelain and Turkish damascened metalwork.[52] In this spirit, John Tradescant wrote a letter to the Secretary of the Admiralty in 1625, asking that he canvass merchants for specimens of foreign birds, animals, plants, and stones; Tradescant appended a long wish list as a postscript to the letter, requesting samples of the skins and bodily fragments of creatures "that be Rare or Not knowne to us," and specimens that were "the Bigest that can be Gotten." Tradescant concluded his list by simply stating that he desired "Any thing that Is strang."[53] The thirst for "wonders" exemplified in Tradescant's letter helped to drive the search for new objects from foreign lands, for once a "marvellous" item became familiar and widely disseminated, it lost the strangeness, the radical quality of difference necessary to excite wonder in European viewers. In 1597 John Gerard noted in his *Herball* that in the past, goldenrod had been highly regarded because it "came from beyond the sea"; however, once it was commonly grown, no one cared about it even though it was valuable for staunching blood, a situation "which plainly setteth forth our inconstancie and sudden mutabilitie, esteeming no longer of any thing, how pretious soever it be, than whilest it is strange and rare."[54]

The ability to command wonder had social and political value in early modern Europe. As James Biester observes, "Wonder was recognized as

overpowering when imposed from without, but empowering when possessed."[55] A man's dazzling but apparently spontaneous eloquence and self-
display were described in terms of wonder; according to Hoby's translation
of Castiglione, the courtier must ensure that "all men wonder at him, and
hee at no man."[56] Like an outsized bird or an unusual artifact, courtly
sprezzatura defied normal categories of assessment, for an astounding exhibition of wit was so suave that it seemed effortless and instinctive rather
than the premeditated result of laborious education. The courtier's mystification of the origins of his skills blurred the boundary between nature and
art, evoking wonder in those around him; in this way, the courtier sought to
represent himself as uniquely awe-inspiring and thus deserving of political
power.

Collecting was complexly related to such harnessing of wonder as a
political and social asset. Like a breathtaking display of courtly wit, the exhibition of physical things in curiosity cabinets was designed to elicit wonder from viewers. Not only were objects selected for their anomalousness,
but the unusual qualities of individual things were emphasized through
their physical juxtaposition with strikingly different items: "Shells, formed
stones, medals, and corals might all be contained in the drawers of the
same cabinet and animals from all over the world were hung together on
the ceiling."[57] Lower down the social scale, wonder books—catalogues of
strange occurrences or the unusual characteristics of natural objects—
afforded the literate paying public with materials for self-improvement and
social advancement. By studying a wonder book, a man could lard his
conversation with nuggets of knowledge in order to win friends and influence people. As the author of *A Helpe to Memorie and Discourse* (1621)
emphasized, his readers would benefit from learning about wonders, since
"that it is that presents education, Gentility, understanding, memory . . .; it
has been a porter to admit many a poor outside for his precious inside, 'to
silken laced and perfumed hindes, / that had rich bodies, but poor wretched
mindes.' "[58]

Just as travel, "wonder," and collecting were bound together in the
procurement and display of foreign objects, so too were they interrelated
in another phenomenon characteristic of the seventeenth century, travel
within Europe. For well-born young men in seventeenth-century England,
a grand tour of Europe, rather than residency at university, became the
approved form of education, a stint on the Continent distinguishing the
crème de la crème from those with less leisure and money.[59] By 1639 Lady
Brilliana Harley could assert her belief that "there are but few noblemen's
sons in Oxford; for now, for the most part they send their sons into France,

when they are very young, there to be bred."[60] Often accompanied by a
tutor, a young gentleman would follow guidebooks to view the remarkable
sights afforded by the Continent. As Bacon noted in his essay "Of Travel,"
"cabinets and rarities" were among the "things to be seen and observed" by
the intelligent traveler.[61] A cosmopolitan network of genteel collectors thus
developed, as would-be visitors arrived on the doorsteps of noteworthy
collectors bearing letters of introduction establishing their social connections—the price of admission, as it were. Visits to well-known collections
were themselves "collected" and displayed by travelers. In writing and publishing their journals—"a genre perfected in particular by the British who
came to Italy"—seventeenth-century travelers exhibited their membership
in cosmopolitan European society, "measur[ing] their success in the number of entries and the quality of access to the leading cultural institutions—
museums, academies, courts, gardens, and homes of learned men."[62] At the
same time, a collector's reputation was enhanced every time the right sort of
person sought to visit his collection: the scholar and naturalist Ulisse Al-
drovandi bragged that "everything in my museum is seen by many different
gentlemen who, passing through this city, visit my *Pandecchio di natura* like
an eighth wonder of the world."[63] Having completed his tour, the well-
traveled young man would return to England, laden with social successes
and curiosities for his own collection. In visiting collections, gathering
rarities, and publishing accounts of their visits to notable collectors, early
modern travelers established their own social credentials while simultaneously enhancing the standing of the collectors whom they visited. By
accumulating amazing material objects from foreign lands and traveling to
view the curiosities possessed by other European collectors, men in early
modern England thus sought to establish themselves as remarkable—that
is, "wonderful"—individuals in a social world which placed a premium on
astonishing novelty.

The Tradescant Collection

The history of the collection of John Tradescant the elder exemplifies
how aristocratic display, humanism, and travel gave social significance to
groupings of material objects in seventeenth-century England. At the same
time, however, the varied meanings which came to be attached to ownership of the Tradescant collection also created new modes of collecting.
Although it began as a direct offshoot of the collecting practices of the
Stuart elite, the Tradescant collection was used to establish innovative

forms of identity by the various "middling sort" people who owned it. An
analysis of the Tradescant collection thus supports Roger Chartier's argument that we need to develop "a way of understanding the circulation of
cultural objects and cultural models that does not reduce circulation to
simple diffusion, usually considered to descend from the upper to the lower
echelons of society." As the history of the Tradescant collection demonstrates, "Processes of imitation and popularization are more complex and
more dynamic: they need to be thought of as competitive efforts in which
any instance of dissemination—whether granted or hard-won—was met
with a search for new procedures for distinction."[64]

The Tradescant collection, located at the Tradescant family home in
South Lambeth, was a "must-see" attraction for nearly half a century. In
1660 the headmaster of Rotherham Grammar School declared that London was "of all places . . . in England . . . best for the full improvement of
children in their education, because of the variety of objects which daily
present themselves to them, or may easily be seen once a year, by walking to
Mr. *John Tradescants*, . . . where rarities are kept."[65] This sense of the sheer
number and diversity of the objects amassed and displayed by the Tradescant family marks contemporary reactions to the collection. In 1638 the
German traveler Georg Christoph Stirn wrote a lengthy description of the
things he had seen during his visit to Lambeth:

[F]irst in the courtyard there lie two ribs of a whale, also a very ingenious little boat
of bark; then in the garden all kinds of foreign plants, which are to be found in a
special little book which Mr. Tradescant has had printed about them. In the
museum itself we saw a salamander, a chameleon, a pelican, a remora, a lanhado
from Africa, a white partridge, a goose which has grown in Scotland on a tree, a
flying squirrel, another squirrel like a fish, all kinds of bright coloured birds from
India, a number of things changed into stone, amongst others a piece of human
flesh on a bone, gourds, olives, a piece of wood, an ape's head, a cheese etc.; all kinds
of shells, the hand of a mermaid, the hand of a mummy, a very natural wax hand
under glass, all kinds of precious stones, coins, a picture wrought in feathers, a small
piece of wood from the cross of Christ, pictures in perspective of Henry IV and
Louis XIII of France, who are shown, as in nature, on a polished steel mirror when
this is held against the middle of the picture, a little box in which a landscape is seen
in perspective, pictures from the church of S. Sophia in Constantinople copied by a
Jew into a book, two cups of "rinocerode," a cup of an East Indian alcedo which is a
kind of unicorn, many Turkish and other foreign shoes and boots, a sea parrot, a
toad-fish, an elk's hoof with three claws, a bat as large as a pigeon, a human bone
weighing 42 pounds, Indian arrows, an elephant's head, a tiger's head, poisoned
arrows such as are used by the executioners in the West Indies—when a man is
condemned to death, they lay open his back with them and he dies of it—an
instrument used by the Jews in circumcision . . . , some very light wood from Africa,
the robe of the King of Virginia, a few goblets of agate, a girdle such as the Turks

wear in Jerusalem, the passion of Christ carved very daintily on a plumstone, a large magnet stone, S. Francis in wax under glass as also of S. Jerome, the Pater Noster of Pope Gregory XV, pipes from the East and West Indies, a stone found in the West Indies in the water, whereon were graven Jesus, Mary and Joseph, a beautiful present from the Duke of Buckingham, which was of gold and diamonds affixed to a feather by which the four elements were signified, Isidor's MS. of de natura hominis, a scourge with which Charles V is said to have scourged himself, a hat band of snake bones.[66]

Although the printed catalogue of the collection, published in 1656, groups the objects into 14 categories under the overarching divisions of "Naturall" and "Artificiall" materials,[67] the incongruous juxtapositions of objects characteristic of accounts such as Stirn's—the stuff of "wonder"—suggest that visitors encountered a less systematic physical arrangement of the objects, akin to the hodgepodge of objects depicted in seventeenth-century engravings of collections displayed on the Continent. It seems likely that the "rarities" were crowded into one or more rooms of the Tradescant house, with some of the specimens hanging from the ceiling, like contemporary continental collections (see Figure 1); and the collection also encompassed the extensive grounds of the house, which contained a garden and orchard filled with hundreds of species of plants and trees, both native and exotic.[68] The Tradescants' garden was not conceived in the apothecary-herbalist tradition: by collecting and propagating rare plants, the elder John Trades- cant "was in the forefront of horticultural innovation," and his son con- tinued to add to the number of rarities contained within the garden at Lambeth, so that by 1656 the Tradescants had accumulated specimens of nearly three-quarters of all the non-native woody plants grown in En- gland.[69] Contemporaries apparently regarded the elder John Tradescant and his son as seventeenth-century Noahs who had gathered together a microcosm of the entire world, for they dubbed the house at South Lam- beth "Tradescant's Ark."[70]

John Tradescant the elder began his collecting career as a professional gardener. By the seventeenth century, gardens had become important status symbols for members (and would-be members) of the English elite; like a country house or an elaborate wardrobe, a garden was a medium of con- spicuous consumption which served as "an effective way of making a state- ment about social standing and political ambition."[71] Employed within this early modern culture of aristocratic display, Tradescant initially collected plants and curiosities on behalf of his wealthy and powerful employers. By 1610 Tradescant was in the service of the Cecils, the Earls of Salisbury, first at Hatfield House and later at Salisbury House and Cranborne as well. The Cecils were extensively renovating Hatfield and its grounds, and in 1611

Figure 1. The collection of Ferrante Imperato, from Ferrante Imperato, *Dell'historia natura* (Venice, 1672), frontispiece. Kenneth Spencer Research Library, University of Kansas.

Tradescant was sent to the Low Countries and France to buy bulbs, plants, and trees suitable for the grand gardens laid out around the rebuilt house. Tradescant went on a horticultural shopping spree, eventually shipping home nearly 1,000 specimens, including roses, currants, vines, and numerous fruit trees. Many of the species with which Tradescant stocked Hatfield's gardens had not previously been seen in England, and when he visited Hatfield three decades later, John Evelyn declared that "the most considerable rarity besides the house . . . was the Garden & Vineyard rarely well water'd and planted."[72] On the same trip, Tradescant likewise bought trees and plants for Sir Walter Cope, Chamberlain of the Exchequer, whose grandiose new house, Cope Castle, needed an equally grandiose garden. Cope was also an avid collector of curiosities, and it has been suggested that through his association with Cope, Tradescant may have seen the politician's wide-ranging display of physical objects and taken it as a model for his own collection.[73]

By 1615 Tradescant had moved on to work for Edward, Lord Wotton at St. Augustine's Palace in Canterbury. In a letter written by Sir Henry Mainwaring to Lord Zouch in 1620, we see how gardening could merge with the competitive displays of novel foodstuffs characteristic of elite conspicuous consumption: Mainwaring explains that he had gone "to see my Lord Wottons garden and to confer with his Gardener, for I do much desire that your Lordship should eat a Muske Mellon of your own in Dover Castle this year."[74] About eight years after he had moved to Canterbury, Tradescant's stature as gardener to the rich and famous was further enhanced when he entered the service of George Villiers, the Duke of Buckingham. Buckingham was energetically styling himself as a princely connoisseur, renovating his recently acquired country house, Newhall, in Essex, and accumulating a dazzling collection of art. Tradescant's role in Buckingham's program of aristocratic self-fashioning entailed more than supervising the Duke's gardens. When Buckingham was sent to France to fetch Henrietta Maria back to England as the bride of Charles I, Tradescant went along; although Tradescant bought trees and plants in Paris, he also acted as baggage master for the Duke's ostentatious wardrobe. In addition, it seems that Tradescant oversaw Buckingham's acquisition of objects for a curiosity cabinet, since, when Tradescant wrote to the Secretary of the Admiralty in 1625 to request samples of "Any thing that Is strang," he did so on behalf of his employer:

I have Bin Comanded By My Lord to Let Yr Worshipe Understand that It Is H Graces Plesure that you should In His Name Deall withe All Marchants from All Places . . . that they will take Care to furnishe His Grace Withe All maner of Beasts & fowells and Birds Alyve or If Not Withe Heads Horns Beaks Clawes Skins Fethers Slipes or Seeds Plants Trees or Shrubs Also from Gine or Binne or Senego Turkye Espetially to Sir Thomas Rowe Who is Leger at Constantinoble Also to Captain Northe to the New Plantation towards the Amasonians With All thes fore Resyted Rarityes & Also from the East Indes Withe Shells Stones Bones Eggeshells Withe What Cannot Com Alive.[75]

The most recent biographer of Tradescant suggests that as merchants, captains, and ambassadors sought to curry Buckingham's favor by showering him with "Rarityes," Tradescant "was in a good position to carry off the duplicates."[76] Certainly his connection with Buckingham allowed Tradescant to develop a network of contacts through whom he enriched his own collection. As April London observes, "In such a system of nepotism as then existed, where men angled for preferment with politic distribution of gifts, Tradescant's position within the Villiers household would have made him a natural beneficiary of courtiers' attentions,"[77] and the list of benefactors included in the *Musaeum Tradescantianum* indicates that many of the people who gave curiosities to Tradescant were linked to Buckingham.

Tradescant found himself unemployed when Buckingham was assassinated in the summer of 1628, and it appears that he acquired his house in Lambeth shortly thereafter.[78] Soon, however, Tradescant was again in the service of the Stuart aristocracy, as he was appointed "Keeper of His Majesty's Gardens, Vines, and Silkwormes" at Oatlands Palace in Surrey in 1630. Apparently Tradescant was also in charge of procuring objects for the King's Cabinet of Rarities.[79] At the same time, as an employee of the King, Tradescant was also able to obtain an interesting new range of royal cast-offs for his own collection: in 1635 the keeper of the Hampton Court Wardrobe was first instructed to "deliver unto John Tredeskyn King Henry the Eight his Capp, his hawking Bagg and Spurres," [80] and then was told to "deliver to John Treidescant king Henry the Eight his Cap, his stirrups, Henry the 7th his gloves and Combcase";[81] several other items of royal clothing may similarly have been given to Tradescant, including "Edward the Confessors knit gloves, Anne of Bullens Night-vayle embroidered with silver, Anne of Bullens silke knit-gloves, [and] Henry 8 hawking-glove, hawks-hood, [and] dogs-collar."[82]

When Tradescant died in 1638, his son—also named John Tradescant—replaced him as keeper of the gardens at Oatlands. Besides his father's position at the royal palace, the younger John Tradescant inherited his father's lease to the house in Lambeth and the collection of rarities contained in the house and garden. In making his will, the elder John Tradescant envisioned that his collection might appropriately return to the context of aristocratic display from which it had arisen, for he specified that if his son did not want to keep his "Cabinett," he must "first offer ye same to ye Prince."[83] Despite his father's doubts, the younger Tradescant did indeed take over the objects housed in the Ark, and years later he described how "my *selfe* with continued diligence have *augmented*, & hitherto *preserved* together" the "*Rarities* and *Curiosities*" which my *Father* had scedulously *collected*."[84] Although the Civil War cut short his employment as a royal gardener, John Tradescant the younger's career as a plantsman and collector in other ways paralleled that of his father. Most important, like the elder Tradescant, John Tradescant the younger procured many rare objects to add to the holdings of the Ark by traveling.

As well as making multiple trips to continental Europe to buy plants for his employers, John Tradescant the elder had also traveled widely to other foreign countries, always managing to bring home new specimens no matter what adverse circumstances surrounded his journey. In 1618 Lord

Wotton apparently gave Tradescant a leave of absence from St. Augustine's Palace so that he could accompany Sir Dudley Digges on a diplomatic mission to Russia. In his *Theatrum Botanicum*, published in 1640, John Parkinson stated that a purple crane's-bill originating in Russia was "brought to us by Mr. *John Tradescant*,"[85] and presumably the "*Rosa Moscovita*" listed in the *Musaeum Tradescantianum* was among the plants that Tradescant mentioned in his diary of his voyage to Russia: "On Munday I had on of the Emperors boats to cari me from iland to iland to see what things growe upon them, whear I found single rosses, wondros sweet withe many other things which I meane to bring withe me."[86] Tradescant was always on the lookout for non-botanical rarities as well: at one point he recounts how "the[re] cam a strang bird abord our shipe, which was taken alive and put to my costody, but dyed within two dayes after being 60 leags from the shore, whos like I yet never sawe, whos case I have reserved."[87] The 1656 catalogue of the collection suggests that Tradescant also acquired several items of clothing and footwear during his time in Russia, including the "Duke of *Muscovy*'s vest wrought with gold upon the breast and armes."[88]

In 1627, while employed by the Duke of Buckingham, Tradescant joined his patron's expedition to the Isle of Rhé. Although Tradescant was praised as "one of our best ingeniers" for his service,[89] he also found time and opportunity to act as a collector rather than an engineer. Parkinson reports that the "greatest Sea Stocke Gillowflower" was "brought out of the Isle of *Ree* by *Rochel* by Mr. *John Tradescant* when the Duke of *Buckingham* was sent with supplies for Mounsieur *Subise*," and the *Musaeum Tradescantianum* describes one of the items housed in the Ark as a "copper Lettercase an inch long, taken in the *Isle of Ree* with a Letter in it, which was swallowed by a Woman, and found"; apparently Tradescant also displayed the silver medal he later received for surviving the disastrous military campaign.[90]

His journey to the Isle of Rhé was not the first time that the elder Tradescant had combined military service with collecting. In 1620, two years after his trip to Russia, Tradescant had again been temporarily released from his service to Lord Wotton, this time to participate in the British blockade of Algiers.[91] Although Tradescant was officially one of the "gentlemen" aboard a ship equipped with 20 guns that was engaged in a military operation, he characteristically found opportunities to gather new plants. In a book published in 1629, John Parkinson noted that "The Argier Apricocke is a smaller fruit than any of the other, and yellow, but as sweete and delicate as any of them, hauing a blackish stone within it, little bigger than a Lacure Cherry stone: this with many other sorts John Tradescante brought with him returning from the Argier voyage, whither hee went voluntary with the Fleete, that went against the Pyrates in the yeare 1620."[92] The garden of Tradescant's employer benefited from this improbable stint of plant-hunting—Parkinson also notes that the wild, double-flowered pomegranate "I thinke was never seene in England, before John Tradescante my very loving good friend brought it from the parts beyond the Seas, and planted it in his Lords Garden at Canterbury."[93]

The double-flowered pomegranate, like the "Muske Mellon" admired by Sir Henry Mainwaring, became part of Lord Wotton's garden, a horticultural rarity valued for its role in the collecting and display practices central to conspicuous consumption among the Stuart elite. By collecting exotic specimens abroad for his employer, Tradescant thus aided in the material representation of Wotton's aristocratic status and power. Yet Parkinson's comments demonstrate how a middling-sort, salaried employee could gain personal prestige from carrying out activities which were intended solely to enhance the image of his elite patron. Similarly, while employed by the Cecils, Tradescant imported a particular kind of cherry tree from the Continent which subsequently became known as "Tradescants Chery"—although Tradescant purchased the plant on behalf of his master, he was credited with a proprietary relationship to the plant.[94] Tradescant's ability to gain authority from activities carried out in the name of his social betters reflects a broad shift in perceptions of agency. Richard Helgerson argues that the early modern period in England was characterized by "a momentous transfer of cultural authority from the patron and the royal system of government of which patronage was an integral part to the individual maker."[95] To explore this phenomenon, Helgerson examines the early modern representations of the set of maps we now know as "Saxton's atlas": although initially depicted as artifacts produced by Thomas Seckford (the gentleman who hired Christopher Saxton as chorographer) and Queen Elizabeth (who ordered the maps in the first place), by the middle of the seventeenth century the maps were instead understood as originating with Saxton, the individual who crafted them, not his elite patrons—hence "Saxton's atlas."[96]

Like Saxton, Tradescant functioned as a subordinate within a system of aristocratic authority and patronage; in 1629 Parkinson described Tradescant as "sometimes belonging to the right Honourable Lord Robert Earle of Salisbury, Lord Treasurer of England in his time, and then unto the right Honourable the Lord Wotton at Canterbury in Kent, and lastly unto the late Duke of Buckingham."[97] As objects gathered by an employee who "belonged" to his wealthy patrons, the rare plants Tradescant obtained

while serving the royally sanctioned blockade of Algiers rightly ended up
"in his Lords Garden." Nonetheless, Parkinson's comments about Tradescant, like the designation "Saxton's atlas," often locate authority in the
skilled plebeian worker rather than his elite sponsors; for Parkinson it is
Tradescant, not the aristocrats who pay him to enrich their showpiece
gardens, who gains status and identity from the act of collecting rare plants.
Parkinson depicts Tradescant as "that painfull industrious searcher, and
lover of al natures varieties" who "hath wonderfully laboured to obtaine all
the rarest fruits he can hear off in any place of Christendome, Turkey, yea or
the whole world."[98] And having established the authority of Tradescant,
Parkinson in turn portrays himself as part of a network of friendships
linking him with Tradescant and other horticultural experts: he refers to
Tradescant as "my louing good friend," writes that the "Trefoil Ladies
smockes" was "sent me by my especiall good friend John Tradescante, who
brought it among other dainty plants from beyond the Seas, and imparted
thereof a roote to me," and praises "Master John Millen, dwelling in Olde
streete, who from John Tradescante and all others that have good fruit, hath
stored himselfe with the best only, and he can sufficiently furnish any."[99]
Parkinson's descriptions of Tradescant thus show how the process of collecting could be understood in mid-seventeenth-century England as the
foundation of non-elite authority, an autonomous identity rooted in a proprietary relationship between the collector and the physical objects he accumulates. And in turn, as he collects plants—both literally and within his
published works on botany—Parkinson fashions his own identity and status
by establishing himself as a friend and colleague of Tradescant. Parkinson's
texts thus construct a kind of non-elite homosociality that is rooted in an
expertise which has been developed and displayed by individual collectors.

As we have seen, in Parkinson's descriptions the elder Tradescant's
plant hunting in foreign countries was integral to the creation of his identity as England's "great Treasurer of Natures rarities."[100] Like his father,
John Tradescant the younger also accumulated new specimens and enhanced his reputation as a plantsman and collector by journeying abroad,
specifically to North America. Even before his son made his first trip to the
New World, Tradescant the elder had obtained specimens of American
plants from intermediaries; for example, Parkinson records that Tradescant
"first received" the "soon fading Spider-wort of Virginia, or Tradescant his
Spider-wort" (now known as *Tradescantia virginiana*) from "a friend, that
brought it out of Virginia, . . . and hath imparted hereof, as of many other
things, both to me and others."[101] As collectors, the Tradescants' interest in
the New World extended beyond botany; in addition to American plants,

by 1656 the Tradescants' collection also contained approximately one hundred zoological and ethnographic specimens of North American origin. While his father knew British travelers to America and was a subscriber to a plantation in Virginia, the younger John Tradescant actually visited America himself.[102] A note in the State Papers, Colonial on the subject of Virginia observes that "In 1637 John Tredescant was in the colony, to gather all rarities of flowers, plants, shells, &c.," and a contemporary letter states that Tradescant had gone to America "under the auspices of the King" and had "brought back a couple of hundred plants hitherto unknown to our world";[103] Parkinson confirms that it was the younger Tradescant who had traveled to Virginia on royal business when he remarks on a "Berry bearing Ferne of *America* . . . which Mr. *John Tradescant* the younger, brought home with him from *Virginia*, this present yeare, 1638, presently after the death of his father."[104] The younger Tradescant returned to North America in 1642 and made a third trip eleven years later. In a catalogue published in 1634, the elder Tradescant listed 750 different plants in his collection; by the time the *Musaeum Tradescantianum* was published in 1656, the number of plants contained within the grounds of the Ark had more than doubled,[105] and it seems likely that the globetrotting younger Tradescant was at least partially responsible for this augmentation of his father's botanical specimens. After their deaths, both father and son were remembered, in part, as travelers. Upon the death of the younger Tradescant in 1662, his widow, Hester Tradescant, had a monument to the family erected in the churchyard of St. Mary in Lambeth. When the tomb was repaired in 1773, it was inscribed with an epitaph which had been composed for but not added to the first incarnation of the monument. The epitaph, written by John Aubrey, describes the elder Tradescant and his son as men who "Liv'd till they had travelled art and nature thro."[106]

In assessing the behavior of seventeenth-century English entrepreneurs, Richard Grassby has argued that there was "a fundamental difference of attitude between the self-employed of every occupation, who had to generate their own income, and those living on salaries or passive, unearned income from property. The former assumed risk in the expectation of profits and initiated change whereas the latter institutionalized their activity and favoured stability."[107] The careers of the Tradescants as collectors straddled this occupational and attitudinal divide. On the one hand, both the elder John Tradescant and his son functioned professionally as hirelings of prominent members of the Stuart elite, gardening, traveling, and collecting on behalf of the aristocrats whose status they were employed to enhance. On the other hand, the Tradescants were accorded personal authority for the work they did; just as early modern surveyors, craftsmen, and authors were increasingly understood as the originators of the artifacts they produced, so the Tradescants, as collectors, were ascribed a kind of artisanal propriety over the objects they gathered for their elite employers.

The ability of the Tradescants to forge autonomous identities as collectors becomes even more apparent when we examine the circumstances under which they displayed their personal collection of rarities in Lambeth. While the nature of the objects displayed within the Ark allied the Tradescant collection with the gardens and curiosity cabinets of their social superiors—and indeed, many of the specimens may well have been acquired in tandem with items procured by the Tradescants for their aristocratic patrons—the Tradescant collection was very different from its elite analogues in terms of its accessibility. Throughout early modern Europe, admission to an individual's collection was normally a privilege extended only to those judged to have adequate social or professional credentials; collectors and visitors used each other to establish personal authority, as a collector's reputation was enhanced by the importance of his visitors, and the would-be cosmopolite increased his status by gaining access to highly regarded displays of objects. The Tradescants, by contrast, commodified the experience of viewing their collection; anyone could see the Tradescants' rarities upon payment of an entrance fee. The family apparently hired a keeper to guide visitors through the collection, and it seems likely that they also sold plants raised in the gardens of the Ark.[108] By thus commercializing their plants and rarities, the Tradescants subverted the elite paradigm of collecting and viewing collections as status markers.

The ideological complexity of the Tradescants' identity as collectors was emblematized in their coat of arms. In early modern England a coat of arms was, theoretically, a sign of an individual's lineage—that is, the antiquity of his family and its landed status. By the sixteenth century in England, "a right to arms had come . . . to be looked on as decisive evidence of gentility," and in Ben Jonson's sardonic formulation, anyone "That ha[d] no pedigree, no house, no coat / No ensigns of a family" was a "mere upstart."[109] The Tradescants proudly displayed their arms in contexts that explicitly associated their insignia—the embodiment of "a hereditary essence of family character"[110]—with their collection. The Tradescant coat of arms decorated an exterior wall of their house at Lambeth, the very first page of the *Musaeum Tradescantianum*, and the family tomb Hester Tradescant commissioned; likewise, after detailing the final disposition of the objects in their collection, both John Tradescant the elder and his son sealed their wills with the family crest, and Hester followed suit.[111] The

Tradescants' display of the family's armigerous status influenced subsequent tributes to them: in 1926, the Gardens Club of Virginia presented the
University of Oxford with a commemorative window which depicted the
family's coat of arms surrounded by a wreath of *Tradescantia virginiana*;[112]
and John Whiteside, Keeper of the Ashmolean Museum from 1714 to 1729,
added labels to the Tradescant family portraits held by the Museum, desig-
nating the father-and-son gardeners as "Sir John Tradescant Senior" and
"Sir John Tradescant Junior."[113] In fact, the Tradescants' coat of arms, and
thus their implicit claim to gentility, were entirely specious, and when
Robert Tradescant, a cousin, applied for arms in 1661 he was denied on the
grounds that he was an "ignoble person" and "no gent."[114] There was
nothing novel about a family manufacturing lineal claims in early modern
England: during the sixteenth and seventeenth centuries, those with short
pedigrees but deep pockets regularly hired antiquaries to concoct genealogies, and periodic county-by-county visitations by the royally appointed
heralds were intended to root out genealogical fraud—or at least, fraud not
aided and abetted (for a fee) by the heralds themselves.[115] The Tradescants'
illicit fabrication and display of a coat of arms both subverted and upheld
their society's ideology of rank; the family successfully claimed a status
which it did not actually have, yet the Tradescants' apparent yearning for
traditional marks of social distinction indicated the continuing power of
the belief that lineage, not personal accomplishment, was the foundation of
social identity. Thus while the Tradescants, by commercializing access to
the Ark and selling plants, created a new identity and career for themselves
as collector-entrepreneurs, they also sought to camouflage—or legitimize—
their innovation beneath signs of membership within a social order predicated on blood.

Elias Ashmole as Collector

Long before Elias Ashmole became involved with the collection displayed in Lambeth's "Ark," the elder John Tradescant had created two
different catalogues of his plants.[116] In the blank pages bound into the back
of a copy of John Parkinson's *Paradisi in Sole Paradisus Terrestris* (which
punningly translates as "The Earthly Paradise of Park in Sun"), Tradescant
recorded a list of plants "Reseved since the Impression of this Booke."[117]
Between 1629 and 1633, Tradescant kept a year-by-year list, mostly in Latin,
of the new plants he added to his collection, often indicating the "forrin
partes" from which exotic specimens originated,[118] as well as the names of

the people who had supplied the plants to him. By creating this catalogue within the physical boundaries of Parkinson's book, Tradescant both linked his burgeoning collection of plants with the authority of Parkinson's work and also literally extended the text, thus representing how Tradescant's garden was expanding the range of plants grown in England. In 1634 Tradescant further textualized his collection of plants by publishing a fifteen-page pamphlet entitled *Plantarum in Horto Iohannem* [sic] *Trades-canti nascientium Catalogus*. The work consists of a list of the Latin names of more than 750 plants, arranged more or less alphabetically, followed by a list of varieties of fruit trees and vines organized by species—apples, pears, plums, cherries, apricots, nectarines, peaches, and grapes, including two varieties named after the author-collector himself, "Tradescants Chery" and "Tradescants doublefloured Peach."[119]

The *Musaeum Tradescantianum*, first published in 1656, was a much more elaborate textual representation of the Tradescants' collection and the identities they had created in relationship to it. Facing the specious Trades-cant coat of arms, the title page reads, "*Musaeum Tradescantianum: or, A Collection of Rarities. Preserved at South-Lambeth neer London By John Tradescant*" (see Figure 2). The book is "By" John Tradescant the younger, and simultaneously the collection of physical objects is "Preserved . . . By" him: the title page syntactically blurs the identity of author and collector. Following the title page appear two Latin anagrams on "Joannes Trades-cantus," and then two English anagrams by Walter Stonehouse; the latter verses are paired with engraved portraits of the elder Tradescant and his son by Wenceslaus Hollar. This prefatory matter immediately situates the cata-logue within a royalist context: Stonehouse was an Anglican clergyman ejected from his living in Yorkshire and imprisoned in 1648, and Hollar had been forced to leave England for some time because he was a royalist sympathizer. Although the catalogue was originally dedicated to the Col-lege of Physicians, when Charles II was restored a new edition of the *Musaeum Tradescantianum* appeared, dedicated to the King by "His Majes-ties most obedient and most Loyal Subject," John Tradescant the younger, who "IN ALL HUMILITY Offereth these Collections."[120] Tradescant likewise exhibited his royalism in the list of "Principall Benefactors" with which both editions of the catalogue conclude: the list is arranged accord-ing to descending social rank, beginning with "King *Charles*" and "Queen *Mary*"; after the Duke and Duchess of Buckingham, the next contributor named is "*William Laud* Archbishop of *Cant.*"[121] Many of the benefactors are designated with titles that were obsolete by the 1650s, suggesting that the list was simply a transcription of a register of patrons which had been compiled by the Tradescants in the 1630s.[122] Whatever the circumstances under which the list was produced, its appearance in the 1656 catalogue has the effect of presenting the origins of the collection as pre-existing the Civil War and Interregnum, transforming both the catalogue and the collection into monuments of a vanished social and political order.

Ironically, the younger John Tradescant's desire to textualize his collection and its associations with aristocratic values left him vulnerable to the predations of another ambitious, middling-sort collector. At the same time that John Tradescant the younger and his wife were displaying the contents of the Ark to a paying public, Elias Ashmole was using collections of objects as part of his lifelong quest for enhanced status. Born the son of a saddler in Lichfield in 1617, Ashmole began his career as a lawyer in London, eventually marrying his way into "the Condition I alwaies desired, which was, that I might be enabled to liue to my selfe & Studies, without being forced to take paines for a livelyhood in the world."[123] Ashmole was at once an arriviste and a staunch royalist who defended the traditional social order, thus exemplifying what Peter Stallybrass has described as the contradictory outlook of the "class aspirant" who "has an interest in preserving social closure, since without it there would be nothing to aspire *to*. But, at the same time, that closure must be sufficiently flexible to incorporate *him*."[124] Ashmole's veneration of tradition combined with his desire for personal authority led him to try to infiltrate the Order of the Garter in the early 1660s. The long association of the Order with the monarchy made it "a quintessential royalist cult,"[125] and Ashmole would later state that he had begun to research a book about the Order during the Interregnum, "a tyme when he could hope neither for preferment or reward, but rather danger & certaine expence."[126] Yet Ashmole's interest in the Order was also shaped by personal ambition. At the Restoration, Ashmole began to lobby for the creation of a new office, "Historiographer and Remembrancer of the Order"—and for the appointment of himself to the position. Despite the King's initial backing for Ashmole's scheme, however, the Chancellor of the Order refused to allow Ashmole to insinuate himself directly into the power structure of the organization. In a scathing speech delivered before the King, Sir Henry de Vic warned that Ashmole was set on becoming "a new Lycurgus," and complained that

nothing will Content Mr Ashmole unlesse hee may have all the partes of thee play hee must act Pyramus and thisbee, the beare and the Lyon, Moonshine, and the rest; he must putt out all the officers of the order out of their places[,] assume to himself the honor that is due to all the noble Companions nay indeed play the soveraigne and bee made dictator of this noble Order.[127]

Musæum Tradescantianum:

OR,

A COLLECTION

OF

RARITIES.

PRESERVED

At *South-Lambeth* neer *London*

By

JOHN TRADESCANT.

LONDON,

Printed by *John Grismond*, and are to be sold by
Nathanael Brooke at the Angel in Cornhill,

M. DC, LVI.

Figure 2. John Tradescant, *Musaeum Tradescantianum* (London, 1656), title page.
William Andrews Clark Memorial Library, University of California, Los Angeles.

By comparing him with Bottom, the weaver-turned-actor in Shakespeare's
A Midsummer Night's Dream, Sir Henry not only ridiculed Ashmole's ego-
tistical officiousness, but also drew attention to Ashmole's lowly social
origins.

Ashmole's avid pursuit of astrology and alchemy similarly embodied
his contradictory blend of conservatism and desire for enhanced status. On
the one hand, his interest in horoscopes and magic was entirely consistent
with his support for the Stuart monarchy, as "Ashmole's view of the world
and of society . . . was always mysterious and hierarchic, buttressing traditional values and social forms rather than challenging them."[128] Yet Ashmole also used astrology and magic as tools with which he could realize his
dreams of social mobility. Ashmole frequently cast magic sigils (talismans
which could harness astrological influences) for such purposes as the "increase of honour and estimation with great men" and he was elated when,
after the death of his genteel but impoverished first wife, a horoscope told
him that he would "labour for a fortune with a wife and get it."[129] Ashmole
hunted for a suitably wealthy second wife to fulfill this prediction and found
the woman of his horoscopes in Lady Manwaring, thrice widowed and
nearly twenty years his senior. Although one of her sons tried to murder him,
Ashmole survived his mercenary courtship and married Lady Manwaring in
1649. Jibing at Ashmole's dual interest in alchemy and marriageable money,
Anthony Wood reported that Lady Manwaring's wealth and property were
"the best elixir that [Ashmole] enjoyed, which was the foundation of his
riches, wherewith he purchased books, rarities and other things."[130]

As part of this program to surround himself with objects suitable for a
man who was no longer "forced to take paines for livelyhood in the world,"
Ashmole began to collect coins in the approved humanist fashion. By the
time most of his collection, housed in the Middle Temple in London, was
destroyed in a fire in 1679, Ashmole had accumulated more than 9,000
items, and his reputation as an expert in numismatics was such that Thomas
Fuller had deemed him to be "critically skilled in Ancient Coins."[131] Ashmole demonstrated his mastery of other bodies of knowledge by assembling
collections of texts, or collections that were displayed in a book-like form.
In 1652 Ashmole displayed his scholarly command of alchemy by publishing
his *Theatrum Chemicum Britannicum*, a collection of alchemical poems
written in English. According to Anthony Wood, Ashmole had also compiled

a large thick paper book, which you may call a double folio (near a yard long)
containing on every side of the leaf two, three or more pictures or faces of eminent

persons of England and elsewhere, printed from copper cuts pasted on them, which Mr. Ashmole had with great curiosity collected: and I remember he has told me that his mind was so eager to obtain all faces, that when he could not get a face by itself he would buy a book wherein a face was set before it, meerly for the face's sake: which being done he would tear out the face or picture, paste it in the said book, and write under it from whence it was taken.[132]

Wood reported that in addition, Ashmole had "another folio as large as the former, containing the pictures of processions at coronations, marriages, interviews, funerals, &c. printed from coppercuts and pasted or fastned therein," and yet a third scrapbook containing "the prospects of cities, towns, houses, &c."[133] Ashmole's scrapbooks thus served both as reference tools and as displays of the knowledge he had accumulated in gentlemanly leisure.

Ashmole's use of physical objects to construct his identity extended to others' collections through his activities as a cataloguer. I have already suggested that early modern collections were used symbiotically by collectors and visitors to establish their mutual status as cosmopolitan men of culture: a collector gained authority if others flocked to see his display of physical objects, while travelers measured their social cachet by the number of curiosity cabinets to which they were granted access. The gathering of physical objects, then, became the site of other self-consciously social (and often subsequently textual) acts of collecting: the collecting of visitors, displayed by the collector as entries in a visitors' book, and the collecting of visits to collections, displayed by the traveler in his journal. In Ashmole's relationships with collectors and collections we find this dynamic intensified, as Ashmole not only viewed but also catalogued the accumulated objects of others, gaining cultural authority and entrée into new social milieus as he did so. As in his attempt to become an officer within the Order of the Garter, Ashmole used his role as cataloguer to "play the soveraigne" within elite environments.

By creating catalogues, Ashmole could both display his royalist politics and gain personal prestige within influential institutions and social circles. In 1644, while employed elsewhere as a Commissioner of Excise, Ashmole had occasion to travel to the royalist stronghold of Oxford on business and ended up studying for about a year at Brasenose College.[134] Later in his life, Ashmole would testify to his sense of "Duty and filial Respect, to my honored mother the University of Oxford,"[135] and in 1656 Ashmole was given the chance to serve his "honored mother" by cataloguing the collection of Roman coins held by the Bodleian Library. Ashmole began work on the catalogue in 1658; in the Latin preface to the finished manuscript, he contextualized his cataloguing activities in terms that were both royalist and self-aggrandizing, stating that "when he began the work in the very difficult times of the Cromwellian tyranny, there were few men left in the University who might have done the like."[136] Ashmole finally completed the three-volume manuscript catalogue in 1666 and was awarded an honorary degree of Doctor of Medicine by the University in 1669; some years later, he complained that the account of him in Anthony Wood's *Historia et Antiquitates Universitatis Oxoniensis* "omitted in his Life what he most valued, viz. his Catalogue of the Collections of Rarities of the University which he did with his owne hand, and was a very laborious worke."[137] Shortly after the Restoration of Charles II, Ashmole was again appointed to produce a numismatic catalogue, this time describing "The Kings Coynes and Medalls." As he compiled the catalogue, however, Ashmole blurred the distinction between the proprietary collector and the nonproprietary cataloguer by simultaneously creating and assembling his own collection of wax impressions of the coins and engraved jewels contained within "The Kings Cabinet."[138] In his arrangement of the wax impressions he had made, Ashmole also elided the boundary between physical objects and their textual representation in a catalogue, for the impressions were ultimately displayed on a series of manuscript pages, with identifying labels written out by Ashmole.[139] Ashmole's identity as royalist cataloguer gained its greatest legitimacy when he was appointed Windsor Herald in June 1660. As a herald, Ashmole became a royally sanctioned arbiter of social distinction and, characteristically, Ashmole responded to his new authority by creating and publishing a catalogue, a broadside entitled *A Catalogue of the Peers of the Kingdome of England, according to their Birth and Creation, in the Raign of Charles the Second, King of England, Scotland, France and Ireland. . . . Collected by E*[lias]. *A*[shmole].[140] By creating catalogues, Ashmole thus gained admission to and asserted his authority over elite cultural circles.

The relationship between collecting, cataloguing, and personal prestige in Ashmole's quest for enhanced status becomes most evident in his attempt to gain ownership of the Tradescant collection. In his prefatory letter "To the Ingenious Reader," Tradescant explains the circumstances under which the catalogue *Musaeum Tradescantianum* was compiled. He maintains that he was persuaded by friends to draw up the catalogue after they argued "*That the enumeration of these Rarities, (being more for variety than any one place known in Europe could afford) would be an honour to our Nation, and a benefit to such ingenious persons as would become further enquirers into the various modes of Natures admirable workes, and the curious*

Imitators thereof "; once his arm had been twisted, Tradescant was helped by "two worthy friends" to prepare the catalogue, a process which entailed "many *examinations* of the *materialls* themselves, & their *agreements* with severall Authors *compared*."[141] The "two worthy friends" were Elias Ashmole and Dr. Thomas Wharton, a physician and "most beloved friend" of the social-climbing lawyer.[142] Ashmole, his wife, and Wharton visited the younger John Tradescant at South Lambeth in June 1650, and Ashmole's wife subsequently stayed with the family;[143] late in May 1652 Ashmole notes that "I & my wife Tabled this Summer at Mr Tredescants."[144] It was probably during this time that Ashmole and Wharton helped Tradescant to compile his catalogue, for in his prefatory remarks to the reader, Tradescant explains that after a draft was completed, work on the catalogue was halted for about a year because "Presently thereupon my *onely Sonne dyed*, one of *my Friends* fell very sick for about *a yeare*, and my *other Friend* by unhappy *Lawsuits* much disturbed"; on top of these problems, Tradescant goes on, he faced another delay because the engraved portraits of him and his father were not ready.[145] The younger Tradescant's son, named John Tradescant like his father and grandfather, died in September 1652 at the age of nineteen; subsequently, Wharton fell ill, and Ashmole became locked in legal combat with his wife's relatives over money he believed they owed her.[146]

Although the catalogue, complete with portraits, was finally published in 1656 under Tradescant's name, Ashmole's role in its creation was to become a contested issue. Henry Oxinden portrayed the catalogue as a testament to Ashmole rather than to John Tradescant the younger: in a poem entitled "To my ever honored Friend ELIAS ASHMOLE Esq. on his explanation of John Tredescants Rarities," Oxinden praises "Elias! whose great partes more wondrous are / Then all Tradescants rarities by far."[147] John Evelyn displayed a similarly Ashmole-centric reaction to the *Musaeum Tradescantianum*: in his account of his visit to the Ark in 1657, Evelyn concluded his list of "the chiefest rarities" of the collection by mentioning "other innumerable things there were too long here to recite, & printed in his Catalogue by Mr. *Ashmole*."[148] Within the *Musaeum Tradescantianum* itself, the names of Ashmole and Wharton appear, after titled members of the gentry, in the list of benefactors with which the catalogue concludes. In addition, although the descriptions of objects in the catalogue rarely name the donors of individual items, Ashmole is specifically credited with giving a bird, "taken upon the *Thames*," to the collection, while Wharton, identified as "T.W.," is named as the donor of a "Civit-Catts-head and bones," a fish head, and a fossil.[149]

Despite the modest textual allusions to Tradescant's "two worthy friends," Ashmole's ties to the catalogue—and ultimately to the collection itself—were made more complicated by the fact that he had paid the costs of publishing the *Musaeum Tradescantianum*. Ashmole maintained that John Tradescant the younger, both touched by the "former paines, care and charge" which Ashmole had expended in producing the catalogue and recognizing how greatly Ashmole "valued" the rarities, decided to give the collection to him.[150] This was accomplished, according to Ashmole, in 1659 when Tradescant arranged for a scrivener to draw up a deed of gift by which Ashmole would receive the collection after both Tradescant and his wife, Hester, had died; in the meantime, the Tradescants would hold the objects in trust for Ashmole. After the deed of gift had been sealed and given to Ashmole, his new proprietary relationship to the collection was symbolized when he was given one of the objects, "a Queene Elizabeth milled shillinge[,] in the presence of severall witnesses."[151]

The fate of a collection after the death of its owner was an issue of great concern to early modern collectors. As John Evelyn wrote to Samuel Pepys in 1689, a "sad dispersion" could threaten "what with so much cost and industry you have collected," a situation most likely to arise "where the next heir is not a virtuoso."[152] In Tradescant's case, this dilemma was particularly acute as his son and namesake had died in 1652.[153] According to Hester, as he considered how best to dispose of his collection after his death, Tradescant was most concerned to ensure that it would be "preserved to posterity"; for that reason, he had altered a previous will in which he had left the collection to the King for fear that some "private person might begg the same of his Majesty."[154] By Hester's account, her husband had come home drunk one evening in the company of four strangers and, without actually reading the document, had signed the deed of gift; when she witnessed the signing, Hester too was ignorant of the contents of the document. According to Hester, when she and her husband realized the next day that while they had meant to leave the rarities to Ashmole in trust for a university, the document they had signed under such strange circumstances specified no such condition, they cut the seal off the deed of gift and obliterated the signatures, believing that they had thus nullified the document. Two years later, Tradescant made what would be the final version of his will, and declared that "I give, devize, and bequeath my Closet of Rarities to my dearly beloved wife Hester Tredescant during her naturall Life, and after decease I give and bequeath the same to the Universities of Oxford or Cambridge, to which of them shee shall think fitt at her decease."[155]

John Tradescant the younger died on 22 April 1662. Less than one month later, Elias Ashmole preferred a Bill of Complaint in Chancery "against Mrs Tredescant, for the Rarities her Husband had setled on [him]."[156] Besides providing his version of the circumstances under which the deed of gift was drawn up and signed, the text of his Complaint reveals that Ashmole was also preoccupied with the authority of the *Musaeum Tradescantianum* as an inventory of what Ashmole now regarded as his personal possessions. Ashmole fumed that Hester had stated that many of the objects listed in the catalogue had been "passed away" by her husband since the *Musaeum Tradescantianum* had been printed in 1656, some of the items having been removed from the Ark after the deed of gift had been signed in December 1659; moreover, while Hester had asserted that her husband had acquired "other Rarities" which he had added to the collection after he had signed the deed of gift in 1659, Ashmole maintained that these objects were "indeed the same individuall things which were conteyned in the said Catalogue, Collection or Abstract."[157]

The case was heard in 1664, two years after Ashmole began legal action against Hester Tradescant, and again, the relationship between Ashmole, the *Musaeum Tradescantianum*, and the Tradescant collection was invested with great significance. Having heard the evidence, the Lord Chancellor declared in favor of Ashmole; the 1659 deed of gift was not revocable, regardless of what Tradescant might have later stipulated in his will, and the collection now belonged to Ashmole. It was reiterated that John Tradescant had been motivated to make the deed of gift because Ashmole, "haueinge Composed a Catalogue or collection of the s[ai]d rarities att his owne Charge & which was published in a printed booke called Musaeum Tredescantianum," had demonstrated "the great Esteeme & value" with which he regarded Tradescant's "Clossitt of raryties"; the deed of gift thus was "made for good & valuable Considerac[i]on" of Ashmole's "composeinge of the s[ai]d Treatise."[158] Hester could keep the objects until she died, but upon her death Ashmole was to "haue & enjoy all & singular the s[ai]d Bookes Coynes Meddalls Stones Pictures Meckanicks & Antiquities & all & euery other the Raryties & Curiosities of what sort or kind soeuer whither naturall or artificiall and whatsoeuer was graunted by the s[ai]d Deed as itt now stands p[ro]ved in Co[u]rt which were in the s[ai]d John Tredescants said Clositt or in or about his said house att South Lambeth the said sixteenth day of Decemb[e]r 1659 when the said deed was executed."[159] Like the 1656 catalogue, the ruling encompassed not only the inanimate objects exhibited inside the Ark, but also the plants located "about" the house in the gardens and orchard. To ensure that Ashmole's possessions were not subject to "Spoyle & Imbezellm[en]t" while they were held in trust by Hester Tradescant, the Lord Chancellor ordered the creation of a commission which would "repaire to Mr Tredescants house & to see the s[ai]d Catalogue of all the Rarities" and check the contents of the Ark against their representation in the *Musaeum Tradescantianum*.[160] The commission was to consist of Sir Edward Bysshe and William Dugdale. Both men were heralds and thus colleagues of Ashmole; in 1668, Dugdale also became Ashmole's father-in-law when Ashmole married his daughter, Elizabeth, seven months after Ashmole's second wife, the wealthy Lady Manwaring, had died.

His legal victory in Chancery was only the first of a series of actions that Ashmole took to secure and display his ownership of the Tradescant collection after the death of John Tradescant the younger. Just as he had earlier tried to become "a new Lycurgus" to the Order of the Garter, Ashmole was firmly on course to "play the soveraigne and bee made dictator" of the Tradescant collection, displacing the Tradescant family as collectors and assuming to himself all the "honor" due the original creators of the collection. Hester Tradescant did not remarry, and she continued to add to the collection and exhibit it at the family home in South Lambeth. In 1674, ten years after Ashmole won his complaint against her, Hester was served the writ of execution of the Chancery decree: she faced the imminent arrival of Ashmole's two friends and colleagues—one of them now also his father-in-law—to inspect the collection. On 15 September 1674 Ashmole asked the stars if he should buy the house which adjoined the Ark, and on 2 October he recorded that "I & my wife first entred my House at South Lambeth."[161] As Prudence Leith-Ross acerbically notes, "Without actually moving in with [Hester Tradescant] Ashmole could not possibly get nearer the coveted collection."[162] Under these circumstances, it was not surprising that the sixty-one-year-old widow anticipated that Ashmole would "come into my house assoone as the breath was out of my Body, & take away my Goods."[163] It seems that the pressure became more than she could bear, for on 26 November 1674, Ashmole recorded that "Mrs: Tredescant being willing to deliver up the Rarities to me, I caried seuerall of them to my House"; likewise, Ashmole noted on 1 December 1674 that "I began to remove the Rest of the Rarities to my house at Southlambeth."[164] Ashmole would later maintain that Hester "forced him" to take away the rarities, "threatning, that if he did not, [she] would throw them into the Streete," and after he first tried to dissuade her and then reluctantly agreed to take in the objects, Hester "voluntarily helped to remove some of them [her] selfe."[165]

Legally, as long as Hester Tradescant was alive Ashmole did not actu-

ally own the rarities now under his roof; Ashmole, however, behaved otherwise. The collection was no longer open to the public, but was now shown
only to selected visitors to Ashmole's Lambeth home—the likes of John
Evelyn, Robert Hooke, and Izaak Walton.[166] By 1675 Ashmole was negotiating with officials at the University of Oxford, specifying that if he were
to donate the rarities to the University, they should be housed in a new,
purpose-built "large Rooem, which may haue Chimnies, to keep those
things aired that will stand in need of it."[167] In October 1677 Oxford agreed
to house the objects to be donated by Ashmole in a new building dedicated
to scientific research. Although John Tradescant the Younger had specified
in his will that the objects in his collection should ultimately be given, at his
wife's discretion, either to Oxford or Cambridge, Ashmole fiercely guarded
the new identity he was crafting for himself as the owner and donor of the
Tradescants' collection. On 1 September 1676 Ashmole drew up a Submission which he forced Hester Tradescant to sign in the presence of a Justice
and seven other witnesses.[168] In the document Hester recants accusations
against Ashmole which caused "the diminution and blemishing of his reputation & good name," averring that contrary to statements that she had
made previously, Ashmole had not harassed her and had not "robde me of
my Closet of Rarities, & cheated me of my estate."[169] Moreover, Hester
also had to disavow her statements "that I had made him promise me to
bestow the said Rarities on the University of Oxford; and that I would force
him to send them thither."[170] Ashmole would not allow Hester to claim any
influence over the final disposition of the Tradescants' collection.

Early in April 1678, Hester Tradescant was found drowned in the
pond located within the grounds of the Ark. In less than three weeks after
her death, Ashmole had "removed the Pictures from Mr Tredescants
House, to myne."[171] Perhaps the loss of his coin collection and scrapbooks in the fire at the Middle Temple in January 1679 made Ashmole even
more determined to possess the Tradescant collection in its entirety, for in
March 1679 Ashmole obtained the lease on the Tradescant house and
garden. Characteristically, Ashmole demonstrated his newly acquired ownership of the horticultural specimens planted around the Ark by creating a
catalogue: in the back of the same copy of Parkinson's *Paradisus* in which
the elder John Tradescant had, nearly fifty years previously, enumerated the
plants he acquired for his garden, Ashmole made his own list, entitled
"Trees found in Mrs Tredescants Ground when it came into my possession."[172] Ashmole thus fashioned a textual representation of his new proprietary status that displayed him subsuming the role of the first owner of
the Tradescant collection.

Ashmole's drive to possess the Tradescant collection was still not satisfied, however. On 2 June 1679 Ashmole was again preferring a Bill of Complaint in Chancery, this time against the two women Hester had named as the principal benefactors of her estate and the executrices of her will, Sara de Critz and Katherine King. Ashmole accused the two women of defrauding him of objects which were part of the Tradescant collection. In their responses to Ashmole's charges, de Critz and King asserted Hester Tradescant's independent identity as a collector, maintaining that Hester had given Ashmole all the rarities to which he was entitled by the deed of gift, keeping only objects which she herself had gathered after her husband's death—objects to which Ashmole had no legal claim. Ashmole had already demanded that the two women hand over "severall Rarityes" to him, and they had given him "severall things and rarityes for to buy their peace and quiettnes which as they beleeve & are informed were not nor are not w[i]thin the graunt of the said Deed."[173] In conclusion, Sara de Critz and Katherine King stated that if Ashmole wanted the remaining items from Hester Tradescant's collection of rarities, they would be willing to sell them to him. There is no record that the case was heard, nor that Ashmole purchased the rest of Hester Tradescant's personal contributions to the collection begun by her father-in-law, John Tradescant the elder.

At the same time that Ashmole was moving into the Ark and bringing legal action against Hester Tradescant's legatees, construction was proceeding on the building in Oxford which would house the new incarnation of the Tradescants' collection.[174] Located near the new Sheldonian Theater, the building was to contain a laboratory in the basement and a lecture theater on the ground floor, with the collection donated by Ashmole displayed on the upper floor. Although the building was inscribed so as to designate its three floors and functions—"*Musaeum Ashmoleanum, Schola Naturalis Historiae, Officina Chimica*"—it was known in its entirety as the "Musaeum Ashmoleanum."[175] When it was finally completed in 1683, Oxford had spent more than £4,500 to erect the building, a sum of money "which so exhausted the university finances that for some years afterwards the Bodleian Library was unable to buy books."[176] In February 1683 Ashmole began to pack the Tradescant collection so it could be transported to Oxford; by the beginning of May the twelve cartloads of objects "were all fixed in their distinct cabinets & places, and the roome furnished in every part of it," and on 21 May 1683 "Ashmoles Musaeum" was opened.[177] The collector Ralph Thoresby visited a year later and enthused that "the *Museum Ashmoleanum* . . . is absolutely the best collection of such rarities that ever I beheld," while another admiring contemporary declared "that it is justly believed, that in a few years it will be one of the most famous Repositories in *Europe*."[178]

The ideological status of Ashmole's collection and the subject positions that it created were complicated. The place of the collection within a royalist social order was symbolized by the fact that the museum was opened by the Duke and Duchess of York, who "were entertained first with the rarities in the upper room, & afterwards with a sumptuous banquet there."[179] To enter the building by the main entrance in the north front, the members of the royal family would have passed beneath "the crowned cypher" of Charles II which was displayed over the doorway.[180] Beneath the insignia of the monarch, a cartouche of Ashmole's coat of arms was located within the pediment of the main door, thus representing Ashmole's rank as a gentleman within a traditional social hierarchy.[181] Despite this facade of elite decorum, however, the museum was not operated like an aristocratic collection, available only to those visitors with approved social credentials: like the Ark, the Ashmolean Museum was accessible to anyone, regardless of rank or gender, who could afford the entrance fee. In 1710 Zacharias Conrad von Uffenbach, a wealthy German traveler, was appalled at the results of such commercial egalitarianism: when he first tried to enter the Ashmolean on a market day, it was so full of "country folk" that von Uffenbach decided to postpone his visit; when he finally did view the collection, he was scandalized that "the people impetuously handle everything in the usual English fashion and . . . even the women are allowed up here for sixpence; they run here and there, grabbing at everything and taking no rebuff from the *Sub-Custos.*"[182] In practice, then, the display of Ashmole's objects at Oxford subverted elite constructions of the collection as a marker of social distinction.

Ashmole's collection—and the identity as a collector which he constructed for himself—came to challenge and sometimes efface other displays of objects. A 1682 draft of the statutes of the Ashmolean Museum reveals that Ashmole intended his collection to subsume all extant or future collections at Oxford, as he specified "That the Rarities now in the Phisick & Anatomy Schoole there (except such as are necessary for the Anatomy Lecture) shalbe brought into the said Musaeum, when Mr: Ashmole sends downe his Rarities thither, & set up with them. And that all such Rarities as shalbe hereafter given to or bestowed upon the University, shalbe placed there, as soone as bestowed."[183] The Anatomy School had a sizeable collection of natural history specimens and "curiosities," including numerous gallstones, two dodos, and a unicorn's horn; as R. F. Ovenell remarks, "With such a collection so similar in character to Ashmole's Museum, and so closely situated, his wish to have the greater part of it transferred and absorbed into his own collections is understandable."[184] Although this stipulation was dropped from the final version of the statutes, Ashmole's

"Rarities" did literally displace another Oxford collection, for the construction of the new building necessitated the demolition of part of the wall, designed and built by Sir Christopher Wren, which housed in its niches specimens of the statues collected by the Earl of Arundel; in this instance Ashmole's collection was responsible for the effacement of remnants of elite Stuart collecting practices.

As he negotiated the meaning of his collection, Ashmole treated the association of the Tradescants with the objects he now owned in different ways. Contemporary descriptions of the collection often portray the Tradescants as its originators/owners, and Ashmole simply as a conduit by which the Tradescants' collection came to Oxford; while Ashmole was still negotiating with Oxford in 1677, Humphrey Prideaux wrote of "John Tredeskins raritys, which Elias Ashmole, in whose hands they are, hath promised to give to the University"; in March 1683 Anthony Wood referred to the cartloads "of Tredeskyns rarities [which] Came from Mr. Ashmole," while the Rev. Thomas Dixon reported that "John Tredeskins Rarities are come downe from London by water."[185] Sir Thomas Molyneux, who visited Oxford in July 1683, described the new building and remarked that the walls of "The Museum Ashmoleanum . . . are all hung round with John Tradescant's rarieties, and several others of Mr. Ashmol's own gathering."[186] Initially, Ashmole used the prestige surrounding the Tradescant collection to enhance his status as a donor to the University. Writing to the Vice Chancellor of Oxford after the museum had opened in May 1683, Ashmole said that he had wanted to indicate his esteem for the University for a long time, "and when Mr: Tredescants Collection of Rarities came to my hands, tho I was tempted to part with them for a very considerable Sum of money, and was also press't by honourable Persons to consigne them to another Society, I firmly resolv'd to deposite them no where but with You."[187] Here, Ashmole tries to impress the Vice Chancellor with his generosity in giving such a famous and sought-after collection to Oxford.

If Ashmole thus turned the history of his collection into cultural capital when constructing his identity as donor, at other times he seemed intent on establishing himself not only as donor, but also as the sole origin of his collection. While Ashmole could not eradicate memories of the Tradescants' relationship to what he often termed "my Rarities," he could shape the institutional framework through which future visitors would apprehend the objects they viewed. As donor, Ashmole was the "new Lycurgus" of the museum which bore his name. Ashmole retained proprietary control over the collection until his death, and he used his ownership of the objects amassed by the Tradescants to represent himself at Oxford as the sole founder of the collection. In their accounts of the founding of the Ashmolean Museum, R. F. Ovenell speaks of Ashmole's "failure properly to acknowledge the name and source from which the greater part of his gift derived," and Martin Welch more bluntly observes that Ashmole "made sure that no reference was made to the Tradescants in the records of the institution built to house his collection" since "He realised that his posthumous reputation would rest on his gift to Oxford University."[188] Although he failed to do so within the Order of the Garter, in the official texts generated by the museum Ashmole fills "all the partes of the play he must act Pyramus and thisbee"—he is depicted simultaneously as owner, donor, and originator of the objects on display. The preamble to the final version of the statutes of the museum makes no mention of the Tradescants, and instead credits Ashmole with assembling the collection and locates its conceptual origins in the events of Ashmole's own life: "Because the knowledge of Nature is very necessarie to humaine life . . . I Elias Ashmole, out of my affection to this sort of Learning, wherein my selfe have taken & still doe take the greatest delight; for which cause aloe, I have amass'd together great variety of naturall Concretes & Bodies, & bestowed them on the University of Oxford, wherein my selfe have been a Student, & of which I have the honor to be a Member."[189] The Benefactors Book of the museum is likewise mute about the role of the Tradescants in creating the collection. The first keeper of the Ashmolean, Robert Plot—whose appointment was entirely at Ashmole's discretion—did not so much as mention the Tradescants in his encomium of Ashmole which was inscribed on the first pages of the museum's Book of Benefactors although, as Ovenell remarks, "there could have been no more fitting context in which to record the Museum's debt to the two Tradescants than in the Benefactors Book."[190] Plot also planned to publish a printed catalogue of the collection adorned with Ashmole's portrait.[191] Although the catalogue never appeared, Plot's Tradescant-free version of the origins of the collection appeared in print in 1686 when he included a panegyric to Ashmole in *The Natural History of Stafford-Shire*: "He hath obliged the learned world with many curious books, and lately the University of Oxford with the best History of Nature, Arts, and Antiquities, to be seen any where in the world; not in print, or Sculpture, but in a generous donation of the real things themselves; wherewith they have furnish't the new Musaeum lately there erected, and gratefully stiled it (as a perpetual memorial of so noble a benefaction) the Musaeum Ashmoleanum."[192]

In the establishment of the Ashmolean Museum at Oxford University, we see how an institution could be used to guarantee the perpetuation of an individual's identity which was rooted in the textualization, ownership, and display of a collection of physical objects. Like John Tradescant the younger, the childless Elias Ashmole died without a male heir and like Tradescant, Ashmole wanted to entrust his collection—and thus the preservation of his identity—to something more reliable than an individual who could easily transform another man's collection into the basis of his own self-fashioning. The epitaph erected to Ashmole in St. Mary's Church in Lambeth proclaims that Ashmole's identity is still embodied by the museum named after him: "Mortem obiit 18 Maii 1692, anno aetatis 76, sed durante Musaeo Ashmoleano Oxon. numquam moriturus," "He passed away on 18 May 1692, at the age of 76, but as long as the Ashmolean Museum at Oxford endures, he will never die."[193]

Chapter 2

Sons of Science

Natural History and Collecting

According to John Aubrey's account of the death of Sir Francis Bacon, the former Lord Chancellor, after having been sent into political exile by James I for accepting bribes, perished in the pursuit of scientific knowledge:

As he was taking the air in a coach with Dr. Witherborne (a Scotchman, physician to the King) towards Highgate, snow lay on the ground, and it came into my lord's thoughts, why flesh might not be preserved in snow, as in salt. They were resolved they would try the experiment at once. They alighted out of the coach, and went into a poor woman's house at the bottom of Highgate Hill, and bought a hen, and made the woman gut it, and then stuffed the body with snow, and my lord did help to do it himself. The snow so chilled him, that he immediately fell so extremely ill, that he could not return to his lodgings (I suppose at Gray's Inn), but went to the earl of Arundel's house at Highgate, where they put him into a good bed warmed with a pan, but it was a damp bed that had not been laid-in about a year before, which gave him such a cold that in two or three days, as I remember Hobbes told me, he died of suffocation.[1]

This story, although probably fictitious, helped to establish the image of Bacon as a keen man of science which persists to this day. In the biographical narrative related by Aubrey we encounter an intrepid experimentalist; Bacon is portrayed as a man whose determination to discover the principles of nature, long frustrated by the demands of his political career, leads him as a frail senior citizen to risk his well-being for the sake of natural history.[2]

In light of the texts he authored, however, what is striking about the tale of Bacon and the lethal chicken is how far it diverges from Bacon's own vision of his proper role in scientific research. Bacon's writings, I shall argue, represent scientific research as a process of collecting which necessitates the prior creation of a collection of men. For Bacon, the gathering of materials fundamental to a reformed natural philosophy becomes the rationale for assembling and organizing a new bureaucracy, a body of men whom Bacon envisions himself administering. In Bacon's writings, we see how the activity of collecting could be conceived as a technology of social innovation in early modern England, a means by which new groups and new forms and positions of status could be created. Bacon never imagined himself as actually having to handle mundane objects like poultry carcasses, but instead envisioned that he would supervise a group of underlings who would gather data for him to assess. During the last five years of his life, however, Bacon bitterly realized that rather than overseeing a group of subaltern "factors," he could pursue his plans to compile a natural history only if he were to get his own hands dirty by gathering material himself. Bacon's chaplain and amanuensis, William Rawley, reported, "I have heard his lordship speak complainingly, that his lordship (who thinketh he deserveth to be an architect in this building) should be forced to be a workman and a labourer, and to dig the clay and burn the brick; and more than that (according to the hard condition of the Israelites at the latter end) to gather the straw and stubble over all the fields to burn the bricks withal."[3] Aubrey's narrative of Bacon's death portrays the one-time Lord Chancellor as being forced to collect the facts of nature for himself, with only an ad hoc assistant like the impoverished woman of Highgate Hill to help him. In the absence of a collection of men for him to administer, the pursuit of natural history proved fatal to Bacon. From this perspective, one could argue that Sir Francis Bacon died because he failed to realize his aspirations as a collector. In the decades after Bacon's death in 1626, however, other men modeled their own natural history projects on Bacon's schema, and more successfully created new social groupings which they organized around the activity of collecting.

The Study of Nature Before Bacon

During the sixteenth and seventeenth centuries, the conceptual frameworks which structured European approaches to the study of nature changed significantly. Although bestiaries, herbals, and lapidaries were popular in the Middle Ages, "natural history as a discipline was an early modern invention."[4] Rooted in the encyclopedic tradition which stretched back to Pliny, sixteenth- and seventeenth-century practitioners of natural philosophy took as their field of study res naturae, all the "things of nature," a vast subject matter which encompassed not only what we would now subdivide into the fields of zoology, botany, entomology, and ornithology, but also cosmology, astronomy, geography, chorography, mineralogy, and meteorology. Unlike their ancient and medieval predecessors, however, early modern naturalists "increasingly saw philosophical inquiry as the product of a continuous engagement with material culture,"[5] and by the late seventeenth century, works of natural history were "grainy with facts, full of experiential particulars conspicuously detached from explanatory or theoretical moorings."[6] During this process of change, as Harold J. Cook has recently argued, natural history became the "big science," the "cutting edge research" of the early modern period.[7]

The seventeenth-century emphasis on individuals' experience of nature departed drastically from earlier concepts of what constituted knowledge of the natural world. Devoted either to medical lore or allegorical commentary, medieval works about natural philosophy were compendia of data gleaned not from firsthand observation, but rather mined from earlier written accounts. The goal of the medieval natural philosopher was not to observe and describe res naturae, but rather "to refine and distill the universal truths he found in books and received from his teachers,"[8] truths concerning the eternal interrelationships between human beings and the natural world. Thus the medieval natural philosopher was a compiler who used his philological skills to elucidate what Foucault has famously described as "the system of resemblances"[9] which was believed to structure God's creation; plants and minerals were analyzed as remedies for the humoral imbalances which caused human disease, and animals were assessed as moral emblems. From a medieval perspective, then, bitter apple (colocynth) was noteworthy for being "hot and dry in the third degree" and thus a powerful antidote to superfluities of phlegm, while the ibis was a feathered object-lesson for sinful Christians:

There is a bird called the YBIS which cleans out its bowels with its own beak. It enjoys eating corpses or snakes' eggs, and from such things it takes food home for its young, which comes most acceptable. It walks about near the seashore by day and night, looking for little dead fish or other bodies which have been thrown up by the waves. It is afraid to enter the water because it cannot swim. This bird is typical of Carnal Man, who goes in for deadly dealings as if they were good spiritual food—by which his miserable soul gets nourished for punishment.[10]

Knowledge of the interconnections between human life and res naturae, gathered in the course of reading authoritative texts, was thus the focus of medieval natural philosophy.

Although inflected by a humanist veneration of classical sources and enthusiasm for emblems, this "dominance of natural history by similitude"[11] continued well into the early modern period. Full of myths and symbolism, works like Konrad Gesner's mid-sixteenth-century *Historia Animalium* exemplify what William B. Ashworth terms "the emblematic

world view" characteristic of much natural history written before the middle of the seventeenth century.[12] At the same time, however, different
conceptual frameworks for analyzing nature were also emerging. Rooted in
humanist scholarship on the writings of Galen and Dioscorides, a move-
ment to reform knowledge of *materia medica* arose in fifteenth-century
Italy which emphasized direct experience of the natural world: by 1550 it
was increasingly common for medical students "to be sent to the surrounding countryside so that they would learn how to recognize the most important medical herbs in the field."[13] This new humanist interest in nature not
only affected the training and practice of physicians, but also came to
suffuse Italian courtly culture. Princes began to patronize research into
natural history by competitively establishing professorships, anatomy theaters, museums, and botanical gardens, and the vogue for studying and
displaying nature was soon taken up by urban patricians as well.[14] At the
same time, Pliny's account of his garden became central to humanist attempts to recreate the built environment of classical antiquity, and "power
gardens," featuring classical sculpture and striking visual effects, became
chic sites for exhibiting one's social status.[15] During the late Tudor period,
this fashionable preoccupation with res naturae crossed the English Chan-
nel as members of the aristocracy came to appreciate and copy elite Italian
modes of the experience and display of nature.[16]

    Other aspects of early modern natural history emerged not from hu-
manist scholarship but from contact with the New World. The European
discovery of previously undescribed plants and animals in the Americas
greatly complicated the relationship of early modern natural philosophers
to ostensibly authoritative texts. As J. H. Elliott remarks, "The superiority
of direct personal observation over traditional authority was proved time
and time again in the new environment of America."[17] Challenging the
time-honored philological approach to analyzing nature, creatures such as
anteaters and toucans did not appear in classical writings on natural history;
these novelties "came to the Old World naked, without emblematic significance," and thus while Gesner could fashion a rich, scholarly "cultural
history" for the fox, an animal known since antiquity, he could provide only
contemporary observations about a recently discovered creature like the
opossum.[18] As Anthony Pagden notes, attempts were made to assimilate
such New World anomalies within the traditional episteme: "American
flora and fauna were forced into classical botanical and biological categories, and Amerindians were located and relocated in a variety of temporal
and spatial relationships to the European and the Asian."[19] Unable to rely
on the likes of Pliny or Alciati for guidance, however, naturalists increasingly turned instead to firsthand, contemporary descriptions of the ap-

pearance and behavior of things found only in the New World. By the middle of the seventeenth century, Joseph Glanvill could warn that by vainly seeking to uphold the authority of Aristotle, "we are not likely to reach the Treasures on the other side of the *Atlantick*, the directing of the World the way to which, is the noble end of true Philosophy."[20] Gradually, then, a philological understanding of the natural world, rooted in knowledge of ancient texts, lost its monopoly over Europeans' apprehension of nature, and a new emphasis on "facts"—the products of firsthand observation—began to shape concepts of the role and practice of natural history within early modern culture.

Bacon's Natural Philosophy

Emerging from this context of imperial expansion and the increasing authority of contemporary experience, the approach to scientific research developed by Sir Francis Bacon was symptomatic of the "dismantling of the emblematic world view" which occurred in sixteenth- and seventeenth-century England.[21] Bacon depicted his blueprint for a reformed study of nature as a logical response to the European voyages of discovery:

It would disgrace us, now that the wide spaces of the material globe, the lands and seas, have been broached and explored, if the limits of the intellectual globe should be set by the narrow discoveries of the ancients. Nor are those two enterprises, the opening up of the earth and the opening up of the sciences, linked and yoked together in any trivial way. Distant voyages and travels have brought to light many things in nature, which may throw fresh light on human philosophy and science and correct by experience the opinions and conjectures of the ancients.[22]

Bacon condemned the bookish natural philosophy of the encyclopedic tradition: "First then, away with antiquities, and citations or testimonies of authors; also with disputes and controversies and differing opinions; everything in short which is philological."[23] By reiterating the ostensibly timeless, universal principles of science articulated by ancient writers, the philologists, Bacon argued, were like "spiders, who make cobwebs out of their own substances," doomed to remain "barren of production of works for the benefit of the life of man."[24] Given the failure of traditional natural philosophy, Bacon maintained, "There was but one course left, therefore,—to try the whole thing anew upon a better plan, and to commence a total reconstruction of sciences, arts, and all human knowledge, raised upon the proper foundations."[25]

Rather than "literature and book-learning," Bacon insisted that natural philosophy should instead "rest on the solid foundation of experience of every kind, and the same well examined and weighed."[26] In scholastic natural philosophy, firsthand experience—facts—were dismissed as epistemologically dubious: according to Aristotle, "sense perception must be concerned with particulars, whereas knowledge depends on the recognition of the universal."[27] Bacon, by contrast, argued that "knowledges are as pyramides, whereof history is the basis: so of Natural Philosophy the basis is Natural History."[28] By establishing the natural history—a catalogue of observations about specific events—as the basis of a reformed, inductive science, Bacon was, as Lorraine Daston observes, "invert[ing] the relationship between natural history and natural philosophy, elevating the former to the status of foundation and corrective to the latter. He redeemed the modest particulars of natural history as the indubitable core of knowledge."[29]

Since natural philosophy was to be rooted in the "fresh examination of particulars,"[30] collecting and collections were essential to the inductive research program envisioned by Bacon. Bacon conceived of his natural history as lists of data, "scrubbed clean of conjecture and severed from theory,"[31] which would be gleaned from books, manufacturing processes, observations of natural phenomena, and directed experiments. Wonders were integral to Bacon's reform of knowledge: as part of the accumulation of material for a natural history, Bacon insisted that he would need to make "a substantial and severe collection of the Heteroclites or Irregulars of nature," entities "which have a digression and deflexion from the ordinary course of generations, productions, and motions."[32] By arguing that "we have to make a collection or particular natural history of all prodigies and monstrous births of nature; of everything in short that is in nature new, rare, and unusual," Bacon thus provided a "scientific" justification for collecting curiosities.[33] In the *Gesta Grayorum*, an entertainment written in 1594, Bacon envisioned the establishment of four new institutions: a lab, a library, a botanical garden which contained a menagerie, aviary, and fish ponds, and "a goodly great cabinet" in which were assembled inanimate natural objects, oddities, and "whatsoever the hand of man by exquisite art or engine hath made rare in stuff, form, or motion."[34] Through a careful process of induction and experimentation, investigators would gradually derive general truths from the massive body of material they accumulated.[35] Bacon insisted that in order to prevent researchers from arriving at premature conclusions, the natural history itself should be deliberately unsystematic, "a granary and storehouse of matters" full of accumulated raw materials: "For no man who is collecting and storing up materials for shipbuilding or the like, thinks of arranging them elegantly, as in a shop, and displaying them so as to please the eye; all his care is that they be sound and good, and that they be so arranged as to take up as little room as possible in the warehouse."[36] Thus, as Julie Robin Solomon has noted, Bacon depicted his reformed natural philosophy "primarily as an activity of collection."[37]

In his descriptions of how research should be conducted, Bacon structures collecting as the basis not only of knowledge, but also of a new social formation. Stressing the sheer volume of labor required to assemble the materials for his natural history, Bacon repeatedly argues that the development of an inductive natural philosophy necessarily entails the prior creation of a vast scientific work force. The immense scope of his project, Bacon insists, requires collaborative effort, since it was quite possible that "the description of the Instances should fill six times as many volumes as Pliny's history."[38] The compiling of the foundational natural history, Bacon maintains, "cannot be done as it should by a private man's industry": "For a history of this kind . . . is a thing of very great size, and cannot be executed without great labour and expense; requiring as it does many people to help."[39] Bacon does not envision this work force as an egalitarian fraternity of scientists, however, but instead advocates the creation of a rigorously differentiated hierarchy of workers, asserting that his program is "one in which the labours and industries of men (especially as regards the collecting of experience) may with the best effect be first distributed and then combined."[40] As John Leary has emphasized, "The plan to rationalize and direct the *activity* of scientific inquiry is also, of course, a plan to direct the *people* to whom the inquiry is entrusted."[41] Mirroring his proposed method of induction, which "proceeds along a strict hierarchy of increasing generality,"[42] Bacon depicts a work force organized into cognitive ranks, with low status investigators gathering data and their superiors first analyzing these collected materials, and then designing and performing experiments to generate more "Instances." At the top of this scientific bureaucracy would preside "the *Interpreter*"—a "new sort of royal judge," as Julian Martin suggests—who would survey all the facts amassed by his underlings and decree what axioms should be derived from the assembled data.[43]

As he contemplated his own role in the preparation of the natural history, Bacon felt that he was best suited to occupy the position of the mastermind Interpreter. In the *Parasceve*, Bacon says that to collect data he will require the labor of others, because "the materials on which the intellect has to work are so widely spread, that one must employ factors and merchants to go everywhere in search of them and bring them in. Besides I hold it to be somewhat beneath the dignity of an undertaking like mine that I should spend my own time in a matter which is open to almost every man's industry."[44] From Bacon's perspective, then, in order to accumulate the "particulars" fundamental to an inductive science, he should first organize a group of men to function as his subordinate assistants. As the "architect" of a reformed natural philosophy, Bacon saw himself *directing* the compilation of a natural history, acting as the scientific arbiter who would derive axioms from the "granary and storehouse of matters" gathered by lesser men. Thus in Bacon's writings collecting becomes not only the basis of scientific knowledge, but also the rationale for a new social order Bacon himself intends to administer.

The Politics of Bacon's Natural Philosophy

Bacon's vision of himself as a mandarin of natural philosophy was inextricably bound up with the relentless quest for political power which shaped his life. Born into a prominent Tudor family—his father, Sir Nicholas Bacon, was Elizabeth I's Lord Keeper of the Great Seal, while his uncle William Cecil, Lord Burghley, served the queen as Lord Treasurer—Bacon "had been apprenticed for power since childhood" and felt that it was only just that he should become a high-ranking political insider.[45] However, when Bacon's father suddenly died in 1579, eighteen-year-old Francis, the youngest of five sons, found himself in straitened circumstances. Lacking an income commensurate with his social status and career expectations, Bacon studied law, and for more than two decades after his father's death lived far beyond his means as he tried to worm his way into royal patronage. Elizabeth never did favor him, but Bacon was knighted by James I in 1603—although, despite his wish not to be "merely gregarious in a troop,"[46] he received his title amid a crowd of 300. The unwillingly "gregarious" Bacon was left to languish in political obscurity for several more years after James's accession, but he finally received preferment and obtained a series of posts and honors from the king, so that when he was impeached for bribery in 1621, Bacon had become Lord Chancellor and held the title of Viscount St. Alban. Simonds D'Ewes cattily remarked that, when Bacon gained this latter honor,

all men [were] wondering at the exceeding vanity of his pride and ambition: for his estate in land was not above four or five hundred pounds per annum at the uttermost, and his debts were generally thought to be near £30,000. Besides, he was fain to support his very household expenses, being very lavish, by taking great bribes in all causes of moment that came before him.[47]

Bacon often presented his plans to reform natural philosophy as springing from unselfish, public-spirited motives. Men should seek knowledge, Bacon piously asserts, not "for superiority to others, or for profit, or fame, or power, or any of these inferior things; but for the benefit and use of life."[48] In the first book of *The Advancement of Learning* (itself written as a bid for James's patronage), Bacon dissociates political careerism from the intellectual pursuits he advocates, lamenting that in the past, men frequently "have entered into a desire of learning and knowledge . . . for lucre and profession" or to secure "a tower of state, for a proud mind to raise itself upon," instead of striving to fashion "a rich storehouse, for the glory of the Creator and the relief of man's estate."[49] Before his political career took off, Bacon claimed that he sought royal preferment "because I hoped that, if I rose to any place of honour in the state, I should have a larger command of industry and ability to help me in my work," which was aimed at "the discovery of new arts, endowments, and commodities for the bettering of man's life."[50]

Despite such claims of altruism, however, Bacon's scheme for the advancement of knowledge and his desire for his own political advancement were inextricably bound together. As Julian Martin argues, Bacon "was a politician and statesman by trade, and he always regarded himself as such, and not as a natural philosopher *per se*."[51] The relationship between Bacon's ideas about natural philosophy and his political ambition is revealed in a famous letter which Bacon wrote to Lord Burghley in 1592. Still shown no favor by Elizabeth, Bacon attempted to spur his uncle to help him:

I confess that I have as vast contemplative ends, as I have moderate civil ends: for I have taken all knowledge to be my province; and if I could purge it of two sorts of rovers, whereof the one with frivolous disputations, confutations, and verbosities, the other with blind experiments and auricular traditions and impostures, hath committed so many spoils, I hope I should bring in industrious observations, grounded conclusions, and profitable inventions and discoveries; the best state of that province. . . . And I do easily see, that place of any reasonable countenance doth bring commandment of more wits than of a man's own; which is the thing I greatly affect. And for your Lordship, perhaps you shall not find more strength and less encounter in any other.[52]

Here, Bacon presents himself as deserving a position of power, entailing "commandment of more wits than [his] own," through which he can realize his "vast contemplative ends." Bacon presents this vision of himself as a commander of wits in overtly political terms: as Martin observes, by depicting knowledge as his "province," Bacon portrays himself as a high-ranking bureaucrat who oversees "an administrative unit of the central government."[53] Bacon attempts to create a political position for himself by imagining the reform of natural philosophy as an endeavor which should be conducted by a new department of state—with Bacon as its director, of course. Thus by insisting that he needs to assemble a large work force to collect data for a natural history, Bacon transforms his inductive method into a bureaucratic machine of the monarchy, with himself as an elite government official.

Like his 1592 letter to Burghley, most of Bacon's writings about natural philosophy were produced when Bacon was trying to gain (or, after his impeachment, *re*gain) the monarch's favor. Martin Elsky comments that Bacon "tended to give serious attention to his scientific pursuits only when his political life flagged," and that he primarily developed and publicized his blueprint for scientific research as "a crutch to lean on during times of political frustration," creating a means by which Bacon could attract the attention of the powerful and imagine himself as a figure of authority.[54] In Bacon's alignment of natural philosophy with his desire for royal favor, we find evidence to support Mario Biagioli's claim that in the early modern period, "Gaining support and legitimation for a new theory or discipline implied an often opportunistic rearrangement of elements of pre-existing social scenarios."[55] Bacon presented his reformed natural philosophy as "a splendid support for the imperial state," not simply in its scope and attendant prestige, but also in its capacity to control sources of intellectual authority which could threaten the ideology of absolutism.[56] Bacon's self-serving quest to bring natural philosophy under royal control thus demonstrates that emergent "scientific sociabilities" were not "predicated on a subversion of the processes whereby court society constructed power and distinction through webs of tense interdependence between subjects and princes,"[57] but rather were modeled on (and intertwined with) courtly social relations.

In seeking the "commandment" of "wits," Bacon's desire to head a department of state was also in part an attempt to engage in a traditional form of aristocratic display: the deployment of a retinue. The bureaucracy which Bacon envisioned himself directing was a professional analogue to the household entourage with which a member of the elite exhibited his status in sixteenth- and seventeenth-century England. In 1617 Bacon was named Lord Keeper, and the lavish festivities which marked his assumption of his father's old office gave Bacon a chance to show off the magnificence of his household. George Gerrard recounted,

Our Lord Keeper exceeds all his predecessors in the bravery and multitude of his servants. It amazes those that look on his beginnings, besides never so indulgent a master. On the first day of the term he appeared in his greatest glory; for to the

Hall, besides his own retinue, did accompany him all the Lords of his Majesty's Council and others, with all knights and gentlemen that could get horses and footcloths.[58]

By 1618 Bacon had more than 120 servants and insisted that they should be opulently clothed for his greater glory, Bacon's retainers wore liveries bearing his crest, and Aubrey reported that "none of his servants durst appear before him without Spanish leather boots; for he would smell the neats leather, which offended him."[59] Thus in attempting to organize a new governmental hierarchy over which he himself would preside, Bacon sought to structure the work force needed for his inductive natural philosophy as a version of his own household, allowing him to display his status in the form of a group of subordinates.

In other ways, however, Bacon's vision of a scientific work force seems less compatible with a courtly social formation rooted in dynastic relations. Perhaps not surprisingly, given that his own father began life as the son of a yeoman, Bacon often expressed opinions that ran counter to his society's preoccupation with lineage.[60] Since, in theory, genealogy and rank were inextricably linked, lineage was considered to be central to a man's social identity in the early modern period: a member of the elite was to regard himself as "a trustee for the handing on of blood, property, and tradition" who was responsible for perpetuating his family by marrying well and begetting legitimate sons.[61] Although Bacon made a financially advantageous marriage when he was forty-five (to thirteen-year-old Alice Barnham, daughter of a wealthy London alderman), he never had children.[62] As scholars have often remarked, some of Bacon's writings present a negative assessment of the impact of family obligations on men's careers. Bacon begins his essay "Of Marriage and Single Life" by observing, "He that hath wife and children hath given hostages to fortune; for they are impediments to great enterprises, either of virtue or mischief. Certainly the best works, and of greatest merit for the public, have proceeded from the unmarried or childless men; which both in affection and means have married and endowed the public."[63] Similarly, in the essay "Of Parents and Children," Bacon stresses the drawbacks of begetting a family: "The perpetuity by generation is common to beasts; but memory, merit, and noble works, are proper to men. And surely a man shall see the noblest works and foundations have proceeded from childless men; which have sought to express the images of their minds, where those of their bodies have failed. So the care of posterity is most in them that have no posterity."[64] Likewise, as he analyzes the myth of Orpheus in *De Sapientia Veterum*, Bacon suggests that if men see children as a means by which they can perpetuate their memories, they become complacent and accomplish less than if they had no offspring:

For true it is that the clearer recognition of the inevitable necessity of death sets men upon seeking immortality by merit and renown. Also it is wisely added in the story, that Orpheus was averse from women and from marriage; for the sweets of marriage and the dearness of children commonly draw men away from performing great and lofty services to the commonwealth; being content to be perpetuated in their race and stock, and not in their deeds.[65]

This notion that childless men will be more motivated to throw themselves into fame-producing public service also shaped Bacon's game plan for assembling "wits" to aid him in his reform of natural philosophy. In 1608 Bacon made a list of prominent men whom he should try to interest in his scientific project. He noted that he should target some, like the Lord of Northumberland and Sir Walter Ralegh, because they were "already inclined to experim[en]ts," but he assessed others as likely prospects on the basis of their childlessness: Richard Bancroft, Archbishop of Canterbury, was a possibility, "being single and glorious, and beleeving the sense," as was Launcelot Andrews, Bishop of Chicester, being not only "a professor to some experim[en]ts," but also "single, rych, [and] sickly."[66]

One could view Bacon's conjunction of childlessness and male accomplishment as reflecting his "subordination of private to public morality," his unselfish conviction that "public life has a higher value than private life."[67] I would argue, however, that the relationship between Bacon's plan to collect the materials for a natural history and the "public life" of early modern England was far from straightforward. Instead of simply reinforcing the aristocratic values of a monarchy, Bacon sometimes structures the homosociality of his natural philosophy project so as to offer an alternative basis for social relations; rather than a "society of blood," in which wealth and status are transmitted by procreation within marriage,[68] Bacon creates a model of a new social formation in which heredity and power are unconnected. By conflating the lineal concerns of an aristocratic patriarch with his inductive research program, Bacon can imagine a society in which dynastic relations of alliance—including those which legitimate the authority of a hereditary monarch—have become irrelevant. Thus in some of Bacon's imaginative writings, the process of collecting data for a natural history becomes the foundation of a social order in which neither kings nor biological fathers exercise power.

William Rawley asserts in his biography of Bacon, "Children he had none; which, though they be the means to perpetuate our names after our deaths, yet he had other issues to perpetuate his name, the issues of his brain; in which he was ever happy and admired, as Jupiter was in the production of Pallas."[69] Rawley's comparison of Bacon with Jupiter, the powerful god who parthenogenetically gave birth to Wisdom, points toward images of self-sufficient male generation in Bacon's own writings. In the monologue *The Masculine Birth of Time*, probably written in 1602 or 1603,[70] an older man explains to a younger man why and how the study of natural philosophy should be reformed in an effort to recruit the young man to the speaker's cause. Throughout the work, the language of kinship is applied to the relationships and activities of men who are not related by blood. From the beginning of his monologue, the speaker calls his silent interlocutor "son" and depicts natural philosophy as an entity which creates a nonbiological family: "science must be such as to select her followers, who must be worthy to be adopted into her family."[71] Most strikingly, at the conclusion of his diatribe the paternalistic speaker declares,

"My dear, dear boy, what I purpose is to unite you with *things themselves* in a chaste, holy, and legal wedlock; and from this association you will secure an increase beyond all the hopes and prayers of ordinary marriages, to wit, a blessed race of Heroes or Supermen who will overcome the immeasurable helplessness and poverty of the human race, which cause it more destruction than all giants, monsters, or tyrants, and will make you peaceful, happy, prosperous, and secure. . . . Take heart, then, my son, and give yourself to me so that I may restore you to yourself."[72]

The final sentence of the speaker's monologue, with its complex, homoerotically charged dynamic of submission and empowerment, foregrounds the relationship which must be established prior to the young man's union with the particulars of natural history: the young man must assume his subordinate role as the speaker's "son." Mark Breitenberg has observed that Bacon's speaker uses contemporary constructions of gender to evoke an image of male inheritance predicated on female chastity, and Evelyn Fox Keller has suggested that this imagery "allows simultaneously for the appropriation and denial of the feminine."[73] What I would emphasize, however, is the subversive potential of the homosocial relationships advocated by Bacon's would-be father figure; along with "the feminine," the speaker also appropriates and denies relations of alliance. Although "*things themselves*" are feminized as a virginal bride whom the "son" should wed, the "marriage" the speaker proposes is, literally speaking, one which cannot generate lineal descendants for the young man. The gendered diction of marriage and chastity thus disguises the fact that as he tries to win over his prospective "son," the father figure is advocating as superior to "ordinary" wedlock a biologically unproductive form of "marriage." In his final appeal, Bacon's speaker asks the young man to accept a place in a new, nonbiological dynasty which will allow him to produce better offspring in the form of knowledge, rather than flesh-and-blood children. Thus the homosocial relations which Bacon hopes will bind his "sons" of science to him provide a fictive example of what Lisa Jardine has described as the "new kinds of liaisons between men . . . [which] came into competition with the more traditional forms of liaison, or bond-forming, between dynastic houses" in Tudor and Stuart England.[74] And if, as Alan Stewart has suggested, in the early modern period "sodomy is by definition a disturbance of alliance/ marriage arrangements,"[75] then the new kind of scientific social grouping Bacon envisions in *The Masculine Birth of Time* is, potentially at least, rooted in sodomitical social relations.

Natural History, Collecting, and Social Innovation in Bacon's New Atlantis

The disjunction between the social relations of Bacon's scientific work force and a social order rooted in dynastic reproduction becomes even more apparent in Bacon's prose fiction *New Atlantis*. This work was published in 1627, the year after Bacon's death, and although one cannot assign a date to its composition, it is tempting to view the narrative as a product of Bacon's political exile, a compensatory depiction of a state in which a man like Bacon could wield immense power.[76] In the *New Atlantis*, Bacon portrays a fictional society in which a scientific research institution, similar to the one Bacon had described decades earlier in the *Gesta Grayorum*, dominates all aspects of life. The narrative is recounted by a Spanish sailor whose ship inadvertently discovers Bensalem, an island in the South Sea, while attempting to navigate from Peru to East Asia. The narrator and his companions are allowed ashore and gradually learn about the history and social order of Bensalem. The story concludes with a detailed account of the activities of the research and development institution called "Solomon's House."[77]

In his representation of Solomon's House, Bacon constructs a model of a scientific community organized to pursue an inductive natural philosophy—a project, as Bacon had advocated, which is rooted in the collection of data. The thirty-six Fellows of the institution are assisted by "novices and apprentices," as well as "a great number of servants and attendants," and the entire work force is structured as a hierarchy of labor and knowledge.[78] Nine of the Fellows, subdivided into teams of three, devote their efforts to gathering "particulars" from books and the "mechanical arts," and to conducting "new experiments" in the House's research facilities—caves, towers, menageries, aviaries, fish ponds, breweries, and "engine-houses."[79] The single largest category among the data collectors consists of the "Merchants of Light," Fellows who travel secretly to foreign countries and bring back to Solomon's House "the books, and abstracts, and patterns of experiments of all other parts."[80] As the European visitors are told, Bensalem thus conducts "a trade, not for gold, silver, or jewels; nor for silks; nor for spices; nor any other commodity of matter; but only for God's first creature, which was *Light*."[81] In their exploitation of knowledge collected from local artisans and foreign nations, the Fellows of Solomon's House are, as Charles C. Whitney has suggested, engaging in a "covert form of colonization," importing into their midst "raw material" from less technically developed social groups.[82] However, the Fellows of Solomon's House are not interested in the military might, territorial conquest, or expansion of markets normally associated with imperialism; rather, they are simply concerned to acquire new "Instances" for themselves. In Bensalem, imperialism is conducted through—and recast as—the activity of collecting.

Taken together, the specialized teams of information gatherers act as the "factors and merchants" Bacon had described in the *Parasceve*, men who are dispatched throughout Bensalem and the world to gather the raw materials for the cognitive "warehouses" of Solomon's House. Next up the bureaucratic ladder of Solomon's House come teams of Fellows who respectively arrange the data into tables, suggest practical applications, and then devise and conduct new experiments. At the apex of the knowledge pyramid preside the three "Interpreters of Nature" who "raise the former discoveries by experiments into greater observations, axioms, and aphorisms."[83] As he enumerates "the riches of Solomon's House" for the visiting Spaniards, one of the head researchers states, "We have large and deep caves . . . We have high towers . . . We have also large and various orchards and gardens . . . We have also precious stones of all kinds . . . we have also perfume-houses . . . We have also . . . novices and apprentices."[84] In this lengthy passage, as Amy Boesky observes, the leader of Solomon's House uses a language of ownership that transforms experimental processes—and the individuals whose labor catalyzes these processes—into physical possessions.[85] In his portrait of this program of research, Bacon presents a scientific community whose activities, work force, and facilities are conceived as collections of objects.

Bacon's depiction of Bensalem seems intended to evoke associations with the reign of James I. The name of the great ruler of Bensalem who founded the research "House," Solamona, immediately calls to mind the Old Testament figure of King Solomon, with whom James was identified in Stuart propaganda.[86] Bacon himself tried to capitalize on James's status as "our *Brittish Salomon*"[87] in the dedication to the *Instauratio magna*, suggesting that a Solomonic ruler worth his salt would finance Bacon's scientific endeavors:

I have a request to make—a request no way unworthy of your Majesty . . . ; namely, that you who resemble Solomon in so many things—in the gravity of your judgments, in the peacefulness of your reign, in the largeness of your heart, in the noble variety of the books which you have composed—would further follow his example in taking order for the collecting and perfecting of a Natural and Experimental History.[88]

James privately complained that the book thus dedicated to him was "like the peace of God, that passeth all understanding," and he did not respond to Bacon's bid for funding.[89] The condition of the monarchy in Bensalem, however, suggests that James acted prudently, for Solamona, his counterpart in Bacon's fiction, has created a research organization which "has taken over most of the functions and privileges of royal power."[90] Although Bensalem is ostensibly ruled by a monarchy, Bacon's text marginalizes the role of the king; we learn of two long-dead monarchs, including Solamona, but the descendants of these legendary rulers are not in evidence. As Robert K. Faulkner observes, "While Bensalem is occasionally called a kingdom, and a king is mentioned, neither a royal person nor a royal action is shown."[91] Into this narrative and political vacuum slip the Fellows of Solomon's House, who act—and are treated—like the de facto rulers of Bensalem. Ian Box notes that "the important political powers exercised by the Fathers of Solomon's House suggest the degree to which the new natural philosophy has become a political program"—a political program which has apparently rendered the king of Bensalem a mere "figurehead."[92] When one of the highest-ranking researchers of Solomon's House enters the city, Bacon dwells at great length on the quality of his clothing, the rich decoration of his "chariot," the splendor of his large retinue, and the deferential parade of city officials who process after him; and when the narrator is later granted an audience, he finds the scientist "set upon a low throne richly adorned, and a rich cloth of state over his head, of blue satin embroidered."[93] We also learn that when the Bensalemites experienced a miraculous conversion to Christianity, this was accomplished only because a member of Solomon's House correctly understood a divine revelation—the scientists thus have the power to authorize religious doctrine. And at the very end of Bacon's text, one of the head researchers casually informs the narrator that the Fellows of Solomon's House, not the king of Bensalem and his government, exercise complete control over the dissemination of the knowledge the scientists amass, as the Fellows prefer to "keep secret" from the state a portion of their work.[94] In considering the ideological ambiguity of these aspects of the *New Atlantis*, Denise Albanese suggests that "The occulted, disembodied monarch of Bensalem can then be read in two ways: as imaginative reconfiguration of the Jacobean monarchy, and as model for a subsequent coexistence between scientific investigation and the dismantling of Stuart absolutism. The text forces recognition that the Bensalemite monarchy contains the possibility not just of its own effacement, but of its own erasure from the system of social and political order."[95] Thus in Bensalem, the scientific collection of particulars has become the material base of a technocratic elite whose political power can nullify that of a hereditary king.

The displacement of traditional forms of authority by the researchers of Solomon's House also appears in Bacon's depiction of the patriarchal family. In the *New Atlantis*, Bacon cannot effectively link the practices and values of Solomon's House with a social order predicated upon lineage. Bacon invites us to view his scientific research institution as an analogue to the family: he designates its leaders as "Fathers," while the term "House" suggests a dynasty. Given that James I habitually depicted himself as the father of his subjects and rooted his version of Divine Right theory in hereditary male succession, Bacon thus uses a highly politicized discourse of patriarchal authority to name Bensalem's scientists and their organization.[96] In Bacon's text, the scientific "House" has also adopted practices of collecting and display associated in Stuart England with aristocratic families. The long gallery in an early modern English country house was intended as "a display of dynastic pride and social success," often containing art objects, sculpture, and portraits of family members and leaders with whom the family wished to be identified, such as past and contemporary kings and queens or Roman emperors.[97] In a parallel to the galleries of elite Stuart country houses, Bacon reports that Solomon's House contains "two very long and fair galleries" which display "patterns and samples of all manner of the more rare and excellent inventions" amassed by the scientists, as well as "the statua's of all the principal inventors," including Columbus, Roger Bacon, and members of Solomon's House who have devised "excellent works."[98] The galleries of Solomon's House, rather than emblematizing the status of members of a hereditary elite, thus exhibit the power of a group of men—the Fellows of the research institution—whose corporate status is derived not from lineage, but from their scientific collection of "particulars."

Some aspects of Bensalemite culture might seem at first to contradict this de-emphasis of bloodlines as the source of identity and power. Bacon's account of the activities of Solomon's House is preceded by a lengthy description of a ceremony which ostensibly honors patrilineage. For Bacon's narrator, this "Feast of the Family" demonstrates that Bensalem is "compounded of all goodness."[99] If the male head of a family—called a "Tirsan"—produces at least thirty living descendants, the state foots the bill for a ritual celebrating the patriarch's reproductive prowess. For two days preceding the ceremony itself, the Tirsan and the governor of the city in which he resides "sitteth in consultation concerning the good estate of the family,"[100] straightening out the finances, morality, marriage plans, and career paths of any problem cases among the Tirsan's offspring and their children. The ceremony itself displays the Tirsan's entire family within an elaborately decorated feasting chamber—although, "if there be a mother from whose body the whole lineage is descended," she is closeted away in a loft "where she sitteth, but is not seen."[101] The Feast is thus structured as a display of male reproductive self-sufficiency, Bensalem's recreation of the myth of Jupiter giving birth to Minerva.

Bacon clearly associates the patrilineal family with the monarchy as institutions in Bensalem. The centerpiece of the ritual leading up to the actual Feast of the Family is the presentation of "the King's Charter," embossed in gold with the king's image, which contains "gift of revenew, and many privileges, exemptions, and points of honour" granted to the Tirsan.[102] According to Bacon's narrator, this royal charter is addressed "*To such an one our well-beloved friend and creditor*" because "the king is debtor to no man, but for propagation of his subjects."[103] After the charter has been bestowed, the feast is then consumed to the accompaniment of hymns, with the Tirsan being served by his sons, but "none of his descendants sit with him, of what degree or dignity soever, except he hap to be of Solomon's House."[104] At the conclusion of the feast, the Tirsan publicly blesses the members of his lineage, who are then allowed to "fall to music and dances."[105]

As Arthur Johnston observes, it seems that Bacon intends the Feast of the Family as a response to Plato's argument in the *Republic* that the family unit should be abolished.[106] Yet if Bacon does not eliminate the family from the social order of Bensalem, his depiction of the Feast of the Family nonetheless calls into question the political importance of biological paternity and lineal descent. While in Sir Thomas More's *Utopia*, the patriarchal kin group serves as the economic and social basis of society,[107] in the *New Atlantis*, by contrast, the relationship between social authority and the family is blurred. The son who is allowed to sit with his Tirsan-father at the Feast of the Family is so honored not because of his place in his father's lineage, but because of his professional relationship with the nonbiological "Fathers" of Solomon's House. Moreover, the social and political authority tacitly accorded the members of Solomon's House by the citizens of Bensalem cannot be aligned with familial structures. Just as Solomon's House seems to obviate the need for a monarch, so too the activities and values of Bensalem's science elite seem functionally unrelated to the celebration of paternity and lineage which Bacon enshrines in the Feast of the Family. Thus rather than underlining the congruence between the patriarchal family and political power—the stuff of James I's claims to Divine Right—the Feast of the Family instead highlights the disjunction which exists between lineage and authority in Bensalem. Despite his attempt to depict Bensalem as a society rooted in patrilineal family values, then, Bacon ends up creating a model of a social formation in which the hereditary foundation of status and authority has become obsolete. The virile Tirsan and his king are, for all practical purposes, politically impotent.

Neither kings nor fathers serve as the true locus of power in Bensalem. The "fair galleries" of Solomon's House, rather than emblematizing the authority of a hereditary elite, instead display the power of men whose status is derived not from the perpetuation of their bloodlines, but from their activities of collecting data within a non-lineal professional group. The collection has lost its function as a signifier of elite status within a political and social order predicated on lineage, and has instead come to constitute a new form of authority. Bacon's text thus presents an uneasy combination of dominant and emergent ideologies: although the patriarchal family is officially celebrated, the "house" as patrilineal kin group has become divorced from the scientific "House" as an infrastructure for the creation and display of non-dynastic status.[108] As modeled in the *New Atlantis*, Baconian science threatens to transform both the monarchy and the patrilineal kin group into powerless anachronisms; in their place, the Father of Solomon's House—the position which Bacon envisioned himself occupying as "architect" of an inductive natural philosophy—becomes a figure of social and political authority.

Ironically, the very form of Bacon's text similarly testifies to the power embodied within the practice of scientific collecting in early modern England. Bacon's narrative ends abruptly, and in his introductory comments to the *New Atlantis*, Rawley observes that Bacon did not compose the account of "the best state or mould of a commonwealth" which he had originally intended. Bacon abandoned such political concerns, Rawley apologizes, because his "desire of collecting the Natural Histories diverted him, which he preferred many degrees before it."[109] Both thematically and structurally, then, Bacon's *New Atlantis* testifies to the formative influence which scientific collecting could exert on early modern English cultural practices. And Rawley's apology for the fragmentary condition of the *New Atlantis*, like Aubrey's story of Bacon's death, indicates how far Bacon fell short of realizing his vision of collecting as a technology of social innovation. Rather than serving as the material base of a new, non-lineal social formation from which he could derive authority, the gathering of scientific data was finally a solitary pursuit for the disgraced Lord Chancellor, an index of his distance from a position of political influence.

After the Fall: Bacon and the Virtuosos

Despite the subversive ideology latent in the *New Atlantis* and other writings, Bacon strove to regain the king's favor during the years following his impeachment. Soon after he was disgraced, Bacon tried to interest the king in "appoint[ing] me some task to write," "since now my study is my exchange and my pen my factor for the use of my talent."[110] At the same time, however, Bacon also endeavored to construct an identity for himself beyond the scope of the Stuart court. After he had presented James with a manuscript copy of the work, Bacon published his *History of the Reign of Henry VII* in 1622, dedicated to Prince Charles; through the double incarnation of the *History*, Bacon attempted to inhabit two social identities at once, as both a courtly writer of manuscripts and an author of printed books who seeks a wider audience.[111] As his enforced retirement wore on, Bacon increasingly embraced print authorship as a mode of identity formation, and by 1625 he could portray his political exile as a fortunate fall: "But for myself, my age, my fortune, yea my Genius, to which I have hitherto done but scant justice, calls me now to retire from the stage of civil action and betake myself to letters, and to the instruction of the actors themselves, and the service of Posterity."[112]

The means by which to secure "Posterity"—descendants—in the absence of biological children became a primary focus of Bacon's activities. As he had done throughout his life, Bacon after his impeachment initially regarded his scientific studies as something to fall back on should he fail to obtain a position of political power: "I am like ground fresh. If I be left to myself I will graze and bear natural philosophy: but if the King will plough me up again, and sow me with anything, I hope to give him some yield."[113] Given his apparently irrevocable status as a political pariah, however, Bacon had no choice but to "bear natural philosophy." Bacon intended that endowed lectureships in natural philosophy should be established in his name at Oxford and Cambridge, but he died so deeply in debt that they could not be founded,[114] and so his posthumous reputation depended on the survival of his ideas in the form of his "works and writings," "that durable part of my memory."[115] Although, as Adrian Johns has documented in great detail, the "fixity" of early modern printed texts was highly problematic,[116] Bacon and his trusted servant Rawley nonetheless turned to print as the vehicle by which the reputation of the fallen Lord Chancellor could be rehabilitated and perpetuated, their textual activities governed, apparently, by Bacon's own maxim that "the images of men's wits and knowledge remain in books, exempted from the wrong of time and capable of perpetual renovation."[117] Scientific print authorship thus became the means by which Bacon attempted to fashion a new, noncourtly identity for himself.

During the last five years of his life, Bacon readied for public consumption the majority of the scientific works for which he would be remembered, and while much of this textual output consisted of the development or revision of works begun earlier, nevertheless it seems that Bacon was suddenly motivated to package his ideas for an audience that was, both in time and space, distant from the court which had rejected him.[118] In 1625 Bacon outlined his progress on his "Instauration," declaring, "I work for posterity," a sentiment repeated by his servant and disciple in natural philosophy, Thomas Bushell, who averred that Bacon had left "his written Works to Posterity."[119] By presenting Bacon's ideas about natural philosophy in printed books—and simultaneously translating many of his English writings into Latin—Bacon and Rawley extended their drive to recruit "factors and merchants" for Bacon's program beyond the former Lord Chancellor's own nation and lifetime. Rawley, as we have already noted, characterized Bacon's written works as his master's progeny, "the issues of his brain" which would outlive their progenitor to "perpetuate his name," and Rawley continued to serve as Bacon's posthumuous textual midwife well into the Interregnum.[120] Upon Bacon's death, Rawley assembled and published a collection of commemorative poems, and he continued to edit, translate, and publish Bacon's work for more than two decades after his master had died.[121]

As Bacon and Rawley had hoped, it was through his written "issues" that Bacon came to influence the conceptualization of natural philosophy in mid-seventeenth-century England—an influence that established collecting as a foundation both of natural history and of new social groupings. Long after Bacon's death in 1626, John Aubrey lambasted the "Paedantry" which, he felt, had dominated intellectual life in Elizabethan and Jacobean England, declaring, "*Things* were not then studied. My Lord Bacon first led that dance."[122] Aubrey's assessment of Bacon as the originator of a new, laudable scientific methodology was typical of the magisterial status Bacon came to be accorded after his death. During the early 1640s, "Bacon's stock as a symbol took a sharp upward turn,"[123] and, as the historian Charles Webster argues, the term "Baconianism" can aptly be used "to describe the dominant tendency in English natural philosophy in the middle decades of the seventeenth century."[124] During the Civil War and Interregnum, "Bacon was posthumously puritanized in England," and men such as Samuel Hartlib developed Baconian proposals for social and educational reform, guided by a utilitarian vision of England as a new Bensalem in which the collaborative efforts of scientists would result in an improved standard of living for the entire populace.[125] Yet Bacon's influence was by no means limited to puritan reformers, since during the 1640s and 1650s royalist members of the gentry and men associated with the London College of Physicians and Oxford University also came to regard themselves as the heirs of Bacon's approach to natural philosophy.[126] Thus by the middle of the seventeenth century, Bacon's works were being used by many English natural philosophers of diverse religiopolitical outlooks "to *justify* a concerted collective program of observational and experimental fact collecting."[127]

An important facet of early modern Baconianism was the adoption— and adaptation—of Bacon's methodology by English virtuosos. Originating from the Italian concept of the virtuoso as "a man with intellectual power (*virtù*) to command any situation," virtuosity became a "cultural ideal" that shaped the sensibility and activities of a self-styled elite in seventeenth-century England.[128] Central to the character of the virtuoso was his highly developed sense of curiosity, "an attitude of mind involving a fascination and admiration for the rare, novel, surprising, and outstanding in all spheres of life."[129] Strange physical objects—"curiosities"—were particularly valued as sites for the evocation and display of this outlook, and thus ownership of a collection of curiosities became an essential part of a virtuoso's program of self-fashioning. When William Rand published his translation of Pierre Gassendi's *Life of Peiresc* in 1657, he dedicated the book to John Evelyn as a man who displayed "the Principalitie of learned Curiositie in England"; although Rand was alluding to Evelyn's translation of the first book of Lucretius's *De Rerum Natura*, Evelyn automatically assumed that Rand was praising him "upon the report (it seemes) of our collection and Cimelium of raritys."[130] Evelyn's instinctive association of his status as a noteworthy individual with his reputation as a collector exemplifies how a virtuoso expected the "curiosity" aroused by the objects he possessed to be transferred to himself as the objects' owner.[131] Rather than symbolizing the collector as the ruler of a microcosm—as did the earlier encyclopedic collections of Francesco I de' Medici or Emperor Rudolph II—the curiosity cabinets of the seventeenth-century virtuosos made no pretense of being comprehensive in their scope; rather, they embodied distinctiveness.[132] Thus Lorraine Daston's characterization of early modern collections is particularly applicable to the curiosity cabinets of the English virtuosos: "The reality they depict is a nominalist one of individuals instead of categories, of cases that break the rules of the normal and predictable, of irreducible diversity."[133] The virtuoso *was* what he collected; he was a "curiosity," a rare individual who deserved admiration for his very anomalousness.

Paradoxically, however, in displaying his ostensible uniqueness, the English virtuoso was also creating and exhibiting his membership in a specific social group. "Curiosity" and "curiosities" were seventeenth-century class markers; as Walter E. Houghton, Jr., has observed, "the virtuoso is clearly a man of wealth and leisure: he is a gentleman."[134] Building on Houghton's classic analysis of early modern English virtuosos, William Eamon argues that the concept of the virtuoso "was born out of the crisis of the aristocracy" which had afflicted the nobility since the reign of Elizabeth I.[135] Beset by a series of social, economic, and political changes, the power and prestige of the English landed elite had gradually been eroding since the mid-sixteenth century. By the Stuart period, there were far more aspirants for court office than positions available, leaving most genteel would-be courtiers unemployed and thus stranded in the country on their estates, where they could easily languish, prone to melancholy and "fruit-lesse, vitious and empty conversations."[136] Under these circumstances, instead of preparation for service to the state, a gentleman's education came to be seen as the source of recreational activities with which the idle aristocrat could both occupy his time and gain status. In *The Anatomy of Melancholy*, Robert Burton declares that "amongst those exercises or recreations of the mind within doors, there is none so general, so aptly to be applied to all sorts of men, so fit and proper to expel idleness and melancholy, as that of study," and under this category Burton includes the appreciation of curiosities—"Indian pictures made of feathers, China works, frames, thaumatur-

gical motions, exotic toys."[137] As he thus warded off boredom, the studious
gentleman simultaneously displayed his social superiority. Peacham grimly
urges the need to distinguish "an ancient descended & deserved Gentleman" from "an intruding upstart, shot up with the last nights Mushroome"
and, as Obadiah Walker observes later in the seventeenth century, "ingenious Studies" are useful to gentlemen precisely because they are "such as
poorer Persons are not able to support."[138] Besides setting the individual
gentleman apart from the hoi polloi, virtuoso activities also allowed for the
fabrication and maintenance of a genteel group identity. "For the companions of your recreation," counsels Peacham, "consort your selfe with Gentlemen of your owne ranke and quality," for "To be over free and familiar
with inferiors, argues a basenesse of Spirit, and begetteth contempt."[139]
Shared participation in virtuoso activities provided seventeenth-century
English gentlemen with a basis for interchanges with social equals and thus
for the creation of a shared class identity.

Bacon had sometimes championed the utility of his brand of scientific
inquiry, arguing that the practitioners of a reformed natural philosophy
could "overcome the immeasurable helplessness and poverty of the human
race," and this aspect of his writings profoundly influenced social reformers
during the Interregnum.[140] The virtuosos, by contrast, conveniently ignored such evocations of practicality and the common good. Indeed, the
conjunction of collecting and class consciousness central to the ethos of
"curiosity" among seventeenth-century English virtuosos made a historically specific form of cultural capital out of a fundamental quality of the
collected object: its nonutility. Krysztof Pomian has stressed that an object
in a collection has been removed from economic circulation and transformed into a "semiophore," that is, an object which "bear[s] meaning": the
semiophore is treated as if it were precious, and thus it has exchange value,
but it carries "no practical or usage value."[141] As he accumulates such items,
the collector fashions himself as a "semiophore-man," exhibiting his social
authority "By abstaining from all utilitarian activities, by distancing himself from those who are forced to carry these out, by surrounding himself
with objects which are not things but semiophores and by displaying
them."[142] The ostentatious non-utility of the objects in a collection was
easily aligned with the early modern construction of genteel male identity.
In seventeenth-century England, as Steven Shapin observes, "the culture
that specified who was and who was not a gentleman laid great emphasis on
how individuals were placed *vis-à-vis* wealth, work, and the production of
goods and services": a gentleman's (ostensibly) landed wealth meant that he
did not have to work to sustain himself, as he exerted "leisured control of

others' labor."[143] In an era of mushrooming upstarts, a virtuoso's collection of curiosities allowed him to display his gentlemanly rejection of the vulgar preoccupation with utility.

This calculated quest for the impractical became central to satirical depictions of natural philosophers. In Thomas Shadwell's *The Virtuoso* (1676), Sir Nicholas Gimcrack conducts experiments in the name of genteel uselessness; as the like-minded Sir Formal approvingly observes, "To study for use is base and mercenary."[144] Later writers more specifically attacked collecting as one manifestation of the virtuoso's obsession with the non-utile. In "The Will of a Virtuoso," which appeared in the *Tatler* in 1710, Shadwell's Gimcrack bequeaths valued possessions such as a humming-bird's nest and a rat's testicles to his family and friends; in another spoof published in the *Tatler*, Gimcrack's widow asks how she should dispose of the "many Rarities and Curiosities" left by her husband: "If you know any one that has an Occasion for a Parcel of dry'd Spiders, I will sell them a Pennyworth. I could likewise let any one have a Bargain of Cockle-Shells. I would also desire your Advice, whether I had best sell my Beetles in a Lump or by Retail."[145] Similarly, the anonymous author of *An Essay in Defence of the Female Sex*, published in 1696, lampooned virtuosos in general (and Dr. John Woodward, a famous collector of fossils, in particular) by defining a virtuoso as

one that has sold an Estate in Land to purchase one in *Scallop, Conch, Muscle, Cockle Shells, Periwinkles, Sea Shrubs, Weeds, Mosses, Sponges, Coralls, Corallines, Sea Fans, Pebbles, Marchasites* and *Flint Stones*; and has abandon'd the Acquaintance and Society of Men for that of *Insects, Worms, Grubbs, Maggots, Flies, Moths, Locusts, Beetles, Spiders, Grashoppers, Snails, Lizards* and *Tortoises*.[146]

Although some aristocratic women, such as Mary Capel Somerset, Duch-ess of Beaufort, did assemble natural history collections, the scientific cul-ture of the period was constructed as masculine—the virtuosos legitimated themselves as a distinctive social group on the basis of gender as well as rank. Hence the author of *An Essay In Defence of the Female Sex* confidently genders virtuoso collecting as a male activity: "This, *Madam*, is another sort of Impertinence our Sex is not liable to."[147]

Virtuoso collections thus functioned as sites where beleaguered male members of a hereditary, landed elite could exhibit their manly defiance of utility, a feature of virtuoso collecting practices also evident in the fad for reading and creating "curiosity books." In addition to gathering anomalous objects, the seventeenth-century English virtuoso was also likely to amass formulas for alchemical procedures, medicines, perfumes, and cosmetics, as well as descriptions of technical processes. As Sir John Hoskyns declared, "Every man has his delight; ingenious information is mine."[148] Books of "conceits" and "secrets" were published to cater to this interest in "curious" information, as well as works on "mathematical magic," a category which encompassed "a grab bag of subjects that included mechanical gadgets, optical illusions, tricks, problems, and various forms of recreational mathematics."[149] Like the Fellows of Solomon's House who ferret out the secrets of the artisans of Bensalem, virtuosos such as John Evelyn engaged in a kind of colonization within their own country, transforming the technical knowledge of vulgar craftsmen and householders into the property of the genteel. Evelyn advocated that a gentleman should accumulate "many excellent receipts to make perfumes, sweet powders, pomanders, antidotes, and divers such curiousities," but he differentiated between vulgar and elite handling of such material: "Commonly indeed persons of mean condition possess them because their necessity renders them industrious; but if men of quality made it their delight also, arts could not but receive infinite advantages, because they have both means and leisure to improve and cultivate them; and, as I said before, there is nothing by which a good man may more sweetly pass his time."[150] In Evelyn's account, while the virtuoso deals with potentially utilitarian subjects, he transforms the pieces of data he gathers into signs of his superior social status by draining them of their original usefulness. In his *Sculptura*, Evelyn mentions a process of mezzo-tinting, shown to him by Prince Rupert, which he refuses to explain in detail for fear that "an *Art* so curious, and (as yet) so little vulgar" might "be prostituted at so cheap a rate, as the more naked describing of it here, would too soon have expos'd it to";[151] elsewhere, Evelyn is similarly loath to publish his insights into techniques of etching, painting, and enamel because he might "debase much of their esteem by prostituting them to the vulgar."[152] Circulating within a genteel social context in which "necessity" is absent, technical knowledge possessed by a virtuoso thus becomes a "semiophore," an artifact which is collected, displayed, and exchanged among members of an elite social group, rather than being put to practical use.

As Evelyn's writings suggest, by the Restoration the English virtuoso had come to share the Baconian natural philosopher's interest in the materials of natural history, and soon the term "virtuoso" was regularly applied to practitioners of the "new philosophy."[153] Houghton points out that in Bacon's program to gather data for a natural history, "the virtuosi not only found their own kind of study recommended, the observation of facts and the collection of specimens to form a vast history of natural and mechanical arts; they found also a glowing appeal for co-operation from men of wealth and leisure, with the assurance that no special training was necessary (great intellects like Bacon's would interpret the phenomena and induce the scientific laws)."[154] Thus seventeenth-century English virtuosos could use Bacon's natural history as a new justification for their own social practices of collection and display. And while Bacon himself had fumed that he deserved to be the inductive "architect" of a reformed natural philosophy rather than a "workman" or "laborer" who accumulated data, the virtuosos, having constructed their collecting activities as intrinsically elite, tacitly elevated the social standing of the men whom Bacon had conceived as subaltern "factors and merchants"; those who gathered the materials of natural history were refashioned into a corps of gentlemanly collectors.

Virtuoso Baconianism and the Royal Society

The congruence between virtuoso activities and aspects of Bacon's natural philosophy was highlighted and exploited by propagandists for the fledgling Royal Society in the 1660s. The Royal Society, founded in 1660 and granted a charter of incorporation in 1662, was a "new type of institution, a public body devoted to the corporate pursuit of scientific research, something unprecedented either in [England] or elsewhere."[155] Viewed with suspicion by the universities, the College of Physicians, and elements of the Church, the early members of the Royal Society attempted to defuse this hostility by aligning their brand of natural philosophy with the social values of Restoration England; despite the diversity of members' approaches to the study of nature, the Royal Society publicly assumed a "unified front of Baconianism, which was readily adopted as a defensive mechanism against critics."[156] The creator of the fictional Solomon's House, "[t]hat Patriark of Experimental Philosophy, the learned Lord *Bacon*," was now cast as the progenitor of the Royal Society and its program.[157] Within Wenceslaus Hollar's frontispiece to Thomas Sprat's *History of the Royal Society* (1666), Bacon—labeled "ARTIUM INSTAURATOR"—and one of the Society's presidents are pictured at either side of a bust of Charles II, which is being crowned by a female personification of Scientia; as Alvin Snider remarks, "Patronage, patriotism, and paternal authority all revolve around the figure of 'Bacon,' who demonstrates the Englishness of science and its harmony with monarchical government."[158] The founders of the Royal Society portrayed their organization as a "structure within the parameters of which people could collaborate without risking the damaging divisions which the Civil War and Interregnum seemed to exemplify":

rather than a site of fractious pedantry or *ad hominem* attacks, the Royal
Society was to be a *"locus neutrum* of gentlemanly pursuit."[159] Bacon's inductive method, with its emphasis on empiricism and cooperative effort,
seemed a safe foundation for the impartial study of natural philosophy, an
activity which was to be rooted in polite, nondogmatic sociability. (Of
course, mid-century English history had to be prudently rewritten so that
the earlier, now embarrassing incarnations of Baconianism among puritan
reformers could be denied.[160]) At the same time, Bacon's elite social status
and political accomplishments were invoked to legitimize natural philosophy as a study suitable for gentlemen; pragmatically ignoring his hero's
impeachment, Abraham Cowley lauds Bacon as "a mighty Man . . . /
Whom a wise King and Nature chose / Lord Chancellour of both their
Laws."[161] Thus Bacon as mythic founder/talisman and his collaborative
method of accumulating data became central to the reassuringly conservative public image displayed by the Royal Society in the 1660s.

   Despite protestations of openness, the early Royal Society was, in fact,
"socially exclusive," its membership consisting largely, as Sprat put it,
of *"Gentlemen,* free, and unconfin'd."[162] Although their differences were
glossed over by Sprat's propagandistic *History,* members of the Royal Society actually subscribed to divergent styles of Baconianism: while men like
Robert Hooke and Robert Boyle "clearly saw the need for a judicious
mixture of theory and observation," others understood Bacon's method as
granting them "a charter for collecting a mass of miscellaneous data about
the natural world."[163] By appealing to this latter group of Baconians, the
Royal Society's program of research into natural history was designed to
"foster participation by those who would have been unqualified to join
in more technical activities of the Society's natural philosophers."[164] As
Thomas Sprat wrote of such keen but unskilled contributors, "And though
many of them have not a sufficient confirmation, to raise *Theories,* or *Histories* on their *Infallibility*: yet they bring with them a good assurance of
likelihood, by the integrity of the *Relators*; and withall they furnish a judicious *Reader,* with admirable hints to direct his Observations."[165] Rather
than turning natural philosophy into an egalitarian project, however, Sprat
was attempting to encourage genteel virtuosos to further their own interests
by joining the Society. Using Robert Boyle, an Anglo-Irish aristocrat, as a
touchstone of the elite nature of the Society's membership, Sprat depicts
the Society as a particularly suitable organization for leisured gentlemen to
join. In a section of the *History of the Royal Society* headed *"Experiments a
proper Study for the Gentlemen of our Nation,"* Sprat appeals to "the *Gentry*
and *Nobility"* of England to pursue natural philosophy.[166] Sprat argues that

unlike utilitarian subjects, "which are made for the beaten tracks of professions, and not for *Gentlemen*," the activities promoted by the Royal Society can offer "the allurements, of *sweeter* and more *plausible Studies*: And for this purpose *Experiments* are the fittest. Their *Objects* [gentlemen] may feel and behold: Their *productions* are most popular: Their *Method* is intelligible, and equal to their capacities: so that in them they may soon become their own *Teachers*."[167] Moreover, the landed gentleman in his country house is especially well placed to enjoy the "freedom of *Observations*" of the natural world, and will find that his usual pastimes such as "hawking, fishing, and fowling" can become "most serviceable to *Experimental Knowledge*."[168] Through such efforts to legitimize their activities and create a base of support among the elite, the Royal Society gained a substantial proportion of virtuosos in the ranks of its membership, and men like John Aubrey gained a new justification for collecting "curious" objects and information, and for visiting and corresponding with other "ingeniose Virtuosi."[169]

While the leaders of the Royal Society sought to construct their organization's genteel public identity by enticing virtuosos to become members—and advertising the consequently elite social make-up of the Society by publishing an annual list of its members[170]—the virtuosos simultaneously used the Royal Society as an institutional framework for enhancing their own individual and corporate identities. The impact of the virtuosos—and thus their distinctive mode of collecting—on the Royal Society became most evident in the development of the organization's "Repository." From its earliest days, the Royal Society had received physical objects as gifts—a bird of paradise, a piece of elephant's skin, samples of ore, an ostrich egg[171]—and in 1664, there were discussions about systematically acquiring specimens for a repository. (These early plans were the stuff of virtuoso dreams—the Society should acquire the carcasses of any exotic birds in the King's aviary which expired, suggested Walter Charleton, while Christopher Merret proposed that the Society should more ambitiously collect "all the rare productions of England, as to beasts, birds, fishes, vegetables, minerals, &c."[172]) It was not until two years later, however, that the Society made a concerted effort to establish a collection of physical objects. At this time, the creation of a repository was seen as vital to renewing interest in the Society, for its members had fled from London during an outbreak of plague in 1665–66, and the organization was financially crippled;[173] the Royal Society needed somehow to invigorate its activities and reassert its identity if it were to survive this hiatus. Giving priority to establishing a collection rather than other facilities—such as a lab, "Optick Chamber," or observatory—the Society purchased Robert Hubert's "Rarities of Nature" for £100, the money having been donated for this purpose by the Society's Treasurer, Daniel Colwall.[174] Addressing Colwall fifteen years later, the botanist Nehemiah Grew stated, "Besides the particular regard you had to the *Royal Society* it Self; which seeming (in the opinion of some) to look a little pale, you intended hereby, to put some fresh Blood into their Cheeks; pouring out your Box of Oyntment, not in order to their Burial but their Resurrection."[175] Michael Hunter suggests that the Society's agenda was shaped by the knowledge that a repository "was a facility which would be widely esteemed among members of the leisured class from which the Society's expectations of support were highest"; Sprat carefully noted that many of the "Noble Rarities" donated to the Royal Society were given not only by "Learned and profess'd Philosophers," but also originated "from the Fishponds, the Parks, the Gardens of *Gentlemen*."[176] Certainly John Evelyn was confident that the acquisition of Hubert's collection would deliver a salutary shot in the arm to the ailing organization: "We are meeting afresh at Gresham College: and have purchased for us, since these days of separation, the fullest, and certainly noblest collection of natural raritys of all kinds that is this day in Europe to be seen: . . . The Royall Society is not at an end, florit floreat."[177]

Like Hubert, who had displayed his accumulation of objects as a source of income and had enhanced its commercial appeal by advertising both the collection and its elite benefactors in published catalogues,[178] the Royal Society used the assembled "Rarities" to attract men (and their membership dues) to the organization. In part, the Repository functioned as an enticing material representation of the Society's institutional identity, for which purpose the collection was made available to the public in different ways. Unlike the meetings of the Society, which a nonmember could attend only through a personal introduction, the Repository was accessible to the public; as a popular tourist attraction, the Repository thus became "one of the most celebrated and 'visible' aspects of the Society in its early years."[179] The collection's publicity value for the Society was heightened by the appearance of a printed catalogue of the Repository in 1681, a folio of more than 400 pages published by subscription, which contained engraved illustrations of some of the items held in the Repository and a list of "those who have Contributed to this Musaeum."[180] The German traveler Zacharias Conrad von Uffenbach attested that "Both in Germany and elsewhere an exalted idea of this Society has been formed, both of it and of the collections they have in their Museum, especially when one looks at the Transactions of this Society and the fine description of the Museum by Grew."[181]

At the same time, the Society also administered the Repository so as to give individuals greater opportunity to experience their gratifying identity as supporters of the organization. As Adrian Johns points out, the Repository operated as "an archive of [members'] material contributions" to the work of the Society—that is, the Repository served as an analogue to the Society's register books.[182] Within the Society's register books, "a matter of fact, experimental technique, theory, or paper could be 'entered' to record the name of its discoverer and the moment of its first discovery."[183] Physical objects such as inventions could similarly be registered by being placed in a sealed box, and the publication of papers in the *Philosophical Transactions* expanded the dynamics of the Society's register into the medium of print.[184] Through such acts of registration, the priority of individual discoveries could be established; even more fundamentally, by registering a contribution, the Society formally legitimated its value, recognizing the worth of its contributor in the process. The Royal Society's methods of "registering" contributions were thus rooted in the practices of gift exchange through which Renaissance collectors "obtained status and maintained authority"[185]—by giving an object to a noteworthy collection, a would-be benefactor both acknowledged the social significance of the collector and attempted to include *himself* within the collection. The Repository, I would argue, similarly provided a physical site of reciprocal identity formation for the Royal Society and its virtuoso supporters.

It was intended that the Keeper of the Repository would "always affix some note to the things in it, by which it might be known what they are, and by whom they were presented," and this official display of objects' provenance was to be complemented by a register of benefactors.[186] By printing the *Musaeum Regalis Societatis* in 1681, the Society even more publicly recognized donors of objects, the book serving as a catalogue of supporters of the Royal Society as well as the physical items in the Repository: we read of "An AEGYPTIAN MUMMY given by the Illustrious Prince *Henry* Duke of *Norfolk*," "A TOOTH taken out of the Testicle or Ovary of a Woman, and given by Dr. *Edward Tyson*," "A piece of a BONE voided by Sir *W. Throgmorton* with his Urine. Given by *Thomas Cox* Esq.," a rhinocerous horn "Given by Sir *Robert Southwell*, present Embassador to the Prince Elector of *Brandenburge*," a canoe from Greenland "Given by Mr. *Hocknel*," "A *Siam* DRUM. Given by Mr. *John Short*," and "A Pot of MACASSAR POYSON. Given by Sir *Phil. Vernatti*."[187]

The function of the catalogue in transforming donors into collected objects possessed by the Royal Society is made explicit in the dedicatory epistle of the *Musaeum*, in which Nehemiah Grew lauds Daniel Colwall as the "Founder" of the Repository. Grew tells Colwall that the members of the Royal Society commissioned the compilation and publication of the catalogue so "that they might always wear this Catalogue, as the Miniature of your abundant Respects, near their Hearts."[188] In this image, the identities of the Repository, the printed book, and Colwall merge: the Catalogue becomes a set of miniature portraits of Colwall worn by his colleagues in the Royal Society, and Colwall is thus transformed into pieces of jewelry which are owned, like the objects in the Repository, by the members of the organization.[189] In financing the purchase of Robert Hubert's collection for the Royal Society, Colwall has not only effaced Hubert's identity as a collector, but has himself become a rarity proudly owned and displayed by the Fellows of the Royal Society. Colwall's identity as an object preserved within the Repository is further heightened by his appearance in the catalogue, opposite the title page, in an engraved portrait (see Figure 3)—paid for, like the other illustrations in the book, by Colwall himself. Colwall is thus displayed like other notable objects depicted in the engraved plates of the *Musaeum*, such as a "Weesle Headed Armadillo," the "Skin on the Buttock of a Rhinoceros" (see Figure 4) and the "Head of the Albitros."[190]

From the beginning of its existence, the capacity of the Repository to objectify and perpetuate the identities of those who contributed to its holdings was extolled. In the *Philosophical Transactions* of October 1666, potential donors were assured that any gifts they gave to the Repository would be "preserved for After-ages, (probably much better and safer, than in their own private Cabinets)."[191] Collectors, especially those with no children, habitually worried about the postmortem fate of their collections (and thus their identities as collectors), and increasingly turned to institutions to preserve them: John Woodward left his collection of fossils to Cambridge, John Bargrave bequeathed his cabinet of curiosities to the Dean and Chapter of Canterbury Cathedral, and John Aubrey, tormented by visions of his life's work being torn to bits by a deceased executor's nieces and nephews, donated most of his manuscripts, books, and antiquities to the Ashmolean Museum.[192] In a letter encouraging Richard Waller to recruit the Bristol naturalist William Cole as a supporter of the Royal Society, Robert Hooke wrote in 1687, "[Cole] can have no better way in the world to present to future ages both his observations & curiousitys then by the Transactions & Repository of the RS. and that will also repay him in some measure at present by returnes of other Observations: and for the future by a Lasting monument of his Name."[193] By creating a Repository, the Royal Society thus provided an institutional focus for virtuosos, a site wherein individuals could display their status as collector-donors, both to their contemporaries and to future generations.

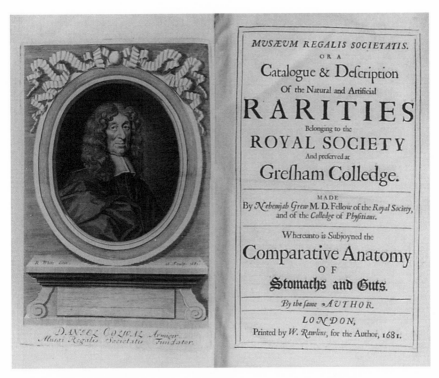

Figure 3. Nehemiah Grew, *Musaeum Regalis Societatis* (London, 1681), title page and frontispiece. Kenneth Spencer Research Library, University of Kansas.

The Repository's status as an institutionalized cabinet of curiosities, like the collections amassed by individual virtuosos, could be justified as a properly Baconian contribution to knowledge—after all, Bacon had called for "a substantial and severe collection of the Heteroclites or Irregulars of nature" as an integral part of his natural history, and had advocated the establishment of a "goodly great cabinet" containing any man-made artifact "rare in stuff, form, or motion" and "whatsoever singularity, chance, and the shuffle of things hath produced."[194] Yet Bacon had also championed the accumulation of "experiments familiar and vulgar," and Sprat suggested that the new Repository would innovatively combine both goals, in that it would become "a General Collection of all the Effects of *Arts*, and the Common, or Monstrous *Works* of *Nature*."[195] Henry Oldenburg wrote of the Society's activities in 1667 that "we have taken to taske the whole Universe,"[196] and the Repository was conceived by some as a research tool in this large-scale effort to create a complete natural history. Robert Hooke,

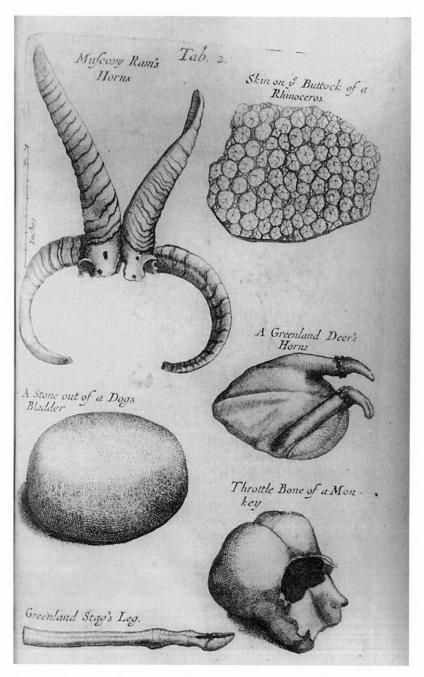

Figure 4. Nehemiah Grew, *Musaeum Regalis Societatis* (London, 1681), Table 2. Kenneth Spencer Research Library, University of Kansas.

appointed Keeper of the Repository, felt that it was important to create "as full and compleat a Collection of all varieties of Natural Bodies as could be obtain'd," and Nehemiah Grew maintained that the collection was to be truly encyclopedic in scope, comprising "not only Things strange and rare, but the most known and common amongst us."[197] This vision of the Repository as a complete collection of all natural history specimens was linked with John Wilkins's project to devise a new, rational language which would include "a universal system of classification which would accurately mirror the natural order."[198] Thus an important segment of the Society's membership felt that "the use of such a Collection is not for Divertisement, and Wonder, and Gazing, as 'tis for the most part thought and esteemed, . . . but for the most serious and diligent study of the most able Proficient in Natural Philosophy."[199]

The conception of the Repository as a taxonomic accumulation clearly flew in the face of the virtuosos' program of self-fashioning—and so they ignored the ideas of hirelings like Hooke. By the time the catalogue of the Repository was published in 1681, the collection contained two or three times the number of objects which had been displayed by Hubert; ironically, however, the Repository had thus become even less like a complete series of natural objects, for whereas Hubert had primarily accumulated "natural rarities," subsequent donations (such as the silver box, presented by Sir Robert Moray, which contained "stones taken out of Lord Belcarre's heart"[200]) had made the Repository much more heterogeneous and "curious." Rather than establishing a new, "scientific" approach to natural history, the Repository helped to perpetuate a mode of collecting—and a mode of self-fashioning—which emphasized the singularity of members of the landed elite. As an organization without an endowment and hence dependent on the good will (and pocketbooks) of its supporters, the Royal Society was vulnerable to the influence of the very men it had attempted to lure into membership in the mid-1660s. The character of the Repository as a curiosity cabinet thus reflected the power of the mode of genteel collecting developed by the seventeenth-century English virtuosos.

At the same time, however, the Repository also became a site for the development of socially transgressive modes of collecting. As we have seen, in Bacon's writings the activity of gathering materials for a natural history can produce new forms of nonhereditary authority; likewise, whereas initially the "curiosity" of a virtuoso's collection was understood to signify the owner's status as a gentleman (that is, a man with inherited, landed wealth who did not have to work for a living), the collection of natural history could also be used to constitute alternative constructions of status and identity. Unlike the catalogues of the collections of Robert Hubert or the younger John Tradescant, the list of benefactors included in the *Musaeum Regalis Societatis* is, with the exception of Prince Rupert's name, arranged alphabetically, not hierarchically. Like the engraved objects, not drawn to scale, which float in groups in the illustrations of the Royal Society's catalogue, the donors to the Repository are equalized by their appearance in the alphabetical list: "A Stone out of a Dogs Bladder" is represented as being as large as a "Greenland Stag's Leg," "Mr. John Malling" is no less notable than "Sir Thomas Millington."[201] Similarly, if the nontechnical, non-utile amateurism of collecting natural objects appealed to self-consciously leisured gentlemen in seventeenth-century England, this mode of collecting also had the potential to give authority to non-elite collectors who could use their collections to constitute new forms of social power, rather than signify an inherited, elite status.

James Petiver and His Rariora Naturae

The career of the amateur naturalist James Petiver provides an example of how a nongentleman could participate in a Baconian mode of collecting in order to fashion an innovative social identity for himself in early modern England. Although he was born the son of a haberdasher, was poorly educated, and earned his living as an apothecary, Petiver could associate with men who were his social betters because of his status as a collector.[202] In Petiver's activities, as Bacon envisioned, the process of collecting materials for the study of natural history served as a means of collecting people: Petiver became an "architect" of his own scientific program, coordinating the labor of others and using his control of this work force to enhance his own social status. Moreover, Petiver enthusiastically combined his identity as a published scientific author with his collecting activities. Thus by examining Petiver's mode of self-fashioning as a collector, we can see how elements of Bacon's natural philosophy could be exploited and adapted in ways that Bacon himself could not have anticipated.

By the time Petiver died in 1718, at fifty-four or -five, he had assembled "one of the largest and most varied collections" of "*Rariora Naturae*" then extant in England.[203] Writing after Petiver's death, Richard Pulteney reported that "The allurement of such uncommon curiosities as Mr. PETIVER exhibited, soon obtained him considerable distinction, and his name became well known, both at home and abroad."[204] Sir Hans Sloane, who was later to found the British Museum with his vast accumulation of objects, purportedly offered £4,000 for Petiver's collection, and later bought the apothecary's rarities after Petiver (unmarried and childless) had died.[205] In a 1711 letter, Petiver observed of his development as a collector,

> I have . . . for more than 20 years dedicated a great many Leasure hours to the contemplations of Natures manifold Wonderfull productions with an inexpressible satisfaction & delight. . . . My first & early progress began at home and after I had made some progress in the knowledge & Collecting all the Plants att London especially the Medicall ones, that part being an absolute necessary branch of my Profession, I then proceeded to the Animal Kingdom, the various classes of these from the greater Animals as Beasts, Birds, & Fish even to the minutest Insect not many of which have escaped [m]y Observation, so that in a few years we have already discovered neer 2000 besides the divers sorts of Land, River & sea Shells, the Fabrick, Beauty, Variety & Use of all these may justly deserve our Admiration as well as Consideration & with the Holy Psalmist say How manifold are thy Works O Lord & in Wisdom has thou made them all.[206]

Petiver's description of the professional origins of his mode of collecting and his objects' pious effect on him barely hints at the complex dynamics of ambition and authorship which shaped Petiver's career as a collector. Although Petiver left England only once, to travel to Holland in 1711,[207] his collection was full of objects from Europe, Africa, Asia, and the Americas. Petiver managed to amass such quantities of exotic items because he built up a vast network of correspondents to supply his insatiable desire for natural "rarities." Like the Fathers of Solomon's House, Petiver commanded his own corps of "Merchants of Light" whose collecting activities served as the foundation of Petiver's personal authority. By 1688, Petiver was beginning to establish a far-flung group of unpaid assistants who would supply him with specimens for his burgeoning collection. Initially, Petiver contacted people who had connections with naturalists he knew in London—his participation in the unofficial Temple Coffee House Botany Club acquainted him with men like Sloane and Martin Lister, whose names he could drop to potential correspondents—but soon he was casting his net more widely, so that by his death, Petiver had corresponded with at least eighty people in America alone.[208]

To recruit these "factors and merchants" with whose labor he built his collection, Petiver constructed and published textual representations of the objects he amassed, and his affiliation with the Royal Society became integral to the identity of collector/author which he developed over the years. When he was still only being considered for membership in the Royal Society, Petiver suggested that Edward Bartar, a surgeon employed by the Royal African Company, would have his name published under the im-

primatur of the Royal Society if he were to collect objects in Guinea for
Petiver: "I shall have far more frequent opportunities of printing more att
large whatever my friends and correspondents abroad shall from time to
time send me," the aspiring Fellow audaciously told Bartar.[209] Petiver was
elected a Fellow of the Royal Society in 1695, and he used his access to the
Society's means of "registering" contributions to entice potential assistants
to gather specimens for him: the subject positions Petiver inhabited as
collector, author, and member of the Royal Society were synergistically
combined when he presented specimens and letters from his donors to the
organization. In 1707 Petiver promised a resident of Guinea that any objects
he might send "shall be communicated to the Royal Society of which
illustrious body I have the Honour to be a Member—shall be shewed to
them and published either in their Transactions or in such Papers I may
have occasion to publish myself . . . and [thereby] let the World know how
much we are beholden to you for the discovery."[210] Petiver also habitually
presented his activities as being undertaken at the behest of the Royal
Society. The year after Petiver was elected to the organization, he effu-
sively thanked Hezekiah Usher for "the Collection of Butterflies you sent,
[which] with your Letter I according to your desire communicated to the
Royal Society"; his colleagues were so smitten with Usher's specimens,
Petiver continued, that they "ordered" him to ask Usher

to continue your (so well begun) Communicating to me, & knowing that I have
correspondence in severall parts of the world & that my inclinations tend to the
promoting of naturall History, viz. the Knowledge of Birds, Beasts, Fishes, Insects,
Shells, Herbs, etc. they have ordered me to give you an Acct. of in order to be
published in the Monthly *Transactions* of what ever of these things shall from
forreign parts come to my hands. This I am now doing for some parts of Africa &
the East Indies in relation to some Plants Shells & Insects I have lately rec'd from
thence and being very willing to do the like for New England I must desire your
farther assistance in furnishing me with more Insects and what plants, Shells, &
Mineralls your parts afford.[211]

In fact, according to the Royal Society's *Journal-Book*, after Petiver had
presented Usher's six butterflies and accompanying letter to the organization, he was asked only to respond "& give the Gentleman thanks for the
pains he had been at";[212] Petiver, however, chose to represent these instruc-
tions as a mandate to impress Usher with Petiver's personal status as a
collector and to urge him to supply Petiver with many more specimens. For
the sake of influencing potential distant correspondents, Petiver was also
prone to overstating his relationship to the Society by calling himself "botanist to the Royal Society," even though no such position existed.[213]

In addition to exploiting the opportunities for publication afforded by the Royal Society, Petiver created his own print venues in which he could display his burgeoning collection—and the network of correspondents who labored on his behalf. In 1695 Petiver published *Musei Petiveriani Centuria Prima Rariora Naturae Continens*, the first of ten "Centuries" in which Petiver listed and described items in his collection, as well as the people who had gathered the objects for him. Before he had published the first of these catalogues, Petiver wrote to Samuel Brown, a surgeon with the East India Company living in Fort St. George in Madras, to promise him

something in print from me relating to the Naturall History of those parts you send me from & be assured your frequent Correspondence & returns from China, Persia, &c with what an acct. you can get of those gums you mentioned & which are in my Catalogue will be so vast a discovery that your name will live as long as the Noble Science of Physick have a being.[214]

At the conclusion of the first "Century," Petiver turned his miniature catalogue-cum-benefactors-book into a recruitment tool, inviting others to take their place with the likes of Samuel Brown in his printed pantheon of helpers:

This *Century* consisting of such *Animals, Vegetables, Fossils, &c.* as have been either observed by my self, or communicated to me not only from many *Very Worthy* and *Learned Assistants at Home*, but also brought me by my *Kind Friends* from divers parts of the World, or transmitted from such *Curious Persons* as do me the Honour to Correspond with me from several parts Abroad: I thought my self highly obliged to acknowledg them as my *Generous Benefactors*; And designing to continue the *Publishing* of these *Centuries* as my *Philosophical Acquaintances* and *Correspondents* Abroad and at Home shall enrich me; I do therefore most humbly beg the Communications and Assistance of all *Curious Persons* and *Lovers of Natural History*, the which shall be *justly* and *faithfully acknowledged*. And if there be any thing in this or the following Centuries which they shall desire to be farther inform'd of, I shall endeavour to serve them in that.[215]

At the conclusion of his fifth "Century," published in 1699, Petiver added "An Abstract Of what *Collections* I have received the *last Twelve Months*, and the *Persons* whom I am Obliged to for them,"[216] and he appended such lists of collected objects and people to all subsequent installments of his "Centuries."

A similar set of publications, *Gazophylacii Naturae & Artis: Decades Decem*, heightened the interrelationships between authorship, collecting and social identity which Petiver was forging. Evocatively, the title of these works refers to the box mentioned in the Old Testament—the "gazophylacium"—in which offerings to the Temple were received.[217] Petiver, as in his earlier "Centuries," acknowledges the donors to his monumental collection within the brief descriptions of the objects he presents in his "gazophyla-cium," thus portraying himself as the focus of a long-distance community of naturalists: "This elegant Snake I received from my worthy Friend Dr. Godfrey Bidloo, Anatomick Professor at Leyden, and Physitian to his late Majesty King William"; "My kind friend Mr Robert Ellis sent me this wonderful Fly from Carolina"; "The Reverend Mr Hugh Jones sent me this beautiful Bird from Mary-Land."[218] Every item described in the text of Petiver's *Gazophylacii* is also depicted in one of a series of "Tables," each "Table" consisting of a group of engraved representations of objects keyed to the catalogue entries; as Pulteney remarks, the one hundred tables of engravings made the *Gazophylacii* a work "of great value at the time of its publication."[219] With these illustrations, Petiver can depict among the do-nations to his *Gazophylacii* objects which, in fact, he possesses only as the pictures in his published book. Through this printed extension of "his" collection, Petiver can thus portray himself not only as the administrator of his correspondents, but he can also represent himself mastering a world where social interactions—and his status—are predicated on collecting: "I have observed this in flower, in the Bishop of London his most curious Garden at Fulham"; "This [fly] is curiously preserved in Mr Joseph Dandridge's Collection, who caught it in Hornsey Wood in June"; a toucan is "Taken from a *Dutch Painting* in Mr Clark's Collection"; a butterfly was "First observed in Mr Tillman Bobart's Collection."[220] Moreover, in de-picting the objects he has accumulated in tables of engravings, Petiver styles himself as inhabiting yet another, more elite social realm by virtue of being a collector/author, for he dedicates each plate to a different person. Some of the dedicatees also appear in the catalogue entries as donors of objects, but many seem to be chosen primarily for the social cachet which they impart to Petiver's collection-book: the Archbishop of Canterbury, the Dowager Duchess of Beaufort, the Earl of Dorset and Middlesex, the Duke of Beaufort, and (the then president of the Royal Society) Isaac Newton.[221] Within each dedicatory caption, Petiver reiterates his own name and his status as a member of the Royal Society: "This TABLE is humbly dedi-cated by JAMES PETIVER, F.R.S." Petiver thus creates and displays his social identity by simultaneously collecting and textualizing objects and people. This dynamic of self-fashioning which structures Petiver's *Gazo-phylacii* is strikingly embodied at the beginning of the sixth "Decade." Within Table 51 (see Figure 5), we find engraved representations of plants, a mushroom, fossils, insects—and a portrait of "that Worthy and Learned

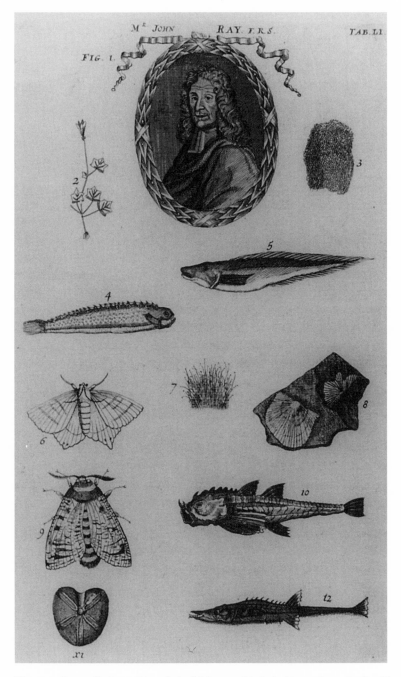

Figure 5. James Petiver, *Gazophylacii Naturae & Artis: Decas Sexta*, in *Jacobi Petiveri Opera*, ed. James Empson and J. Millan (London, 1767), Table 51. Kenneth Spencer Research Library, University of Kansas.

Naturalist Mr *John Ray* done a little before his Death."[222] John Ray, the renowned naturalist, like Petiver's far-off correspondents and the Archbishop of Canterbury, becomes a specimen gathered and exhibited in a printed book by James Petiver, Fellow of the Royal Society and collector/author.

*   *   *

In early modern England the study of natural history was inextricably bound up with practices of collecting which were structured to create new social groups. Sir Francis Bacon envisioned the establishment of a department of state through which he could gain commandment of other men's wits; later in the century, virtuosos adopted a Baconian interest in natural history as part of their project to construct an elite circle of singular gentlemen; the Royal Society developed its Repository so as to align its own quest for members with the virtuosos' program of individual and corporate self-fashioning; and James Petiver used the process of accumulating natural rarities to assemble and display a collection of "assistants," many of them his social superiors. The role of collecting in the development of early modern natural philosophy was thus intrinsically social: the natural history collection became a technology with which diverse new social formations could be created. At the same time, however, the collector himself was always more than a member of a group; like Bacon, the virtuosos and Petiver asserted uniquely individual, authoritative selves even as they sought to secure membership in a corporate endeavor, class, or institution. And as the seventeenth century wore on, the role of printed texts in the construction of collections of natural history and men, and thus in the fashioning of collectors' identities, became more important. While Bacon may not have wanted to "father" an upstart apothecary, James Petiver was, in his creation of a new social identity as a collector/author, very much a self-styled heir of Bacon's innovative reconfiguration of the study of natural philosophy.

Chapter 3

The Countryside as Collection

Chorography, Antiquarianism, and the Politics of Landscape

Thou several artists dost employ to show
The measure of thy lands, that thou mayest know
How much of earth thou hast . . .
—Thomas Randolph[1]

According to the social theory of early modern England, a man's identity and authority were, in large part, determined by his relationship to land. The social formation was understood as "a graduated ladder of dominance and subordination," and within this patriarchal hierarchy of status, fathers were, on the basis of their gender, uniformly entitled to be the heads of their respective households. Outside the home, however, men's differential "claims to land" in large part determined their standing in society.[2] As Steven Shapin observes, sixteenth- and seventeenth-century English culture "laid great emphasis on how individuals were placed *vis-à-vis* wealth, work, and the production of goods and services."[3] At the top of the status pyramid stood England's "gentlemen," the members of the peerage and gentry, men who (ostensibly) did not labor for their incomes. In William Petty's formulation, a gentleman was "able to subsist without the practise of any mercenary employments" because he had "annuel riches, especially in Terra Firma."[4] Landed wealth—an estate, worked by others, which provided an income largely in the form of land rents—was thus considered an essential foundation of elite status. At the same time, land and lineage were, in theory, inextricably bound together. A gentleman not only possessed landed wealth, but did so as a member of a family which had for generations derived its "annuel riches" from the same substantial tracts of "Terra Firma": as Lord Burghley maintained, "Gentilitie is nothing but *ancient riches*."[5] Although humanists and Puritans proposed other criteria of social merit, "their ideas were tamed, and, purged of their radical critique, were incorporated into or made compatible with the traditional framework of legitimation."[6] Thus despite ideological challenges, men in sixteenth- and seventeenth-century England were still looked upon "as standing at the apex of a double helix intertwining land and blood,"[7] and the hereditary possession of substantial amounts of land continued to be regarded as the basis of gentle status in the early modern period.

Implicitly, this concept of a hereditary, landholding elite was rooted in a vision of a static social hierarchy. However, as Lawrence Stone has demonstrated, in the late sixteenth and early seventeenth centuries "families were moving up and down in the social and economic scale at a faster rate than at any time before the nineteenth and twentieth centuries."[8] Members of the landed elite in Elizabethan and Stuart England faced a daunting set of financial challenges: "exceptional temptations and compulsions to overspend on conspicuous consumption, royal service, or marriage portions, exceptional need for adaptability in estate management, novel opportunities and exceptional dangers in large-scale borrowing."[9] Gentlemen were particularly vulnerable to ruin by "the two great agents of destruction, sterility and stupidity,"[10] and estates often were sold as the result of a family's genetic or economic failure. In addition, the sale of Crown lands greatly increased the size of the land market in early modern England. The buyers for estates were found not only among the landed class; men who had amassed wealth through "mercenary employments" sought to secure a social status commensurate with their financial standing by purchasing land. Since wealth acquired through an individual's labor, whether in trade, finance, the professions, government administration, or farming, had no place in the traditional model of the English social hierarchy, men with non-landed fortunes bought estates to repackage their wealth in the garb of "Gentilitie" and further sought to cloak their lowly origins beneath purchased titles, forged genealogies, and new manor houses. Thus despite the notion of a hereditary landed elite presiding over an unchanging social hierarchy, early modern England was subjected to social mobility on a vast scale—and to equally widespread attempts to align the influx of *nouveaux riches* with traditional landed values.

Under these circumstances, the preoccupation with the hereditary possession of land—and the display of such proprietorship—was a vital feature of early modern English culture. In this chapter, I explore how the construction of landed identity in this period was intertwined with modes of representation by which the English countryside came to be portrayed as a space filled with physical objects. In works inflected by chorography and antiquarianism, I argue, early modern writers became collectors, gathering, arranging, and exhibiting artifacts that symbolized the identity of genteel

English landowners. Although such texts participated in the widespread cultural attempt "to define gentility, to display legitimate signs by which it might be recognized, and to offer resources to justify and maintain it,"[11] they were also ideologically volatile. During the Tudor and early Stuart eras, writers like William Camden and Richard Carew used the representational modes of chorography and antiquarianism to legitimize emergent concepts of property, concepts which not only sanctioned controversial agrarian practices but also created a new identity for landowners which, potentially at least, dissociated the landed gentry from the centralized monarchy. During the Caroline era, however, texts written by chorographers and antiquarians frequently were rooted in a self-consciously conservative politics and were intended to buttress the status quo. As the traditional social order was challenged and, it seemed, eclipsed during the Civil War and Interregnum, antiquarians and chorographers attempted to salvage the physical remnants of an elite culture on the brink of destruction. For midcentury authors like John Weever and William Dugdale, the chorographic/antiquarian text came to be understood as a superior physical object, a repository of symbolic artifacts which would endure even as funerary monuments were defaced by iconoclasts and grand homes were battered and sequestrated. Within this context, we can also better appreciate the shifting strategies of collecting which inform many of the works of Sir Thomas Browne; although Browne is often interpreted as a religiopolitical conservative, I argue that an examination of Browne's antiquarianism reveals his equivocal stance toward social authority. Browne thus represents a transition between the ideology of collecting exemplified by Dugdale and the Restoration portrayal of the landscape as owned objects which characterizes both the county natural histories of Robert Plot and late seventeenth-century country house poems. By the third quarter of the seventeenth century, the cultural understanding of the English countryside as a site of hereditary landholding had decisively eroded, giving way to a new landscape of possessive individualism constituted by objects and their owners.

Chorography

During the early modern period in England, the concept of landed property underwent striking modification. In the Middle Ages a manorial lord was not considered to "own" land; rather, he was understood to have customary rights to revenue (including payments from the farmers who worked the land) as part of an overarching network of reciprocal obligations linking all his subordinates and superiors within a hierarchical community.[12] This notion of landed property as "some right in the land" gradually eroded, however, and by the sixteenth century landlords were increasingly understood to possess "actual parcels of land" over which they had absolute rights.[13] At the same time, the Crown was selling substantial quantities of land, including properties it had acquired at the dissolution of the monasteries, thus catalyzing an unprecedented rate of land transfers.[14] Amidst these conditions of great conceptual and material change, innovative modes of representing landed property arose in Tudor England.

The emergence of the notion that landed property was a tangible *thing* rather than a set of rights was accompanied by an increased emphasis on depicting land as a physical entity. Sixteenth-century shifts in the practice of surveying were one facet of the ongoing struggle to redefine landownership. The medieval and early sixteenth-century surveyor was an estate supervisor who was expected to measure and describe land: the "survey" he produced was not a map but a written text, a detailed description of the estate which could be used in managing work on the land.[15] In addition to these formal written descriptions, topographical plans, not drawn to scale, were also created ad hoc as aids for specific projects conducted on medieval and early sixteenth-century English estates; estate maps per se—cartographic representations of landed property, drawn to scale, which were intended for general reference or display[16]—did not appear until the 1570s. From that point in time, however, the estate map came to supplement (and sometimes replace) the traditional written survey of a landlord's holdings, and by the late seventeenth century the estate surveyor was primarily regarded as a mapmaker.[17] The estate map thus embodied the new concept of land as a physical object which was owned, like the map itself, by the landlord. As Andrew McRae observes of the emergent association between surveying and mapping, these "new geometric methods of land measurement effectively strip[ped] away moral concerns," representing the land as a tangible, personal possession, rather than a site of reciprocal community obligations.[18]

The estate map offered both economic and social advantages to the landowner of early modern England. With a detailed map on hand, legal disputes could be settled more readily, controversial "improvements" to an estate (emparking, enclosure) could be conducted more efficiently, and, as John Norden observed early in the seventeenth century, an estate's profitability could be enhanced: "Lords of Tenants haue due regard of their owne estates, namely of the particulars of all their Tenants lands, and that

by a due, true, and exact view and suruey of the same, to the end the Lord
bee not abused."[19] The landowner could also enjoy increased social status
by displaying his property in the form of a map. Some estate maps were
highly ornamental: colored, embellished with the owner's coat of arms, and
illustrated with pictures of the manor house and scenes of activities (agricultural work, hunting, hawking) carried out on the property.[20] Removed
from its place among an estate's records, such an elaborate map was intended to function as an ornate status symbol, and decorative estate maps
were often commissioned by arrivistes to legitimize their new social position as landowners.[21] Thus early modern English estate maps, like cartography in general, functioned as "a form of political discourse concerned with the acquisition and maintenance of power,"[22] constructing
and displaying the proprietary identity of the landlord in relation to the
countryside.

The same ideological matrix which gave birth to the estate map also
engendered a keen interest in chorography in early modern England. A
Jacobean writer defined chorography as "an Arte, whereby wee be taught to
describe any particular place, without relation unto the whole, delivering all
things of note contained therein."[23] Chorography thus entailed a type of
local history in which the important features of a town or county were
enumerated. As Howard Marchitello observes, whereas cartographic por-
trayals of the land (such as estate maps) "aim at synchronic representation,"
chorographic depictions of the countryside, by contrast, "opt instead for the
diachronic," constructing a topographically organized, historical account of
a specific area. Hence, in Marchitello's formulation,

Chorography is the typically narrative and only occasionally graphic practice of
delineating topography not exclusively as it exists in the present moment, but as it
has existed historically. This means not only describing surface features of the land
(rivers, forests, etc.), but also the "place" a given locale has held in history, including
the languages spoken there, the customs of its people, material artifacts the land
may hold, and so forth.[24]

To describe particular landscapes and their historical significance, English
chorographers initially created works which were, above all, compilations
of names: names of communities, both vanished and extant; names of
rivers; names of local landmarks; names of buildings; names of people,
living and dead. Drawing on the techniques of humanist textual scholarship, sixteenth-century English chorographers such as William Lambarde
"concentrated on place-names and made etymology their principal tool";
by the seventeenth century, however, as middling gentry and *nouveaux*

riches families tried to establish their legitimacy as landowners, "local genealogies were drawn up in response to a search for ancient and respectable
roots that would allow this group to enter the ranks of the armigerous
gentry,"[25] and chorographies came to reflect this preoccupation, becoming
"little more than undigested collections of manorial and genealogical records," "books where county gentry [could] find their manors, monuments,
and pedigrees copiously set forth."[26]

Like an estate map decorated with a property owner's coat of arms, the
chorography became a means of constructing and displaying elite identities
rooted in (theoretically) hereditary title to land. By selecting and assembling noteworthy estates—and thus the estates' owners—within his text, the
early modern chorographer became, in effect, a collector of physical entities, and his descriptions of estates provided narratives of ownership
which legitimated individuals as genteel landlords. In *Britannia*, first published in Latin in 1586, William Camden established landowners and their
genealogies as essential features of early modern English chorography. In
his preface to the enlarged 1607 edition of *Britannia*, Camden states that in
addition to listing "what Dukes, what Earls, what Barons there have been,"
he has also "set down some of the most ancient and honourable Families,"
although "'tis impossible to mention them all." (Camden attempts to fore-
stall protests by families he has not included by equating such criticism with
low birth: "But whoever takes it so hainously, may probably be of the
number of those who have been the least serviceable to their Country, and
who claim their nobility from a modern date."[27]) In his county-by-county
descriptions of the English countryside, Camden locates geographical features in relation to the estates of important landed families: thus in his
account of Cornwall, for example, Camden notes that, "More to the East,
stands Godolcan, a hill famous for store of tinn-mines, (they now call it
Godolphin,) but much more noted for its Lords of that name, whose
virtues are no less eminent, than their family is ancient. The name in
Cornish comes from a White Eagle; and this Family has still bore for their
Arms, in a shield gules, an eagle display'd between three flower-de-luces
argent."[28] As Camden's narrative proceeds, topography becomes the backdrop for the display of the landed elite, and the hill Godolcan is replaced in
the mind's eye of the reader by the coat of arms symbolizing the Godolphin
family and their legitimate possession of their estates.[29] In Berkshire, the
course of a river leads Camden to an estate which he describes in terms of
its owners' pedigree: "And now the Kenet having run a long way, passes at
last by Aldermaston, which Henry I gave to Robert Achard, from whose
posterity by the De la Mares it came at length by right of marriage to the

Fosters, a Knightly family."[30] The landscape similarly yields family trees in Surrey: "Near to this place [Croydon] is Beddington, where is a most neat and curious house, adorn'd with pleasant orchards and gardens, built by Sir Francis Carew Knight. For 'tis an ancient seat of the Carews, who are descended from Nicholas Baron Carew of Moulesford (the Carews of Devonshire are of the same family too) and have flourish'd a long time in this County; especially, since J Carew marry'd the daughter and coheir of the noble Baron Hoo."[31] For Camden, the topography of a county is comprised, in large part, by the ancient families who have possessed landed estates therein.

In *The Survey of Cornwall*, published in 1602, Richard Carew similarly transforms geography into genealogy. Carew's designation of his work as a "survey" calls to mind the association between emerging concepts of the land as an "ownable" physical entity and the evolving nature of the survey as a representation of landownership. Aware that his home county may be regarded as a backwater, Carew evokes the contemporary concern with gentility to aggrandize his subject: "The most Cornish Gentlemen can better vaunt of their pedigree, then their liuelyhood: for that, they deriue from great antiquitie, (and I make question, whether any shire in England, of but equall quantitie, can muster a like number of faire coates-Armours)."[32] Throughout his chorography, Carew represents the landscape of Cornwall as a collection of pedigrees which are embodied architecturally in the houses of the gentry: "In following the course of Lymer, you fall downe by Master Bonds auncient house of Earth, descended to his auncesters, from the daughter and heire of that name. . . . Bond married with Fountaine, his father with Fits: his Armes are Ar[gent], on a Cheuron Sa[ble,] three Besants"; Sir William Treffry at Fowey possesses a "faire & ancient house, Castle-wise builded, and sufficiently flanked, [which] ouerlooketh the towne and hauen with a pleasant prospect, and yet is not excluded from the healthfull ayre, and vse of the country, which occasioned his auncestours (though endowed elsewhere, with large reuennues, of their owne and their wiues inheritance) for many discents, to make here their ordinary residence, as is witnessed by their toombestones, which I haue seene in the church"; Sir Johnathan Trelwyny owns "Poole, for his low and moyst seate, [which] is not vnaptly named . . . farre beneath his worth & calling," and also "hath a large priuiledged Mannour of the same name" in the parish.[33] Carew is less concerned to describe Sir Johnathan's estate than he is to draw attention to the gentleman's lineage: he mentions that Sir Johnathan "married Sir Henry Killigrews daughter: his father, the coheire of Reskimer: his graundfather Lamellyns Inheritrix," and further notes that "Out of Sir

Ionathans house is also descended Master Edward Trelawny, a Gentleman qualified with many good parts. Their armes are A[rgent] a Cheuron, S[able] betweene three Oke-leaues Vers."[34] Here, the architectural house becomes the embodiment of lineage as a vision of Sir Johnathan's coat of arms rises from the landscape, and the chorographer provides the narrative—a kind of catalogue entry—to explain the significance of the artifact he has chosen to gather and display in his text.

This urge to represent the landscape as a series of estates, pedigrees, and coats of arms becomes even more explicit in William Burton's *The Description of Leicester Shire*, published in 1622. Rather than organizing his work according to topography—by following rivers, say—Burton abandons any pretence that the natural features of the landscape are primary and instead lists the places he describes in alphabetical order. Just as the activity of surveying became less narrative and more graphical as it was allied with mapmaking, so in Burton's text his narrative is often sandwiched between diagrams of family trees and illustrations of armorial bearings: Burton thus represents visually on the printed page a geography conceived in terms of the hereditary ownership of land. A former lawyer, Burton shows a distinctive interest in the tortuous details of land transfers, and his style of chorography often superimposes chunks of legal records on the landscape as he explains families' claims to their estates. Burton's description of Tilton, for example, begins with a focus on genealogy familiar from earlier authors like Camden and Carew: "This Mannor (for many yeeres passed) hath beene the inheritance of the ancient family of *Digby*." At this point, however, Burton abandons the ancient Digbys and instead sketches the outlines of a court case involving a more recent Digby and his ownership of Tilton: "Sir *Euerard Digby* Knight, after attainted for the gun-powder Treason, conueyed this Mannor (before any Treason committed) to his sonne and heyre in tayle. Concerning the wardship of which heyre, a question after came in 7. *Iac.* whether it belonged to the King or no."[35] A lengthy summary of the court case follows in which Tilton becomes a physical site where the relationship between genealogy, possession of land, and the law is contested and clarified. Thus by focusing on the legal bases of land transfers as well as the pedigrees of landholding families, Burton emphasizes the concept of land as something individuals own; and by festooning his chorography with coats of arms and diagrams of family trees, Burton creates a text which portrays the landscape as a collection of elite individuals and the signs of their landed status.

As a representational mode, chorography could create different forms of identity. The increasing emphasis on landholders and their lineage helped to reinforce the concept of gentle status as a function of a wealthy family's long-standing title to a landed estate. Yet this focus on the gentry and their lineage paradoxically weakened the dynastic claims of the centralized monarchy. By representing the autonomy of individual landowners and localities, early modern chorographers depicted a national identity rooted in allegiance to the land rather than to the monarch. Whereas chronicle history was "almost by definition, a story of kings," chorography replaced this view of the past and the nation with a story of the land in its local particularity, marginalizing the monarch as a focus of loyalty.[36] Here, perhaps, may be discerned the origins of the opposition between the monarch on the one hand, and county men and Parliament on the other which would erupt violently in the Civil War.[37]

At the same time that chorography thus fostered a sense of local identity among elite landowners, it also afforded new positions of authority for writers who worked within the genre. As Richard Helgerson observes, "Not only does the emergence of the land parallel the emergence of the individual authorial self, the one enforces and perhaps depends on the other"; put another way, "authors are enabled by the authority they confer on the land they describe."[38] Richard Carew and William Burton, for example, included themselves among the elite landowners they gathered and displayed in their published texts. Carew represented two boroughs of Cornwall in Parliament, and by organizing his "survey" according to the county's hundreds, he implicitly places a grid of "administrative practicalities" over the landscape.[39] Carew's legitimacy as a leader of his native county emerges from his description of his family's place in the countryside. In describing Mount Edgecumb and its builder, Sir Richard Edgecumb, Carew first provides a detailed account of the house and its environs, and then launches into a paean to Sir Richard, a gentleman notable for his "mildnes & stoutnes, diffidence & wisdome, [and] deliberateness of vndertaking"; after this eulogy, Carew disingenuously cautions that he must restrain himself, "least a partiall affection steale, at vnwares, into my commendation, as one, by my mother, descended from his loynes, and by my birth, a member of the house."[40] Shortly after thus lauding his maternal grandfather, Carew embarks upon an extended description of East Antony, his ancestral home, providing the reader with a lengthy narrated pedigree, a poem about his immediate family, and a description of his coat of arms. Carew's excursion into autobiography ends with an account of a fish pond on his estate (including a poem in which Carew declares, "My fishfull pond is my delight") and a description of a "little woodden banqueting house" which Carew would like to erect "on the Iland in my pond."[41]

The relationship between chorography and authorial self-fashioning is even more apparent in Burton's *Description of Leicester Shire*. By ensur-

Figure 6. William Burton, *The Description of Leicester Shire* (London, 1622), title page. Photo courtesy of the Newberry Library, Chicago.

ing that "my natiue Countrie should [not] any longer lye obscured with darknesse," Burton also brings his own status as a landed gentleman to light.[42] In the body of his text, Burton provides a detailed pedigree for himself and his ancestral seat, Lindley Hall—on the estate of which, Burton reports, "therein was neuer seene Adder, Snake, or Lizzard, though in all the bordering confines haue bin seene and found very often"—and he explains how the heraldry of the Burton family evolved.[43] Burton's depiction of himself within the text as the heir of an ancient landholding dynasty is emphasized at the very beginning of his book, for the title page bears a map of Burton's estate which features a profile picture of Lindley Hall (see Figure 6); an engraved portrait of Burton, surrounded by his family's armorial bearings, appears on a subsequent page. As a chorographic author, Burton thus portrays himself as a preeminent specimen of the elite houses (simultaneously architectural and lineal) which he amasses and displays in his text.

William Camden, by contrast, used his work as a chorographer to establish an identity rooted in a genealogical mode of expertise. The son of a London painter, Camden initially earned his living as an undermaster (eventually headmaster) of Westminster School; but after he was appointed as Clarencieux King of Arms in the College of Heralds in 1597, Camden was able to devote himself to the kind of research which underpinned *Britannia*.[44] As Lesley B. Cormack observes, "The appointment of England's most important chorographer to this heraldic position of honor demonstrates more clearly than anything else the prominent position of genealogical research in the program of chorographical study."[45] At the same time that Camden's career path indicates the integral relationship between chorography and lineage, however, it also suggests how a non-elite man might convert his specialized knowledge—knowledge greatly valued by the landed gentry of early modern England—into professional activities which were identical to some of the pastimes cultivated by leisured country gentlemen. In providing the materials by which members of the gentry could legitimate their identities as pedigreed landowners, Camden was thus able to forge a new subject position for himself as a genealogical/geographical expert.

Antiquarianism

Early modern English chorography was deeply intertwined with antiquarianism—indeed, a historian recently termed Camden's *Britannia* a "book of topographical antiquities."[46] The humanist program of philology had led Renaissance scholars in Italy to appreciate the value of material remains in the study of classical texts, and this outlook soon shaped scholarship—and elite culture—throughout Western Europe. In England, as discussed previously, ambitious Elizabethan and Stuart aristocrats emulated their peers on the continent by collecting Greek and Roman artifacts and statuary, while men with shallower pockets trendily amassed collections of ancient coins; by the 1630s, knowledge of classical antiquities was firmly established as part of the repertoire of the English virtuoso. At the same time, this voguish interest in the material culture of antiquity also inflected an emerging preoccupation with English national identity, giving rise to antiquarian research into the past of England itself.

Like early modern English chorography, which was dedicated to assembling and displaying the noteworthy parcels of land (and their owners) which comprised a particular region, antiquarianism was distinguished from chronicle history by its focus on physical *things*. History, as it was conceived in the sixteenth and seventeenth centuries, consisted of an account of particular occurrences, usually a narrative of important political or military events: according to a description published in Elizabethan England, "Hystories bee made of deedes done by a publique weale, or agaynst a publique weale, and such deedes, be eyther deedes of warre, of peace, or else of sedition and conspiracie."[47] The historian's job was to recount the acts of individuals involved in such high politics: "euery deede, be it priuate, or publique must needs be done by some person, for some occasion, in sometyme, and place, with meanes & order, and with instruments, all which circumstaunces are not to be forgotten of the writer, and specially those that haue accompanyed and brought the deede to effect."[48] The chronological narrative the historian thus constructed was regarded as "a storehouse of timeless examples for the use of the moral philosopher or, somewhat belatedly, of the political pragmatist."[49]

By contrast, rather than res gestae, the antiquarian delved into what Sir Francis Bacon termed "history defaced, or remnants of history which have casually escaped the shipwreck of time."[50] Comparing the fragmentary physical artifacts of past societies to "the spars of a shipwreck," Bacon depicted antiquarianism as a kind of salvage operation:

though the memory of things be decayed and almost lost, yet acute and industrious persons, by a certain persevering and scrupulous diligence, contrive out of genealogies, annals, titles, monuments, coins, proper names and styles, etymologies of words, proverbs, traditions, archives and instruments as well public as private, fragments of histories scattered about in books not historical,—contrive, I say, from all these things or some of them, to recover somewhat from the deluge of time.[51]

To construct this type of "Imperfect History," as Bacon called it,[52] the researcher needed to assemble a group of "spars" of the shipwrecked past and arrange them in some type of order other than that of the grand narrative of political leaders. Thus antiquarianism was conceived and practiced in early modern England as an activity of *collecting*.

During the Tudor period, the category of "antiquities" usually comprised texts—documents and records regarded as "monuments" of the past—from which the antiquarian would make "collections," that is, transcriptions of and notes about the written material he had unearthed.[53] Paralleling the evolution of the estate survey, however, the focus of antiquarianism began to shift to nontextual materials, and by the seventeenth century an interest in physical objects such as coins, fossils, tombs, inscriptions, bones, and ruins increasingly came to characterize English antiquarianism.[54] John Leland, appointed the "King's Antiquary" in 1533, spent ten years gathering materials for a chorography of England; although Leland spent much time sifting through libraries, he also was interested in coins, sculptures, and archaeological remains.[55] In his Jacobean chorography of Cornwall, not published until 1728, John Norden provided illustrations of archaeological ruins; earlier, in his chorography of Middlesex published in 1593, Norden had asserted the value of copying the inscriptions and coats of arms adorning funerary monuments—a practice previously limited to the manuscript "collections" compiled by heralds—and he included engravings of armorial bearings in his text.[56] That Norden, a surveyor who also created estate maps, should thus innovatively extend the boundaries of chorography into antiquarianism suggests how emerging concepts of property, a new interest in physical objects, and a preoccupation with genealogy affected Tudor and Stuart perceptions of the landscape and its past.

This interaction of chorography with a mode of antiquarianism focused on physical artifacts was part of the ongoing modification of the early modern English concept of the collection. Beginning in the sixteenth century, there occurred a vitally important conceptual shift: rather than understanding the collection solely as a series of texts which had been produced in the course of research from original documents, people began to view the collection as an assemblage of physical *things*. The relationship between textuality and objects remained fluid, however; some written records, falling outside the province of the historian, were treated as antiquarian "spars" of the shipwrecked past, while artifacts such as funerary monuments, coins, and inscriptions were prized for the writing they bore. (Indeed, until 1803 the British Museum kept all its coins and medals in the department of manuscripts.[57]) At the same time, though, writers began to further the new notion of the collection as a group of physical objects. In addition to manuscripts for his famous library, Sir Robert Cotton also accumulated Roman and English coins, as well as many seals and medals from around the globe,[58] and illustrations of some of Cotton's coins were included by Camden in the 1600 edition of *Britannia*. As he prepared his *Theatre of the Empire of Great Britaine*, first published in 1611, John Speed likewise used coins lent to him by "the worthy repairer of eating times ruines, the learned *Sir Robert Cotten*, Knight Baronet, another *Philadelphus* in preseruing old Monuments, and ancient Records: whose Cabinets were vnlocked, and Library continually set open to my free accesse."[59] The relationship between Cotton's collection of physical objects and his printed text informed Speed's construction of both his historical narrative and the readers of his book. In his *History*, engravings of coins illustrate each of Speed's accounts of the monarchs who have ruled Britain, forming "the visual backbone of the narrative"[60] and merging the activities of the historian and the antiquarian, the author and the collector. Despite his access to Cotton's extensive collection, however, Speed could not find coins to illustrate every ruler he discusses; to compensate for these omissions, Speed provides blank "coins" at appropriate points in his book so that future readers, armed with previously undiscovered antiquities, can supplement the physical objects which Speed has depicted (see Figure 7).[61] Speed thus constructs the reader as an antiquarian collector/editor who will collaborate with him in simultaneously perfecting both Speed's text and Cotton's collection of coins.

A similarly dynamic interpenetration of textual and artifactual concepts of the collection also underlay the evolution of Camden's *Britannia*. Like Bacon, who championed firsthand observation over philology as a research method in natural philosophy, Camden's practice as a chorographer became increasingly focused on the examination and representation of physical objects. Initially, Camden intended to establish Britain's identity as one of the European nations originating from the Roman empire by researching place-names. As he informed his readers in the preface to the 1607 edition of *Britannia*, "That which I first proposed to myself, was to search out and illustrate those places, which Caesar, Tacitus, Ptolemy, Antoninus Augustus, Provinciarum Notitia, and other ancient writers have recorded; the names whereof Time has either chang'd, lost or corrupted."[62] With each revision and expansion of his text, however, Camden added

R ufinus ſlaine.

rrapped, or elſe himſelfe in thoſe dangers, ſet vp as the more ſufficient.But theſe things thus dangerouſly complotted by *Ruffinus*, were as politically preuented by the *Emperor*, although a *Child*: for before the *Seed* of this *Treaſon* could bring forth either *Bud* or *Blade* it was diſcouered, and the *Author* ſlaine by an *Italian* Band, his Head (which as ſome affirme, firſt tooke breath in *Britaine*) was advanced ouer a *Gate* in *Conſtantinople*.

Stilicho ſet at haz rd the whole Empire.

(4) Thus *Peace* obtained by the *Deaths* of theſe two *Traitors*, the *Third* ſtood vp with more danger in the *weſt*. For *Stilicho,Tutor* to yong *Honorius*,thought it not ſufficient honour for him to haue his *Daughter* an *Empreſſe* by the *Marriage* of his *Ward*;but ſet at hazard (for himſelfe and ſonne) his own *Conſcience*,both their *Liues*, and the fatall ruine of the *Now-declining Empire*. For firſt,ſowing ſeditions amongſt the *Lieutenants* of the *Prouinces*, picked alſo quarrels in the *Emperors* Court, *Caſhiering* with diſgraces thoſe *Gothes* that had ſerued with good proofe of their fidelitie aboue twenty yeeres, ſince their entertainment by *Theodoſius*. Theſe to reuenge their *Wrongs*, choſe for their *Cheiftaine* a valiant *Gothe* named *Alaricus*,which

Alaricus the ſcourge of Rome.

ſhortly proued the *Scourge of Rome* : wich whom ioyned the *Vandals, Alanes*, and *Sueuans*, who ioyntly with great fury beganne to warre in *Auſtria* and *Hungarie*, increaſing their *Powers* with ſuch *Multitudes*,

Paulus Oroſius.

that as *Paulus Oroſius*, an Author of that time ſaith, The *World* was am azed and ſtood in feare. For vnto

Rad gaſius with tvo hundred thouſand Gothes.

theſe *Colonies* reſorted two hundred thouſand *Gothes*, more,vnder the leading of *Radagaſius* their *King*,who together with vnited forces,ſubdued all *Thraſia, Hungary, Auſt ich,Sclauonia,and Dalmatia*,and ſpoiled all in ſuch manner, that it ſeemed *Diuels* and not *Men* had

Hieron. in epiſt. ea Paul.& Euſt.

paſſ'd that way, as Saint *Ierome* (who liued at that time)expreſſeth : *Theſe brute Beaſts* (ſaith he) *ſuffered by the wrath of God in this warre, haue laid Cittes waſte, ſlaine the People, and left the very Fields bare and deſolate, whereof the Prouinces of Thracia, and Sclauonia,with the Country wherein my ſelfe was borne,beare too true,but lamentable Records.*

Marcus choſen Emperor. Marcus murthered, Subellicus Ene. 7. lib.9.

(5) The *Roman Empire* thus daily declining, and theſe fierce *Nations* making hauock where they came, left the Armies in *Britaine* were put in great feare, leſt the Flames of their *Neighbours fire* might *Flaſh* out, and take hold of them alſo. Therefore prouidently to preuent that danger, they elected one *Marcus* their *Lieutenant* for *Emperor*, yeelding him their obedience ſome ſhort time, and then finding his defects, immediatly murthered him.

Gracian choſen Emperor. Gracian murthered.

In whoſe ſtead they Inthroned one *Gracian* a *Britaine* : whoſe carriage not anſwering their expectations, they *Murthered* alſo, within *Foure Moneths* after his Royall ſolemnity.

The features and Imperiall Titles ſtamped on the

Romiſh Mony of theſe two *Vſurpers*, (according to the vſuall manner of the like in Eſtate) we finde not, neither ſtands it with credit of our Hiſtory to faine them at pleaſure:therefore till time bring them forth, from the Caues of obſcurity wee haue allowed them place onely by theſe Circles inſerted, that others may ſupply what preſentlie wee want, and accompliſh by pencile what we cannot by Preſſe.

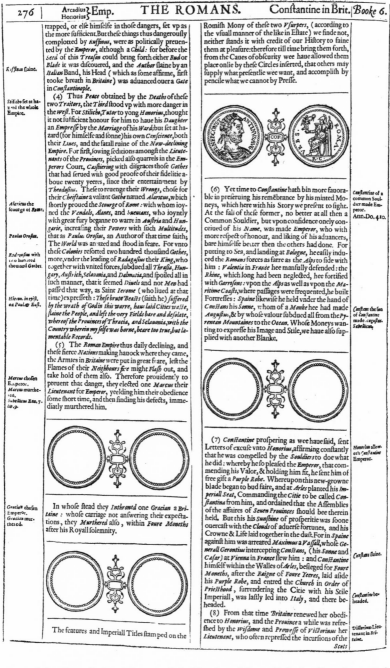

Conſtantine of a common Souldier made Emperor. Ann.Do. 4 10.

(6) Yet time to *Conſtantine* hath bin more fauorable in preſeruing his remēbrance by his minted Moneys, which here with his Story we preſent to ſight. At the fall of theſe former, no better at all then a Common Souldier, but vpon confidence onely conceiued of his *Name*, was made *Emperor*, who with more reſpect of honour, and liking of his aduancers, bare himſelfe better then the others had done. For putting to Sea, and landing at *Bologne*, he eaſily induced the *Romans* forces as farre as the *Alps* to ſide with him : *Valentia* in *France* hee manfully defended : the *Rhine*, which long had been neglected, hee fortified with *Garriſons* : vpon the *Alps* as well as vpon the *Maritime Coaſts*,where paſſages were frequented,he built *Fortreſſes* : *Spaine* likewiſe he held vnder the hand of *Conſtans* his *Sonne*, whom of a *Monke* hee had made

Conſtans the ſon of Conſtantine made auguſtus. Sabellicus,

Auguſtus,& by whoſe valour ſubdued all from the *Pyrenean Mountaines* to the *Ocean*. Whoſe Moneys wanting to expreſſe his Image and Stile,we haue alſo ſupplied with another Blanke.

Honorius alloweth Conſtantine Emperor.

(7) *Conſtantine* proſpering as wee haue ſaid, ſent Letters of excuſe vnto *Honorius*,affirming conſtantly that he was compelled by the *Souldiers* to doe what he did : whereby he ſo pleaſed the *Emperor*, that commending his Valor, & holding him fit, he ſent him of free gift a *Purple Robe*. Whereupon this new-growne blade began to bud faire, and at *Arles* planted his *Imperiall Seat*, Commanding the Citie to be called *Conſtantina* from him, and ordained that the Aſſemblies of the affaires of *Seuen Prouinces* ſhould bee therein held. But this his *Sunſhine* of proſperitie was ſoone ouercaſt with the *Clouds* of aduerſe fortunes, and his Crowne & Life laid together in the duſt.For in *Spaine*

Conſtans ſlaine.

againſt him was arreared *Maximus* a *Vaſſall*,whoſe Generall *Gerontius* intercepting *Conſtans*, (his *Sonne* and *Caſar*) at *Vienna* in *France* ſlew him : and *Conſtantine* himſelf within the Walles of *Arles*, beſieged for *Foure*

Conſtantine beheaded.

Moneths, after the *Raigne* of *Foure Yeeres*, laid aſide his *Purple Robe*, and entred the *Church* in *Order* of *Prieſthood*, ſurrendering the Citie with his Stile Imperiall, was laſtly led into *Italy*, and there beheaded.

Victorinus Lieutenant in Britaine.

(8) From that time *Britaine* renewed her obedience to *Honorius*, and the *Prouince* a while was refreſhed by the *wiſdome* and *Proweſſe* of *Victorinus* her *Lieutenant*, who often repreſſed the incurſions of the

Scots

Figure 7. John Speed, *The Theatre of the Empire of Great Britaine* (London, 1611), p. 276. Reproduced by permission of the Huntington Library, San Marino, California.

material which diverged from this plan, and in the process *Britannia* came
increasingly to emphasize artifacts. The 1586 edition of *Britannia* contained
the first archaeological illustration to appear in an English book, a representation of a medieval inscription; the second edition, published in 1590,
incorporated four drawings of coins; and the 1600 edition featured even
more illustrations, including a map of early Britain and "archaeological
insets" engraved on the title page, plates depicting coins, an engraving of
Stonehenge, and pictures of Romano-British altars.[63]

The interrelationship between Camden's increasingly antiquarian
mode of chorography and emergent practices of collecting was cemented in
1600, when Camden traveled to Hadrian's Wall with his former student
Robert Cotton. Together, Camden and Cotton hunted for physical traces
of the past; many of the inscriptions Camden gathered appeared in the 1607
edition of the *Britannia*, while many of the stones which bore these inscriptions eventually ended up among Cotton's burgeoning collection of
antiquities at his seat in Huntingdonshire. These stones, never part of the
renowned antiquarian library Cotton maintained at his Westminster residence, were one aspect of Cotton's display of his social authority in his
home county. Transported with great cost and difficulty to Cotton's country estate in the fens, the inscribed stones were arranged in an octagonal
summer house in the garden at Conington Castle. Like the long gallery
Cotton added to Conington and the funerary monuments he erected in the
local church to commemorate his forebears (including the Scottish ancestors he shared with James I), the stones were intended to exhibit Cotton's
credentials as a Huntingdonshire gentleman.[64] In the 1607 edition of *Britannia*, Camden described Cotton as "a singular lover and searcher of
antiquities, [who,] having gathered with great charges from all places the
monuments of venerable antiquitie, hath heere [i.e., at Conington Castle]
begunne a famous Cabinet, whence of his singular courtesie, he hath often
times given me great light in these darksome obscurities."[65] Thus by 1607,
Camden's *Britannia* had evolved into a work which depicted the British
landscape as physical things, and Cotton had begun to fashion himself as a
powerful member of the gentry by collecting antiquities; in the process,
Camden's book came to emphasize both pieces of real estate owned by
gentlemen and artifacts from the past, objects which themselves became
intertwined with the construction of landed identity through Sir Robert
Cotton's activities of collection and display.

The relationship between early modern English antiquarianism and
new concepts of landownership took other forms as well. While deeds and
pedigrees could be exhibited as signs of their owners' gentle status,[66] they

were also useful weapons in legal battles over land rights. An examination of Sir Robert Cotton's practice as an antiquarian/landlord reveals how attention to the "spars" of the past could have practical benefits for the owner of an estate. As Roger B. Manning has demonstrated, Cotton "considered research into manorial records and chancery practice to be necessary for sound estate administration because it enabled the lord of the manor to retrieve ancient precedents for higher rents and entry fines, to revive long forgotten seigneurial dues and to extract higher profits from his tenants in an age of rising prices," and in several instances of Cotton's antiquarian legal wrangling about his properties, it seems that tenants became antiquarian collectors themselves by stealing manorial documents which they subsequently used or hid to their own advantage.[67] Such exploitation of antiquarian research to secure a more profitable relationship to land was by no means limited to Cotton and the tenants he attempted to best. Cotton's library, which he made available to many scholars and gentlemen, was closed by Charles I in 1629 because it seemed to be the source of "[m]uch of the information about parliamentary rights and precedents and procedures that were invoked against the King"; however, previous to its closure the library was often consulted by members of the gentry who were less interested in high politics than in their own attempts to legitimate their claims to land or titles.[68] Thus like chorography, antiquarianism in early modern England came to be inextricably bound up with the identities of individual gentlemen, identities rooted in the intertwined histories of genealogy and landownership.

Salvaging Society: Chorography, Antiquarianism, and the English Civil War

As the political crisis deepened in Stuart England, the collecting and textualization of British antiquities assumed new ideological functions. By the middle of the seventeenth century, chorography and antiquarianism were imbued with the grim aura of an increasingly desperate rescue mission, and the antiquarian author became a cultural Noah who gathered and protected endangered specimens on the verge of extinction within the ark of his text. The dynamics of Caroline and Interregnum antiquarianism are clearly revealed in authors' growing emphasis on funerary monuments. Funerary monuments were primarily an elite cultural form in seventeenth-century England, and churches were used as theaters for the posthumous display of status through commemorative art works.[69] An early modern funerary monument was intended to "sustain social differentiation," to counteract Death's disregard for status through a representation of a deceased individual's "social body" and thus reaffirm the enduring, hierarchical structure of his community.[70] Just as living family members competed with other dynasties for the best pews in their local church, so they sought to bury their dead in the most socially prestigious locations within the church, angling for coveted positions near the altar which were now associated with superior social rank rather than sanctity. As David Cressy notes, "With their heraldic arms representing the past, and their progeny pointing to the future," deceased but commemorated family members filled "a crucial place in the maintenance of gentle dynastic continuity," a group of family monuments serving as "a striking reminder of power, continuity, and cohesion" to the community which gathered in the local church.[71]

Not coincidentally, at the same time that social mobility and an active land market were causing an unprecedented turnover in landed families, there arose a building boom in funerary monuments. "From the 1580s onwards," Graham Parry remarks, "English churches were acquiring more inscriptions, epitaphs and monuments than ever before"[72] as members of the elite sought to legitimize their families' ostensibly ancient wealth and blood. Born of these preoccupations with continuity and social identity, a funerary monument was thus a site on which an elite family displayed its lineage: inscriptions would record the deceased's parentage and descendants, and the coats of arms associated with him and his family would further exhibit his status.[73] Family trees, often wildly fictitious, were included on the tomb itself or placed nearby on a wooden panel to stress the family's continuity. Sculpture, tablets, painting, and stained glass were all media available to the gentleman who wished to advertise the glories of his ancestry in his local church, and the ostentation of funerary display was equated with a family's importance. As John Weever observed in 1631, "Sepulchres should bee made according to the qualities of degree of the person deceased, that by the Tombe euery one might bee discerned of what ranke hee was liuing"; however, Weever goes on to lament that this principle was being undermined by upstarts: "for by some of our epitaphs more honour is attributed to a rich quondam Tradesman, or griping usurer, then is giuen to the greatest Potentate entombed in Westminster: and their tombes are made so huge great, that they tak vp the Church, and hinder the people from diuine Seruice."[74]

In their enthusiasm for the commemorative family trees, epitaphs, and heraldry found in the churches of particular locales, chorographers furthered this association between the identity of elite landowners and memorializing objects. In 1600 William Camden anonymously published the first printed survey of the inscriptions in Westminster Abbey,[75] and two decades later William Burton explained to the reader of his chorography of Leicestershire,

I haue added all the Armes in all the Church windowes in the shire, and the inscriptions of the Tombes, which (for the most part) I haue taken by my own view and trauell, to this end, for that perhaps they may rectifie Armories and Genealogies, and may giue testimony, proofe, and end to many differences. For of my owne knowledge I can affirme, that the Antiquity of a Church window, for the proofe of a match and issue had, hath beene deliuered in euidence to a Iury at an Assises, & been accepted.[76]

By the early 1630s, however, Burton's lawyerly interest in funerary monuments as repositories of genealogical information was giving way to the anxious sense of mission expressed by John Weever. Unlike other European nations in which funerary monuments are carefully preserved and their epitaphs diligently collected and printed, Weever chides,

how barbarously within these his Maiesties Dominions, they are (to the shame of our time) broken downe, and vtterly almost all ruinated, their brasen Inscriptions erazed, torne away, and pilfered, by which inhumane, deformidable act, the honourable memory of many vertuous and noble persons deceased, is extinguished, and the true vnderstanding of diuers Families in these Realmes (who haue descended of these worthy persons aforesaid) is so darkened, as the true course of their inheritance is thereby partly interrupted.[77]

In Weever's lamentation we find the specter of past iconoclasm which would increasingly come to haunt English ceremonialists. Protestant reformers—"puritans"—stressed the primacy of scripture and faith (as opposed to works), and this outlook entailed an abhorrence of the use of man-made objects and rituals in worship.[78] From the time of Henry VIII, funerary monuments were supposed to be excluded from iconoclastic reforms of the fabric of churches: as long as funerary monuments were simply commemorative, they were not to be defaced or removed, a position codified during the reign of Edward VI by a statute that proscribed damage "to any image or picture set or graven upon any tomb in any church, chapel or churchyard, only for a monument of any king, prince, nobleman or other dead person, which hath not been commonly reputed and taken for a saint."[79] Later in the sixteenth century, bursts of iconoclasm spurred Elizabeth I to reiterate this royal policy against damaging funerary monuments.[80] Despite this official stance, however, tombs and monuments nonetheless were targeted by zealous Tudor reformers: in 1551–52, a bishop ordered that "tombs" and "sepulchres" should be removed from churches in the dioceses of Gloucester and Worcester, since such monuments were a type of "provocation of idolatry," and, as Margaret Aston notes, "John Stow's repeated laments show [that] the damage to funeral monuments in London churches was ancient history by the later years of Elizabeth's reign."[81]

The iconoclast who attacked a gentleman's tomb crossed the line between acceptable Protestant ideology and subversion of the social order: since funerary monuments functioned to preserve the integrity of the corporate "social body" of the landed elite, the destruction of such place-holders constituted a threat to the hereditary social formation as a whole. As fears of a resurgence of iconoclasm heightened, seventeenth-century English antiquarians created texts which could serve as surrogate churches full of funerary monuments, books which could reconstruct the social bodies of dead gentlemen and preserve them from the predations of an increasingly hostile culture. John Weever frets,

And nothing will be shortly left to continue the memory of the deceased to posteri-tie; pilfery and the opinion some haue, that Tombes, and their Epitaphs, taste somewhat of Poperie, hauing already most sacrilegiously stolne, erazed, and taken away, almost all the Inscriptions and Epitaphs, cut, writ, inlaid, or engrauen vpon the Sepulchres of the deceased; and most shamefully defaced the glorious rich Tombes, and goodly monuments of our most worthy Ancestours. It could bee wished that some order might be taken for the preseruation of these few which are as yet remaining: for to mine owne knowledge, by the obseruation I haue made in many Churches, the Monuments of the dead are daily thus abused.[82]

From the late 1620s, the Church of England had come increasingly under the influence of proponents of ceremonialism. Ceremonialist clergy such as Matthew Wren, John Cosin, Richard Neile, and William Laud instituted a new emphasis on the externals of worship, "corporeal images, material objects, and aesthetic formalism" as well as "ritualized, regulated bodily practices and gestures."[83] Integral to this focus on the physicality of worship was the refurbishment of churches; as part of a campaign to restore the ecclesiastical fabric of England, communion tables were moved to the east end of churches and railed, while new religious paintings, statues, stained glass, crucifixes, chalices, candlesticks, and altarcloths were used to ornament ecclesiastical spaces.[84] During the Civil War, such physical ob-jects were targeted in attempts to root out ceremonialism, and in 1643 and 1644, Parliament passed ordinances mandating the obliteration of "Monu-ments of Superstition or Idolatry."[85] Lamenting the effects of this mid-century assault on ecclesiastical art, John Aubrey observed that "When I came to Oxford Crucifixes were common in ye glasse in the Studies window: and in the Chamber windowes were canonized Saints. . . . But after 1647 they were all broken: Down went Dagon. Now no religion to be found."[86] As in the sixteenth century, this program of iconoclasm was supposed to exclude any funerary monuments commemorating a "dead person which hath not been commonly reputed or taken for a saint";[87] however, these injunctions to spare tombs were not always obeyed. An ostensibly eyewitness account of the ransacking of Peterborough Cathedral by parliamentary troops in 1643 asserts that once the organs, service books, communion table, altar rails, stained glass, and "painted or carved work" had been destroyed, the men began to demolish the tombs located in the cathedral; a few years later, a funerary monument was erected in the nearby village of Marholm with the inscription, "To the courteous souldier / Noe crucifix you see, noe Frightful Brand / Of Superstition's here. Pray let me stand. / Grassante bello civili."[88] Likewise in 1643, as Bishop Joseph Hall would later recount, iconoclasts vigorously sought to "reform" the fabric of Norwich Cathedral:

Lord, what work was here, what clattering of glasses, what beating down of walls, what tearing up of monuments, what pulling down of seats, what wresting out of irons and brass from the windows and graves! What defacing of arms, what demolishing of curious stonework, that had not any representation in the world, but only of the cost of the founder and skill of the mason.[89]

Similarly, it was reported that parliamentary troops "violated the monuments of the dead" in Canterbury Cathedral in 1642, and John Evelyn found when he visited Lincoln Cathedral in 1654 that "the Souldiers had lately knocked off all or most of the Brasses which were on the Gravestones, so as few Inscriptions were left: They told us they went in with axes & hammers, & shut themselves in, till they had rent & torne off some barges full of Mettal; not sparing the monuments of the dead, so helish an avarice possess'd them."[90]

Although one should not exaggerate the scope of the wartime destruction of funerary monuments—the art historian Nigel Llewellyn has recently argued that Victorian reformers inflicted far more damage on English funerary monuments than Cromwell's troops[91]—many antiquarians during the Civil War and Interregnum nonetheless perceived themselves to be facing a wholesale destruction of the physical remains of the social order of the past. Some antiquarians, especially those interested in the history of law (Sir Simonds D'Ewes, Sir Edward Dering), sympathized with Parliament, and indeed Thomas, Lord Fairfax, a parliamentary general, was known for "the peculiar respect he had for Antiquities."[92] For many other antiquarians, however, their interest in the past was inextricable from their loyalty to the Church of England and the monarchy. With cathedrals and country houses under attack in the 1640s, "The Civil War gave an urgency to the recording of endangered objects"; later, during the Protectorate, "many royalists excluded from public life took refuge in scholarship" and nostalgically recreated a landscape which bespoke traditional religious and political authority.[93] Thus many of the antiquarian studies undertaken and published during the 1640s and 1650s were highly politicized texts of resistance and consolation.

The works of Sir William Dugdale exemplify this political stance. Dugdale was born in 1605 to a family "of yeoman background" which had recently moved from Lancashire to Warwickshire.[94] Dugdale was conscious of the precariousness of his social status; in the preface to his chorography of Warwickshire, Dugdale apologizes that as an "undertaking . . . this would have been more proper for such a one whose ancestors had enjoyed a long succession in this Countie, whereunto I cannot pretend. . . . But I presume, that the less my relations are, the more acceptance will my endeavours find with the ingenuous, and learned, to whose Judgment I only submit both myself and it."[95] After his father died, Dugdale bought Blythe Hall, located near Coleshill, Warwickshire, and adopted the lifestyle of a country gentleman, which included antiquarian research into his family and estate. In his *Antiquities of Warwickshire*, Dugdale concludes his account of Blythe by representing his chorographic text as a product of his ownership of the Warwickshire country house: "Which Sir Walter (afterwards Lord *Aston* of *Forfare* in *Scotland*) by his Deed of bargain and sale . . . conveyed it unto me *William Dugdale*, it being the place of my residence, and where I compiled the present Work."[96] Thus, like Richard Carew and William Burton, both of whom he mentions in the dedicatory epistle of his study of Warwickshire, Dugdale initially pursued scholarship in chorography and antiquarianism to enhance his own standing as a member of his county's elite, a status about which he, as a *parvenu*, apparently felt rather insecure. At the same time, Dugdale's representation of his chorography as emanating from Blythe Hall also testifies to the geographically circumscribed life he was forced to lead as a royalist under the Protectorate, for Dugdale was largely confined to a radius of several miles from Blythe Hall.[97]

As a young man, Dugdale's quest for elite status and identity had offered prospects beyond the bounds of Warwickshire. His early research drew him into contact not only with the local gentry but also with a national network of antiquarians, and Dugdale was appointed to the College of Heralds in 1638 and eventually rose to the position of Garter King-at-Arms and received a knighthood in 1677. During the 1640s and the Interregnum, however, Dugdale's antiquarian activities became imbued with an urgent politics of resistance. In 1641, Dugdale and a heraldic painter went on a textual rescue mission, attempting to make "a speedy view of what Monuments [they] could, especially in the principall Churches of this realm; to the end, that by Inke and paper, the Shadows of them, with their Inscriptions might be preserved for posteritie, forasmuch as the things themselves were so neer unto ruine."[98] When, as Dugdale put it, "the flames of our civill dissentions" began "breaking violently out," he served the king in his capacity as a heraldic officer and delivered royal warrants demanding loyalty from towns held by parliamentary garrisons, and he accompanied the king to Oxford when the city became the royalist head-quarters in October 1642.[99] Dugdale's loyalty had financial consequences: his estate was sequestrated and, as his allowance from the king went un-paid, it seems that Dugdale made his living as a herald by overseeing the elaborate funerals of prominent royalists;[100] he also did antiquarian research and continued his studies even when he went to France for several months after the king was defeated in 1648.[101]

During the 1650s, Dugdale began to publish his antiquarian works, books which strove to recreate the social body of an Anglican and royalist England. The first of the three volumes of Dugdale's *Monasticon Anglicanum* appeared in 1655, by which time "The function of the Church of England had been suspended, its bishops deposed, its clergy purged, and its services banned."[102] Comprised mainly of charters, the *Monasticon* docu-ments the foundation and growth of the monastic orders of England, and the various rights and privileges to be exercised by secular landowners who obtained ecclesiastical property after the Dissolution. Thus besides chroni-cling the history of the defunct English Church, Dugdale's text also pre-serves information about the elite and their ownership of property. As James Wright later noted in the abridged English edition of the *Monasti-con*, "this Book is of great use in matters of Heraldry and Genealogies," and many of the plates in the 1655 volume bear the names and armorial bearings of the gentlemen who paid for them to be engraved.[103] In this way, through the publication of his *Monasticon* Dugdale collected and preserved the identities of defiant Anglican royalists, as well as the churches and cathe-drals he discussed and depicted in his text.

The genealogical emphasis of his chorography of Warwickshire was similarly politicized when the book appeared in 1656. In his preface, Dug-dale laments the sparse evidence of Warwickshire life in Saxon times, asking, "what likelyhood there is, that Memorialls of any thing could be preserved, where War did so much abound," implicitly comparing the destructiveness of the Saxon conflicts with the effects of the recent Civil War. In the dedicatory epistle to the gentry of Warwickshire, Dugdale characterizes his book as "a *Monumentall Pillar*" to their ancestors and praises those gentlemen who assisted his research for exhibiting their dynastic loyalty "by representing to the world a view of the [ancestors'] Tombes, and in some sort preserving those Monuments from that fate, which *Time*, if not contingent mischief, might expose them to";[104] Dugdale's book will rescue the Warwickshire elite from the ravages of war and republican hostility and give them an immortality denied to their Saxon forebears. Dugdale's preoccupation with the genealogical value of *Warwickshire* caused him to stay in London while the book was printed, "by reason that the ordinary Correctors were not skyll'd in the Pedigrees."[105] In Dugdale's chorography, the landscape becomes a backdrop for the display of local pedigrees, armorial bearings, funerary monuments, and epitaphs, and he suggests he has thus fashioned a kind of genealogical ark of "*Monuments and Memorialls*" which will ensure "the continued welfare and lasting honour" of the Warwickshire gentry.[106] In addition, by representing Warwickshire's topography in terms of elite landownership, Dugdale promoted a vision of genteel "social solidarity" which had the potential to override political differences; indeed, as Ann Hughes observes, the Warwickshire gentry who helped Dugdale to publish his *Warwickshire* included parliamentarians and neutrals, as well as royalists.[107] Dugdale makes clear, however, that inclusion in his ark of a book entails a reciprocal relationship between his text and the gentry it honors, and in his preface, Dugdale names heads of families whose monuments he would have excluded from his chorography if he had known that they would not subsidize the cost of the relevant illustrations, as well as skinflints who refused outright to help finance "the preservation of their memories" and who thus forfeited commemoration through engraved plates.[108] Thus, in the context of the 1650s, the text and the conditions of its publication reaffirmed the shared values of the landed gentry as transcending political divisions; but at the same time, *The Antiquities of Warwickshire* also served to aggrandize Dugdale's position as an elite "insider" in his county and an arbiter of genteel behavior and commemoration.

In 1658 Dugdale published his work on St. Paul's Cathedral, the building which had been the first stop on his 1641 mission to record the antiquities of English churches. The royalist origins of *The History of St. Pauls Cathedral* are foregrounded in Dugdale's dedication of his work to Christopher, Lord Hatton, whom Dugdale identifies as "Comptroller of the Household to the late King Charles, and one of his Majesties most honourable Privy Councill," and later in the text Dugdale declares himself "a son of the Church of *England*" and laments how the cathedral was used as a "Horse quarter for Souldiers" during the war, its "Pavement torn up, and Monuments, either utterly demolish'd or defaced."[109] Dugdale regarded St. Paul's Cathedral as a particularly valuable genealogical archive that must be transcribed in order to preserve the identities of England's ancient families, and he writes that he sought to preserve and disseminate the antiquarian information embodied within the fabric of the cathedral "[o]ut of a sad contemplation . . . that so glorious a structure, thus rais'd, inricht, and beautified by the piety of our deceased Ancestors, should be utterly destroyed, and become a wofull spectacle of ruine."[110] The text is illustrated with engravings of funerary monuments, and in addition Dugdale provides enlarged representations of armorial bearings and epitaphs adorning the tombs portrayed; the expense of producing the plates was borne "by the helpe and favour of sundry worthy persons."[111] Just as he depicted Warwickshire as a geography of pedigrees and escutcheons, so in his account of St. Paul's Cathedral Dugdale transforms ecclesiastical architecture into a landscape of tombs and inscriptions, artifacts which testify to the identity of elite families who own individual sections of the English countryside. As a whole, then, Dugdale's antiquarian and chorographic texts act as cabinets within which the author gathers and displays physical objects that embody the individual and collective identities of beleaguered members of the gentry.

Sir Thomas Browne as Antiquarian Author

A more equivocal social stance may be discerned in the antiquarianism of the works of Sir Thomas Browne. New Historicist criticism of Browne's *Religio Medici* (1642–43) has stressed the work's engagement in the politicized discourse of the Civil War era and has revealed that Browne's celebrated tolerance is neither apolitical nor moderate, but "deeply, committedly, and indeed polemically, conservative."[112] An analysis of Browne's antiquarianism in later texts allows us to develop and qualify Michael Wilding's perception that in *Religio Medici*, Browne's religious views are intertwined with an elitist social vision.[113] More specifically, I would argue, Browne's antiquarian works often buttress the social authority of the propertied class; yet at other times, Browne more ambivalently explores new

criteria of cultural authority. By depicting himself as a virtuoso with expertise in antiquarianism, Browne can choose to uphold a genteel cultural
economy founded upon traditional social distinctions; but he can also emphasize that he possesses a new form of power rooted in his activities as an
antiquarian collector/author. Browne's works thus reveal how antiquarianism, like other forms of collecting, could become a site of conflicting
ideologies and identities in seventeenth-century England.

   Pseudodoxia Epidemica, published in 1646, clearly establishes Browne's
allegiance with the landed gentry and his disdain for the plebeian rabble
which he dismissed in *Religio Medici* as "those vulgar heads, that rudely stare
about."[114] By compiling and publishing *Pseudodoxia Epidemica*, Browne was
responding to Sir Francis Bacon's suggestion that a catalogue of popular
errors was needed as a foundation for the advancement of knowledge. In the
context of the 1640s, however, Browne's portrayal of a society on the verge of
being overwhelmed by the errors of the vulgar also resonates politically:
"And being now at greatest distance from the beginning of Error, [we] are
almost lost in its dissemination, whose waies are boundless, and confess no
circumscription" (2:25). In his prefatory remarks to the reader of *Pseudodoxia* Browne asserts, "Nor have we addressed our Pen or Stile unto the
people (whom Books do not redress, and are this way incapable of reduc-
tion), but unto the knowing and leading part of Learning" (2:5). Browne's
display of his collection of popular errors is socially exclusive: he presents
himself as a virtuoso who seeks to improve the condition of society by
sharing his erudition with other learned, leisured men. In a social world
turned upside down by war, Browne's catalogue of virtuoso knowledge
functions as a rallying point for the beleaguered or exiled "ingenuous Gentry" (2:4) to reassert their class identity and influence—and his book simultaneously constructs Browne as a member of this elite. Like Dugdale,
Browne in the *Pseudodoxia* champions a traditional social order, exploiting
his potential autonomy as a collector only to align himself with his social
betters.

   Allegiance to landed values, suffused with nostalgic respect for what
had been, before the Civil War, the established Church, likewise underpins
Browne's *Repertorium*. Significantly, the very title of Browne's work emphasizes its affiliation with physical objects, for the term "repertorium"
means "the things so gathered"—that is, a collection. As its subtitle, *Some
Account of the Tombs and Monuments in the Cathedrall Church of Norwich*,
indicates, the *Repertorium* is Browne's version of Dugdale's *History of St.
Pauls Cathedral*, a textual reconstruction of artifacts threatened or destroyed
by the predations of war and iconoclasm. As a longtime puritan stronghold,

Norwich "had become the special target of Laudian reform" during the late 1630s and thus faced particularly acute puritan backlash in the 1640s.[115] As Bishop Hall recounted, Norwich Cathedral was attacked and damaged by iconoclasts, and Browne narrates how "richly embroydered" vestments "were formally carryed into the market place, some blowing the organ pipes before them, and were cast into a fire provided for that purpose, with showting and Rejoyceing" (3:140–41). Although the *Repertorium* was not published during Browne's lifetime, it was written in 1660 as an act of political allegiance, as Browne later reported in a letter to Aubrey:

a clark of the church told mee that in the late times above an hundred brasse inscriptions were stolne out of the church, and therefore to prevent all oblivion of the rest I tooke the best account I could of them at the Kings returne from an understanding singing-man of 91 yeares old and sett them downe in a booke which otherwise would have in a short time been forgotten, the churchmen litle minding such things. (4:373)

Geoffrey Keynes suggests that Browne composed the *Repertorium* "purely as a pious labour, a duty to the memory of former Norwich worthies" and observes that Browne took "considerable pains over it," as evidenced by the fact that he wrote it out twice.[116] Like the spire of the cathedral, which was repaired "at His majesties Restauration" (3:142), Browne's *Repertorium* stands as a highly politicized reconstruction of physical objects and the cultural values they embody.

Throughout the work, Browne depicts himself in the service of the landed elite, dutifully restoring the funerary monuments—and thus the genealogical identities they commemorated—which had been defaced. Because so many inscriptions were removed, Browne notes, "the distinct places of buryall of many noble and considerable persons, becomes now unknowne" (3:123), and he attempts to replace these lost objects with his own text. As an antiquarian trying to compensate for the destruction of the Civil War, Browne recreates Norwich Cathedral as a heraldry-encrusted display of landed power, a great exhibition hall of elite identities rooted in lineage. Like Dugdale and the chorographers, Browne is primarily concerned to preserve the information about genealogies and landholdings inscribed onto funerary monuments: Browne informs us that a ruined tomb, "now broken, splitt and depressed by blowes," commemorates Miles Spencer, "Lord of the mannor of Bowthorp and Colney, which came unto the Yaxleys from him" (3:123); "In the middle Isle and under a large stone, and allmost over which a branch for lights hangeth, was buryed Sr Frances Southwell of a family of great name and estate, and which formerly pos-

sessed Wood Rising" (3:125); "Next unto it is the monument of Richard
Brome Esquire, where his Armes or Achievement is to bee seen, bearing
Ermynes, and for the crest a bunch or branch of broome with golden
flowers" (3:128). Browne also restores to the mind's eye of the reader heraldic devices obliterated by whitewash: of the monument of Randolph Pul-
vertoft, Browne writes, "Above the Inscription there is an escocheon, and
his coat of Armes was thereupon, six eares of wheat, with a border of cinque
foyles, butt now washed out since the wall was whitened"; and he likewise
provides biographical information about Sir Thomas Erpingham, since the
painted inscriptions on the pillars of his tomb have been "washed out" and
the brasses "torne and taken away in the late time" (3:126–27). In addition,
as part of his mission to recreate the hierarchical social body of Norfolk,
Browne also resurrects the history of the cathedral—and the Anglican
Church—by recreating the ruined monuments of the bishops of Norwich,
and he depicts himself as a friend of the expelled Bishop Joseph Hall, "A
person of singular humillity, patience and pietie," who was regarded as a
symbol of the persecution of the Anglican clergy.[117]

At the same time that Browne attempts to reconstruct the prewar
fabric of Norfolk's elite culture, however, he also sketches an order of objects—and thus an order of society—which is not entirely coextensive with
the ruined monuments of the cathedral and the landed values they (and
Browne's "repertorium") commemorate. The destruction of the fabric of
Norwich Cathedral has created a physical and social space which Browne
fills with his text, and in the process he fashions different identities for
himself. Browne sometimes draws our attention beyond his text to the
antiquities he himself owns and has assembled in order to create the *Repertorium*: he remarks how "The northern wall of the cloyster was handsomely
beutified with the Armes of some of the nobility," goes on to describe the
heraldic wall, but then concludes, "The figures of these coates in their
distinguishable and discernible colours are not beyond my remembrance,
butt in the late times when the lead was faultie & the stone work decayed,
the rayne falling upon the wall washed them away, butt a draught of them
all I have by mee" (3:137–38). And at one point, Browne stresses the role his
antiquarian collections will play in the future: after he enumerates the
heraldic devices found "upon the inside of the steeple over the Quire"
(3:135), Browne says that since they are "litle taken notice of, and time being
still like to obscure and make them past knowledg, I would not omitt to
have a draught thereof sett downe, which I keepe by mee" (3:136). As the
possessor of antiquarian "collections" about the cathedral—another repertorium—and a living, documentary source for his own text, Browne thus

allies himself with a group of men whose memories have likewise provided material for the reconstruction of the physical fabric of the cathedral. During the years of tumult and disrepair, Browne tells us, the lost brasses and whitewashed escutcheons of Norwich Cathedral survived in the memories of non-elite functionaries of the Church: "John Wright a clark above 80 yeares old," "Mr John Sandlin one of the Quire" (presumably the "understanding singing-man" Browne mentioned to Aubrey), and "old Mr Spendlowe, who was a prebend fiftie yeares" become Browne's authoritative sources of information, and without them, the tombs of Sir Thomas Windham, the Bigot family, and Bishop Henry le Spencer would remain anonymous (3:123, 127). By assembling this group of sources—a collection of men who provide the material for Browne's collections of notes—the author can imaginatively piece together the ruined monuments of the cathedral in his text. Simultaneously, though, Browne also presents himself as a member of a parallel, though more socially exclusive circle whose members are united by their monetary efforts to restore physical objects in the cathedral: Browne reports that the organ destroyed by iconoclasts was replaced by "Another fayre well tuned organ" which was "afterward paynted and beutifully adorned by the care and cost of my Honourd freind Dr Herbert Astley the present and worthy Deane of Norwich" (3:140), while the burned vestments have been replaced by a new cope "which was presented by my Honord freind Philip Harbord Esqr and present High Sheriffe of Nottingham" (3:141); in addition, part of the cloister floor, previously "broaken and the stones taken away," is "now handsomely paved by the beneficence of my worthy freind Wm Burghleigh Esquier" (3:138). The *Repertorium* thus positions Browne in a series of overlapping subject positions: royalist, Anglican author in the service of a traditional social order; owner of a private collection of antiquities; county insider. In all these roles, Browne's identity is rooted in the activities of gathering and assessing antiquarian objects—activities which have specific social coordinates, as Browne simultaneously assembles groups of men to help him restore the lost artifacts of Norwich Cathedral. In Browne's display of his multifaceted ability to shape the social order of the present by gathering the shipwrecked spars of the past, he underlines the collector's power to create new positions of cultural authority for himself.

This potential for self-fashioning literally haunts the margins of the printed text of Browne's *Hydriotaphia* (or *Urne-Buriall*). The ideological stance of the *Urne-Buriall* cannot be fully understood without considering Browne's portrayal of the work's social context. A wide-ranging meditation on humankind's attempts to commemorate the dead, *Urne-Buriall* is firmly rooted in a local antiquarian discovery: the unearthing, "In a Field of old *Walsingham*, not many moneths past," of "between fourty and fifty Urnes, deposited in a dry and sandy soile, not a yard deepe, nor farre from one another" (1:140). *Urne-Buriall* can, in part, be viewed as a defense of cere-monialism because it implicitly attacks puritan prohibitions against funer-ary rites. When Browne published *Urne-Buriall* in 1658, the Church of England's "Order for the buriall of the dead" had been banned for more than a decade; rather than follow the ritual outlined in the Book of Com-mon Prayer, mourners were to obey the injunctions of the *Directory for the Public Worship of God* and bury a corpse "without any Ceremony."[118] In this context, as Achsah Guibbory has suggested, the catalogue of funerary customs which comprises much of Browne's *Urne-Buriall* defiantly speaks to "the universality of burial ceremonies, . . . making it evident that the puritan abolition of burial rites radically disrupts and violates human prac-tices that go back to the earliest recorded antiquity."[119] Yet the political charge of this emphasis on ritual is complicated by the apocalyptic conclu-sion of *Urne-Buriall*, in which Browne reveals the futility of men's "Cere-monies of bravery":

But the sufficiency of Christian Immortality frustrates all earthly glory, and the quality of either state after death makes a folly of posthumous memory. God who only can destroy our souls, and hath assured our resurrection, either of our bodies or names hath directly promised no duration. (1:169)

This paradoxical religiopolitical stance of *Urne-Buriall*, I would argue, is intertwined with the contradictory social visions presented in the work. By focusing exclusively on the theological implications of *Urne-Buriall*, one can overlook how Browne both establishes the text's origins in an elite social milieu but also constructs alternative modes of authority.

Although in *Pseudodoxia Epidemica* he styles himself as a leisured virtuoso and in the *Repertorium* he salvages the monuments of landed families, Browne's relationship to elite culture was not straightforward. Browne was born the son of a well-to-do London mercer. After attending Winchester College and Oxford, Browne went to the Continent to con-tinue his medical studies and began practicing medicine in Norwich, where his wife's family had connections, in 1637 or so.[120] His title, as C. A. Patrides has wryly observed, "was gained by default" in 1671 when, after the mayor of Norwich refused to be knighted by the visiting Charles II, "Browne was proposed as a substitute, and *found* himself a knight."[121] Although he was not a member of the landed gentry, Browne nonetheless cultivated the interests of a typical seventeenth-century virtuoso: he collected objects (especially natural history specimens), sent curiosities—including "a great

Bone petrifyed, [and] a whole Egg in an Egge"[122]—to the Repository of the Royal Society, wrote observations on medals and the natural history of Norfolk, and corresponded with other virtuosos on such topics as ancient barrows.[123] More explicitly than *Religio Medici*, *Pseudodoxia Epidemica*, or the *Repertorium*, *Urne-Buriall* portrays the middling-sort Browne as an intimate of members of both the Norfolk gentry and a national community of antiquarians. *Urne-Buriall* is dedicated to Thomas Le Gros, the son and heir of Browne's former friend and patient Sir Charles Le Gros; Thomas had inherited his ancient family's Norfolk manor house, Crostwick Hall, upon his father's death in 1656.[124] Browne's choice of Le Gros as his dedicatee would seem to indicate his veneration for ceremonialist as well as genteel values, since Le Gros was known for helping to support Thomas Campbell, the destitute former Rector of Swafield, after Campbell had been ejected from his living.[125] In his dedicatory epistle, however, Browne suggests that Le Gros is a particularly appropriate audience for *Urne-Buriall* given his own experience as an appreciative collector of antiquarian objects: "We present not these as any strange sight or spectacle unknown to your eyes, who have beheld the best of Urnes, and noblest variety of Ashes; Who are your self no slender master of Antiquities, and can daily command the view of so many Imperiall faces [i.e., a collection of Roman coins]" (1:132). Browne thus depicts Le Gros as an accomplished virtuoso and implicitly contrasts his own lack of time for such pursuits with the moneyed leisure of his genteel dedicatee: "We are coldly drawn unto discourses of Antiquities, who have scarce time before us to comprehend new things, or make out learned Novelties" (1:132). In the first edition of 1658, *Urne-Buriall* was paired with *The Garden of Cyrus*, and Browne's epistle to Le Gros was immediately followed by his dedication of the latter work to Nicholas Bacon, whom Browne praises as "a flourishing branch of that Noble Family" of "the most worthy Sʳ *Edmund Bacon* prime Baronet, my true and noble Friend."[126] The prefatory matter of the book thus seems to establish Browne's deferential respect for his social superiors.

Despite Browne's choice of a ceremonialist gentleman as his dedicatee, however, the social values of Browne's text are not consistently conservative, for Browne also establishes an equivocal relationship between the genteel identity of Le Gros and the antiquarianism of the *Urne-Buriall*. Although Browne says he hopes that "these Urnes might have the effect of Theatrical vessels, and great *Hippodrome* Urnes in *Rome*; to resound the acclamations and honour due unto [Le Gros]," he nonetheless maintains that his antiquarianism will not enhance Le Gros's status as the product of a distinguished pedigree: "In the offer of these Antiquities we drive not at ancient Families, so long out-lasted by them; We are farre from erecting your worth upon the pillars of your Fore-fathers, whose merits you illustrate" (1:133). The concluding paragraph of the dedicatory epistle thus distinguishes *Urne-Buriall* from the county histories of Burton, Carew, and Dugdale, which ally antiquarianism with elite genealogy. Instead of celebrating Le Gros's lineage, Browne asserts the value of his personal knowledge of Le Gros's character, Browne's "long experience of [Le Gros's] friendly conversation, void of empty Formality, full of freedome, constant and Generous Honesty," and he declares in conclusion, "I look upon you as a Gemme of the Old Rock" (1:133). It may well be that this last comment is meant to allude to Le Gros's status as his father's son;[127] yet Browne's marginal gloss on the term "Old Rock," *Adamas de rupe veteri praestantissimus* ("The most outstanding diamond comes from ancient rock"), seems also to refer punningly to Le Gros's relationship to Adam, the pedigree-free father of the human race.[128] Thus even as Browne dedicates his work to a royalist gentleman, he minimizes the importance of Le Gros's inherited status and emphasizes instead Le Gros's unassuming recognition of his shared humanity—his descent from Adam—as revealed in his courteous treatment of a non-elite friend such as Browne.

At the same time that he downplays the significance of Le Gros's gentility, Browne underlines his own status as a man who must work for his living. Early in the dedicatory epistle, Browne links his identity as the author of *Urne-Buriall* with his professional duties:

to preserve the living, and make the dead to live, to keep men out of their Urnes, and discourse of humane fragments in them, is not impertinent unto our profession; whose study is life and death, who daily behold examples of mortality, and of all men least need artificial *memento's*, or coffins by our bed side, to minde us of our graves. (1:132)

This association between the identity of the physician and the practice of the antiquarian would later be humorously echoed by Robert Thoroton, who writes in the preface to his 1677 county history of Nottinghamshire,

The Art of Physick, which I have professed (with competent success) in this County, not being able for any long time to continue the people living in it, I have charitably attempted, notwithstanding the difficulty and almost contrariety of the study, to practise upon the dead; intending thereby to keep, all which is, or can be left of them, to wit, the shadow of their Names (better than precious Oyntment for the body,) to preserve their memory, as long as may be in the World.[129]

Like Thoroton, Browne aligns the workaday life of the physician with the endeavors of the antiquarian, both of whom strive (unsuccessfully, in Thoroton's experience) to "preserve the living"; however, whereas Thoroton goes on to catalogue funerary monuments and enumerate the past and present owners of landed estates, Browne's *Urne-Buriall* finally rejects attempts to preserve elite identities after death:

We cannot hope to live so long in our names as some have done in their persons, one face of *Janus* holds no proportion unto the other. 'Tis too late to be ambitious. The great mutations of the world are acted, our time may be too short for our designes. To extend our memories by Monuments, whose death we dayly pray for, and whose duration we cannot hope, without injury to our expectations in the advent of the last day, were a contradiction to our beliefs. (1:166)

In keeping with Browne's earlier refusal to celebrate Le Gros's lineage, he argues late in *Urne-Buriall* that funerary monuments, those elite representations of genealogy, are ineffective:

Grave-stones tell truth scarce fourty years: Generations passe while some trees stand, and old Families last not three Oaks. To be read by bare Inscriptions like many in *Gruter*, to hope for Eternity by Ænigmaticall Epithetes, or first letters of our names, to be studied by Antiquaries, who we were, and have new Names given us like many of the Mummies, are cold consolations unto the Students of perpetuity, even by everlasting Languages. (1:166–67)

Unlike Thoroton, Browne's professional identity as someone who strives to "make the dead to live" does not entail the preservation of funerary monuments and their displays of elite lineage.

As we have seen, in seventeenth-century England the pursuit of antiquarianism was initially constructed as an elite class marker. The possession of British antiquities was linked to landholding not only because a collector needed moneyed leisure to study and assemble such objects, but also because landlords were usually entitled to objects found on (or buried beneath) their property.[130] This connection between antiquities and the emergent concept of land as absolute property also increased the number of artifacts available for display, since antiquarian objects often were discovered when innovative "improvements" such as enclosure were carried out on estates. In a brief text written in 1667, "Concerning Some Urnes Found in Brampton Feild in Norfolk," Browne reports how urns were found when workmen "made severall diches" in "A part of the feild being designed to bee enclosed, . . . & fell upon divers urnes"; three months later, Browne concludes, "my noble & honor'd freind, Sr. Robert Paston, had the curiosity to open a part of ground in his park at Oxned wch adjoyned unto the former feild where fragments of potts were found" (1:233, 238). In *Urne-*

Buriall, however, Browne establishes other social frameworks for the circulation of antiquarian objects and the construction of their cultural meanings, for as he lists various English discoveries of urns, Browne's marginal notes create a parallel collection of men which surrounds the body of his text. Ten urns found in recent years "in a Field at *Buxton*" enter into Browne's personal network of friends via a marginal note in which Browne specifies that the objects were discovered "[i]n the ground of my worthy Friend *Rob. Jegon* Esq. Wherein contained were preserved by the most worthy Sir William Paston, Bt." (1:142 n. *c*). Another gloss transforms some coins, described in the body of the text as having been unearthed at Caster, near Yarmouth, into personal possessions and gifts circulated as tokens of friendship: more specifically, Browne tells us, they were "found in a place called *East-bloudy-burgh furlong*, belonging to Mr *Thomas Wood*, a person of civility, industry and knowledge in this way, who late hath made observation of remarkable things about him, and from whom we have received divers Silver and Copper Coynes" (1:142 n. *e*). Similarly, coins described in the body of the text as having been discovered "at *Burghcastle* and *Brancaster*" are metamorphosed in the margins of *Urne-Buriall* into personal property which betokens the owner's standing in Browne's circle of friends; in his gloss, Browne identifies these coins not only in terms of their geographic location, but in social terms as "Belonging to that Noble Gentleman, and true example of worth Sir *Ralph Hare* Baronet, my honoured Friend" (1:142 n. *f*). Browne reports that one of the urns dug up at Walsingham contained "some kinde of *Opale*," which the accompanying gloss reveals has become Browne's personal property, "sent me by my worthy friend Dr *Thomas Witherley* of *Walsingham*" (1:141 n. *a*). The collection of men which Browne thus assembles in the margins of *Urne-Buriall* reaches out to encompass the authors of other antiquarian texts as well. Perhaps gesturing toward the need to salvage English culture in the face of civil war and its aftermath, Browne asserts in his epistle to Le Gros, "'Tis time to observe Occurrences, and let nothing remarkable escape us; The Supinity of elder dayes hath left so much in silence, or time hath so martyred the Records, that the most industrious heads do finde no easie work to erect a new *Britannia*" (1:132). In addition to implicitly invoking Camden as inspiration and authority for his own project, Browne adds another intellectual heir of Camden to the roster of men commemorated in his marginal notes by remarking in an accompanying gloss, "Wherein Mr *Dugdale* hath excellently well endeavoured, and worthy to be countenanced by ingenuous and noble persons," thus reflexively including Browne himself among the "ingenuous and noble" who recognize Dugdale's virtues (1:132 n. *h*).

The specificity of the names Browne lists in his margins contrasts sharply with the posthumous anonymity which, in the body of his text, Browne deems the inevitable fate of all members of the human race. The textual apparatus of *Urne-Buriall* thus bears a contradictory relationship to the content of Browne's work. Although he mocks antiquarians for inventing rather than discovering the identities of the men whose artifactual remains they study—mummies, Browne observes in a marginal note, are at the mercy of those who "giv[e] them what names they please; and unto some the names of the old Ægyptian Kings out of Herodotus" (1:167)—he simultaneously ascribes to scholars like himself an Adamic power of naming, the authority to decree the identities of lesser creatures. While Browne earlier declares that the identities of the men and women whose ashes fill the Walsingham urns "were a question above Antiquarism" (1:165), here he suggests that the antiquarian has the ability to construct a new reality out of the objects he studies. Extending Bacon's description of the antiquarian's task as the gathering and assembling of fragments, Browne depicts scholars like himself as creators of mosaics of identity: "We have enough to do to make up our selves from present and passed times, and the whole stage of things scarce serveth for our instruction. A compleat peece of vertue must be made up from the *Centos* of all ages, as all the beauties of *Greece* could make but one handsome *Venus*" (1:132). Like the mythical Zeuxis, the antiquarian is an artist who fashions new composite beings whose perfection exceeds their disparate individual origins. This concept of the antiquarian as collector/creator, I would argue, underlies the process by which Browne constructs his own identity in relation to the community of antiquarians he assembles outside the body of his text. Through his marginal notes, Browne follows the accepted scholarly practice of his era by indicating the sources of his information; as Anthony Grafton observes, because they were concerned with physical artifacts, antiquarians were "highly conscious of the importance of seeing their evidence at first hand" and consequently "took care to tell their readers who had seen a particular object, and in what conditions."[131] At the same time, however, Browne creates in the margins and dedicatory epistle of his text a catalogue of his antiquarian friends; by establishing the provenance of the objects he describes, Browne assembles a group of men, a collection of like-minded individuals who confer social and authorial legitimacy upon Browne even as he, Zeuxis-like, shapes them into a corporate body of antiquarians allied with Browne himself.

In *Urne-Buriall*, Browne thus uses the resources of print and the residual ideology of manuscript culture to forge a new identity for himself

as an antiquarian collector/author. In his marginal glosses, Browne represents the social networks through which he has accumulated cultural capital by exchanging knowledge and physical objects with other virtuosos. As
William W. E. Slights observes, in Renaissance books marginalia often do
not simplify the text they surround, but instead "provide perspectives on the
text that greatly complicate and sometimes radically destabilize it."[132] In
Urne-Buriall, Browne's marginal evocation of himself as the center of a
circle of past and present antiquarians constructs a narrative of identity and
immortality which the body of the text does not address. To some extent,
Browne's glosses function like the marginalia in printed Renaissance literary texts which provide "a residual, protective overlay of the marks of
manuscript circulation," thus evoking a cultural community which both
legitimizes the writer and serves to construct a desired readership for his
text.[133] Rather than representing his *text* as circulating among a coterie,
however, Browne depicts in the margins of *Urne-Buriall* a collection of
artifacts whose circulation among a group of men has forged a new kind of
community which, while elite in aspects of its interests and membership,
nonetheless establishes the possession of particular kinds of objects and
knowledge, rather than lineage and landed wealth, as the hallmark of social
authority. And by publishing *Urne-Buriall*, Browne extended his social
network even further, as he "acquired an immediate reputation as an opin-
ionist on the remains of the ancient world" upon the work's appearance in
print.[134] Thus in the name-dropping textual apparatus of *Urne-Buriall*, the
power of the antiquarian author to create new, hybrid forms of identity and
authority is enacted and displayed.

The potential subversiveness of Browne's perception that the antiquarian author fashions new social realities is most fully explored in his
Musaeum Clausum. This brief text takes the form of a thank-you note to
another erudite collector (perhaps Dr. Walter Charleton)[135] who had lent
Browne the catalogue of a collection of "Books, Rarities and Singularities
of Art and Nature" (3.109). Browne's work is, in many ways, of a piece with
his other correspondence, for his letters are full of references to books,
rarities, and arcane knowledge: he had, for example, sent a letter accompanying a gift of bird carcasses and flies to Christopher Merret, requested
information about whales from Arthur Bacon, and received a letter from
Henry Power asking a follow-up question about "the Vipers head" which
Power had seen in Browne's collection at Norwich (4:351, 381, 263). In the
Musaeum Clausum, Browne compares the collection inventoried in the
catalogue he had borrowed to the famous curiosity cabinets of Europe, and
he backhandedly reminds his correspondent that Browne, too, has an esti-

THE COUNTRYSIDE AS COLLECTION 133

mable collection of similar objects and that Browne has regarded his correspondent highly enough to grant him access to it: "Of what in this kind I have by me I shall make no repetition, and you having already had a view thereof" (3:109). After this statement, Browne launches into the body of his letter, "the List of a Collection, which I may justly say you have not seen before" (3:109), and the rest of the text consists of an inventory of fantastical objects, subdivided into the categories "Rare and generally unknown Books," "Rarities in Pictures," and "Antiquities and Rarities of several sorts" (3:109, 112, 116). The letter is a *jeu d'esprit*: the curiosity cabinet containing such wonders as "The Skin of a Snake bred out of the Spinal Marrow of a Man" does not exist, as Browne makes clear when he concludes his tantalizing list by saying, "He who knows where all this Treasure now is, is a great Apollo. I'm sure I am not He" (3:118, 119).

How are we to interpret this fiction of a catalogue? C. A. Patrides has argued that the work is a parody in which Browne aims "to underline the inherent absurdity" of the "indiscriminate" collecting habits of his culture, and Patrides links the *Musaeum Clausum* with Donne's *Catalogus Librorum Aulicorum incomparabilium et non vendibilium* and the works of Rabelais.[136] Yet I would argue that Browne's ironic humor is even more subversive than Patrides suggests, for in the *Musaeum Clausum* Browne demonstrates how the antiquarian writer, like Sidney's poet, can create a golden world by ranging only within the zodiac of his own wit—and his own social ambitions. The *function* of Browne's letter—its furthering of Browne's relationship with the man who loaned him the catalogue—is finally more important than its *content*: the collection Browne describes, whether extant or fictional, is used instrumentally as an object in a social exchange, and the antiquarian writer stands revealed not as a neutral documenter of truth, but as someone who self-servingly transforms collections of objects into cultural capital. Thus the *Musaeum Clausum*, like Browne's other antiquarian works, demonstrates that the textualizing of a collection of objects—whether in the form of an ecclesiastical "repertorium," secular marginalia, a catalogue, or a letter—is, first and foremost, a social act; the antiquarian collector/author creates social networks through the circulation of artifacts, metamorphosing groups of physical objects into collections of men.

Taken as a whole, then, the antiquarian works of Sir Thomas Browne register ambivalence toward lineage as the basis of status, and Browne sometimes uses his texts to construct alternative models of cultural authority which legitimize his own standing as a non-elite collector and author. My analysis of the writer's antiquarianism necessarily complicates previous assessments of Browne's politics which have been rooted primarily in an

examination of the conservative religious and social views underpinning
Religio Medici. As we have seen, Browne's works embody shifting concepts
of social authority, sometimes extending the chorographers' veneration of
genealogy and the established Church, yet at other times creating new roles
for Browne himself within a social formation that has been constructed
through the gathering and ownership of groups of physical objects. Writing
during the tumultuous decades of the Civil War and Interregnum, Browne
thus is not a reactionary but rather a transitional figure who wavers between
celebrating a hereditary landed elite and searching for an understanding of
possessive individualism as a source of new forms of social legitimacy.

Robert Plot and the Restoration County History

As a glance at the subjects of Browne's correspondence reminds
us, seventeenth-century English antiquarians, being good virtuosos, were
often interested not only in urns, funerary monuments, and coins, but in
the rarities of natural history as well. By the Restoration, as Stan A. E.
Mendyk observes, "more and more antiquaries originated from, or involved
themselves in, the scientific circles of the time," and when such men turned
their attention to the landscape, they tended to describe the countryside in
terms of Baconian natural history, rather than the pedigrees and armorial
bearings of landed families.[137] Earlier English chorography was not, of
course, devoid of concern with natural phenomena, and Camden himself
sometimes set aside his focus on antiquarianism long enough to comment
on such noteworthy entities as the superior potter's earth located near
Nonesuch Palace in Surrey, or a toothsome fish called the "Ruffe" which
could be caught in the River Yare near Norwich.[138] However, whereas
earlier seventeenth-century English chorographers emphasize the genealogies of landowners as defining the significance of a landscape, the authors of
regional studies written after 1660 often conceive of the countryside as a
treasure-trove of naturalia instead.

Although he borrowed material from previous chorographers, the
schoolmaster and clergyman Joshua Childrey explains that the reader of his
Britannia Baconica is not going to find the landscape depicted as a genealogical display: "I have not at all medled with matter of Antiquity, Pedigrees, or the like, those being copiously handled by several of our Coun-
treymen already."[139] In this work, published in 1661, Childrey focuses on the
distinctive natural phenomena of each county and the specialized ways in
which inhabitants exploit locally available resources: we learn that in Dev-

onshire, "they use . . . sea-sand to mend and enrich their Land"; that near Portsmouth "is a race of small Dogs, like Beagles, that they use there to hunt Moles with"; that in 1653, it rained blood in Poole in Dorsetshire; and that in certain parts of Lancashire, "the people use Turfs for fire and candle both."[140] Like Dugdale and his ilk, Childrey addresses his book to the gentry, but not as a representation of their lineal identities:

I intend this Book for the service of the Gentry, that they may see England is not void of those things which they admire abroad in their travels. And that those ingenious Gentlemen whose occasions carry them into several Counties, or who are otherwise disposed to see the sports of Nature about them, may know by this Portable-book, in what parts of what Counties to find them. . . . And what is there worth wonder abroad in the world, whereof Nature hath not written a Copy in our Iland? I would have those that know other Countreys so well, not to be strangers to their own, which is a compendium of all others.[141]

Childrey thus depicts the English countryside as his own, truthful version of Browne's *Musaeum Clausum*: his book reveals to learned English gentlemen that their nation is a cabinet of natural wonders, with each region affording distinctive kinds of stone, metals, plants, animals, and farming techniques to interest the discerning viewer. At the same time, however, Childrey also democratizes his perspective on the landscape—like Tradescant's Ark, his book is available to anyone who will pay to see its contents, and Childrey hopes that his collection of natural rarities will confer a new sense of identity upon "the Vulgar" as well: "This book doth not shew you a Telescope, but a Mirror, it goes not about to put a delightful cheat upon you, with objects at a great distance, but shews you your selves."[142] In Childrey's book, then, we find the beginnings of a new construction of identity, ostensibly not rooted in lineage or rank, that is achieved through an individual's relationship with the regionally specific objects which constitute the landscape he inhabits.

The focus on local natural history and concomitant de-emphasis of genealogy which distinguish Childrey's *Britannia Baconica* from earlier English chorography indicate how the countryside was reconceptualized in the wake of the Civil War and Interregnum. Like the earlier questioning of lineage which we find in Browne's *Urne-Buriall*, Childrey's book could be interpreted as one facet of a widespread shift in the social meaning of landownership; as Felicity Heal and Clive Holmes observe, "The tenuous nature of the hold of gentry families upon their lands and their social power was more acutely apparent in the 1640s and 50s," and this new sense of precariousness led to a franker acknowledgment of "wealth as the essential foundation of claims to status."[143] With less emphasis placed on lineage, neither heraldry nor funerary monuments were regarded as the socially potent symbols they had been before the Civil War, and the antiquarian representation of a genealogical landscape declined accordingly. Just as chorography in previous decades had responded to and helped to shape the process by which "the meaning of agrarian England shifted . . . from a site of manorial community and moral economy toward a modern landscape of capitalist enterprise,"[144] its reconfiguration in Restoration England as the genre of the county natural history furthered the conceptualization of the land as a collection of absolute properties.

This new mode of representing the countryside emerged as landowners struggled to overcome adverse economic conditions. After a long period of steadily rising prices, English agriculture entered a trough of depression in the middle of the seventeenth century, a situation exacerbated by the dire financial losses inflicted by the Civil War and its aftermath. During the conflict, both Parliament and the king sequestered estates, sometimes leaving landowners stranded without incomes for years, and royalists had to pay composition fines to recover their sequestrated property; landowners of all political persuasions were more heavily taxed after 1643, and rents fell. Under these circumstances, landlords searched for new ways to increase the profitability of their estates, instigating an upsurge in agricultural innovations and the development of new cottage industries. In Joan Thirsk's words, "[v]ariety, diversity, and unique specialization" came to characterize English agriculture in the second half of the seventeenth century, "and in every decade more distinctive regions came into existence as a result."[145]

The county natural histories written by Robert Plot celebrate this frankly profit-driven landscape of proliferating subregions. Plot's career was intertwined with modes of collecting distinctive to seventeenth-century England. Born in 1640 to a family which owned property in Kent, Plot became a tutor and later a fellow at Oxford. His professional life dovetailed with the ambitions of another collector when Elias Ashmole appointed Plot as the first Keeper of the Ashmolean Museum; Oxford University subsequently named Plot as its first Professor of Chemistry as well.[146] Plot seemed the logical choice for these posts since he had established his reputation as a disciple of Baconian natural history several years earlier with the publication of *The Natural History of Oxford-shire, being an Essay towards the Natural History of England* (1677). When he first began work on his natural history, Plot aimed "to make search after the Raritys both of Nature & Arts afforded in the Kingdome, for the Information of the Curious, and

in order to an Historical Account of the same,"[147] a wildly ambitious project the scope of which Plot later pragmatically narrowed to a study of the
county of Oxfordshire alone. "Leaving the *Antiquities* and Foundations of
Churches and *Religious Houses*, . . . with the *pedigrees* and *descents* of *Families*
and *Lands*, *&c.* as sufficient matter for another *Historian*," Plot instead
gathered information for a Baconian natural history of the region.[148] Plot
made extensive personal observations during his own fieldwork on the
project and gleaned further particulars from questionnaires which he circulated among those inhabitants of the county—gentlemen and clergymen—
whose testimony could be trusted.[149] Upon its publication, Plot's *Oxford-
shire* was acclaimed by proponents of "the new philosophy," and Plot was
offered a fellowship of the Royal Society, eventually rising to the position of
joint secretary and editor of the *Philosophical Transactions*.[150] Plot thus
achieved national prominence thanks to his new method of analyzing the
regional landscape. In 1686 Plot published his second study of the English
countryside, *The Natural History of Stafford-Shire*, billing himself on the
title page as "Keeper of the Ashmolean Musaeum and Professor of Chym-
istry in the University of Oxford."[151] Despite this show of pride in his
professional identity, Plot resigned both posts several years later and "re-
tired to the life of a country gentleman on his Kentish property" until his
death in 1696.[152]

Like his Baconian contemporaries, recent scholars have tended to
emphasize the novelty of Plot's approach to local studies and stress how he
"discarded the conventions of the chorographies published at the end of the
sixteenth and the beginning of the seventeenth centuries, based as they
were primarily on the history of properties, families and landowners, and
institutions."[153] What has been overlooked in discussions of Plot's work are
the *continuities* between Plot's ostensibly newfangled "natural history" and
the earlier chorographic/antiquarian tradition; in particular, I would argue,
one needs to appreciate the ways in which Plot extends the chorographic
depiction of the landscape as a collection of discrete physical objects owned
by specific individuals. Despite his claims of disinterest in "the *pedigrees* and
descents of *Families* and *Lands*," the body of Plot's first book is preceded by
an elaborate, foldout map of the county which is framed by the coats of
arms of all the noblemen and gentry of Oxfordshire, each coat of arms
being numbered so readers can match the numbered manor houses represented on the map with the men who own them. In his prefatory remarks to
Oxford-shire, Plot says he hopes that his map will have a salutary effect on
the county's landlords, suggesting *"That the Gentry hereby will be somwhat
influenced to keep their* Seats, *together with their* Arms, *least their* Posterity

hereafter, not without reflexions, *see what their* Ancestors *have parted* with"
("To the Reader"). Plot also explains that he intends the heraldry-ringed
map as an aid to the correct interpretation of the landscape: *"for the* Houses
of the Nobility *and* Gentry, *this* Map *is so contrived, that a* Foreigner *as well
as* English-man, *at what distance soever, may with ease find out who are the*
Owners *of most of them; so as to be able to say that this is such or such a*
Gentlemans *House"* ("To the Reader"). Plot created a similarly coded map
for his study of Staffordshire, in which he also included twenty-three engraved representations of the houses of the county's elite. None of the plates
illustrating his study of Oxfordshire depict a country house, and the nature
of the engravings in Plot's second county history thus represents an intensified focus on the houses of the landed elite as the most significant features
of the landscape. Plot's emphasis on the houses of a county's landowners
still makes a nod toward the time-honored concept of "house" as lineage
(hence his display of armorial bearings on his maps and expressed desire for
multigenerational ownership of property), but Plot's work also reveals a
new sense of the "house" primarily as a physical object, a *thing*, the ownership of which betokens one's status in relation to the landscape. Garrett
Sullivan argues that as part of the transition from feudalism to capitalism,
the country house was "reimagined" in early modern England, metamorphosing from a feudal "community site" to a new role as "private
property,"[154] and in Plot's county histories we see a late stage in this process.

Throughout Plot's natural histories, houses as material entities—not
the genealogical symbolism of coats of arms or pedigrees—come to represent their owners' identities in relation to the English landscape. Earlier
chorographers such as Carew sometimes describe country houses, all the
while stressing the buildings' significance in terms of the lineage of their
owners. Although Burton incorporates a hybrid ground plan/prospect of
his own seat, Lindley, on the title page of his chorography of Leicestershire, and Dugdale includes one plan and several prospects of country
houses in his study of Warwickshire, houses as material entities are com-
pletely subordinate in importance to lineal houses in the works of both
writers. Plot, by contrast, transforms houses into noteworthy physical
structures, both in terms of their material characteristics and their proximity to other phenomena. In Plot's representation of the countryside, a
landlord is distinctive not for his family tree, but for the memorable physical features of the house and section of the countryside which he owns.
Although the iconography of the introductory maps represents each house
as being identical, Plot's texts (and, in *Stafford-Shire*, the engraved plates)
differentiate the houses from each other in physical terms. Plot confers

status on houses and their owners by discussing and illustrating particular buildings in his text, and he assures the reader of *Stafford-Shire* that "Of the private structures, the most eminent in the County, are those whose prospects, the Reader has or will find engraven in this Work" (358). Plot's landscape—and his books—are thus constructed around country houses which are conceived as distinctive physical objects rather than symbols of lineage.

Country houses are the reference points by which Plot maps the phenomena of a county's natural history, and in *Stafford-Shire* Plot's accounts of Baconian particulars often seem no more than convenient excuses to include more grand homes within the bounds of his book. In a section entitled "The Art of making Fryingpans," for example, Plot informs us that "there are flat round plates hammer'd out of barrs at a forge for that purpose at the parish of Keel," and quickly relates local industry to landownership by explaining that the frying pans are manufactured "not far from the fair Mansion of the Worshipfull and judicious William Sneyd Esq; a worthy Benefactor to this work" (*Stafford-Shire*, 335): the significance of regional manufacturing becomes a double-page engraving of the "South-West Prospect of Keel-Hall." Similarly, to describe unusual natural phenomena, Plot often takes his reader on a walking tour of the grounds of a country house, as he does when pursuing echoes: "such a tremulous Echo there is (for I cannot fit it with a better Epithet) at Elmhurst-Hall on the tarras walk in the Garden behind the house, where the various windings and angles of the walls, return a hum or clap with the hands (the weather being calm) ten or a dozen times" (*Stafford-Shire*, 30); Elmhurst Hall itself subsequently appears as an engraved plate. Likewise, a county's weather becomes noteworthy on the basis of its interaction with the houses of the landed elite: Plot recounts that

a more unusual accident . . . was shewed me at *Statfold*, by the foremention'd worthy *Gentleman* the Worshipful *Francis Wolferstan* esquire, who having built a new Gate before his house Anno 1675. and placed fair Globes of the finest and firmest stone over the Peers of it (whereon He depicted with his own hand two Globe Dials in oyl colours, and on the terrestrial the several Empires and Kingdoms of the World, that He might see how day and night succeeded in each of them) in January 1677. had them both struck with lightening in the same point. (*Stafford-Shire*, 8–9)

Walter Lord Aston has had frogs rain on his house at Tixall, Plot believes, "for as I was told by that severely inquisitive Gent. the Worshipful Walter Chetwynd of Ingestre Esq; a near neighbour to the place, they have been sometimes found in great numbers upon the Leds of the stately Gate-

House there" (*Stafford-Shire*, 24). Likewise in Plot's house-centric land-scapes, notable plants are not simply regional phenomena, but are described in relation to specific county seats: thus in *Oxford-shire*, Plot mentions "the *Glastenbury Thorn*, in the Park and Gardens of the Right Honorable the Lord *Norreys*, that constantly buds, and somtimes blossoms at or near *Christmas*"; praises the plentiful elms "in the *Avenues* to the House of the Honorable the Lady *Cope*, the Relict of the most Ingenious Sir *Anthony Cope* of *Hanwell*, where there is a whole Walk of them planted in order, beside others that grow wild in the *Coppices* of the *Park*"; and draws the reader's attention to the "*Nurseries* [of fir and pine] planted in the *Quincunx* order, at *Cornbury*, in the *Park* of the Right Honorable the Earl of *Claren-don*" (156, 158, 172).

Plot's natural histories also celebrate the process of diversification, driven by landlords' search for new sources of profit, characteristic of English agriculture in the second half of the seventeenth century. Plot's accounts of the "Arts" of Oxfordshire thus become a catalogue of notable "improvements" made to estates, such as "a contrivance for *Fish-ponds*, that I met with at the Right Worshipful Sir *Philip Harcourt's* at *Stanton Harcourt*, where the *stews* not only feed one another, as the *Ponds* of the Right Honorable the Earl of *Clarendon* at *Cornbury*, Sir *Timothy Tyrrils* at *Shot-over-Forrest*, and the worshipful *Brome Whorwoods* at *Holton*" (234). Plot similarly remarks on distinctive goods produced in the county, again describing these physical objects according to their proximity to estates; he notes, for example, that "At *Caversham*, near the Right Worshipful Sir *Anthony Cravens* (and at some other places) they make a sort of *brick* 22 inches long, and above six inches broad" (*Oxford-shire*, 251). On the subject of the "Tobacco-pipe clays" found in Staffordshire, Plot openly discusses the economic relationship between landholding and local rarities. He begins by telling us that "the Clay that surpasses all others of this County is that at Amblecot, on the bank of the Stour, in the parish of old Swynford yet in Staffordshire, in the lands of that judicious and obliging Gent. The Worshipfull Harry Gray of Enfield Esq; whose beautifull Mansion, perhaps the best situat of any in the County, is here represented [in an adjacent plate]"; Plot then goes on to remark that this clay is in such demand "that it is sold on the place for sevenpence the bushell, whereof Mr. Gray has sixpence, and the Workman one penny" (*Stafford-Shire*, 121). Plot further exhibits his commitment to the cause of local specialization (and local landlords' profits) when he describes an Oxfordshire "earth" that is "of a fat close texture, and greenish colour": "At present 'tis accounted of small or no value, but in recompence of the signal favors of its present *Proprietor*, the

Right Worshipful Sir *Timothy Tyrril*, who in person was pleased to shew me the *pits*, I am ready to discover a use it may have, that may possibly equal that of his *Ochre*" (*Oxford-shire*, 55). For Plot, ownership of land is inextricable from the right to prosper economically from the physical characteristics and products of that land, and he strives not only to celebrate but to develop new economic benefits for landowners. Thus, in Plot's regional studies, the gathering of particulars fundamental to Baconian natural history merges with chorography's depiction of the countryside as an assemblage of the owners of physical objects, resulting in a new landscape of country houses and the profitable natural resources which the houses' owners exploit.

In the midst of this reconceptualization of the country house as a site and symbol of elite possessive individualism, the authorial self which emerges from Plot's regional studies is explicitly that of a collector. For Plot, the act of authorship is inseparable from the act of collecting. He assures us at the beginning of his account of Oxfordshire

that most of the Curiosities, whether of Art, Nature, or Antiquities engraven in the Cuts, are so certain truths, that as many as were portable, or could be procured, are in the hands of the Author. But for such things as are inseparable from their places, they remain to be seen as in the History directed, there being nothing here mention'd, but what either the Author has seen himself, or has received unquestionable testimony for it. (*Oxford-shire*, "To the Reader")

So that he may assemble an appendix in the future, Plot asks his "Gentry" readers "to bring in their Arms in colours" which he had omitted, along with "any other Curiosity of Art or Nature" which likewise deserves inclusion in his text, to the Keepers of the Bodleian Library: objects which are literally carried to Plot will be added both to his personal collection of rarities and its textualized incarnation as the natural history of Oxfordshire. Plot's book thus embodies and yet cannot fully encompass an order of material objects external to the text, for the author's collecting continues even as the book is being printed, and Plot must try to realign his textualized version of the rarities he has accumulated with its ever-expanding material counterpart: "since the Printing the beginning of this *Chapter*, I received from the Right worshipful Sir *philip Harcourt* of *Stanton Harcourt*, two kinds of *Selenites*"; "even since the Printing the first Chapter of this Treatise, I have found here at home just such another Echo, as at Mr. Pawlings at Heddington" (*Oxford-shire*, 142, 357). And as these examples suggest, Plot regularly enters his text as a character in the narratives which describe the objects he displays in his county histories, reminding us that

Plot's own labor has shaped the landscape and social networks he depicts. We learn, for example, that Plot found a heart-shaped stone at Shetford, weighing about twenty pounds, "which being much too heavy for my Horse-portage, was afterward upon my direction, fetch'd away by that miracle of Ingenuity Sir *Anthony Cope*" (*Oxford-shire*, 127). At one point, he recounts how he used a house as a lab for conducting an experiment in natural history:

> at *Blechington* 'twas confidently believed, that a *Snake* brought from any other place, and put down there, would instantly die, till I made the *experiment* and found no such matter: Whereupon I got leave (in the absence of the *Family*) to inclose my *Snake* in the *Court*, before the Right Honorable the Lord *Anglesey*'s house, to see what time would produce, leaving the *Gardiner* in trust to observe it strictly, who found it indeed, after three weeks time *dead*, without any sensible external hurt. (*Oxford-shire*, 187)

On another occasion, Plot assumes the role Jonson assigned himself in his poem on Penshurst and becomes a dinner guest in the home of an elite patron; but rather than praise his host's feudal hospitality in Jonsonian style, Plot instead displays a Baconian appreciation of rare foodstuffs: "at the Worshipfull Walter Chetwynds of Ingestre Esq; I tasted potted Otter so artificially order'd by his excellent Cook, that it required a very nice and judicious palat to distinguish it from Venison" (*Stafford-Shire*, 390). Plot thus inserts himself into the life of the landscape—and the country houses—which he portrays in his text.

In a similar vein, Plot regularly depicts himself as the recipient of gifts from the landed elite. We learn, for example, that a specimen of the mineral "Metallophytum . . . was dug, and kindly bestowed upon me by the Worshipful *William Bayly* Esq."; Plot describes a fossil "found in the *Chiltern* Country, near *Stonorhouse*, [which was] sent me by the Worshipful *Tho. Stonor* Esq; the Proprietor of the place, and one of the *Noblest Encouragers* of this Design"; and he gratefully recalls that a coin "was dug up at *Wood-Eaton* this present Year 1676. near the House of the Worshipful *John Nourse* Esq; amongst old *Foundations*, and kindly bestowed on me by the same worthy *Person*" (*Oxford-shire*, 65, 106, 309). Plot's county histories thus serve, in part, as the autobiography of their author's career as a collector and intimate of his society's elite. In the gift-giving relationships which Plot establishes between landowners and himself as collector/author, Plot reciprocates by turning the proffered objects and their donors into textualized items within Plot's book. As an act of gratitude, Plot can transform a gift into the physical form which most fully embodies its donor's identity: his country house. Thus at one point, Plot recounts, "I was presented with the lower jaw of some Animal with large teeth in it, dugg up in a marle-pit somewhere in the grounds of the Worshipfull William Leveson Gower of Trentham Esq; who hath been so noble a Maecenas in promoting this Work, that I could doe no less than present the Reader with a double Prospect of his magnificent Seat" (*Stafford-Shire*, 267). And there is, of course, a more mercenary relationship between Plot and his gift giving benefactors than such an account might suggest. Like Dugdale's *Warwickshire*, the publication of Plot's natural history of Staffordshire required the financial backing of the elite men it commemorated, and thus the engraved plates of country houses featured in Plot's text were actually engendered by commercial exchanges between the author and his subscribers; but such stark economic realities are submerged beneath narratives of collecting and the bestowal of gifts.

Unlike Sir Thomas Browne, who depicts a social network fostered by the exchange of physical objects only within the margins of his *Urne-Buriall*, Plot weaves his own collecting activities and their social cachet firmly into the fabric of his main narrative; there is no competing view of the cultural meaning of objects and their role in the social formation within Plot's county histories. Plot's regional studies thus construct their author as a collector of naturalia whose personal connections with members of the landed elite, forged in the process of collecting, allow him to include the rarities wealthy landlords own, display, and exchange within the textualized collections that comprise his books on Oxfordshire and Staffordshire. At the same time that Plot fashions his authorial identity in this way, his texts help to naturalize a concept of the countryside as an amalgam of physical objects which are possessed and exploited to create wealth for individual landowners. In Plot's county histories, then, genealogy is depicted as a residual aspect of social authority, overshadowed by a newly dominant ideology that equates status with the financial ability to possess and profit from an artifactual landscape. Thus an analysis of Plot's works reveals how agricultural innovations in England during the late seventeenth century were bound up with changing models of proprietary identity constructed through activities of collecting.

The Late Seventeenth-Century Country House as Collection

Plot's distinctive representation of country houses as the points of reference in a landscape of owned objects also leads him to examine the decor of elite houses. Plot often remarks on objects displayed within a house which began their existence as naturalia discovered on the surrounding estate: for example, we are invited to examine an engraving of a fish "taken in the river Tame in the damm near Fasely bridg, by Goodyer Holt Free-Mason, as he was repairing it Aug. 11.1654, who presented it to Colonell Comberford of Comberford, who caused it to be drawn to the life, and placed in his Hall, where it still hangs, and whence this draught was taken in a less proportion"; Plot describes "the Eagle in Beaudesart Hall kill'd in the park" and a grosbeak "found and kill'd somewhere about Madeley-Manor"; and he remarks on the stone quarried at Bilston which is "curiously streaked black, whereof there are elegant patterns, in the Garden at the right worshipful Sr. Henry Gough's at Pury-Hall" (*Stafford-Shire*, 240, 229, 230, 168). Similarly, we learn that "a sort of *gray Marble* [is] dug in the Parish of *Blechington*, in the Lordship of the Right Honorable *Arthur* Earl of *Anglesey*, Lord *Privy Seal*: Of this there are several *Chimny-pieces* and *Pavements*, in his *Lordships* House there, well worth the notice; as also at the Right Honorable the Earl of *Clarendon*'s at *Cornbury*" (*Oxford-shire*, 78). Huge pieces of stone are cut in the quarry located in Purton park, and "of these large stones there are very good examples in Purton house belonging to the right Worshipful Sr. Walter Wrottesley Baronet" (*Stafford-Shire*, 168). After explaining that there are two different varieties of "curled and twining grain" in ash, Plot informs us that

With the *Molluscum* of *Ash* there is a whole Closet wainscoted, at the much Honored Mr. *Stonor*'s of *Watlington* Park, the grain of the panes being curiously waved like the *Gamahe*'s of *Achats*. And at the Worshipful Mr. *Reads*, of the Parish of *Ipsden*, the *Bruscum* of an old *Ash* is so wonderfully figured, that in a Dining-table made of it (without the help of fansie) you have exactly represented the figure of the Fish, we commonly call a *Jack*... and in some other *Tablets* the figures of a *Vnicorn*, and an old *Man* from the navel upwards. (*Oxford-shire*, 171)

These objects function as synecdoches of landownership, as Plot makes clear in his description of "Cannel-coal" mined at Wednesbury:

They cut it also into Salts, Standishes, and carve Coats of Armes in it, witness that of the right Honorable William Lord Paget, in the Gallery of his stately Seat at Beaudesart, which as a thankfull memorial of the Encouragement He so readily afforded this Work, is here represented Tab. 8. And the rather here because this Coale is dug in the Park adjoyning, also belonging to his Lordship." (*Stafford-Shire*, 126)

Plot's account of "Cannel-coal" reveals how a sign of lineage is fashioned from a substance unearthed from a particular landowner's property and how it becomes a decorative object displayed among other rarities in the gallery of a country house; but rather than pursue the genealogical significance of the landowner's coat of arms—his lineal house—Plot emphasizes instead the man's status as an owner of objects by depicting his physical house.

The narratives of elite identity-as-ownership (of houses, of naturalia) which Plot constructs in his texts depart markedly from the representation of country houses in the poetry of the earlier seventeenth century. Rather than depict a "natural order of productivity" and familial continuity as do Jacobean and Caroline country house poems,[155] Plot presents objects which embody rupture, innovation, or personal ownership and profit. Instead of the suicidal creatures of Ben Jonson's Penshurst or Thomas Carew's Saxham, which eagerly offer themselves as foodstuffs so they may have the honor of feeding the manorial lord and his household full of guests,[156] Plot depicts animals being caught and killed not for the sake of communal need, but for private display. A landlord's possession of objects, not his participation in the communal life of his estate, excites Plot's admiration, as evidenced by his praise of "that great *Virtuoso*, the Right Worshipful Sir *Anthony Cope* of *Hanwell*, . . . whose House me thought seemed to be the real *New Atlantis*" (*Oxford-shire*, 73). And unlike earlier seventeenth-century representations of estate life which sought to efface labor, Plot frankly depicts work and its economic motives: the forcible extraction of stone or clay from the ground, the repair of deteriorating structures, the manufacture of bricks and pots, the inequitable distribution of profits among landlords and their hirelings. The natural bounty and reciprocity—the ideological mystification—of the country houses portrayed by Jonson and Carew have vanished, and the earlier writers' emphasis on the manorial lord's relationship with his community as a sign of his social and moral stature has been replaced in Plot's works by a new fascination with the landlord's relationship to objects and his ability to profit from his ownership of them.

Even though they were writing at a time when landlords were amassing collections of art and rarities to signify their status, most pre-Restoration authors of country house poems were reluctant to acknowledge this form of elite self-fashioning. While Sir John Beaumont in 1621 called Burley, owned by the Duke of Buckingham, "a cabinet," alluding to Buckingham's art collection,[157] few English poets in the first half of the seventeenth century portrayed elite landowners as collectors. More typically of the genre in this period, Carew contrasts the Earl of Kent's participation in traditional hospitality with the self-aggrandizement of collecting when he praises Henry

Gray and his wife as *non*-collectors: at Wrest, Carew approvingly observes, "Instead of statues to adorn their wall / They throng with living men their merry hall."[158] Similarly, although known as an agent who procured art for Charles I and the Earl of Arundel as well as a collector in his own right, Endymion Porter nonetheless emerges from a poem written by Robert Herrick as an old-style manorial lord. In Herrick's verse, repeated possessive pronouns suggest an emergent concept of Porter as an owner of absolute property—"thy cornfields," "thy teams," "thy large sleek neat," "thy flocks"; at the same time, though, Herrick tries to incorporate these hints of Porter's proprietary identity within a portrayal of him as a feudal magnate: "thy ambition's masterpiece / Flies no thought higher than a fleece, / Or how to pay thy hinds." Herrick alludes to Porter's status as a collector in the term "masterpiece," only to deny Porter's interest in anything unrelated to the agrarian well-being of his estate.[159] Ben Jonson likewise hints at Sir Robert Sidney's interest in growing novel varieties of fruit at Penshurst: "The early cherry, with the later plum, / Fig, grape, and quince, each in his time doth come: / The blushing apricot and woolly peach / Hang on thy walls." However, this collection of unusual plants, rather than betokening Sidney's status as a virtuoso, merges with the communal life of the estate, for Jonson maintains that "every child may reach" to pluck an apricot or peach from Sidney's orchards, and the daughters of the estate's farmers bring baskets of plums and pears, "An emblem of themselves," as gifts to the lord and lady of Penshurst.[160] As Don E. Wayne observes, this passage of the poem depicts the farmers' payment of rent in kind as the bestowal of a present, and Jonson thus attempts to transform Sidney's collection of exotic fruit trees into part of the reciprocal life of a feudal landscape.[161]

Later poetry, however, exhibits Plot's frankness in depicting landlords not as benign feudal magnates, but as owners and collectors of *things*. In celebrating Golden Grove, the seat of Richard Vaughan, Earl of Carberry, in 1660, Rowland Watkyns enthuses about the estate in terms which foreshadow Plot: "There are parks, orchards, warrens, fishponds, springs: / Each foot of ground some curious object brings."[162] By depicting the estate as a curiosity cabinet, Watkyns avoids any portrayal of Vaughan interacting with his subordinates—a necessarily tactful strategy, perhaps, given the account of Vaughan dispossessing tenants after he had first cropped their ears and cut their tongues.[163] Sometime between 1656 and 1666, Mildmay Fane wrote that, "Whoso desires, that, earnestly to see / The statued marbles of antiquity" should visit Thorpe Hall, owned by the parliamentarian Oliver St. John, "Where stand such trophies wherein he'll descry / The lively figures of old history"; as Alastair Fowler remarks, St. John's collection of trophy statues, like that of Cromwell, may have come from the royal collection.[164] Similarly, in contemplating the Earl of Devonshire's Chatsworth in the late 1670s or early 1680s, Charles Cotton declared his powers as a poet overwhelmed by the grandeur and sheer proliferation of objects contained by the house:

And should I be so mad to go about
To give account of everything throughout—
The rooms of state, staircases, galleries,
Lodgings, apartments, closets, offices;
Or to describe the splendours undertake
Which every glorious room a heaven make,
The pictures, sculpture, carving, graving, gilding—
T'would be as long in writing as in building.[165]

Unlike Plot, who confines his descriptions of the interior decor of country houses to objects found or produced locally, some later poets also stress the ability of a landlord to amass collections of objects originating from beyond the bounds of the estate. Extending the demystification of labor characteristic of Plot's county histories, some post-Restoration country house poets revel in a wealthy landlord's capacity to command the labor not only of his own estate's work force, but of entire classes and races of unfortunates who must toil to fulfill his desire for physical objects. Thus in a paean to Belvoir Castle written in 1679, Thomas Shipman describes at length the paintings, tapestries, carpets, and chimney-pieces of the house, concluding cheerfully,

Belvoir! thou must the world's chief wonder be,
    Since nature is turned upside down for thee.
    The lofty fir stoops down thy floors to frame;
        And though laborious miners cry
        That lead does at the centre lie,
    Thy lofty roof is covered with the same.[166]

This celebration of the landlord as a vicarious owner of others' labor is inflected by a racialized discourse of colonialism in another poem on Belvoir, also written in 1679, in which an anonymous writer catalogues the "boundless stores" of foreign luxury goods displayed to the "curious eyes" of a visitor:

The rarities rich China send,
Fair Bantham, Goa, and Japan;
The treasure western caverns lend,
Dug by the miserable American.
[And] [a]ll the black negro dives for in the deep.[167]

As these representations of Belvoir indicate, by the late 1670s the country house was no longer depicted as a "manorial matrix of duties and responsibilities,"[168] but rather was portrayed as a structure designed to impress visitors with its display of wealth in the service of possessive individualism: an elite house, no longer primarily understood as a symbol of lineage, was to dazzle in its profuse display of rarities, all of which bespoke the owner's financial ability to amass objects of no use-value which were provided to him by a subordinate labor force both within and beyond his estate.

Thus the logic of the early modern English landscape as a collection culminates in the late seventeenth-century country house poem. During the last decades of the seventeenth century, an amalgam of residual, dominant, and emergent modes of collecting makes for complex representations of the late seventeenth-century English landscape, as chorography, antiquarianism, and natural history are inflected by mercantilism to depict a regional social terrain that bears traces of the feudal past, celebrates land-ownership, and yet also absorbs objects from outside its own boundaries. Although coats of arms still appear on county maps and engraved plates of country houses, feudal rights and responsibilities have conclusively given way to a concept of the countryside as a space filled with physical objects which embody the identities of their owners, elite possessors of property whose buying power, rather than lineage, is displayed in a landscape of rarities, both indigenous and exotic. At the same time as they participated in this refashioning of the countryside and the identity of the landed elite, writers like Camden, Dugdale, Browne, and Plot created innovative identities for themselves as collectors in their own right, authors who assembled rarities—and rare men—in ways that ascribed new social authority to such activities. Seventeenth-century writers who worked within and extended the modes of chorography and antiquarianism thus developed new models of subjectivity and the social formation rooted in the material practice of collecting. In the process, they created both new literary forms and the artifactual landscape of early modern England.

Chapter 4

The Author as Collector

Jonson, Herrick, and Textual Self-Fashioning

A writer is not necessarily an author. In distinguishing between these two categories, Adrian Johns suggests that, "An *author* is taken to be someone acknowledged as responsible for a given printed (or sometimes written) work; that is, *authorship* is taken to be a matter for attribution by others, not of self-election. A *writer* is anyone who composes such a work. A writer therefore may or may not attain authorship."[1] These definitions immediately elicit questions from the literary historian. In what ways might one be considered "responsible" for a written work? Or, to use slightly different terms, what characteristics have different cultures understood as constituting "authorship"? If a writer cannot unilaterally decree himself an "author," how might he present himself and his work to gain the social assent necessary to claim such a status? And why would a writer want to become an "author" in the first place? This chapter explores these issues by examining how two seventeenth-century writers, Ben Jonson and Robert Herrick, used practices of collecting to create new modes of authorship for themselves.

Rooted in the humanist "notebook method" of reading and writing, the composition and circulation of texts in sixteenth- and seventeenth-century England was often conceptualized and practiced as a process of collecting. Within manuscript culture, collections of texts established and maintained the identity of elite social groups. As his classicism (and his contemporaries' charges of plagiarism) indicate, Ben Jonson was himself a practitioner of the "notebook method," treating texts as bundles of fragments which could be appropriated by readers and writers. Jonson's much heralded construction of himself as a proprietary author, I argue, should be viewed as a revision of this "notebook method" using the technology of print. In his 1616 folio *Workes*, Jonson becomes the collector of his own texts, removing them from their earlier contexts of use-value and recontextualizing them within a printed book. Through his selection of texts and the editorial apparatus with which he surrounds them in the folio, Jonson constructs a narrative of proprietary authorial identity which both subverts and capitalizes upon the social relations of seventeenth-century England. After the publication of his folio, however, Jonson reverted to older constructions of authorial identity, circulating his works in manuscript and constructing himself as a progenitor of literary sons until his death in 1637. Ironically, the emerging cultural association between the printed book and closure was further cemented when Jonson's identity was enshrined (both before and after his death) as it had been presented in the 1616 folio. As a collector, Jonson thus inadvertently helped to create the very cultural norms by which the last decades of his career would come to seem irrelevant.

Several years after Jonson's death, one of his literary "sons," Robert Herrick, developed and revised Jonson's practice as an author/collector. In *Hesperides*, published in 1648, Herrick created an oeuvre in the form of a printed book which contained more than 1,400 of his poems. Herrick conceives of the self as an assemblage of discrete objects, and he constructs *Hesperides* as a catalogue of his life's experiences, a textual ark which will preserve the artifacts comprising his identity in the face of social tumult. Herrick deliberately exploits and politicizes the association of the printed collection with posthumous fame, depicting his book as an arrangement of "pieces" which monumentalizes the life of a royalist clergyman who had become a cultural nonentity during the Civil War.

The strategies of textual self-fashioning developed by Jonson and Herrick thus reveal how differing constructions of identity rooted in proprietary authorship could emerge from subject positions associated with collecting in seventeenth-century England. Both Jonson and Herrick combined practices of collecting with the technology of print to constitute new identities as collector/authors. Conceiving of their writings as physical objects which they owned, Jonson and Herrick fashioned new forms of authorial selfhood as they transformed their individual texts into collections. By analyzing Jonson's folio *Workes* and Herrick's *Hesperides* in light of early modern practices of collecting, we may better understand the dynamics of authorial identity they embody.

Authorship in Seventeenth-Century England

In contemporary parlance, an "author" is a unique individual who creates original literary texts. Legally, the author is recognized as possessing the written works he has created; copyright gives the author "the right to exclude others from a temporary monopoly in a copyable commodity" (the text he has generated),[2] and thus the author has the right to profit from others' consumption of the literary property the author has produced. These notions of authorship and authorial copyright rest on two premises: first, the writer, as originator of the works he fashions, "owns" the literary commodities he produces; and second, the literary property—the text—the writer creates and owns can be abstracted from the physical form in which it appears.[3] Thus we conceive of authorship as a kind of possessive individualism: the proprietary author both writes and possesses a text which is not co-extensive with the physical object conveying that text.

In sixteenth- and seventeenth-century England, by contrast, it was understood that a writer owned the *manuscript* he produced, rather than a text existing independently of the manuscript, and it was this physical object, termed a "copy," which a writer could offer for sale to a bookseller. As John Feather observes, the fact that writers were paid for their copy "at least suggest[s] that the booksellers recognized that in acquiring a copy for entry [into the Stationers' Register] and publication, they were acquiring something which had already taken on the status of property"; nonetheless, authors were paid "for little more than the scribal labor of generating a unique but reproducible text—a scribal and not a creative act."[4] After a manuscript had been purchased, a writer had no further rights over the commodity he had fashioned; and since "the principle of literary property did not exist, any bookseller had the right to publish any manuscript which he had managed to procure without consulting the author."[5] In buying the manuscript of a play, theater companies similarly gave limited recognition to the writer as owner of his copy by paying him for the literary object he had produced. Once the manuscript was sold, however, a play—its initial script often created piecemeal by several writers—was owned by the acting company which had commissioned and bought the copy, not the individual(s) who had written the manuscript in the first place. As Stephen Orgel observes,

The text thus produced was a working model, which the company then revised as seemed appropriate. The author had little or no say in these revisions: the text belonged to the company, and the authority represented by the text—I am talking now about the *performing* text—is that of the company, the owners, not that of the playwright, the author.[6]

Thus Ben Jonson lived and wrote in a culture in which, by our standards, only a rudimentary concept of proprietary authorship had been established.

It is useful to consider how we might apply Foucault's concept of the "author-function" to the situation of early modern writers like Jonson.[7] According to Foucault, the "author" is a product of ideology, a "privileged" notion of "individualization" by which discourse is socially categorized and controlled.[8] Foucault thus helpfully disabuses us of any illusions we may have about authorship as a "natural," unpoliticized relationship between writers and texts; however, Foucault's analysis is problematic insofar as it presents a simplistic view of historical process and denies any role to human agency in the creation of selfhood or culture. As Louis A. Montrose suggests, we should develop Foucault's concept of the author-function "by giving greater historical and cultural specificity and variability both to the notion of Author and to the possible functions it may serve" and by examining how writers in particular historical circumstances *used* the discourses and material practices of their cultures to forge new modes of authorship.[9]

With regard to sixteenth- and seventeenth-century England, of course, one must consider how writers could exploit the process by which printed books were created. Countering a tendency in earlier scholarship to treat printing as "a nonsymbolic form of material reality" that was intrinsically imbued with qualities of closure and fixity, historians of the book now recognize that the shifting "meaning" of print has been negotiated within specific cultural contexts.[10] Thus in understanding how author-functions were constructed in early modern England, we must acknowledge that authorship bore no inevitable relationship to printed books. I would argue, moreover, that we should not privilege the cultural role of print to the extent that we fail to consider how other material practices might also have offered writers new models or resources for authorial self-fashioning. In his fascinating biography of the seventeenth-century English clergyman and collector John Bargrave, Stephen Bann asks, "Did the practice of collecting, in this historical period, have an author-function of its own, as . . . literary creation became inseparably linked with authorship?"[11] I would suggest that we might reverse the terms of Bann's provocative question and instead consider if the practice of writing had a *collector*-function during the early modern era. More precisely, as this chapter demonstrates, we should recognize that the collector and the author were not necessarily separate identities in seventeenth-century England. Drawing initially on humanist notions of reading and writing, writers like Jonson and Herrick could innovatively construct author-functions which were conceived as activities of collecting and cataloguing.

The Humanist Text as Collection

As discussed in Chapter 1, the humanist veneration of classical antiquity had an important influence on the scope and cultural meaning of collections of objects in early modern England. Humanism not only inflected elite collecting practices, however, but also established a new mode of identity rooted in a specifically textual practice of collecting. Building upon the *florilegia* and compilations of *exempla* spawned by "the medieval addiction to texts as such," humanist educators in the late fifteenth and early sixteenth centuries developed a distinctive "notebook method" of reading and writing.[12] Students were taught to view texts as fields of sayings—exempla, analogies, aphorisms, proverbs, adages—which should be "harvested" as they were read.[13] Each student would keep his own commonplace book—an exercise book organized by a series of headings—at his elbow. As the student read, he would record memorable sayings under the appropriate headings, creating a "personal, subject-organized dictionary of quotations" to which he could refer when writing his own compositions.[14] For a humanist reader, "The point of reading a book was not to provide an 'anatomy' or an understanding of its argument or structure; rather, the end was a harvesting or mining of the book for its functional parts—useful to borrow for the reader's own writing or to serve as practical conduct rules or stylistic models."[15] The educational program promoted by humanists such as Agricola and Erasmus thus entailed the "rhetorical disintegration of texts" and the simultaneous development of the reader's own collection of textual fragments.[16] The influence of this fragmenting mode of reading on the literary culture of early modern England was profound, and during the Tudor period, printed commonplace books proliferated, forming both "the staple of the ordinary man's reading" and the "building blocks" of the imaginative literature of the period.[17]

The humanist notebook method of reading and writing fostered new concepts of the relationship between textuality, collecting, and identity. Rhetorical *copia* had a long association with notions of material abundance, and sixteenth-century descriptions of the notebook method emphasize the physicality of the reader's collection of sayings, often figuring the gathered textual fragments as a treasury of jewels or a storehouse of bricks.[18] This impulse to conceive of sayings *as* material objects led some writers to advocate the display of sayings *on* material objects. Erasmus suggested that to inculcate virtue in a youngster, sayings "should be engraved on rings, painted in pictures, appended to the wreaths of honor, and, by using any other means by which that age can be interested, kept always before him."[19] Sir Thomas Elyot similarly argued that a nobleman should transform his home into an architectural commonplace book:

concernynge ornamentes of halle and chambres, in Arise, painted tables, and images containyng histories: wherein is represented some monument of vertue, most cunnyngly wroughte, with the circumstance of the mater briefly declared, wherby

other men in beholdynge, may be instructed, or at the lest wayes to vertue persuaded. In like wise his plate and vessaile wolde be ingraved with histories, fables,
or quicke and wise sentences . . . whereby some parte of tyme shall be saved, whiche
else by superfluouse eatyng and drinkyng wolde be idely consumed.[20]

Sir Nicholas Bacon agreed with such a philosophy of interior decoration
and inscribed the walls of the great chamber at Gorhambury with sayings.[21]
The humanist practice of reading thus encouraged the conceptualization
and display of texts as personal material possessions.

A humanist's collection of sayings gleaned from authoritative classical
authors was a form of cultural capital which testified to the owner's learning
and thus to his credentials as a political advisor. Erasmus argued that the
educated man could use his store of sayings in the service of his prince,
providing good precepts "now by a suggestive thought, now by a fable, now
by analogy, now by example, now by maxims, now by a proverb";[22] and in
the court of Henry VIII, where a premium was placed on gathering evidence to support the king's positions on marital and religious issues, the
"skillful citation of maxims and commonplaces became a way of displaying
the fruits of humanist education when seeking preferment."[23] If the humanist collection of textual fragments was thus understood and deployed as
a tool of absolutist monarchy, it could also engender concepts of identity
less readily compatible with hereditary authority of any kind. Most obviously, the project of humanism stressed that a particular type of education, rather than lineage, qualified a man for positions of political influence.
In analyzing Tudor humanism, Mary Thomas Crane argues that this distinctive humanist mode of subjectivity challenged landed values:

> In opposition to aristocratic codes of honor, violence, and frivolous display [elite
> pastimes such as dancing and hunting], humanist teachers and writers sought to
> instill respect for learning, hard work, and serious devotion to duty. The very
> process of reading through approved texts, selecting their most pithy and useful
> bits, and laboriously transcribing them in a notebook reinforced these values.[24]

This potentially subversive form of humanist identity was bound up with
collecting. While the elite collection of art or rarities was intended to
display an ostensibly pre-existing social status, the textual fragments contained within a commonplace book were a physical manifestation of the
humanist subjectivity which had been constructed through the process of
creating the book.

The notebook method of reading—the methodical gathering, arrangement, and display of sayings—was thus simultaneously a process of
self-fashioning; the humanist subject was constituted through and repre-

sented by a collection of textual fragments. The humanist identity so constructed was at once "profoundly unique and profoundly derivative."[25] On the one hand, as Barbara M. Benedict argues, the notebook method "empowers readers over culture by allowing them to reshape printed literature to complement their own subjectivity," the resulting commonplace books standing as monuments to the authority and independence of their compilers.[26] At the same time, however, the autonomy of the humanist reader/writer was delimited by communal norms, for "in theory at least, all texts formed a common storehouse of matter, validated by existing cultural codes, from which all educated people could gather and through which all educated subjects were framed."[27] This interrelationship between the individual subject and a larger social group was extended to the political realm, for the wise ruler would assemble a group of singular men as his advisors—a collection of textual collectors.[28]

The creation and representation of individual and social identities through the practice of textual collecting was also a vital dynamic in early modern manuscript culture. Like the commonplace book, the manuscript miscellany of poems grew out of the humanist practice of collecting textual artifacts. Just as sayings were inscribed on walls and furnishings in early modern England, so poems, as fundamentally occasional writings, were often integrated with physical objects: funeral elegies were pinned to coffins, while verses in other genres appeared "on rings, on food trenchers, on glass windows (scratched with a pin or diamond), on paintings, on tombstones and monuments, on trees, and even (as graffiti) on London's Pissing Conduit."[29] This habitual merging of what we would differentiate as texts and things, I would suggest, enhanced the quality of the manuscript miscellany as a collection of *objects* which was possessed by its compiler(s). In seventeenth-century England, manuscript miscellanies were often produced by groups of individuals—frequently associated with the court, the universities, the Inns of Court, or elite households—who exchanged texts and compiled manuscript anthologies to create and define the identity of their specific social circles. As Harold Love explains, "Networks of friends or associates would regularly exchange texts with each other either by a process of chain copying or by a member making copies for the entire group," the manuscripts thus formed "serving to nourish a shared set of values and to enrich personal allegiances."[30] Within these closed circles of manuscript transmission, poems would elude both authorial control and the democratizing tendency of print;[31] shared (and often revised and supplemented), the poems gathered and displayed in a manuscript miscellany became the collective cultural property of the community which created the anthology, the assembled verses constituting and epitomizing the identity of the group as a whole. Thus Renaissance humanism fostered not only a vogue for antiquities as physical objects, but also catalyzed the development of new subject positions for collectors of literary artifacts which situated readers and writers at complicated junctions of the textual and the material, the individual and the communal.

Ben Jonson and the "Culling Muse"

A professional writer held a very dubious social standing in early modern England. The playwright and poet Ben Jonson faced particularly difficult obstacles—the circumstances of his own history—in his quest to achieve cultural authority. Born the posthumous son of a clergyman and forced to truncate his education so he could take up his stepfather's craft of bricklaying, Jonson began his literary career as a hack writer for the Elizabethan public theaters. Determined to gain greater respect for his abilities and accomplishments, Jonson struggled to elevate his status as a producer of literary commodities by constructing himself as an author through practices of collecting.

As scholars like Richard S. Peterson have exhaustively demonstrated, Jonson's mode of authorial self-fashioning was, in part, rooted in his devotion to humanist *imitatio*.[32] Displaying his prodigious stores of *copia* in the texts he wrote, Jonson used the humanist notebook method as one basis of his literary art, and his relentless exhibition of his classical knowledge became a means by which a lowly bricklayer-turned-writer, a "self-made man with no *given* status, constantly under pressure to justify himself,"[33] could claim authority for the texts he produced in early modern England. An extension of his training as a student at Westminster School,[34] Jonson's stockpile of learned quotations and allusions became a fund of cultural capital which he exploited in new ways as a professional writer.

Jonson's notebook method is both described and embodied in his treatise *Timber, Or, Discoveries, Made upon men and matter, as they have flowed out of his daily readings, or had their reflux to his peculiar notion of the times*.[35] *Timber* is, in Peter Beal's words, "little more than a patchwork of quotations from classical and Renaissance literature, intermingled with some original comments, and is evidently based on some kind of commonplace book if not virtually amounting to one in itself."[36] The two Latin epigraphs which appear below the title underline *Timber's* emphasis on physical material gathered and redistributed. The first epigraph, from Persius, commands, "Live in your own house, and recognize how poorly it is furnished."[37] The second epigraph defines its own heading, "Silva," with a passage from Statius:

Silva, or the rough timber of facts and thoughts, so called from the multiplicity and variety of their contents. For just as we are wont commonly to call a great mass of trees growing indiscriminately a *wood*, so the ancients called those of their books in which varied and diverse materials were randomly crowded together *woods*: timber trees.[38]

Juxtaposed in this way, the two epigraphs suggest that one should remedy sparse (intellectual) decor by gathering "timber trees" (passages from other authors) and converting this raw material through craftsmanship into serviceable "furnishings" of the mind. Jonson's opening emphasis on the assembling and refashioning of physical objects recurs in different guises throughout *Timber*. In a subsequent passage, Jonson insists that a poet must practice "imitation," which, drawing upon the traditional image of *copia* as treasure, he defines as the ability "to convert the substance or riches of another poet to his own use" (*Timber*, 2490–92). The "substance or riches" of other writers becomes, in turn, "the treasure of [the poet's] mind" which he "must be able by nature and instinct to pour out" (*Timber*, 2435–36). William Hodgson's laudatory analysis of Jonson's "elaborated Art-contrived Playes," published in 1640, develops this concept of Jonson's notebook method as the accumulation of valuable materials, depicting Jonson's practice of *imitatio* as a kind of mercantilism:

Each [play] like an Indian Ship or Hull appeares,
That tooke a voyage for some certaine yeares,
To plough the sea, and furrow up the main,
And brought rich Ingots from his loaden brain.
His Art the Sunne; his Labours were the mines;
His solide stuff the treasure of his lines.[39]

Jonson also described his imitative art as the gathering and digestion of food, another standard metaphor for the humanist process of reading and writing.[40] Drawing ultimately on Seneca and Horace,[41] Jonson asserts in *Timber* that the poet imitates

Not as a creature that swallows what it takes in crude, raw, or indigested, but that feeds with an appetite, and hath a stomach to concoct, divide, and turn all into nourishment. Not to imitate servilely (as Horace saith) and catch at vices for virtue, but to draw forth out of the best and choicest flowers, with the bee, and turn all into honey: work it into one relish and savour, make our imitation sweet, observe how the best writers have imitated, and follow them. (*Timber*, 2495–2503)

Whether represented as a woodlot, food, or nectar-filled flowers, classical authors become the source from which the Jonsonian poet gathers his own raw literary materials.

Jonson insists that this activity of accumulating material and shaping it into a work of literature is laborious. He proudly characterizes the poet as "a maker" and describes writing as an artisanal activity: "A poem, as I have told you, is the work of the poet, the end and fruit of his labour and study. Poesy is his skill or craft of making" (*Timber*, 2370, 2398–2400). For Jonson, labor, not formal qualities of genre or rhyme, distinguish a "poem" from other, lesser forms of writing, and he thus includes his plays and masques in the category of poetry.[42] Jonson's construction of the author as a laborer leads him to develop further the humanist concept of the literary text as a material object. He asserts that if the poet's "wit"

will not arrive suddenly at the dignity of the ancients, let him . . . come to it again upon better cogitation, try another time with labour. If then it succeed not, cast not away the quills yet, nor scratch the wainscot, beat not the poor desk, but bring all to the forge, and file again, turn it anew. . . . It is said of the incomparable Virgil that he brought forth his verses like a bear, and after formed them with licking. (*Timber*, 2459–66)

In Jonson's poetics, the physicality of the imitative poet's *copia* is transformed by great effort into the materiality of the newly created text, which must be forcibly shaped into cogent wholeness by the laboring artisan/poet. Rather than indicating the poet's ineptitude, laborious hours spent writing ensure the immortality of his art works: in *Timber*, Jonson recounts how Euripides, after he had produced only three verses in three days of strenuous effort, responded to the taunts of a more prolific writer by asserting, "But here is the difference: thy verses will not last those three days, mine will to all time"; as an amen to Euripides's speech, Jonson adds, "Indeed, things wrote with labour deserve so to be read, and will last their age" (*Timber*, 2477–89).

Jonson's theory of laborious poetry is, characteristically, steeped in the writings of Aristotle, Horace, and Seneca. "What is different," Richard Dutton observes, "is that Jonson is not writing as a detached theorist, but as a writer who needs to sell and justify himself in the marketplace. . . . He deploys notions of the poet as maker not in a selfless perpetuation of accepted wisdom, but in order to establish spaces and shapes for himself in a world where none pre-exists and to which he has no given right."[43] Jonson's concept of the author as artisan flew in the face of the elite ideology of poetry as a leisure-time activity for the courtly amateur; as Richmond

Barbour notes, "Against an aristocratic code of *sprezzatura* that he, by birth and disposition, could never embody, [Jonson] proposed a classical ethic of deliberately cultivated skill."⁴⁴ The strongly artifactual quality of the literary text as Jonson conceived it linked his compositional method as a writer with his earlier career as a craftsman and left him open to class-based attack: Jonson was, sneered a detractor in 1601, "A meere Empyrick, one that getts what he hath by obseruation, and makes onely nature priuy to what he indites, so slow an Inuentor that he were better betake himselfe to his old trade of Bricklaying, a bould whorson, as confident now in making a booke, as he was in times past in laying of a brick."⁴⁵

Jonson's most radical innovation in poetic theory was to associate authorial labor with property. By insisting that his agency as a literary "maker" entailed his ownership of his writings, Jonson transformed his class-marked concept of intellectual labor into the basis of a new mode of identity: authorial possessive individualism.⁴⁶ The Jonsonian imitator dynamically transforms the materials he has selectively gathered from other writers into a new, original art work which forever "belongs" to its author, whom Jonson conceives as an artisan retaining "proprietary rights" over the commodities he has produced.⁴⁷ By linking labor and ownership, Jonson thus anticipates Locke's theory of possessive individualism, according to which "Whatsoever then [the individual] removes out of the State that Nature hath provided, and left it in, he hath mixed his *Labour* with, and joyned to it something that is his own, and thereby makes it his *Property*."⁴⁸ Richard Handler's analysis of Locke's theory of possessive individualism can be usefully applied to Jonson's artisanal, proprietary concept of authorship:

By objectifying labor as an individual's property, Locke allowed the individual to mix detachable pieces of himself into natural objects. Yet the individual does not thereby alienate his labor; rather he draws the contacted objects to himself. . . . Moreover, if [the things he acts upon] become his property, on the other hand the individual comes to be defined by the things he possesses.⁴⁹

Extending the notion of *copia* as a stockpile of textual goods gathered and owned by the compiler of a commonplace book, Jonson thus sought to construct the imitative literary work as the inalienable possession of its laboring writer.

As part of his program to fashion a new concept of proprietary authorship, Jonson strenuously attacked other writers if they failed to meet his standards of successful imitation. Jonson was one of the first English writers to use the term "plagiary" (from *plagiarius*, meaning "kidnapper"),⁵⁰ which for Jonson designated the antithesis of the beelike imitator. In *Tim-*

ber, Jonson heaps scorn on would-be imitators who cannot pursue their own cogent line of discriminating thought, who "write out of what they presently find or meet, without choice: by which means it happens that what they have discredited and impugned in one work, they have before or after extolled the same in another" (*Timber*, 732–35). In Jonson's scathing estimate, such an inept reader/writer commits serial servility, for he randomly parrots whatever author he has just read, rather than carefully choosing and synthesizing his models: "Nothing is more ridiculous than to make an author a dictator," Jonson cautions (*Timber*, 2114–15). Moreover, there seems to be no line separating the "ridiculous" literary slave from the reprehensible plagiarist, for Jonson also condemns "fox-like thefts . . . as a man may find whole pages together usurped from one author" (*Timber*, 750–52).

The generalized scorn Jonson exhibits toward plagiarists in *Timber* becomes much more personal and defensive in works where Jonson contemplates the theft of his own writings by others. Jonson recognizes the power of collecting as a means of creating authorial subjectivity, and he strenuously attacks other would-be collectors for attempting to appropriate components of Jonson's own self-fashioned identity. Poet-Ape, who "makes each man's wit his own," has "robbed" Jonson, according to one epigram; in another, Jonson reveals that Playwright made a play out of five "toys" which he had purloined from Jonson; elsewhere, Jonson disdainfully analyzes the thieving ways of the writer "Old-End Gatherer," and warns Prowl the Plagiary,

> I will not show
> A line unto thee till the world it know,
> Or that I've by two good sufficient men
> To be the wealthy witness of my pen:
> For all thou hear'st, thou swear'st thyself didst do;
> Thy wit lives by it, Prowl, and belly too.[51]

Jonson thus reveals and indicts the unscrupulous hacks who cobble together texts out of fragments stolen from other men's work, asserting his proprietary claim to his own literary products—and his identity as an author—as he does so.

Jonson's fierce insistence that he owned the texts he wrote was, perhaps, shaped by his personal experience of the individual's precarious relationship to chattels in early modern England. Although his grandfather, Jonson told William Drummond, "was a gentleman," Jonson's own father "lost all his estate under Queen Mary; having been cast in prison and forfeited"; after losing everything he possessed, Jonson's father "at last turned minister" and died before Jonson was born, leaving his posthumous son to be "brought up poorly" by his mother and stepfather.[52] Jonson himself forfeited all his possessions in 1598 when, after having killed the actor Gabriel Spencer in a duel, he escaped being hanged by pleading benefit of clergy; as his more lenient punishment for committing manslaughter, Jonson's thumb was branded and all his goods were confiscated.[53] The Crown was not the only consumer of Jonson's property: he told Drummond that "Sundry times he hath devoured his books, i.[e.], sold th[e]m all for necessity,"[54] and in 1623 a fire destroyed much of his remaining library. Thus Jonson's construction of his literary texts as inalienable property may have been a response to his own background of material *dis*possession: as a writer, Jonson strove to create a kind of chattel which could never be taken from him.

Embarrassingly, however, neither Jonson nor his contemporaries could distinguish the proprietary imitative author from the literary thief. Jonson maintained that his poetry was filled with "high and noble matter" rather than the "commonplaces, filched, that take these times," and Lucius Cary concurred that Jonson "writ past what he quotes, / And his *Productions* farre exceed his *Notes.*"[55] Nonetheless, Jonson's concept of proprietary authorship, his insistence that his literary texts were inalienable possessions, contradicted his own humanist practice of reading and writing. As Bruce Thomas Boehrer observes of Jonson's illogic,

> On one hand, the poet seems to regard others' texts . . . as an open invitation to copy, imitate, and assimilate; on the other hand, he expends great effort to protect the boundaries of his own work—to render it inimitable and unassimilable. . . . In short one moral of Jonson's poetics would seem to be "I write; more or less everybody else steals." Within Jonson's self-created realm of authorial property rights, this moral has a corollary: "My work is mine; everybody else's . . . is more or less mine too."[56]

John Dryden acerbically critiqued this authorial double standard, commenting that Jonson "invades authors like a monarch, and what would be theft in other poets is only victory in him."[57] The disjunction between Jonson's insistence that authors *owned* their texts and his continuous appropriation of other writers' work was acknowledged even by Jonson's keenest admirers. In an elegy published after Jonson's death, for example, his disciple William Cartwright attempted to praise Jonson's practice of *imitatio*:

What though *thy* culling Muse did rob the store
Of Greeke, and Latine gardens to bring ore

Plants to *thy* native soyle? Their vertues were
Improv'd farre more, by being planted here.[58]

The elegist's horticultural imagery draws on the conventional depiction of
the humanist reader/writer as a discriminating literary harvester who
plucks only the choicest flowers for inclusion in his notebook; moreover, I
would argue, by the time Cartwright's poem was published in 1638—the
year that John Tradescant the younger returned from his first voyage to
North America bearing hundreds of plants never before seen in England—
this gardening metaphor also associated the humanist gathering of texts
with other contemporary practices of collecting and display. Cartwright,
however, undermines Jonson's status as a literary collector by describing
Jonson's relationship to classical authors with the damning monosyllable
"rob": Jonson's plant-hunting muse filches interesting artifacts from the
likes of Horace and Seneca. In seventeenth-century terms, Cartwright's
revealingly equivocal defense of Jonson's compositional method questions
Jonson's *propriety*:[59] Cartwright inadvertently suggests that Jonson did not
really "own" the textual fragments, gleaned by reading classical authors,
which he displayed in his literary works. Cartwright's elegy thus depicts
Jonson's mode of writing as being rooted in a kind of collecting which,
despite its respectable humanist origins, raises vexing issues of textual
ownership. Jonson's insistence that a writer "owned" the works he produced
thus came to exist in tension with the notebook method. The claims of the
proprietary author could not be reconciled with the claims of the textual
collector who, like Jonson, was inspired by a "culling Muse."

The Collector as Editor: Jonson's Workes

Jonson's attempt to found his identity as a proprietary author on humanist *imitatio* was rendered deeply problematic by the internal contradic-
tions of his own poetic theory and practice. By contrast, Jonson was much
more successful in establishing his authorial status by collecting the literary
artifacts he himself had produced. This strategy did not address the issue of
plagiarism, but instead changed the material basis of Jonson's claims of
authorship as a collector. As Richard C. Newton has argued, during the
course of his career Jonson became "the poet of printed books," shaping the
notion of the printed text as both "the primary object of literature" and as
the embodiment of an author's proprietary identity.[60] In 1616, extending his
earlier use of print to negate others' claims to the texts he had written,

Jonson assembled and exhibited his literary output as a collection in his folio *Workes*. By selectively gathering and reconstructing his texts in the form of an ostentatious printed book, Jonson represented his career as a collection of literary artifacts, removing the art works he had fashioned from their original contexts of commercial or aristocratic use-value and instead displaying them as Jonson's own property. Thus as the collector/editor of his own literary commodities, the cataloguer of the texts he claimed to own, Jonson used the technology of print to create a new mode of authorial identity.

Years before he published his *Workes* in 1616, Jonson had been using print as a medium through which he could innovatively assert his ownership of the plays, masques, and entertainments he had written. As previously discussed, neither plays nor playwrights were highly esteemed when Jonson decided to trade his trowel for a pen; dramas were, in Richard Helgerson's words, the "semianonymous, rarely respected by-products of the Elizabethan entertainment industry" over which acting companies and booksellers, not writers, exercised ownership.[61] Similarly, a masque or aristocratic pageant was authorized not by its writer, but by its patron and the occasion for which it had been created. Thus, for Jonson, exploiting the resources of print to construct a new form of proprietary authorship was necessarily "an act performed *on* or *against* the theatrical script, so as to efface its real conditions of production."[62]

Jonson turned to print for the first time in 1600 with the publication of *Every Man Out of His Humour*. As David Riggs observes, by selling his copy of *Every Man Out* to a bookseller soon after the play had been performed, Jonson "was claiming, in effect, that the author continued to own his work after the players had purchased a copy of it."[63] Given the unusual features of the published text, it seems likely that Jonson himself was involved in preparing *Every Man Out* for the press. "Contrary to usual practice," Richard Dutton observes, "the title-page mentions nothing of the acting company involved" in the play's performance in 1599.[64] Not only is the legitimate "owner" of the play, the Lord Chamberlain's Men, thus unacknowledged, but the title page also distinguishes the (authentic) printed text from its (inauthentic) staged adaptation, informing the reader that the printed version conveys the drama "As It Was First Composed by the Author B. J. Containing more than hath been publicly spoken or acted."[65] The identity of *Every Man Out* as a text intended to be read, rather than a script to be performed, is further emphasized by the appearance of Latin mottos on the title page—highly unusual for a play at this time—and "elaborate characters for the dramatis personae."[66] Jonson thus constructed himself as the proprietary author of his play by presenting it in print.

As he published more of his dramatic works, Jonson developed a repertoire of tactics by which he could regain authority over his plays, masques, and entertainments after they had been performed and thus were no longer his property. In most of his texts printed after *Every Man Out*, Jonson's full name, rather than his initials, appeared on the title page; references to acting companies were carefully omitted; and, although printed plays were conventionally undedicated (since copy texts were owned by theater companies rather than writers), with the publication of *Volpone* in 1607 Jonson also began to dedicate his plays.[67] Latin mottos, and, in the case of *Poetaster* (1602), a Latin preface to the reader, established Jonson's plays as texts to be studied by an educated readership, rather than ephemeral entertainment consumed by the masses; and in imitation of classical convention, Jonson divided his printed plays into acts and scenes, rather than following contemporary stage practice and using the entrance or exit of main characters to determine the structure of scenes.[68]

The quarto of *Sejanus*, published in 1605, exemplifies many of the strategies Jonson devised to assert his authorial propriety over his individual printed texts. Jonson tells the reader of *Sejanus* that, like the printed text of *Every Man Out*, "this Booke, in all numbers, is not the same with that which was acted on the publike Stage,"[69] and he goes on to explain that whereas the 1603 staged version of the play had been written in collaboration with another author (whom Jonson pointedly never names), for the printed "Booke" Jonson has replaced everything his collaborator wrote with new material created by Jonson himself; as Douglas Brooks notes, Jonson thus suggests that the "Booke" and the "Stage" afford different conditions for the construction of authorship, and "Jonson makes it clear that the publication process has given him the power to transform the authorial status of the work from a collaborative performance text to an individualized printed quarto text."[70] Jonson further legitimizes the printed version of *Sejanus* by prefacing it with a series of eight commendatory verses, an "altogether unusual procedure."[71] Moreover, Jonson emphasizes the play's new status as a readerly text rather than a theatrical script—and his own status as an erudite author rather than a common hack—by encrusting each page of *Sejanus* with Latin marginalia, a practice Jonson also followed when publishing his entertainments for James I and most of his masques in quarto. As Joseph Loewenstein remarks in analyzing Jonson's printed masques, "In many ways the annotations destabilize the format of Jonson's page, announcing, gravely insisting, that these are not scripts."[72]

Indeed, some pages of *Sejanus* are so heavy with scholarly apparatus that the marginal notes "overspill their column to make inroads into the 'play' itself."[73] Stephen Orgel observes that by transforming the original script in these ways, Jonson's published incarnation of *Sejanus* "has succeeded in *suppressing* the theatrical production, and has replaced it with an independent, printed text."[74] Thus by exerting editorial control over the publication of his dramatic texts, Jonson represented himself as a proprietary author whose claims to the literary artifacts he had produced both preceded and superseded the rights of any mere consumer of his works: Jonson forged his identity as the owner of his texts by creating, through print, a new material existence for his writings.

The construction of authorial propriety through the publication of individual texts did not satisfy Jonson, however. In 1616 Jonson combined some of his editorial practices as a published writer with the technology of the collection in his printed book, *THE WORKES of Beniamin Jonson.* Jonson's *Workes* consists of more than 1,000 folio pages, comprising nine plays, a collection of 133 verses entitled *Epigrammes,* another group of fifteen poems entitled *The Forrest,* and a series of aristocratic dramatic works categorized as "Entertaynments," "Panegyre," "Masques," and "Barriers." Bibliographic studies of the *Workes* indicate that Jonson was involved in proofing and correcting the book as it was printed, and scholars concur that "Jonson exercised some influence during the initial stages of the Folio's planning, directing the choice of format, layout, ornamentation and even type use."[75] Moreover, Jonson introduced new material—notably the text of *The Golden Age Restored* and the Earl of Pembroke's title of Lord Chamberlain—into the folio as late as the winter of 1615–16.[76] Adapting his own compositional practice as a "culler" of classical texts, Jonson thus became the collector of the literary artifacts he had produced and "owned."

In early seventeenth-century England, the physical size of Jonson's new book was culturally meaningful—and provocative. As D. F. McKenzie has argued, the nonverbal physical characteristics of books should be regarded as having "an expressive function,"[77] and Jonson exploited the symbolism of the book as a material object by publishing his collection of texts as a folio, the most substantial format in which a book could appear. During Jonson's lifetime, the size of a book was equated with its status.[78] With quadruple the perimeter and a cost twenty to forty times more than a play printed in quarto,[79] a folio's physical and financial heft meant that it was also associated with elite and institutional reading, with libraries that could afford such an expensive book and the space within which it could be laid flat to be read; moreover, the folio format was favored by scholars because

166

the greater legibility of its text meant that "it was an easier form in which to trace references."[80] As Roger Chartier observes, "a hierarchy exists that links the format of the book, the genre of the text, and the moment and mode of reading," and thus the folio format was "generally reserved for sermons, geographies, the classics, royal books like *The Works of King James*, and other such literature thought to be of permanent significance."[81] In this material system of registering literary value, the inconsequential status of plays was indicated by their customary appearance in quarto form: "Before 1616," Gerald Eades Bentley has observed, "nearly all plays which got printed had appeared on bookstalls looking like almanacs, joke books, coney-catching pamphlets, and other ephemera."[82] A flimsy quarto was not intended to last: "After it was read it lay around, the top leaf and the bottom leaf got dirty and torn, then the string broke, and it disintegrated and was thrown away."[83] Thus by presenting plays written for the commercial theater in folio form rather than quarto, Jonson was audaciously claiming a new cultural importance for his literary products.

The title of Jonson's book was as defiantly unconventional as the volume's physical size. By translating the Latin term *opera* to designate his writings, Jonson was boldly claiming a place for himself amidst the ranks of the most venerated authors in the classical tradition: "as Horace had his *Opera*, so the 'English Horace' had his *Workes*."[84] Jonson's title asserts the artistic monumentality of the scripts and poems written by the former bricklayer—including his commercial plays, the likes of which Sir Thomas Bodley banned from his library as contemptible "riffe-raffes."[85] The elaborate engraved title page of Jonson's book further symbolizes the aspirations embodied by its physical size and charged title (see Figure 8). Framed within a triumphal arch that is richly adorned with Corinthian columns, cartouches, laurel-entwined obelisks, and allegorical statues associated with classical drama, a proscenium contains the title of the volume and a Latin motto from Horace. As Margreta de Grazia notes, "By locating the origins of theatre in the ancient past, by representing its genres through classical icons and Latin names, by incorporating the proscenium stage into the monument's architectonics, the engraving visually converts the transitory play texts, the contents of the book, into enduring art."[86] Predictably, Jonson was attacked for his pretensions: an anonymous detractor sarcastically inquired, "Pray tell me Ben, where doth the mystery lurk, / What others call a play, you call a work."[87]

Literary historians rightly regard Jonson's *Workes* as "a landmark," a monument to the theory of possessive individualism which "stands alongside Locke's essay 'Of Property' as a significant historical document," and

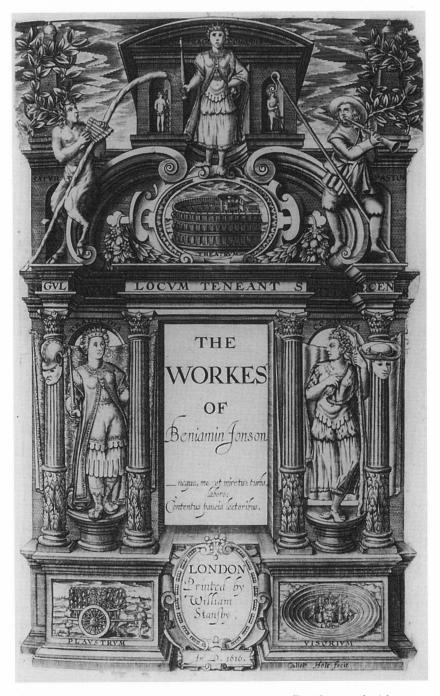

Figure 8. Ben Jonson, *The Workes of Beniamin Jonson* (London, 1616), title page.
Kenneth Spencer Research Library, University of Kansas.

argue that the publication of Jonson's folio constitutes "the single most important event in the social history of English authorship before the Statute of Anne."[88] What sometimes is minimized in such assessments of the volume, however, is the folio's overwhelmingly tautological nature: insofar as most of the items published in the folio had already been printed, one could argue that the contents of the new book were largely redundant.[89] Given the extent to which Jonson was recycling previously printed plays and masques, it seems, as Richard Dutton proposes, that in the folio Jonson "was making a further statement about himself and the status of his own writings."[90] Our analysis of the folio thus should not simply conclude that the form of print authorship Jonson constructed in the texts he had previously published "became the model for his relation to the dramatic and lyric texts of the 1616 Folio."[91] Rather, it was the nature of the *Workes* as a collection that gave it a signifying power which Jonson's earlier published books lacked. As a collection, the folio created and embodied a new kind of authorial identity which Jonson could not attain by publishing his plays and aristocratic entertainments piecemeal.

Richard C. Newton has argued that as a poet, Jonson developed a literary form Newton terms the "critical collection." In contrast to a sonnet sequence or a poetic miscellany, the critical collection "depends on an established notion of a 'collection' as a structural idea . . . to which it brings the application of critical readings, not just of the individual poems but of the collection as a whole."[92] Acting as his own editor to create *The Forrest*, Newton suggests, Jonson retrieves his poems from their past occasions and functions, treating each one "as an autonomous object, a thing, movable from context to context, and variously interpretable therein," and places each literary object "in a context defined precisely by the poet's current critical intelligence." This process of decontextualizing and assembling a group of poems thus becomes "the expression of a mind looking back over its own productions, its own artifacts, and considering them as part of the poet's present self."[93] Newton's analysis of *The Forrest* could be usefully applied to the 1616 folio as a whole: that is, the volume in its entirety should be assessed as a "critical collection" through which Jonson creates a new authorial persona as an editor/collector.

Insights from scholarship in collections studies can help us to understand why Jonson should republish his plays and masques in the form of a critical collection. Jean Baudrillard argues that a collection embodies the collector's "independence from the world" and allows him to create an "alternative discourse" whose "ultimate signified" is the collector himself;[94] thus collections can, in Susan Pearce's words, "act as material autobiographies" for their collectors.[95] As a material display of personal identity, the collection does not simply reflect a pre-existing self, but rather functions as a technology through which selfhood is simultaneously constructed and represented. In analyzing the seventeenth-century collection of John Bargrave, Stephen Bann observes how individual objects in Bargrave's cabinet open out onto "episodes of biography," and Bann argues that to be a collector "is not merely an attribute of the self but also, in a real sense, the model through which the unity of the self is, progressively and retrospectively, achieved."[96] Thus unlike the previously printed quartos of Jonson's plays and masques, the folio's nature as a collection allowed Jonson to construct an autobiographical representation of his identity. By simultaneously gathering and cataloguing the artifacts he had produced, Jonson constructed a model of authorial selfhood in the material form of the folio: the book does not record but *fabricates* an account of Jonson's career. In preparing the folio for publication, Jonson became both the consumer and the producer of his own texts, his own plagiarizer: Jonson-the-collector "culls" the literary art works Jonson-the-writer had previously created and assembles them in a critical collection which is a masterpiece of editorial self-fashioning. Through the narrative Jonson materially constructs in his folio, he rewrites his own history.

So that the individual literary artifacts within the folio may appear to comprise Jonson's professional autobiography, Jonson restores information to indicate the historical specificity—the provenance—of some of his dramas, information which he had excised from the plays' previous incarnations as printed quartos.[97] The tendency to assume that the *Workes* is necessarily a culmination of Jonson's earlier authorial strategies, rather than the embodiment of different dynamics of self-fashioning, has led some scholars to overstate the anti-theatricality of the folio. Several recent commentators have maintained that in the folio, Jonson attempts to exclude "the sustaining features of public theatre" from his book, "[d]isabling the proprietary intrusion of acting companies" to construct the volume as "anti-theater" and raise the status of the poet "from playhouse employee to autonomous creator."[98] Yet in many ways Jonson presents his texts in the folio as being *more* theatrical than in their previous printed versions. Richmond Barbour observes that whereas the title page of the 1600 quarto of *Every Man Out* omitted any reference to the conditions of the play's original performance, other than to assert the printed text's greater fidelity to the play as Jonson had composed it, the title page of *Every Man Out* in the folio re-establishes Jonson's relationship with the theater by stating that the play was "Acted in the yeere 1599. By the then Lord Chamberlaine *his Seruants*"; all the title pages of the folio plays similarly acknowledge when and by which company the dramas were originally staged, and after each play Jonson lists the individual actors who performed it.[99] In preparing *Sejanus* for inclusion within the folio, Jonson also cut the quarto's epistle "To the Readers" and most of the marginal annotations; as John Jowett comments, "In this normalized text the theatrical work begins to re-emerge."[100]

Certainly the construction of authorial propriety which Jonson foregrounds in his quartos is still an issue in the folio. Jonson omits entirely from the book the civic pageants he wrote, as well as all of the collaborative plays he had churned out in the 1590s; and he further erases the contributions of his collaborator from the text of *Sejanus* by not even mentioning in the folio that the play originally had a co-author.[101] Moreover, as James K. Bracken has observed, Jonson's right to republish in his folio the works which had previously been printed was dubious: the texts had become the property of the stationers who had published them, and "several of the works were no longer even the property of the publishers to whom Jonson had originally sold them."[102] Many of the texts appearing in Jonson's folio were thus doubly abstracted from their original status as commodities which had been collaboratively produced, first in the playhouse as staged dramas and then in the printing house as published quartos; the act of collecting his texts, of arranging and displaying them, removes them from their earlier contexts of use-value (both as plays and as printed books) and thus exhibits Jonson's proprietary identity as a collector. Nonetheless, while Jonson asserts his authorial propriety in the very republication of these works in the folio, he also pursues a different agenda of self-fashioning through the presentation of his texts in their new format, constructing an identity that is conceived less as a challenge to the proprietary claims of theater companies, aristocratic patrons, or stationers than as a revised account of Jonson's own history as a writer. Through the folio, Jonson constructs and asserts his authorial ownership not only of his texts, but also of his own history.

The Latin tags inscribed on the title page of the folio provide insight into Jonson's conception of the artistic principles embodied by the book. The motto beneath the title—"*neque, me ut miretur turba, laboro: Contentus paucis lectoribus*" ("I do not work so that the crowd admires me: I am satisfied with a few readers")—emphasizes Jonson's lofty disdain for popular approval. This sentiment is surmounted by the inscribed frieze which stresses that the rarefied art contained by the book is rooted in the skill of editorial arrangement: "SI[N]GVLA QVAEQV[E] LOCVM TENEANT S[O]RTITA DECEN[T]ER" ("Let each particular variety hold the place properly allotted it").[103] This latter slogan evokes the humanist notebook method, the culturally authoritative ability to choose texts as a reader and writer. As Timothy Murray observes, "Neither comedy, tragedy, poetry, nor poetic theory is extolled explicitly by this motto. Issues intrinsic to classical dramatic form are here supplanted by contemporary philosophical notions of selection, placement, and arrangement. The folio advertises itself as an exemplum of the *ars inveniendi*."[104] Jonson thus extends the collecting practices associated with the humanist notebook method to his own material practice as the editor of his *Workes*.

The title page mottos' characterization of Jonson's folio as an entity which is both intended for an exclusive audience and governed by skilled placement is reinforced by other aspects of the editorial apparatus which shape the reader's experience of the book. Following the title page is a table of contents for the volume, "The Catalogue" (see Figure 9). Most of the Catalogue is comprised of two columns of names: the titles of the nine plays included in the folio and the *Epigrammes* appear in the left-hand column, while directly in line with the appropriate titles, the names of the dedicatees of each item are listed in the right-hand column. The Catalogue then concludes with five undedicated items—*The Forrest*, Entertaynments, Panegyre, Masques, and Barriers—which are presented in a single, centered column, suggesting "the apex of a hierarchy of genres."[105] The *Oxford English Dictionary* distinguishes the original definition of "catalogue" as "a list, register, or complete enumeration" from a later sense of the term as an itemization marked "by systematic or methodical arrangement, alphabetical or other order, and often by the addition of brief particulars, descriptive, or aiding identification." Although the Oxford English Dictionary cites Pepys's 1667 reference to his "Catalogue of books" as the earliest use of this latter meaning,[106] I would suggest that Jonson's folio Catalogue is an example of this more rigorous, contextualizing inventory. The dedicatees in the Catalogue appear in a socially ascending order, beginning with William Camden and concluding with the Earl of Pembroke, placing the literary works they accompany in a social trajectory rather than simply a chronological or generic ranking. As Richmond Barbour comments, the Catalogue "at once historicizes and canonizes the career" of its author by recording Jonson's "social dependencies."[107] The Catalogue thus schematically represents how, in the folio, Jonson assembles not only his own texts but a collection of people as well, situating his professional autobiography within a social context of increasing prestige.

Other features of the structure of the folio similarly reveal the editorial strategy behind Jonson's critical collection. The quality of the folio as an

The Catalogue.

Euery Man in his Humor,   To Mr. CAMBDEN.

Euery Man out of his Humor, To the INNES of COVRT.

Cynthias Reuells,   To the COVRT.

Poëtafter,   To Mr. RICH. MARTIN.

Seianus,   To ESME Lo. Aubigny.

The Foxe,   To the VNIVERSITIES.

The filent Woman,   To Sir FRAN. STVART.

The Alchemift,   To the Lady WROTH.

Catiline,   To the Earle of PEMBROK.

Epigrammes,   To the fame.

The Forreft,

Entertaynments,

Panegyre,

Mafques,

Barriers.

Figure 9. Ben Jonson, *The Workes of Beniamin Jonson* (London, 1616), "The Catalogue." Kenneth Spencer Research Library, University of Kansas.

autobiographical assemblage of both texts and people is enhanced by the fact that Jonson chose not to dedicate the volume in its entirety to a single individual. Although the plays and *Epigrammes* are, as the Catalogue suggests, separately dedicated, only Jonson's name is associated with—authorizes—the book as a whole, a fact underlined by the preliminary dedicatory poems which praise Jonson. The effect of the opening material is, in Baudrillard's words, to construct Jonson as the "ultimate signified" of the folio.[108] The selection and presentation of the individual texts work to the same end, shaping the biographical narrative of a writer whose consistent genius has won him increasing acclaim and prestige. For example, Jonson craftily revised the first play in the folio, *Every Man In his Humour*, by setting it in London rather than Florence, dedicating it to the teacher and mentor of his youth, William Camden, and adding a Prologue in which Jonson proclaims the play "what other playes should be"[109]: in the absence of his earlier hackwork, by placing *Every Man In* at the beginning of the volume, Jonson leads his reader to understand that this play is *"the first" "of the fruits"* of his career[110] and creates the impression that from the beginning, he knew that London would be the setting for his mature comedies. In addition to the work he had written before 1598, Jonson also omits *The Case is Altered* and *Bartholomew Fair* from the folio. David Riggs observes,

By placing *Catiline* last in the folio ordering and keeping *Bartholomew Fair* out of print, Jonson superimposed a definitive and logical shape on his artistic development. The final transition from *The Alchemist* to *Catiline* takes him out of the native and into the classical tradition and marks his passage from the lesser genre of comedy to the greater one of tragedy; his career as a dramatic poet is now complete.[111]

The career path Jonson thus represents in the folio was, however, contrary to historical reality, for between *Catiline* (1611) and the publication of the folio, Jonson wrote *Bartholomew Fair* and began *The Devil Is an Ass*—in Riggs's words, "His investment in comedy, and in native literary traditions, had actually increased since the completion of *Catiline* in 1611."[112] By selecting—and selectively revising—his plays for inclusion in the folio, Jonson thus "minimized the discrepancies among the canonical works and created the impression that he had foreseen the course of his career from its very outset," retrospectively imposing "a striking unity" on a professional life that was, in actuality, much less coherent and unswerving than the folio suggests.[113] Moreover, by revising his dramas yet dating them from their original performances, Jonson further enhanced the illusion that the unity of his career was innate, rather than retrospectively imposed.

The inset collections of poetry, the aristocratic entertainments, and the masques which conclude the folio are integral to the authorial identity fabricated by the volume. Unlike the 1623 folio of Shakespeare's works, which contained only plays, Jonson's folio depicts a multifaceted career. Jonson's characterization of the *Epigrammes* as the most lofty of his achievements, "the ripest of my studies,"[114] is further underlined by their dedication to the highest ranking of Jonson's dedicatees, the Earl of Pembroke. While the *Epigrammes* are integrally related to the rest of the folio, the poems, both individually and as a group, nonetheless exhibit a strongly independent, artifactual character. Encompassing poems that are datable from 1595 to 1609, the *Epigrammes* chronicle Jonson's life as a poet of occasions.[115] Jonson had apparently considered publishing the *Epigrammes* several years before the folio appeared,[116] and he did not remove the verses, including the three introductory epigrams, which refer to the poems as "my book," an entity clearly not the folio itself.[117] The designation given on the title page of the collection in the folio—*Epigrammes. I. Booke*—similarly demarcates the poems as a separate, unified entity. This artifactual quality also characterizes the *Epigrammes* on the level of the individual poem. Epigrams were, traditionally, associated with physical objects, and Jonson refers to the contents of the *Epigrammes* as "pieces," a term which he habitually used to designate both fragments and complete art works.[118] This sense of epigrams as physical artifacts merges with the collector's desire to assemble people in Jonson's consistent representation of his epigrams as versified names. As Stanley Fish has argued, many of Jonson's epigrams of praise are strangely antirepresentational, presenting a community of admirable individuals whose names embody their virtuous essences: in the dedicatory epistle, Jonson tells the Earl of Pembroke that as dedicatee, he is "leading forth so many good and great names as my verses mention on the better part," and then later in a laudatory epigram, suggests that Pembroke's name makes Jonson's poetry redundant—"I do but name thee, Pembroke, and I find / It is an epigram on all mankind."[119] When Jonson does attempt to describe the named exemplars of his *Epigrammes*, he tends to depict them *as* physical objects, usually monumental architecture or statuary: thus Sir John Radcliffe is "like a column," while Sir Thomas Roe's "gathered self" is "round . . . and straight," a pillar of virtue which "stand[s] well to."[120] The individual epigrams thus seem to aspire to the condition of statues inscribed with names, further enhancing the artifactual quality of the verses. At the same time, though, this assemblage of objectlike poems finally adds up to the identity of Jonson, their writer/collector. Early poems about Camden and Jonson's dead children establish a biographical, chronological framework for the *Epigrammes* as a whole, while an increasing number of poems praising powerful members of the Pembroke faction in the latter half of the collection signals that "Jonson has firmly ensconced himself in a patronage network of rising power."[121] No longer occasional verse circulating in manuscript, removed from their contexts of use-value within an economy of patronage, the *Epigrammes* proclaim Jonson's participation in elite culture even as the collection reinscribes and exhibits that participation within the more democratic realm of print. Furthermore, as W. H. Herendeen observes, "all the dedicatees (including representatives from the Inns of Court, the universities, and the court) are absorbed into the *Epigrammes*":[122] the *Epigrammes* provide provenance for the dedicatees Jonson collects and displays in the Catalogue and dedicatory epistles of the folio. Thus the *Epigrammes*, a collection within a collection, embodies the editorial principles of the folio as a whole, constructing an inset narrative of Jonson's professional history as social ascent.

This arrangement of individual literary artifacts to suggest social advancement similarly marks the rest of the works in the folio. By placing *The Forrest*, the royal entertainments, and the masques at the conclusion of the volume, Jonson-the-editor encourages the reader to understand that Jonson-the-author has progressed from being a successful writer in the public theater to living as the favored companion of aristocratic patrons. *The Forrest*, another inset collection of verses, is the first undedicated item in the folio; the exclusive social coordinates of the collection do not require further legitimation. Whereas some poems in the *Epigrammes* are addressed to non-aristocrats, the speaker of *The Forrest* apparently consorts only with titled landowners: Jonson constructs himself as "an amateur poet attached to a noble household" who dabbles in love lyrics when not producing occasional verse for patrons like the newly powerful Pembroke and his family.[123]

The entertainments and masques are the capstone of the folio's shaping of Jonson's identity. It is true that Jonson does not entirely remove signs of his authorial propriety from these texts; the annotations of the masques still proclaim Jonson's mastery over aristocratic occasion, and, as Joseph Loewenstein points out, Jonson sometimes omits names of elite participants he had included in the masque quartos.[124] At the same time, though, where Jonson does alter his self-presentation in the masques, he seems primarily concerned to de-emphasize his authorial autonomy. Comparing the quarto and folio incarnations of Jonson's 1604 entertainment for James I, Douglas Brooks points out that "the title page of the folio version offers up a text that is considerably less proprietary—especially in terms of its printing and authorship"—than the quarto; moreover, Brooks notes, unlike the title pages for the plays, "none of the masques included in the folio has a separate title page nor any indication of authorship."[125] As the folio triumphantly concludes with *The Golden Age Restored*, a dramatization of the new authority of the Pembroke faction,[126] the book definitively removes Jonson from his earlier life among commoners and the scrum of the commercial theaters.

The Beniamin Jonson who has collected and catalogued his *Workes* thus emerges from the latter part of the folio not as a creature of print and protocapitalism, but as the darling of his society's most wealthy and powerful aristocrats. By assembling the folio, Jonson-the-editor (who lived as a member of Lord Aubigny's household)[127] fabricated a narrative which depicted Jonson-the-author as moving inexorably toward the transcendence of the very commercialized market relations which enabled the publication of the book itself. When his *Workes* appeared in 1616, Jonson's life merged with the fictive autobiography he had fashioned by collecting and cataloguing his own literary texts. The narrative of social ascent which the folio constructs became valorized when Jonson was awarded a royal pension in 1616; David Riggs suggests that "The imminent publication of the 1616 folio helped to justify, perhaps even to motivate, James's decision to make [Jonson] his unofficial poet laureate."[128] Thus while the authorial identity which the folio created was, in many ways, a fiction, it was a fiction that had the power to shape reality.

"Thy BOOKE shall be thy Tombe": Jonson's Folio and the Death of the Collector

Upon the publication of his folio, Jonson assumed the authorial persona of the courtly writer which he had shaped as the culminating subject position of his autobiographical collection. For nine years after *The Devil Is An Ass* was performed in 1616, Jonson did not write another play for the public theater. He also ceased to publish his texts: neither *The Devil Is An Ass* nor *Bartholomew Fair* was printed until the 1630s, and Jonson similarly did not commercially publish any of his later masques until *Love's Triumph through Callipolis* appeared in print in 1630.[129] Likewise, although Jonson wrote verse for private circulation in manuscript, no more collections of his poetry were published during his lifetime.[130] When Jonson did return to the commercial stage and the printing house after the death of King James, it seems likely that he did so out of financial need, since both his health and his popularity at court were in decline.[131] As Richard Dutton remarks, the folio thus stands as "an equivocal milepost" in Jonson's career, for rather than ushering in a period during which Jonson further exploited the self-fashioning possibilities of print authorship, the *Workes* served as a threshold of identity from which Jonson instead embraced a traditional mode of authorship legitimated by patrons and scribal communities: "having so resoundingly identified himself with the emerging print culture, he now effectively abandoned it in favour of the private circulation of what he wrote, the hallmark of the courtly amateur."[132]

Jonson's retreat to a form of authorship which supported and was supported by a hereditary elite was paralleled by his assemblage of a literary lineage, the Tribe of Ben. In a society in which genealogy and identity were still closely allied, Jonson was, as both son and father, a victim of failed biological paternity: the death of his own genteel, educated father left him at the mercy of his bricklaying stepfather, and all four of Jonson's legitimate offspring died as young children.[133] As a medium of self-fashioning, the collection in early modern England could serve as an alternative to lineage; rather than accepting his identity as determined by membership in kin groups, the collector could become a self-made man whose accumulation of objects allowed him to construct his subjectivity—and social authority—on a nonbiological basis. Like contemporary nouveaux riches, however, who converted the economic power they had gained through trade or commerce into the socially prestigious signs of hereditary wealth (landed estates, forged genealogies, dubious armorial bearings), Jonson used his folio collection as the material basis for constructing a neoconservative identity as a patriarch. The Tribe of Ben was a London-based, all-male literary coterie comprised of Jonson and a band of younger admirers, including Richard Brome, Thomas Carew, Lucius Cary, William Cartwright, William Cavendish, Kenelm Digby, Sidney Godolphin, Robert Herrick, James Howell, Thomas Killigrew, Richard Lovelace, Shakerley Marmion, Jasper Mayne, Thomas Nabbes, Thomas Randolph, Joseph Rutter, John Suckling, and Edmund Waller. By the early 1620s, the group was meeting, eating, and drinking together, most famously in the Apollo Room of the Devil and St. Dunstan Tavern, where the members were governed by Jonson's code of behavior, the *Leges Convivales*, which was engraved in gold letters on a marble tablet over the mantlepiece.[134] The group described itself in metaphors of biological kinship: Jonson was the "father" of his "Tribe" of adoring "sons."

Thus after 1616, Jonson strove to construct subject positions for himself which were allied with genealogical succession: he served a hereditary elite and became the self-styled patriarch of a literary dynasty. Like Sir

Francis Bacon, Jonson transformed his activities as a collector into a kind of paternity, simultaneously upholding and undermining the value traditionally accorded patriarchal descent. Jonson was able to exploit modes of authority rooted in patrilineage because his folio proved to be such a culturally powerful means of self-fashioning, allowing him to rise above the circumstances of his own birth and his failure as a biological father. However, collections and collectors exist reciprocally; a collection is not simply the product but also the *producer* of its collector, and Jonson's printed folio, as a physically extant collection, continued to construct Jonson's identity within early modern English culture. Baudrillard suggests that a collection transcends the death of its collector: "The man who collects things may already be dead, yet he manages literally to outlive himself through his collection, which, originating within this life, recapitulates him indefinitely beyond the point of death."[135] On this basis, early modern collectors were concerned to guarantee the survival of their collections after they died. But the merging of the collection and the collector's identity also means that the completion of a collection "in effect denote[s] the death of the subject."[136] Like print, though, the cultural meaning of the collection is not predetermined but socially constructed, and we may observe how these dynamics evolved by examining the cultural status of Jonson's folio during his lifetime.

Jonson's folio had appeared in print when Jonson was only forty-three years old, but to Jonson's contemporaries it implied closure, the end rather than the midpoint of his career. The status of an edition of works as a complete collection, translated into the self-contained, finite materiality of the printed book, encouraged readers to perceive such a volume as a posthumous monument, and Arthur Marotti points out that in the seventeenth century, "collected editions of living authors" were anomalous.[137] Jonson exploited the self-fashioning possibilities of the collected edition in his folio, but seems not to have anticipated its signifying power as an apparently *complete* collection of artifacts. Jonson's attempts after 1616 to revise his identity could not supplant the continuing material presence and representational power of his *Workes*. As a self-fashioning subject, Jonson fell victim to his own earlier project of authorial collecting.

As Jonson outlived the publication of his *Workes*, his career after 1616 came to be perceived as belated, an affront to the self monumentalized in the folio. Jonson had often worried that his chosen medium of self-assertion, the printed book, was physically too fragile a medium to ensure the survival of Jonson's textual identity, and like collectors who feared the dissipation of their collections after their deaths, Jonson mordantly envisioned his texts being disintegrated and used as food wrappers or toilet paper.[138] Ironically, though, Jonson's printed folio became more real than its creator, for, as Jennifer Brady observes, "By the last decade of Jonson's life, the Folio had gained a canonical life independent of its author and maker."[139] Contemporaries yearned to remedy the disjunction between the authorial identity embodied in the collected texts of Jonson's book and the life of the man himself, a man who was increasingly, embarrassingly, out of favor as a writer. A poem written in 1629 commands,

> Die, Johnson: crosse not our Religion so,
> As to bee thought immortall. Lett us know
> Thou art a Man. Thy workes make us mistake
> Thy person; and thy great Creations make
> Vs idol thee, and 'cause wee see thee doe
> Eternall things, thinke Thee eternall too.
> . . . .
> Die: seemes it not enough, thy Writing's date
> Is endlesse, but thine owne prolonged Fate
> Must equall it? For shame, engrosse not Age,
> But now, thy fifth Act's ended leave the stage,
> And lett us clappe.[140]

While he was alive, Jonson's adopted "sons" likewise impatiently viewed the authority of the folio as superior to the authority of their ageing flesh-and-blood "father," and members of his Tribe chided Jonson when he tried to champion his post-folio texts. In one poem, Carew scolds Jonson for the "immodest rage" he had expressed in the ode "Come, leave the loathed stage," explaining bluntly that *The New Inn* had failed, in part, because "Thy comique Muse from the exalted line / Toucht by thy Alchymist, doth since decline / From that her Zenith"; after this dressing down, Carew comforts Jonson that, by contrast, "Thy labour'd workes shall live."[141] Another poem on the same topic similarly counsels Jonson to sheath his angry pen and instead think about how *Catiline* and

> The other workes, rais'd by thy skillfull hand,
> pittying the Worlds old wonders, they shall stand
> As Monuments of thee, more firme, amids
> all enuies blasts, then *AEgypts Pyramids*.[142]

As mentioned earlier, the difficulty of guaranteeing the posthumous survival of a collection was an issue which an early modern collector would regard with great anxiety, as he needed to ensure that after he died his collection—and thus his identity—would remain intact. By founding a coterie of "sons" on the strength of the identity he had fashioned in his folio, Jonson used his printed collection to gather together people who would further enhance his social authority and who, as his "heirs," would perpetuate his fame as their legacy after Jonson's death. While Jonson was still alive, however, his "sons" championed the authorial selfhood constructed by the folio in the face of any new form of identity Jonson might try to develop. Jonson had assembled a group of men who were concerned to safeguard Jonson's status as the kind of "father" from whom they could inherit desirable cultural capital—and the Father Ben the members of the Tribe wished to acknowledge was the Beniamin Jonson constructed by the folio. Just as Elias Ashmole jealously insisted that the Tradescant collection must remain exactly as it had been represented in the *Musaeum Tradescantianum*, so the Sons of Ben, the would-be inheritors of their father's collection, maintained that Jonson's identity should not diverge from its embodiment in the folio. As Henry Coventry shrewdly observed in his elegy on Jonson,

... th'art requited ill, to have thy herse,
Stain'd by prophaner *Parricides* in verse;
Who make mortality, a guilt, and scould,
Meerely because Thou'dst offer to be old.[143]

Not surprisingly, when Jonson finally did show the good grace to die in 1637, many of the elegies written to mourn his passing portrayed his career as coextensive with the 1616 folio. Sidney Godolphin declared, "Heere lies BEN : IOHNSON, every *Age* will looke / With *sorrow* heere, with *wonder* on *his* BOOKE,"[144] while John Ford advised that if one could not learn enough about the author from Jonson's lengthy entry in the *"Booke of Fame,"* "Survey *him* in *his* WORKES, and know *him* there."[145] John Rutter acknowledged the self-serving motives of such adulation of Jonson as author of the folio:

But *thou* art gon, and *we* like greedy Heires,
That snatch the fruit of their dead Fathers cares,
Begin t'enquire what *meanes thou* left'st behind
For *us* pretended Heires unto *thy* mind.
And *my-selfe* not the latest 'gan to looke
And found the Inventory in *thy* Booke.[146]

Thus Jonson's self-fashioning collection ultimately took on a life of its own: long before his died, Jonson's *Workes* came to embody the only authorial identity that his culture was willing to attribute to him. Henry King's elegy explained what Jonson apparently could not foresee—that rather than wrapping fish, the paper of his 1616 folio would come to encompass Jonson himself:

Thus in what low *earth*, or neglected *roome*,
So ere *thou* sleepst, *thy* BOOKE shall be *thy Tombe*,
Thou wilt goe downe a *happie Coarse*, bestrew'd,
With *thine* own *Flowres* and feele *thy selfe* renew'd,
Whilst *thy immortall*, never with'ring *Bayes*
Shall yearely flourish in *thy Readers* praise.
And when more *spreading Titles* are forgot,
Or, spight of all their *Lead* and *Seare-cloth*, rot;
Thou *wrapt* and *shrin'd* in *thine* owne *sheets* wilt lye
A *Relique* fam'd by all *Posteritie*.[147]

The pages of the folio became Jonson's shroud, culturally smothering any further attempts at self-fashioning. Monumentalized by the literary artifacts he had assembled in the folio, Jonson's skill as an editor/collector killed his own identity into art two decades before he actually died. The men comprising the Tribe of Ben would acknowledge as their "father" only the Beniamin Jonson who had created the magisterial *Workes*, and they edited Jonson's existence, both before and after his death, to reconcile it with the authorial self Jonson had so powerfully constructed in his folio. Thus after 1616, Jonson's collection and the identity it embodied were preserved by his "sons"—but at the expense of nullifying part of Jonson's life itself.

"Piece by Piece": Robert Herrick's Hesperides

Robert Herrick's volume of poetry, *Hesperides*, provides another example of how a seventeenth-century writer could combine practices of collecting with the technology of the printed book to construct a new mode of authorial identity. A member of a well-to-do family of London goldsmiths, educated at Cambridge and "adopted" as one of Jonson's "sons," Herrick initially exhibited his poetry in the genteel form of manuscript circulation. Alastair Fowler suggests that "to judge by numbers of early manuscripts, he was better known than Carew or Marvell," and in 1625 Herrick was ranked as a poet of the stature of Drayton and Jonson.[148] Herrick left the fleshpots and elite scribal communities of London in 1630, however, to take up the position of vicar in the remote Devonshire community of Dean Prior. As a royalist and a Laudian cleric, Herrick was forced to return to London in 1647, having been ejected from his living, and he was not able to return to Dean Prior until 1660.[149] It was during this period of dislocation and civil war that the fifty-seven-year-old Herrick saw fit to publish the book *Hesperides*, a volume which acknowledges, yet also diverges from, the model of authorship constructed in Jonson's folio. In *Hesperides*, I argue, we encounter a subjectivity represented as a collection of discrete, artifactual moments of experience—the self as curiosity cabinet. By textualizing this identity in a printed book, Herrick assumed the roles of both collector and cataloguer of his own identity, recording the varied artifacts which, taken together, comprise a natural history of Robert Herrick.

With the publication of *Hesperides* in 1648, Herrick became "the only Renaissance poet who gathered together the work of his lifetime into one polished, self-presented and self-presenting volume."[150] *Hesperides* consists of 1,402 poems, most of them very brief. They are written in a bewildering variety of modes and genres: the book includes pastorals, georgics, odes, hymns, an eclogue, dialogues, epithalamia, a country house poem, and a panoply of epigrams.[151] In *Hesperides*, what are now Herrick's frequently anthologized lyrics about beautiful women and flowers, such as "*To the Virgins, to make much of Time*" and "Corinna's *going a Maying*," jostle incongruously with brief glimpses of sordid members of the lower social orders—"Batt he gets children, not for love to reare 'em; / But out of hope his wife might die to beare 'em"—and versified aphorisms that seem lifted straight from a commonplace book—"To safe-guard Man from wrongs, there nothing must / Be truer to him, then a wise Distrust."[152] Moreover, as Leah Marcus has observed, in *Hesperides* the heterogeneity of Herrick's poems is emphasized by the volume's typography and the varying lengths and shapes of the poems.[153] Like the objects of a curiosity cabinet which have been displayed to maximize their quality of "wonder," the poems comprising Herrick's book seem arranged to defy categories of assessment.

Faced by the kaleidoscopic variety of *Hesperides*, scholars continue to debate how we should interpret Herrick's work. Some critics have attempted to refute T. S. Eliot's description of *Hesperides* as lacking a "continuous conscious purpose"[154] by insisting that the poems in their entirety constitute a narrative. In two influential articles published in the early 1970s, John L. Kimmey argued that Herrick's book is unified by a "fictive character" who progressively ages and finally dies.[155] More recently, Ann Baynes Coiro has similarly found in *Hesperides* an "extraordinary sense of sustained narrative," but she combines a focus on genre with a New Historicist emphasis on Herrick's political ideology to argue that we should interpret *Hesperides* as an "epigram book" structured by a "fictive autobiography" of a persona increasingly disillusioned and alienated by the trauma of the Civil War.[156]

These characterizations of *Hesperides* as a narrative have been cogently questioned from several perspectives. Randall Ingram points out that in a significant number of verses, Herrick invites readers to approach his poems selectively, rather than treat his book as a unified whole which must be read front to back. While Herrick does sometimes seem to hope that his audience will read "my Booke unto the end," he also accepts the fact that some readers will "light" on individual poems (7.1), and at times Herrick even encourages such a piecemeal approach to *Hesperides*, as when he tells Joseph Hall, Bishop of Exeter, that if, "to sanctifie my Muse / One onely Poem out of all you'l chuse; / And mark it for a Rapture nobly writ, / 'Tis Good Confirm'd; for you have Bishop't it" (64.2.7–10). Like the poet's own fondness for *sententiae* and translated gobbets of classical verse, Ingram suggests, Herrick's poems to selective readers demonstrate the continued influence of the notebook method in seventeenth-century English literary culture, and Ingram argues that instead of reducing the complexity of *Hesperides* to a single, overarching narrative, we should recognize that the book is "multiply coherent, permitting multiple readers to participate in the making of multiple patterns."[157] Ingram's argument dovetails with Alastair Fowler's reading of *Hesperides* as a silva, "a collection type characterized by apparent spontaneity and random variety."[158] Like the notebook method, the early modern silva was a product of humanism, a classical literary genre which was revived as collections and collecting assumed new cultural importance in Western Europe.[159] Similarly analyzing the structure of Herrick's book as non-narrative, Robert B. Hinman has related the subject matter and structure of *Hesperides* to the precepts and practice of Baconian natural history. Hinman notes that "close observation, like that of the empiricists, provides the often minute and sometimes unpalatable data of Herrick's world," and he argues that Herrick presents this "data" in a book which is "the product of an obviously creative intellect, yet . . . appears to be a miscellaneous gathering of observations made about phenomena," a book which is "analogous to the universal natural history Bacon desired."[160]

Ingram, Fowler, and Hinman thus helpfully insist on the fundamental discontinuities of Herrick's book. They are not as successful, though, in illuminating how the fragmentary structure of *Hesperides* conveys such a strong sense of Herrick's identity. If the diverse contents of *Hesperides* finally cannot be reduced to a narrative, how does the book seem to embody its author? The critics who have sought to find a narrative in *Hesperides* have responded to what Eliot called the "unifying personality" which imbues the book.[161] Appropriating Eliot's terms, I would argue that this "unifying personality" *is* the "continuous conscious purpose" underwriting the book: Herrick's book functions as a collection through which Herrick constructs and represents his own identity. But the self which Herrick creates and displays in *Hesperides*, unlike the identity Jonson created in his folio, does not take narrative form. Patricia Fumerton has suggested that in early modern England, elite selfhood was rooted in "its experience of the fragmentary, peripheral, and ornamental,"[162] and I would argue that Herrick's poems, taken in their entirety, depict such a mode of subjectivity. Analyzing *Hesperides* as a textualized museum of the self thus allows us to understand how Herrick's identity emerges from a wildly varied, non-narrative group of discrete poems.

Printed as an octavo volume, *Hesperides* does not embody Herrick's authorial aspirations in the charged shape of a folio, but the book's subtitle, *"OR, THE WORKS BOTH HUMANE & DIVINE OF ROBERT HERRICK Esq.,"* links it, unlike the posthumously published editions of Donne or Herbert, with the claims of Jonson's *Workes*. The collection is divided, as the volume's subtitle indicates, into a body of secular verse followed by a grouping of sacred poetry, the latter of which Herrick names on a separate title page as *"HIS NOBLE NUMBERS: OR, HIS PIOUS PIECES."*[163] Like the *Musaeum Tradescantianum*, which divides the multifarious contents of Tradescant's Ark into the "Artificiall" and the "Naturall," Herrick categorizes the items which comprise his subjectivity as either man-made or divinely inspired.

Initially, we might feel that Herrick effaces his own propriety and agency from *Hesperides* by emphasizing the effect of the royal family on his poetry.[164] As we turn over the main title page of the book, the iconic crown it depicts is replaced by a versified compliment to the Crown, a dedicatory poem to the Prince of Wales. Herrick concludes his poem to Prince Charles by exulting, "Full is my Book of Glories; but all These / By You become *Immortall Substances*" (3.10–11). The validity of this statement is immediately undercut, however, by the list of errata, located on the opposite page, which emphasizes Herrick's authorial concern for his text.[165] Apparently Herrick, like Jonson, was involved in the actual production of his collected works, for collation of copies of the text reveals that Herrick was fine-tuning and correcting *Hesperides* as it was being printed.[166] Mistakes that escaped his proofreading are enumerated in the errata, prefaced by a brief poem in which the poet asks the reader to blame the printer for the mistakes, since Herrick *"gave him forth good Grain, though he mistook / The Seed; so sow'd these Tares throughout my Book"* (4). As Marcus comments, Herrick's "insistence on surveillance over the book and the image of him it communicates" is unusual for a poet of his era.[167] Rather than the influence of Prince Charles, Herrick continually insists that it is the

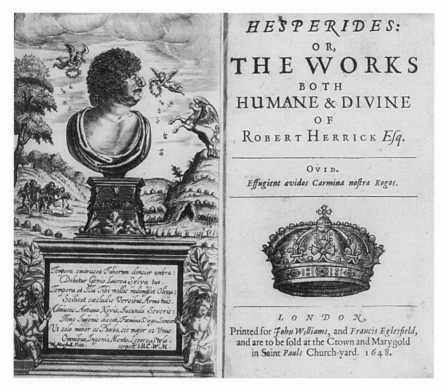

Figure 10. Robert Herrick, *Hesperides* (London, 1648), frontispiece and title page. Photo courtesy of the Newberry Library, Chicago.

poet/collector who has shaped the artifact which he repeatedly calls "*my* Book."

In claiming ownership of *Hesperides* and all its component verses, Herrick puts himself quite literally in the reader's face, creating a more overtly obtrusive authorial presence than Jonson constructed in his 1616 folio. Like the title page and list of errata, the engraved frontispiece of *Hesperides* leads us to associate the book with the identity of the poems' author. Prominently displayed within the frontispiece is a bust, presumably of Herrick himself, which is depicted in profile so it seems to gaze at the main title page of *Hesperides* (see Figure 10). Located in the midst of a rural landscape rife with mythological references to poetic inspiration (Pegasus, Mount Parnassus, the Spring of Helicon) and flanked by hovering putti laden with floral garlands, the bust stands on an ornate plinth; the plinth itself rests upon a tomb which has been inscribed with a Latin verse that

speaks of a poet who deserves laureate status.[168] As Marcus observes, when
Herrick published *Hesperides*, "Frontispiece portraits were usually memorial in function," and thus "if a reader encountered a frontispiece portrait
attached to a volume of poetry, he or she could be reasonably certain that its
author was defunct."[169] Under these conditions, the depiction of Herrick as
a bust perched on a tomb both confirms and displaces the writer's identity;
as Marcus argues, in a seventeenth-century volume containing a frontispiece portrait, "The poet is no longer to be found in the corrupted physical body memorialized as it had been in life through the portrait, but can be
located instead in the printed words that constitute the less ephemeral body
of the book."[170] Herrick strengthens this association of the collected edition
with the death of its author by presenting himself as a funerary monument
in the frontispiece of *Hesperides*, emphasizing that his subjectivity is now
embodied by his book. As with Jonson's folio, the completed collection
represents the demise of the collector, though Herrick seems to have inten-
tionally embraced this dynamic.

Herrick's representation of his book as his authorial self is continued
in the versified catalogue with which the body of the collection begins.
Whereas Jonson's folio "Catalogue," which enumerates his dedicatees as
well as his works, outlines a trajectory of social advancement, Herrick's
"The Argument of his Book" presents an inventory that cannot be contained
within a linear narrative:

I sing of *Brooks*, of *Blossomes*, *Birds*, and *Bowers*:
Of *April*, *May*, of *June*, and *July*-Flowers.
I sing of *May-poles*, *Hock-carts*, *Wassails*, *Wakes*,
Of *Bride-grooms*, *Brides*, and of their *Bridall-cakes*.
I write of *Youth*, of *Love*, and have Accesse
By these, to sing of cleanly-*Wantonnesse*.
I sing of *Dewes*, of *Raines*, and piece by piece
Of *Balme*, of *Oyle*, of *Spice*, and *Amber-Greece*.
I sing of *Times trans-shifting*; and I write
How *Roses* first came *Red*, and *Lilies White*.
I write of *Groves*, of *Twilights*, and I sing
The Court of *Mab*, and of the *Fairie-King*.
I write of *Hell*; I sing (and ever shall)
Of *Heaven*, and hope to have it after all. (5.1)

While the title of the poem emphasizes the status of *Hesperides* as one
physical entity that belongs to its author—*"The Argument of his Book"*—the
poem itself depicts both the contents of that book and the subjectivity of its
creator as radically discontinuous. Immediately, one is struck by the author-

ial self-referentiality of the poem, achieved through the emphatic repetition of the pronoun "I": seven lines, including the first, begin with "I," and the monosyllable is reiterated within several lines as well, for a total of ten appearances in only fourteen lines. This unsubtle focus on the poet as the speaking subject of his book is complicated, however, by the fact that the *"Argument"* depicts Herrick as alternating between two modes of poetic discourse, that which "I sing" and that which "I write": Herrick's "I" is thus split into different personae, the singer and the writer.[171] The *propositio* "I sing" acts as a generic marker of epic, but "I write" suggests epigram: the poet intends his book to combine the cosmic scope of epic with the brief specificity of epigram and its association with physical objects.[172]

This tension between epic expansiveness and epigrammatic particularity is further accentuated by the paratactic inventory of topics which the speaker promises to cover in his book. The poet's determination to transform the vastness of nature (brooks, blossoms, birds) and human experience (maypoles, wassails, wakes) into discrete, lapidary forms is also evidenced by his richly ambiguous declaration, "I sing of *Dewes*, of *Raines*, and piece by piece / Of *Balme*, of *Oyle*, of *Spice*, and *Amber-Greece*." As in Jonson's writing, the term "piece" in Herrick's poetic vocabulary can refer both to a fragment and to a complete art work. Here, the multivalence of the word "piece" suspends the reader in an evocative confusion: "piece by piece," whether meaning "fragment by fragment" or "work by work," could refer to the many poems in *Hesperides* which, one after another, describe precious unguents and perfumes; but the sentence also suggests that the speaker "sings" about *pieces* of the exotic substances he enumerates, transforming liquids like balm and oil into solidified, isolated artifacts—into collectible objects. Herrick's impulse to metamorphose poetic and physical material into discrete "pieces" also inflects the prosodic form of his *"Argument."* The poem is a sonnet of sorts, being fourteen lines long and thematically divided so as to suggest both the Italian and English sonnet forms. The first eight lines list natural phenomena and human festivals which have positive connotations, while the more troubling references to mutability, darkness, the fairies (traditionally viewed as evil spirits)[173] and hell appear in the sestet/quatrain and concluding couplet, before the poem concludes hopefully by referring to *"Heaven."* The poem does not adhere to any conventional sonnet rhyme-scheme, however, as it is written entirely in couplets, each of which ends with a different rhyme. As Hinman suggests, "in fracturing the sonnet's customary mould," Herrick "emphasizes the separateness, the discreteness of things and moments perceived, even when the perceptions are organized."[174] The very structure of the *"Argument"* thus reflects the nature of *Hesperides* as an amalgamation of isolated artifacts.

The nature of the aesthetic of "thingness" which informs *Hesperides* is strikingly revealed in several poems about collectors. Madam Ursly, for example, transforms herself into an ambulatory curiosity cabinet:

For ropes of pearle, first Madam *Ursly* showes
A chaine of Cornes, pickt from her eares and toes:
Then, next, to match *Tradescant's* curious shels,
Nailes from her fingers mew'd, she shewes: what els?
Why then (forsooth) a Carcanet is shown
Of teeth, as deaf as nuts, and all her own. (232.4)

Madam Ursly creates a new identity by turning herself into the raw materials of her own collection, harvesting and arranging the discrete objects produced by her body to form decorative art works with which she adorns herself. The poem's reference to the "curious shels" gathered and displayed within Tradescant's Ark allies Madam Ursly's mode of self-fashioning with the most famous collection of rarities in England: like the Tradescants—and the author of *Hesperides*—Madam Ursly creates herself "piece by piece." Similarly, in a trilogy of poems Herrick depicts the diminutive fairy king, Oberon, as a virtuoso collector. In "Oberons *Palace*," Herrick provides a guided tour of the monarch's grand home, which is full of wonder-inducing artifacts:

Throughout that *Brave Mosaick* yard
Those Picks or Diamonds in the Card:
With peeps of Harts, of Club and Spade
Are here most neatly inter-laid.
Many a Counter, many a Die,
Half rotten, and without an eye,
Lies here abouts; and for to pave
The excellency of this Cave,
Squirrils and childrens teeth late shed,
Are neatly here enchequered
With brownest *Toadstones*, and the Gum
That shines upon the blewer Plum. (166, 47–58)

Herrick's description of Oberon's palace evokes the hodgepodge of rare objects exhibited in a curiosity cabinet. Like the Tradescants or Sir Thomas Browne, Oberon and his queen, Mab, have accumulated a collection of unusual artifacts which they display as part of their home's interior decor. Rather than trafficking in dairy products or human babies like the fairies of folklore,[175] Oberon and Mab participate in a trade in naturalia: the fairies' ornamental paving materials include "The nails faln off by Whit-flawes" and "those warts, / Which we to others (from our selves) / Sell, and brought hither by the Elves" (166, 59–62), while "The tempting Mole, stoln from the neck / Of the shie Virgin, seems to deck / The holy Entrance" (166, 63–65). Queen Mab's bedclothes are fashioned from "the Caule / That doth the Infants face enthrall, / When it is born" (167, 90–92), and the palace is festooned with

> . . . the blew skin
> Of shifted Snake: enfreez'd throughout
> With eyes of Peacocks Trains, & Trout-
> flies curious wings; and these among
> Those silver-pence, that cut the tongue
> Of the red infant, neatly hung. (166, 66–71)

In "Oberons *Palace*," Herrick depicts the fabric of the fairy palace as an artful exhibition of physical objects, transforming the fairies' traditional association with cleanliness and domestic order into an architecture of painstakingly arranged artifacts.[176]

Combined with a strong evocation of authorial presence, *Hesperides* in its entirety is characterized by an aesthetic that transforms all aspects of experience into collections of discrete *things*. As an assemblage of lapidary poems, the versified "particulars" of *Hesperides* are united only by each poem's relationship to its creator/collector. As Marcus observes, "The most obvious unifying feature of the collection is that on nearly every page we are made emphatically aware that it belongs to Herrick, the poet, its author."[177] The reiteration of authorial propriety on the title page of *Noble Numbers*— "*HIS NOBLE NUMBERS; OR, HIS PIOUS PIECES*"—typifies Herrick's construction of his relationship to *Hesperides* and the individual poems which comprise it. Likewise, the titles and bodies of Herrick's verses are full of tellingly superfluous possessives that establish Herrick as the owner of his poems, both individually and collectively: in "*When he would have his verses read*" (7.3), for example, he calls his poems "my Enchantments" and "these Lines of mine," while eleven poems share the same title, "*To his Booke.*" The authorial self-referentiality of the volume is further emphasized by the number of times Herrick names himself, either with third-person pronouns—twenty-four poems are entitled "*On Himselfe*" or "*Upon Himselfe*"—or with his surname, which appears twenty times.[178] Moreover, although they are not arranged to form a sustained narrative, some poems are overtly autobiographical: Herrick includes in his collection verses about his "*Discontents in Devon*" (19.3), speaks of "the *Golden-cheap-side*, where the earth / Of *Julia Herrick* [his mother] gave to me my Birth" (316, 15–16), and nervously approaches the grave of his father, who committed suicide when Herrick was an infant (27.1).[179] The autobiographical nature of *Hesperides* is also stressed by the frequency with which Herrick presents verses to his kin, friends, and members of his household. Unlike Jonson, who is concerned to depict the men and women he commemorates in his poetry as moral exemplars, the individuals whom Herrick includes within his book are notable primarily for their relationship to the proprietary poet. As many of Herrick's titles indicate, the relatives and companions displayed in *Hesperides* are "his": "*To his honoured kinsman Sir* William Soame" (131.1), "*Upon his kinswoman Mrs.* M. S." (257.1), "*To M.* Leonard Willan *his peculiar friend*" (298.6), "*To his maid* Prew" (151.3), "*Upon his Spaniell* Tracie" (302.1).

Like the mid-seventeenth-century English antiquarians who frantically collected funerary inscriptions within printed books to save them from an increasingly iconoclastic world, Herrick constructs his book as a superior site of commemoration, a cross between Noah's Ark and a reliquary which will eternally preserve the identities of those whom Herrick gathers within its bounds.[180] Herrick visually highlights the artifactual quality of his verses to the dead or soon-to-be-dead in his shaped poems. Appearing on the page as outlines of material objects, these poems assert that the physicality of a printed verse included within Herrick's book is superior to the funerary monument for which it substitutes. In "*His Poetrie his Pillar*," for example, each four-line stanza is shaped like a little column. The poet, anticipating his imminent death, asks, "How many lye forgot / In Vaults beneath? / And piece-meale rot / Without a fame in death?," answering his grim query by gesturing toward the superior monument he is constructing even as he writes:

5.   Behold this living stone,
        I reare for me,
        Ne'r to be thrown
     Downe, envious Time by thee.
6.   Pillars let some set up,
        (If so they please)
        Here is my hope,
     And my *Pyramides.* (85.1)

In the plethora of poems he writes about named friends and relatives, Herrick similarly uses his collection to transform people into objects over which Herrick exerts the author/collector's power of life and death. Herrick is keenly aware that he safeguards the people he assembles by turning them into artifacts and recontextualizing them within the physical confines of his book, and he thus often characterizes his poetic collection as a material object or space set apart from quotidian existence in which he physically places those whom he chooses to memorialize. Playing with the connotations of the title *Hesperides* as a garden of immortality[181] and the *silva* as a collection of poems, Herrick metaphorically turns *"his peculiar friend Sir* Edward Fish" into a tree as he transforms him into a poem:

Since for thy full deserts (with all the rest
Of these chaste spirits, that are here possest
Of Life eternall) Time has made Thee one,
For growth in this my rich Plantation. (152.4.1–4)

In another poem, *"his Honoured Kinsman, Sir* Richard Stone" becomes a statue so that Herrick may add him to his collection:

To this *white Temple* of my *Heroes,* here
Beset with stately Figures (every where)
Of such rare *Saint-ships,* who did here consume
Their lives in sweets, and left in death perfume.
Come thou *Brave man*! And bring with Thee a Stone
Unto thine own *Edification.*
High are These Statues here, besides no lesse
Strong then the Heavens for everlastingnesse. (185.3.1–8)

Herrick similarly transforms *"his deare Valentine, Mistresse* Margaret Falconbrige" into a precious stone so that she, too, can be added to Herrick's collection of poem-objects: "Now is your turne (my Dearest) to be set / A Jem in this eternall Coronet" (264.3).

The identity which emerges from the poems bespeaking Herrick's personal and social history must be understood as only one aspect of the multifaceted authorial self which Herrick constructs in his book. The subjectivity of the collector displayed within *Hesperides* also, for example, encompasses the many verses in which Herrick recounts his amorous adventures with "a thousand thousand" mistresses (62.1.11), a bevy of perfumed, pearly-toothed supermodels, among whom *"his* Julia" (138.1) is "prime of all" (15.3.3). Again, Herrick's amatory verse is marked by both the poet/speaker's self-referentiality and possessiveness—"his" and "my" regularly modify the word "mistresses" and the individual names of the women Herrick celebrates—and by his habit of breaking up large vistas into groups of objects which he then gathers within the confines of a poem. Herrick frequently depicts women in terms of their jewelry and clothing, and he ogles selected anatomical fragments of his favorite, Julia, devoting separate poems to her legs, hair, breasts, nipples, and lips. Like the epic cosmos Herrick sketches in his *"Argument,"* the female body in *Hesperides* is often presented as discrete physical artifacts:

How rich and pleasing thou my *Julia* art
In each thy dainty, and peculiar part!
First, for thy *Queen-ship* on thy head is set
Of flowers a sweet commingled Coronet:
About thy neck a Carkanet is bound,
Made of the *Rubie*, *Pearle* and *Diamond*:
A golden ring, that shines upon thy thumb:
About thy wrist, the rich *Dardanium*.
Between thy Breasts (then Doune of Swans more white)
There playes the *Saphire* with the *Chrysolite*.
No part besides must of thy selfe be known,
But by the *Topaz*, *Opal*, *Calcedon*. (30.1)

In this poem, Herrick presents a vast expanse of beauty—Julia's body—which he transforms into and displays as separate "parts." Rings, crowns, and necklaces reappear time and time again in Herrick's amatory poems; here, such jewelry encircles and demarcates various sections of Julia's body and thus visually fragments her. Herrick's transformation of Julia into a collection of precious stones is also enhanced by the stasis he verbally imposes upon the woman's body. As Herrick inventories Julia's "parts," only the jewels are granted active verbs by the poet—a golden ring "shines," as does a bracelet of "rich *Dardanium*," while a sapphire "playes" with chrysolite in Julia's cleavage. Through his use of syntax, Herrick depicts Julia as a kind of human Christmas tree, a motionless entity decorated by unseen hands. She plays no role in the process of her adornment: the coronet of flowers "is set" on her head, a necklace "is bound" around her neck by the poet. Like Margaret Falconbrige, whom Herrick converts into "A Jem" for safekeeping in his immortalizing book, Herrick transforms Julia into the enduring, nonhuman substance of beautiful stones. Julia becomes a conglomeration of bejewelled objects, a collection which Herrick, as the creator/owner of "my *Julia*," assembles and exhibits.[182]

The identity which Herrick fabricates in *Hesperides* is thus a cabinet of self-generated and self-generating curiosities, an assemblage of experiences and relationships conceived of and transformed into artifacts owned by the poet. In the frontispiece portrait of *Hesperides*, Herrick depicts himself as the posthumous author of his book, encouraging readers to regard *Hesperides* as the poet's remains, the swirling mosaic of a life represented as versified *copia*. The factual data of his family relationships and career are no more or less constitutive of Herrick's identity than his fantasy worlds populated by Oberon or Anthea, Perilla, and their gorgeous sisters. Aphorisms, often expressing positions diametrically opposed to each other, testify to Herrick's participation in literate notebook culture without committing him to one specific viewpoint. Friends and relatives, royalists and parliamentarians alike, become funerary monuments forever preserved within Herrick's book, testifying both to the poet's personal attachments and to his power, as an author/collector, to immortalize others. Taken as a whole, then, *Hesperides* is an autobiographical repository, a poetic archive of Herrick's life which encompasses his imaginings, his reading, and his observations about the things and people in the world around him. The author has selected the meaningful moments from his social, intellectual, and imaginative existence, turned them into discrete poems, and gathered them together as a textualized museum of the identity of Robert Herrick.

In 1648 Herrick was leading a marginal existence as an unemployed clergyman whose royalist and Laudian ideals were being forcibly eradicated from England. It is said that after he was ejected from his living at Dean Prior, Herrick "was subsisted by Charity, until the Restoration."[183] Socially and culturally abject, Herrick constructed his collection of poems to commemorate a life that had ended, in the hopes that the identity stripped from him by history would survive in artifactual form. Both exploiting and revising the dynamics of possessive individualism by which Jonson had prematurely memorialized himself, Herrick fabricated a new mode of selfhood, creating *Hesperides* as the everlasting incarnation of its collector/author. Although the parish register at Dean Prior records Herrick's burial in 1674, his grave is unmarked; a childless bachelor, Robert Herrick died leaving neither a funerary monument nor a family to perpetuate his identity.[184] Transforming himself into a collection, Herrick changed the material basis of the endurance of the self. By cataloguing the components of his subjectivity, Herrick fashioned a printed monument—an ark—of his authorial selfhood. More than 350 years after it was published, *Hesperides* continues to embody the complexities of the life and mind which created it. Herrick's book has, in fact, preserved him for posterity—piece by piece.

Epilogue: An Ornament to the Nation

When Peter Mundy entered John Tradescant's "Ark" in 1634 to gaze, spell-bound, at Tradescant's collection of taxidermy, minerals, coins, art work, and plants, he unknowingly crossed the threshold of modernity. Possessive individualism, the concept of the self-as-owner which would later come to dominate Western culture, emerged in England during the sixteenth and seventeenth centuries amidst a rapidly expanding world of physical objects. Shaped by the social, economic, and political conditions peculiar to the early modern period, collections of material things began to proliferate among the English, affording new opportunities for the construction and display of possessive identity. To understand early modern English modes of selfhood and social identity, I have demonstrated, we must consider how individuals and groups used collections of physical objects as sites of self-fashioning.

This study has argued that collecting was often used as a technology of social innovation in seventeenth-century England. Initially pursued as an elite cultural form, the collection was soon adopted—and adapted—by ambitious, middling sort men. Although the Tradescants began their careers as the hirelings of Stuart aristocrats, they capitalized on their employers' social connections and the nascent exploitation of the New World to construct new identities—and a livelihood—for themselves as collector/entrepreneurs. The Tradescants' urge to textualize their collection proved their downfall, however, when the creation and publication of the *Musaeum Tradescantianum* allowed another collector to claim possession of the contents of the Ark. In thus transforming his role from that of cataloguer to owner of the Tradescant collection, Elias Ashmole, the son of a saddler, gained a new foundation upon which to claim enhanced social authority. Knowing from this firsthand experience just how vulnerable an individual's collection was to posthumous predation, Ashmole created a museum to keep "his" collection intact, seeking to guarantee the perpetuation of his identity by entrusting it to the architectural and institutional stability of a custom-made building at Oxford University.

Although he was born with greater social cachet than Ashmole, the politically disappointed Sir Francis Bacon also turned to collecting as a means by which to improve his status. Bacon envisioned himself obtaining power and influence as a scientific mandarin who would oversee the collecting activities of a new bureaucracy. After his death, Bacon's blueprint for natural history research was amended to legitimate the self-consciously genteel collecting practices of virtuosos and the Royal Society.

Other fields of knowledge were also shaped by the new emphasis on artifacts and collecting. Chorographers and antiquarians like William Camden, Richard Carew, William Burton, and Sir William Dugdale functioned as collectors to create texts which portrayed the English landscape as a space filled with objects. While these authors gathered and displayed objects which symbolized landownership in genealogical terms, after the Civil War other writers such as Sir Thomas Browne and Robert Plot came increasingly to depict the countryside as an amalgam of *owned* objects, implicitly questioning the social authority of bloodlines in a polity which had endured regicide.

The interpenetration of concepts of text and artifact so characteristic of early modern collecting also gave rise to innovative literary forms. Exploiting the blurred boundary between writings and physical things, Ben Jonson and Robert Herrick combined an artifactual concept of the text with the technology of the printed book to create new modes of proprietary authorship for themselves. In his folio *Workes*, Jonson collected his literary texts to present them as one unified entity—and underestimated the cultural power this apparently complete collection would exert over the reception of his literary output after 1616. By gathering his poems together in the volume entitled *Hesperides*, Robert Herrick constructed a vision of the self as a collection of textualized moments of consciousness, creating a printed ark to preserve his multifaceted identity.

In many ways, the collecting practices which flourished during the seventeenth century reached their culmination in the immense collection of rarities amassed by Sir Hans Sloane (1660–1753). Despite his title (he was created a baronet in 1716) and his coat of arms (which he applied to register in 1726), Sloane, like so many of the collectors examined in this study, was a self-made man. Hans Sloane was born the youngest son of a Scottish family which had settled in Ireland, where his father worked as an agent of the estates owned by James Hamilton, first Viscount Clandeboye.[1] Throughout his adult life, Sloane displayed a great talent for acquiring large sums of money. Moving to England at the age of nineteen to pursue medical studies, Sloane embarked on what would prove to be a lucrative career as a fashionable London physician. Sloane's marriage also brought him financial benefits, as his wife inherited estates both from her father, a London alderman, and her first husband, a doctor who had emigrated to the West Indies.

In keeping with his interest in natural history, Sloane became a Fellow of the Royal Society in 1685, and would eventually serve as Secretary and then President of the organization. Sloane's activities as a collector began in 1687, when he travelled to Jamaica as the personal physician of the newly appointed governor, the Duke of Albemarle. Practicing the "everyday Baconian empiricism" which was the hallmark of the seventeenth-century virtuoso,[2] Sloane accumulated a diverse collection of natural history "Curiosities" during his fifteen months in Jamaica: "Plants, fruits, Corralls, Minerals, stones, Earth, shells, animals, Insects & c: collected by him with greate Judgement."[3] Commanding a hefty salary as Albemarle's physician, Sloane also used his time in Jamaica to acquire a large quantity of "Peruvian bark"—the source of quinine. He later transformed this botanical stockpile into a financial windfall by promoting the unconventional use of the drug for many ailments, both in his own practice as a physician and in the pages of the Royal Society's *Philosophical Transactions*.

Sloane's interests as a collector later became less rigorously focused, and he went on to acquire not only more natural history specimens, but also antiquities, ethnographic items, art works, books, and manuscripts. As his ambitions expanded and his pockets deepened, Sloane began to acquire entire collections assembled by others, including James Petiver's natural history collection (for which Sloane paid £4,000); botanical specimens accumulated by Nehemiah Grew; and the renowned herbarium of Leonard Plukenet. Upon his death in 1702, William Courten (also known as William Charleton) bequeathed his huge collection of curiosities, valued at £50,000, to Sloane on condition that Sloane honor several legacies and keep Courten's collection "intire."[4] As von Uffenbach marvelled when he visited Sloane's collection in 1710, "He has here the whole Charleton collection and many objects which Dr. Sloane brought from India [i.e., the West Indies] himself, while he is daily increasing them in England for vast sums of money."[5] By collecting collections, Sloane was able to amass nearly 80,000 artifacts in addition to a herbarium and library.[6] His collection was, in William Stukeley's opinion, "the greatest that ever was a private mans possession."[7]

Sloane's self-fashioning activities were similar to those of other early modern collectors. He diligently transformed the physical objects he accumulated into texts by creating catalogues of the items he acquired, sometimes inscribing on the objects themselves the information—the narrative—

which would comprise the catalogue entry.[8] In 1696 Sloane published his *Catalogus plantarum*, a Latin catalogue of the plants he had found in Jamaica. He also produced a two-volume *Natural History* of Jamaica. With his collection growing rampantly, however, Sloane faced many practical dilemmas which affected his relationship to the objects he gathered.

By commodifying the activity of collecting into a kind of cannibalism, buying up the lifetimes' work of other collectors, Sloane created a collection which ballooned to the limits of one individual's ability to possess it effectively. The sheer physical space required to accommodate all his objects necessitated that Sloane first acquire a house adjacent to his own in Bloomsbury, and later move his entire collection to an even larger manor house in Chelsea. And as the collection lost its original homogeneity and became more complicated and unwieldly, Sloane also had to employ assistants to help him care for and catalogue his objects. Moreover, his omnivorous consumption of other men's collections hampered Sloane's efforts to textualize his own identity as a collector: he complained that it took him so long to reorganize Petiver's messy collection that Sloane's work on the second volume of his *Natural History* was delayed for years. The fame of his collection brought other problems as well: a would-be robber tried to set fire to Sloane's Bloomsbury house in 1700; and even legitimate visitors could endanger precious artifacts, as when George Frideric Handel stained one of Sloane's valuable manuscripts by setting a buttered muffin on it. The greatest challenge Sloane faced, however, was how to devise a plan whereby he could ensure the survival of the collection beyond his own lifetime.

As we have seen, early modern collectors agonized over what should become of their collections after their deaths, and the problem was particularly acute for collectors like Sloane who died without a male heir. John Tradescant the elder left his collection to his namesake son; but in the absence of male offspring to whom he could entrust the Ark, John Tradescant the younger tried, unsuccessfully, to transfer the collection to a university, only to have it intercepted by Elias Ashmole. Like Ashmole, Sloane's own acquisitiveness had allowed him to see firsthand how the previous owner of a group of objects could become absorbed—dissolved—within another man's collection. Yet collections left to institutions rather than individuals did not necessarily receive sufficient care and attention either: although Sloane himself solicited donations to the Repository of the Royal Society,[9] the organization did not have adequate funds to staff the collection properly, and by 1710 the Repository had fallen into a state of disarray, the objects "covered with dust, filth and coal-smoke, and many of them

broken and utterly ruined."[10] Sloane had also given objects to the Ashmolean Museum, but had become disillusioned when its collections, too,
suffered from neglect after Ashmole's death.[11]

Collections of objects, I have argued in this study, could be used in the
early modern period to create collections of people. If Sloane wanted his
collection to survive him, he needed to entrust it to an even larger group of
individuals—and their financial resources—than were available at either a
university or a voluntary organization like the Royal Society. So Sir Hans
Sloane looked to the nation itself to become the custodian of his collection.
The nation, however, did not immediately recognize the utility of the new
role of collection keeper which Sloane hoped to foist upon it.

When the Prince of Wales visited Sloane's collection in 1748, he
praised it in suggestively nationalistic terms: "he express'd the great pleasure
it gave him to see so magnificent a collection in *England*, esteeming it an
ornament to the nation; and expressed his sentiments how much it must
conduce to the benefit of learning, and how great an honour will redound to
Britain, to have it established for publick use to the latest posterity."[12] In his
will, first written in 1739 and revised in subsequent codicils, Sloane ensured
that Britain would have the opportunity to buy his collection; and if the
nation refused to purchase it, the collection would be offered to foreign
academies of science or, as a last resort, to private buyers. Shortly after
Sloane died in 1753, his trustees, as instructed, offered to sell the collection to
the King for £20,000 (estimated as one-fifth to one-quarter of the collection's true market value). Despite the earlier royal effusions about the magnificence of Sloane's collection, however, the King said he could not afford
the price tag. The Sloane trustees next turned to Parliament, which was also
dubious that the nation could afford the "ornament" Sloane posthumously
wanted to bestow upon it. After negotiating with Sloane's trustees, however, Parliament decided "that it will be for the Honor and advantage of this
country to accept of Sir Hans Sloane's Legacy" for £20,000. As the MPs'
thoughts turned to collections, they further agreed that the nation should, at
long last, house the Cotton Library properly. (Sir Robert Cotton's library
had been bequeathed to the nation half a century earlier, but the collection
had been dumped into a dormitory in Westminster School in 1631, where,
"in great Confusion and Disorder," it still lay, coated in dust.[13]) In its new
collecting mood, Parliament also decided it should buy the Harleian manuscripts, now being offered to the nation at the discount price of £10,000.[14]
Reaffirming the early modern association between texts and collecting,
Parliament laid the foundation for the British Library at the same time as it
covetously regarded Sir Hans Sloane's curiosities.

During the parliamentary wrangling over this plan, the new amalgam of collections had become known as the "British Museum," and the British Museum Act took effect on 7 June 1753, with the collections of Sir Hans Sloane, Sir Robert Cotton, and the Harleys as the museum's foundational holdings. Money, however, was still a problem, and Parliament had to organize a national lottery to raise enough funds both to buy the Sloane and Harleian collections and to house and care for the new institution in its entirety. Despite rampant corruption, the lottery brought in £95,000. Located in Montagu House, very near Sloane's former residence in Bloomsbury, the British Museum opened in January 1759. Sir Hans Sloane's collection had become national property, its purchase reluctantly authorized by Parliament and paid for by the gambling British public. Amalgamated within one institution, the artifacts and texts of the Cotton, Harley, and Sloane collections were now owned by Great Britain. The early modern impulse to collect had been transformed to create a new social group: the nation.

In 1707 the Act of Union joining England and Scotland created the nation of Great Britain. Governmental fiat alone, however, could not forge a new British national identity; as Benedict Anderson insists, a nation must be imagined into existence, and he points to the novel and the newspaper as examples of innovative cultural forms which allowed people in eighteenth-century Britain to conceive of themselves as citizens of a nation, rather than as the subjects of a king.[15] According to Jürgen Habermas, this development of the eighteenth-century nation-state was accompanied by the emergence of civil society within a new "public sphere," the discursive space between the private realm and the government in which citizenship was experienced.[16] Building on these ideas, other scholars have emphasized the role of museums in creating ideologies of national identity and civic virtue. "Because the state is abstract and anonymous, it is especially in need of potent and tangible symbols of its powers and attributes," Carol Duncan and Alan Wallach observe, and they contrast the social relations structured by a royal collection to those embodied by a national museum:

A visitor to a princely collection might have admired the beauty of individual works, but his relationship to the collection was essentially an extension of his social relationship to the palace and its lord. The princely gallery spoke for and about the prince. . . . In the museum, the wealth of the collection is still a display of national wealth and is still meant to impress. But now the state, as an abstract entity, replaces the king as host. This change redefines the visitor. He is no longer the subordinate or a prince or lord. Now he is addressed as a citizen and therefore a shareholder in the state.[17]

According to this narrative, the national museum emerges logically from the elite collections of the absolutist era.[18] As my study has shown, however, the foundation of the British Museum occurred not simply as the inevitable, top-down imposition of an instrument of nationalism. Rooted in the seventeenth-century practices of virtuosos and middling-sort collectors, the British Museum instead originated within a tradition of non-princely collections—and, more specifically, from one individual's search for a haven of posthumous identity.

By transforming his cultural capital as a collector into an "ornament" of the British nation, Sir Hans Sloane participated in the realignment of the potentially subversive social force of the middling-sort collector with the interests of the state. As Sloane's collection of collections became national property, the forces of possessive individualism and capitalism combined with nationalism to create a new institution which constructed the visitor as a subject of the mercantilist state. The dynamics at work in Tradescant's Ark had been nationalized; the visitor to the new British Museum would view not simply the "wonderful" identity of an individual collector, but rather a tangible representation of both the nation's identity and the viewer's own status as a citizen. The possessive quality of viewing early modern collections, like Herrick's gathering of experiences to create a curiosity cabinet of selfhood, had become literalized: as a British subject, the viewer now was a part-owner of the objects he gazed upon in Montagu House. As an instrument of national integration, the British Museum thus transformed the wonder-filled Peter Mundys of the seventeenth century into the collecting citizens of the eighteenth century, and recast the class identity of the virtuosos into the collective identity of the nation.

Nonetheless, the advent of the national museum did not foreclose all possibility of individual self-fashioning through the practice of collecting. While the museum whose foundation he catalyzed does not bear his name, we remember Sir Hans Sloane today primarily as a collector; as he had hoped, Sloane's collection and thus his identity have been bought and preserved by a new owner, the nation of Great Britain. Likewise, in tandem with the establishment of national collections such as the British Museum in the eighteenth and nineteenth centuries, myriad types of private collections have continued to flourish in Britain and her former colonies to this day. Although a "middling sort" collector might now obsess about Beanie Babies rather than bezoar stones, or electronically hunt for new treasures on eBay rather than ask sea captains to procure "any thing that is Strang," the twenty-first century collector can trace her history back to the richly diverse possibilities for self-fashioning unleashed by the likes of the Tradescants and Elias Ashmole. We are still discovering—and transforming—the heritage of the early modern culture of collecting.

Notes

Introduction

1. Peter Mundy, *The Travels of Peter Mundy, in Europe and Asia, 1608–1667*, Hakluyt Society ser. 2, 45 , 3:1–3. In the 1656 catalogue of the Tradescant collection, the "Cherry stone" mentioned by Mundy is described as having "upone one side S. George and the Dragon, perfectly cut: and on the other side 88 Emperours faces" (J. T. [John Tradescant the younger], *Musaeum Tradescantianum; or A Collection of Rarities Preserved at South-Lambeth neer London*, 38). For contemporary drawings of the "Cherry stone," see Arthur MacGregor, ed., *Tradescant's Rarities: Essays on the Foundation of the Ashmolean Museum*, Plate CLXXIII.

2. John Evelyn, *Numismata*, 282.

3. Oxford English Dictionary, s.v. "collection," "collector."

4. John Evelyn, *Diary and Correspondence of John Evelyn*, ed. William Bray, 3:305 (from a letter to Pepys, 12 August 1689).

5. R. Malcolm Smuts, *Court Culture and the Origins of a Royalist Tradition in Early Stuart England*, 119, 121; Arthur MacGregor, "King Charles I: A Renaissance Collector?" 154. On aristocratic Stuart art collections, see also David Howarth, *Lord Arundel and His Circle*; Ronald Lightbown, "Charles I and the Tradition of European Princely Collecting"; Linda Levy Peck, "Building, Buying, and Collecting in London, 1600–1625"; Smuts, "Art and the Material Culture of Majesty in Early Stuart England"; and Timothy Wilks, "The Picture Collection of Robert Carr, Earl of Somerset (c. 1587–1645), Reconsidered."

6. Sir Francis Bacon, *Gesta Grayorum*, in *The Works of Francis Bacon*, 8:335.

7. Lorraine J. Daston, "The Factual Sensibility," 458.

8. Eilean Hooper-Greenhill, *Museums and the Shaping of Knowledge*, 86–88; John Evelyn, *The Diary of John Evelyn*, ed. de Beer, 3:594. Evelyn particularly commended Browne's extensive accumulation of birds' eggs.

9. Thomas Platter, *Thomas Platter's Travels in England, 1599*, 171–73.

10. Stephen Bann, *Under the Sign: John Bargrave as Collector, Traveler, and Witness*, 14, 15, 7; in the 1630s, Arundel had attempted to buy the same obelisk (Howarth, *Lord Arundel and His Circle*, 111–12, 138). On the design of Bargrave's cabinets, see David Sturdy and Martin Henig, *The Gentle Traveller: John Bargrave, Canon of Canterbury and his Collection*.

11. James Petiver, "An Account of a BOOK. *Musei Petiveriani Centuria Prima.*"

12. P. C. D. Brears, "Ralph Thoresby, a Museum Visitor in Stuart England," 213–14. Thoresby produced a catalogue of his collection, the *Musaeum Thoresbyanum*, which is bound into his chorography of Leeds, *Ducatus Leodiensis*.

13. For a brief description of Dee's library, see Anthony G. Medici, "John Dee."

14. Samuel Pepys, *The Diary of Samuel Pepys*, 7:243.

15. On Pepys's library, see Esther Potter, "'To Paul's Churchyard to Treat with a Bookbinder.'"

16. Arthur MacGregor, "The Cabinet of Curiosities in Seventeenth-Century Britain," 150.

17. R. H., alias Forges [Robert Hubert], *A Catalogue of part of those Rarities Collected in thirty years time with a great deal of Pains and Industry* (n.d.), title page, 25–27.

18. Robert Hooke, *The Posthumous Works of Robert Hooke*, 338.

19. Michael Hunter, *Establishing the New Science: The Experience of the Early Royal Society*, 123–39.

20. Hunter, *Establishing the New Science*, 149; quotation cited in David Murray, *Museums: Their History and Their Use*, 1:200.

21. The British Museum opened to the public in 1759, its holdings largely comprised of the collections of Sir Hans Sloane. The Royal Society offered its Repository to the British Museum in 1779. On Sloane's collections and the foundation of the British Museum, see Epilogue, below; on the transfer of the Royal Society's collection to the Museum, see Michael Hunter, *Establishing the New Science*, 154–55.

22. James Deetz, *In Small Things Forgotten: The Archaeology of Early American Life*, 7, quoted in Susan M. Pearce, *Museums, Objects and Collections: A Cultural Study*, 5.

23. Neil McKendrick, John Brewer, and J. H. Plumb, *The Birth of a Consumer Society: The Commercialization of Eighteenth-Century England*. On the historiography of the "backdating" of consumer culture to the early modern period, see Jean Christophe Agnew, "Coming Up for Air: Consumer Culture in Historical Perspective," 23–26.

24. Lisa Jardine, *Worldly Goods: A New History of the Renaissance*, 10.

25. Chandra Mukerji, *From Graven Images: Patterns of Modern Materialism*, 13.

26. Joan Thirsk, *Economic Policy and Projects: The Development of a Consumer Society in Early Modern England*, 179.

27. James Clifford, *The Predicament of Culture: Twentieth-Century Ethnography, Literature, and Art*, 217.

28. C. B. Macpherson, "Capitalism and the Changing Concept of Property," 106.

29. Richard A. Goldthwaite, *Wealth and the Demand for Art in Italy, 1300–1600*, 255.

30. Influential anthropological accounts of the social meanings of objects include Arjun Appadurai, "Introduction: Commodities and the Politics of Value," in *The Social Life of Things: Commodities in Cultural Perspective*, ed. Appadurai, 3–63; Mary Douglas and Baron Isherwood, *The World of Goods*; and Daniel Miller, *Material Culture and Mass Consumption*. These writers reject Macpherson's Marxist view of consumption as an intrinsically alienating activity. For a summary and critique of Marxist approaches to consumption, see Miller, *Material Culture*, 34–49.

31. Margreta de Grazia, Maureen Quilligan, and Peter Stallybrass, eds., *Subject and Object in Renaissance Culture*, 2.

32. See, e.g., Peter Stallybrass, "Worn Worlds: Clothes and Identity on the Renaissance Stage"; Jonathan Gil Harris and Natasha Korda, eds., *Staged Properties: Props and Property in Early Modern English Drama*; Susan Frye, "Sewing Connections: Elizabeth Tudor, Mary Stuart, Elizabeth Talbot, and Seventeenth-Century Anonymous Needleworkers"; Lena Cowen Orlin, "Three Ways to Be Invisible in the Renaissance: Sex, Reputation, and Stitchery"; Patricia Fumerton, "Secret Arts: Elizabethan Miniatures and Sonnets," in her *Cultural Aesthetics: Renaissance Literature and the Practice of Social Ornament*, 67–110.

33. Susan M. Pearce, *On Collecting: An Investigation into Collecting in the European Tradition*, 3. As Susan Stewart observes, "In acquiring objects, the collector replaces production with consumption: objects are naturalized into the landscape of the collection itself" (*On Longing: Narratives of the Miniature, the Gigantic, the Souvenir, the Collection*, 156).

34. Oliver Impey and Arthur MacGregor, Introduction to *The Origins of Museums*, ed. Impey and MacGregor, 1. Other traditional, untheorized histories of the development of the museum include Germain Bazin, *The Museum Age*; Murray, *Museums: Their History and Their Use*; and Niels Van Holst, *Creators, Collectors and Connoisseurs: The Anatomy of Artistic Taste from Antiquity to the Present Day*.

35. Werner Muensterberger, *Collecting, An Unruly Passion: Psychological Perspectives*, 27.

36. Tony Bennett, *The Birth of the Museum: History, Theory, Politics*, 38. This section of Bennett's book draws upon the analysis presented by Carol Duncan and Alan Wallach in "The Universal Survey Museum"; Duncan develops her ideological assessment of the Louvre in "From the Princely Gallery to the Public Art Museum: The Louvre Museum and the National Gallery, London," in her *Civilizing Rituals: Inside Public Art Museums*, 21–47.

37. Hooper-Greenhill, *Museums and the Shaping of Knowledge*, passim.

38. Clifford, *Predicament of Culture*, 220.

39. Pearce, *Museums*, 35.

40. Pearce, *On Collecting*, 28.

41. Grant McCracken, *Culture and Consumption: New Approaches to the Symbolic Character of Consumer Goods and Activities*, 135, 137. McCracken's comments about the innovative potential of goods in general apply equally well to the collection in particular.

42. Recent studies of collecting in early modern Europe include Genevieve Warwick, *The Arts of Collecting: Padre Sebastiano Resta and the Market for Drawings in Early Modern Europe*; and Paula Findlen's magisterial *Possessing Nature: Museums, Collecting, and Scientific Culture in Early Modern Italy*.

43. Lisa Tiersten, "Redefining Consumer Culture: Recent Literature on Consumption and the Bourgeoisie in Western Europe,"136–37.

44. MacGregor, "Cabinet of Curiosities," 147; Richard Helgerson, *Forms of Nationhood: The Elizabethan Writing of England*, 13.

45. I am using a cultural materialist model of the relationship between social formations, cultural production, and individual agency; that is, I assume that while an historically specific social formation "sets limits and exerts pressures, agency

takes place within those limits and pressures, and takes the characteristic form of an unavoidably material production, and subjectivity, though socially produced and shared, is nonetheless both real and active" (Andrew Milner, *Cultural Materialism*, 101).

46. Patricia Fumerton, "Introduction: A New New Historicism," 12.

47. Transcribed by H. J. Braunholtz, *Sir Hans Sloane and Ethnography*, 34–35; the inscribed spoon is pictured in Plate 16.

48. Robert Hubert, *A Catalogue of Many Natural Rarities, With Great Industry, Cost, and Thirty Years Travel in Foraign Countries, Collected by Robert Hubert, alias Forges* (1664), 16, 9. Hubert published two editions of his catalogue, apparently in an effort to generate interest among prospective buyers of his collection. The undated edition of Hubert's catalogue (see Bibliography) appears to be a later, expanded version of the 1664 edition.

49. Hubert (n.d.), 29, 36–37.

50. Hubert (1664), 59.

51. The published travel journal could also function like a catalogue: men would record their visits to private collections, displaying their ability to negotiate the elite culture of foreign countries by collecting their experiences of desirable collections. Within these journals, early modern travelers would thus turn the collections of others into the framework of a personal narrative of social and intellectual success.

52. Michael Warner, *The Letters of the Republic: Publication and the Public Sphere in Eighteenth-Century America*, 7; see also Wendy Wall, *The Imprint of Gender: Authorship and Publication in the English Renaissance*, 1–22.

53. Walter J. Ong, *Orality and Literacy: The Technologizing of the Word*, 132.

54. Tradescant, *Musaeum Tradescantianum* (1656), 179. For an analysis of the political factions represented in the list of benefactors, see April London, "*Musaeum Tradescantianum* and the Benefactors to the Tradescants' Museum."

55. Hubert (1664), 58, 21.

56. Ibid., 69.

57. On visitors' books, see Findlen, *Possessing Nature*, 136–46.

Chapter 1. Cultures of Collecting in Early Modern England

1. On the concept of "magnificence," see Richard A. Goldthwaite, *Wealth and the Demand for Art*, 152–55; and Felicity Heal, *Hospitality in Early Modern England*, 24. On the display of magnificence in Stuart court culture, see R. Malcolm Smuts, "Art and the Material Culture of Majesty," 87–93.

2. Smuts, "Art and the Material Culture of Majesty," 103. For accounts of Charles's acquisition of the Gonzaga collection, see Francis Haskell, "Charles I's Collection of Pictures," 211–14; and Jonathan Brown, *Kings and Connoisseurs: Collecting Art in Seventeenth-Century Europe*, 40–45.

3. Haskell, "Charles I's Collection of Pictures," 203, 204.

4. Quoted in Smuts, "Art and the Material Culture of Majesty," 99. For an account of seventeenth-century princely art collections in Spain, see Jonathan

Brown, *Kings and Connoisseurs*, 95–145; on Lord Roos's travels in Spain, see John Stoye, *English Travellers Abroad, 1604–1667*, 262–66.

5. Smuts, "Art and the Material Culture of Majesty," 103–7. Jonathan Brown observes that in 1613 the gold and silver lace for one of Princess Elizabeth's gowns cost £1,700, a price tag "which would have made it more valuable than all but a few paintings in the famous collection of her brother, Charles I" (*Kings and Connoisseurs*, 8).

6. Ronald Lightbown, "Charles I and the Tradition of European Princely Collecting," 59.

7. Lightbown, "Charles I and European Princely Collecting," 60; Brown, *Kings and Connoisseurs*, 244. See also Goldthwaite, *Wealth and the Demand for Art*, 243–45.

8. As Pierre Bourdieu observes, "art and cultural consumption are predisposed, consciously and deliberately or not, to fulfil a social function of legitimating social differences" (*Distinction: A Social Critique of the Judgement of Taste*, 7).

9. Henry Peacham, *Peacham's "Compleat Gentleman," 1634*, 107.

10. Michael Vickers, "Greek and Roman Antiquities in the Seventeenth Century," 227. For a detailed account of Arundel's collecting activities, see David Howarth, *Lord Arundel and His Circle*.

11. One room alone at Arundel House contained more than 30 paintings by Holbein (Howarth, *Lord Arundel and His Circle*, 69).

12. Goldthwaite, *Wealth and the Demand for Art*, 249. See also Thomas DaCosta Kaufmann, "From Treasury to Museum: The Collections of the Austrian Habsburgs," 139–40; and Vickers, "Greek and Roman Antiquities," 224.

13. Anthony Alan Shelton, "Cabinets of Transgression: Renaissance Collections and the Incorporation of the New World,"184–85.

14. Brown, *Kings and Connoisseurs*, 148. Julius von Schlosser's *Die Kunst- und Wunderkammer der Spätrenaissance* focuses on princely Austrian collections, especially that of Archduke Ferdinand in Schloss Ambras.

15. Brown, *Kings and Connoisseurs*, 107, 149; Kaufmann, "From Treasury to Museum," 144.

16. Fynes Moryson, *An Itinerary*, 1:321–22. Moryson's description dates from 1594.

17. As Michael Rinehart observes, "the very existence" of the *studiolo* was apparently secret, as it was "never included in sixteenth-century inventories of the palace" ("A Document for the Studiolo of Francesco I," 278).

18. The interior of the *studiolo* was also adorned with bronze statues of the gods and circular portraits of Francesco's parents; the ceiling was decorated with painted figures representing the elements, such as Prometheus.

19. Eilean Hooper-Greenhill, *Museums and the Shaping of Knowledge*, 106. My account of Francesco's *studiolo* also draws upon Glenn Andres, John M. Hunisak, and A. Richard Turner, *The Art of Florence*, 2:1275; and Frederick Hartt, revised David G. Wilkins, *History of Italian Renaissance Art*, 657.

20. On the collections of Duke Albrecht V, see Lorenz Seelig, "The Munich *Kunstkammer, 1565–1807*."

21. Giuseppe Olmi, "Science-Honour-Metaphor: Italian Cabinets of the Sixteenth and Seventeenth Centuries," 10.

22. Kaufmann, "From Treasury to Museum," 143.

23. Thomas DaCosta Kaufmann, "Remarks on the Collections of Rudolf II: the *Kunstkammer* as a Form of *Representatio*," 25; see also Kaufmann, "From Treasury to Museum," 143.

24. Kaufmann, "From Treasury to Museum," 145.

25. As I discuss later, Renaissance humanism also established new, specifically textual collecting practices; see below, Chapter 4.

26. Mary Thomas Crane, *Framing Authority: Sayings, Self, and Society in Sixteenth-Century England*, 56.

27. Richard Halpern, *The Poetics of Primitive Accumulation: English Renaissance Culture and the Genealogy of Capital*, 34–35; Felicity Heal and Clive Holmes, *The Gentry in England and Wales, 1500–1700*, 30. On the "social doctrine" of Tudor humanists, see also Alistair Fox, "Facts and Fallacies: Interpreting English Humanism," 25–27.

28. Lightbown, "Charles I and European Princely Collecting," 54. On the appropriation of humanistic collecting practices by political elites, see also Krysztof Pomian, *Collectors and Curiosities: Paris and Venice, 1500–1800*, 35–39. On the elision of birth and education as hallmarks of gentility in early modern England, see Heal and Holmes, *Gentry in England and Wales*, 30–33.

29. Peacham, "*Compleat Gentleman*", 104–5.

30. Vickers, "Greek and Roman Antiquities," 227; Lightbown, "Charles I and European Princely Collecting," 65.

31. Peacham, "*Compleat Gentleman*", 107, 112, 108. Many of Charles's statues were from the Gonzaga collection and the ruined Temple of Apollo on Delos (Lightbown, "Charles I and European Princely Collecting," 65).

32. Peacham, "*Compleat Gentleman*", 123–24.

33. John Evelyn, *Numismata*, 1.

34. Elias Ashmole, *Elias Ashmole, 1617–1692*, ed. C. H. Josten, 4:1635.

35. Lorraine J. Daston, "The Factual Sensibility," 456.

36. Alexander Brown, ed., *The Genesis of the United States*, 1:357.

37. John Evelyn, *Navigation and Commerce*, 9–10.

38. Nicholas Thomas, *Entangled Objects: Exchange, Material Culture, and Colonialism in the Pacific*, 141.

39. Daston, "The Factual Sensibility," 455. On the importance of travel in early modern culture, see also Lisa Jardine, "Strange Specimens," in her *Ingenious Pursuits: Building the Scientific Revolution*, 223–72.

40. Margaret T. Hodgen, *Early Anthropology in the Sixteenth and Seventeenth Centuries*, 111–12; Anthony Pagden, *European Encounters with the New World: From Renaissance to Romanticism*, 31.

41. Lorenzo Magalotti, *Travels of Cosmo III, Grand Duke of Tuscany, through England (1669)*, quoted in Michael Hunter, *Science and Society in Restoration England*, 67; Pepys, *The Diary of Samuel Pepys*, 6:215. As Kim F. Hall observes, in seventeenth-century England "the objectification of black people in material culture signifies both the rarity of foreign luxury goods and the subjectivity and value of white owners" (*Things of Darkness: Economies of Race and Gender in Early Modern England*, 212).

42. Stephen Bann, *Under the Sign: John Bargrave as Collector, Traveler, and Witness*, 83.

43. Peter Mason, "From Presentation to Representation: *Americana* in Europe," 9.

44. Thomas Platter, *Thomas Platter's Travels in England, 1599*, 173. As Christian F. Feest notes, the term "Indian" could designate both Asia and America during the Renaissance ("The Collecting of American Indian Artifacts in Europe, 1493–1750," 335).

45. Feest, "The Collecting of American Indian Artifacts," 334; Hodgen, *Early Anthropology*, 166; John Evelyn, *The Diary of John Evelyn*, ed. E. S. de Beer, 5:48 (16 April 1691).

46. Joseph M. Levine, *Dr. Woodward's Shield: History, Science, and Satire in Augustan England*, 318 n.25.

47. Steven Mullaney, "Strange Things, Gross Terms, Curious Customs: The Rehearsal of Cultures in the Late Renaissance," 77–78; Anthony Alan Shelton, "Cabinets of Transgression: Renaissance Collections and the Incorporation of the New World," 203. Amy Boesky similarly suggests that early modern collections signified "the West's capacity to tame and culture the exotic" (" 'Outlandish-Fruits': Commissioning Nature for the Museum of Man," 310).

48. Paula Findlen, *Possessing Nature*, 27.

49. Stephen Greenblatt, *Marvelous Possessions: The Wonder of the New World*, 20; James Biester, *Lyric Wonder: Rhetoric and Wit in Renaissance English Poetry*, 9. Greenblatt contrasts "wonder" with an analytical, contextualizing mode of perception he terms "resonance" ("Resonance and Wonder").

50. Martin Kemp, " 'Wrought by No Artist's Hand': The Natural, the Artificial, the Exotic, and the Scientific in Some Artifacts from the Renaissance,"185. On early modern collectors' interest in objects which blurred distinctions between art and nature, see also Horst Bredekamp, *The Lure of Antiquity and the Cult of the Machine*, esp. 1–80.

51. Joy Kenseth, "The Age of the Marvelous: An Introduction," 33–34. This cultural fascination with natural "wonders" is criticized in Marvell's poem "The Mower against Gardens": "Another world was searched, then oceans new / To find the *Marvel of Peru*" (Andrew Marvell, *The Complete Poems*, 105, ll. 17–18). Since the mower attacks these foreign flowers (now commonly called "four o'clocks") as part of a hysterical indictment of horticultural perversions, it is difficult to gauge Marvell's own attitude toward wonders and collecting here.

52. Kenseth, "Age of the Marvelous," 42.

53. Mea Allan, *The Tradescants: Their Plants, Gardens and Museum, 1570–1662*, 114–15.

54. John Gerard, *The Herball Or Generall Historie of Plantes*, 430.

55. Biester, *Lyric Wonder*, 13.

56. Quoted in Biester, *Lyric Wonder*, 10–11.

57. Katie Whitaker, "The Culture of Curiosity," 87. As Whitaker observes, although early modern catalogues sort the components of collections into different categories, the collections themselves were usually arranged in a deliberately unsystematic fashion.

58. Anon., *A Helpe to Memorie and Discourse; with Table-Talk* (London, 1621), quoted in Katharine Park and Lorraine Daston, "Unnatural Conceptions: The Study of Monsters in Sixteenth- and Seventeenth-Century France and England," 39.

59. Stoye, *English Travellers*, 11.

60. Quoted in Roger Hudson, *The Grand Tour, 1592–1796*, 21.

61. Sir Francis Bacon, *The Essays*, 113.

62. Findlen, *Possessing Nature*, 132–33.

63. Quoted in Paula Findlen, "The Museum: Its Classical Etymology and Renaissance Genealogy," 72.

64. Roger Chartier, *The Cultural Uses of Print in Early Modern France*, 10.

65. Charles Hoole, *A New Discovery of the Old Art of Teaching Schoole, In four small Treatises*, 284–85.

66. Herman Hager, transcription of Bodl. Add. B. 67, Appendix II to his review of K. H. Schaible, *Geschichte der Deutschen in England*, 450.

67. John Tradescant, "To the Ingenious Reader," *Musaeum Tradescantianum* (1656).

68. On the probable appearance of the Tradescant collection, see Prudence Leith-Ross, *The John Tradescants: Gardeners to the Rose and Lily Queen*, 152; and Martin Welch, *The Tradescants and the Foundation of the Ashmolean Museum*, 7. David Sturdy has speculated that the inanimate objects could have been housed in a gallery within the garden itself ("The Tradescants at Lambeth,"11).

69. P. J. Jarvis, "The Introduced Trees and Shrubs Cultivated by the Tradescants at South Lambeth, 1629–1679," 247, 248.

70. In a poem first published in 1651, John Cleveland refers to "*Tredeskin* and his ark of Novelties" ("Upon Sir Thomas Martin" in *The Poems of John Cleveland*, 53, l. 6), while Thomas Powell writes of "*John Tredeskin's* Ark in *Lambeth*" in a book published in 1661 (*Humane Industry: Or, A History of Most Manual Arts*, 187).

71. Andrew Cunningham, "The Culture of Gardens," 43.

72. Evelyn, *Diary*, ed. de Beer, 2:80 (11 March 1642). On Tradescant's career at Hatfield, see also Allan, *The Tradescants*, 34–60; and Leith-Ross, *The John Tradescants*, 28–43.

73. Arthur MacGregor, *Tradescant's Rarities*, 18. Thomas Platter's description of Cope's collection is quoted above. Tradescant's trips to the Continent to buy plants may also have allowed him to visit the collection displayed in the Anatomy School in Leiden, as well as a French collection of curiosities.

74. Quoted in MacGregor, *Tradescant's Rarities*, 7. For a detailed description of seventeenth-century melon growing techniques, see Leith-Ross, *The John Tradescants*, 46.

75. Public Record Office (hereafter PRO), State Papers Domestic, Charles I, IV, 1625, nos. 155–56, quoted in MacGregor, *Tradescant's Rarities*, 19.

76. Leith-Ross, *The John Tradescants*, 80.

77. April London, "*Musaeum Tradescantianum* and the Benefactors to the Tradescants' Museum," 30. London analyzes the benefactors connected to Buckingham on pp. 29–37.

78. As Leith-Ross explains, it is impossible to determine exactly when Tradescant first leased what would become known as his "Ark"; however, beginning in 1629, Tradescant began to record all the new plants he acquired for his garden (Leith-Ross, *The John Tradescants*, 86–88).

79. As Leith-Ross observes, a letter was sent to the Court of the East India Company in 1633 which indicated "His Majesties pleasure, that the Company

should write for such varieties as are expressed in a paper thereinclosed, and being returned to deliver them to John Tradescant to be reserved by him for His Majesties Service" (*The John Tradescants*, 97).

80. Quoted in MacGregor, *Tradescant's Rarities*, 21.

81. Tradescant, *Musaeum Tradescantianum* (1656), 49.

82. Leith-Ross, *The John Tradescants*, 97.

83. Quoted in Leith-Ross, *The John Tradescants*, 103.

84. Tradescant, "To the Ingenious Reader," *Musaeum Tradescantianum* (1656).

85. John Parkinson, *Theatrum Botanicum, The Theater of Plantes*, 705.

86. Tradescant's diary is transcribed in Leith-Ross, *The John Tradescants*; the passage quoted is found on p. 58. In his attempt to collect previously unknown plants, Tradescant faced a hazard typical of early modern travel—the propensity of ships' crews to eat specimens. Tradescant describes a dogwood whose berries he gathered for seed, and then laments that "the Boys in the ship, befor I pe[r]seved it, eat of the berries" (Leith-Ross, *The John Tradescants*, 63; Allan, *The Tradescants*, identifies the fruiting shrub as a dogwood on p. 87).

87. Leith-Ross, *The John Tradescants*, 55.

88. Tradescant, *Musaeum Tradescantianum* (1656), 49.

89. MacGregor, *Tradescant's Rarities*, 9.

90. Parkinson, *Theatrum Botanicum*, 622, 624; Tradescant, *Musaeum Tradescantianum* (1656), 54, 68. The catalogue entry for what was presumably Tradescant's medal, found under the headings "Medalls" and "Silver," reads "*Upon the* Isle of Ree *Voyage*" (Tradescant, *Musaeum Tradescantianum* (1656), 68).

91. Allan (*The Tradescants*, 94–100) and Leith-Ross (*The John Tradescants*, 69–70) provide accounts of the blockade and its background.

92. John Parkinson, *Paradisi in Sole, Paradisus Terrestris*, 579.

93. Parkinson, *Paradisus*, 430. Parkinson was incorrect that the wild pomegranate had never been seen in England before Tradescant brought it back from Russia—John Gerard had mentioned the plant in his 1597 herbal. Since this species "was apparently unknown to Parkinson, it must have been extremely rare if it had not died out altogether" (Leith-Ross, *The John Tradescants*, 71).

94. "Tradescants chery" is listed in Tradescant's own 1634 catalogue of his garden at Lambeth (Leith-Ross, *The John Tradescants*, 224); the cultivar originated either in France or Germany, and was still named after Tradescant as late as 1823 (Leith-Ross, *The John Tradescants*, 34).

95. Richard Helgerson, *Forms of Nationhood: The Elizabethan Writing of England*, 111.

96. Helgerson, *Forms of Nationhood*, 108–39. During the same period, as Helgerson notes, plays came to be designated by their authors' names—William Shakespeare, for example—rather than by the aristocratically affiliated companies which staged them—such as the Lord Chamberlain's Men (ibid., 111).

97. Parkinson, *Paradisus*, 152.

98. Ibid., 575.

99. Ibid., 388, 389, 575.

100. Gerard, *The Herball*, 260.

101. Parkinson, *Paradisus*, 152.

102. John Smith was apparently a friend of Tradescant, as he willed some of

his books to Tradescant (Allan, *The Tradescants*, 159); and while George Sandys was in Virginia, he corresponded with Tradescant (MacGregor, *Tradescant's Rarities*, 12 n. 82). On Tradescant's involvement in the plantation established by Captain Sam Argall, see Leith-Ross, *The John Tradescants*, 47–49.

103. State Papers, Colonial, 1574–1660, v.i, no. ii; Leith-Ross, *The John Tradescants*, 102.

104. Parkinson, *Theatrum*, 1044–45. For a list of other new American plants that Parkinson attributes to Tradescant's first trip to Virginia, see Leith-Ross, *The John Tradescants*, 189.

105. John Dixon Hunt, "Curiosities to Adorn Cabinets and Gardens," 201.

106. Allan, *The Tradescants*, 198; epitaph quoted in MacGregor, *Tradescant's Rarities*, 15.

107. Richard Grassby, *The Business Community of Seventeenth-Century England*, 408.

108. Leith-Ross, *The John Tradescants*, 90–92. It seems that it cost sixpence to enter the Tradescants' museum (Leith-Ross, 91).

109. Anthony Richard Wagner, *English Genealogy*, 120; Ben Jonson, *Catiline*, 2.1.119–21. On lineage and heraldry in early modern England, see also Heal and Holmes, *Gentry in England and Wales*, 20–30.

110. Frank Whigham, "Elizabethan Aristocratic Insignia," 333.

111. Leith-Ross, *The John Tradescants*, 105.

112. Ibid., 148.

113. Allan, *The Tradescants*, 182n, 221.

114. Quoted in Leith-Ross, *The John Tradescants*, 105.

115. On the creation of fictitious genealogies, see Heal and Holmes, *Gentry in England and Wales*, 36–37; on heraldic visitations, see Wagner, *English Genealogy*, 122.

116. Another catalogue in manuscript, known as "Tradescant's Orchard," consists of watercolor drawings of a hazelnut tree, grape vines, and fruit trees, arranged according to the dates by which the different fruits ripened; it has been suggested that the manuscript may have been made for Tradescant during his stint as gardener at Hatfield (A. C. de la Mare, "Manuscripts and Printed Books Associated with the Tradescants in the Bodleian Library," 352–53).

117. Leith-Ross, *The John Tradescants*, 199; Leith-Ross transcribes the entire plant list on pp. 199–203.

118. Ibid., 199.

119. Ibid., 221–24.

120. John Tradescant, *Musaeum Tradescantianum*, 2nd ed. (London, 1660). Only the dedication was changed in the 1660 edition; Leith-Ross, *The John Tradescants*, reproduces the 1660 dedication on p. 123.

121. Tradescant, *Musaeum Tradescantianum* (1656), 179.

122. London, "Benefactors," 25.

123. Ashmole, *Elias Ashmole*, ed. Josten, 2:448.

124. Peter Stallybrass, "Patriarchal Territories: The Body Enclosed," 134.

125. Michael Hunter, *Elias Ashmole, 1617–1692: The Founder of the Ashmolean Museum and his World*, 13.

126. Ashmole, *Elias Ashmole*, 3:891. Ashmole published *The Institution, Laws & Ceremonies of the most Noble Order of the Garter* in 1672.

127. Ashmole, *Elias Ashmole*, 3:846–47.

128. Michael Hunter, *Ashmole*, 6.

129. C. H. Josten, "Biographical Introduction" to Ashmole, *Elias Ashmole*, 1:226, 1:33; on Ashmole's first wife, Eleanor Manwaring, see ibid., 1:16–18. Although Ashmole's first two wives shared a surname, they apparently were not related; see ibid., 2:320 n.1 and 2:495 for details of their pedigrees.

130. Josten, in Ashmole, *Elias Ashmole*, 1:62.

131. Quoted by Michael Hunter, *Ashmole*, 19.

132. Ashmole, *Elias Ashmole*, 4:1635–36.

133. Ibid., 4:1636.

134. Josten, in Ashmole, *Elias Ashmole*, 1:20.

135. Quoted by R. F. Ovenell, *The Ashmolean Museum, 1683–1894*, 28.

136. Josten, in Ashmole, *Elias Ashmole*, 1:124.

137. Ashmole, *Elias Ashmole*, 4:1394.

138. Ibid., 2:781 n.1.

139. For a photograph of one of the pages of Ashmole's collection of wax impressions, see Michael Hunter, *Ashmole*, 87.

140. On the evidence for attributing this work to Ashmole, see Ashmole, *Elias Ashmole*, 3:813 n. 5.

141. Tradescant, "To the Ingenious Reader," *Musaeum Tradescantianum* (1656).

142. Josten, in Ashmole, *Elias Ashmole*, 1:70.

143. Despite his origins as a saddler's son, Ashmole clearly regarded the Tradescants as social inferiors, for when his wife suggested that she might stay at the Ark for a time, Ashmole asked the stars "Whether my wife shall have any disgrace by going to Mr. Tradescants to live" (Ashmole, *Elias Ashmole*, 2:612).

144. Ibid., 2:613.

145. Tradescant, "To the Ingenious Reader," *Musaeum Tradescantianum* (1656).

146. Ashmole, *Elias Ashmole*, 1:99–102.

147. Quoted by Josten in Ashmole, *Elias Ashmole*, 2:687.

148. Evelyn, *Diary*, ed. de Beer, 3:198–99.

149. Tradescant, *Musaeum Tradescantianum* (1656), 4, 6, 8, 19.

150. PRO: C 7/454/1.

151. PRO: C 7/454/1.

152. John Evelyn, *Diary and Correspondence of John Evelyn*, ed. William Bray, 3:304, 300.

153. Although Tradescant still had another child living, his widowed daughter Frances Norman, he apparently did not see fit to leave the collection to her. Under the English system of coverture, if Frances were to remarry—a scenario Tradescant envisioned in his will—her legal identity, and thus her property, would pass to her husband, someone whose behavior Tradescant could not foresee. On the effect of coverture on the disposition of property in the seventeenth century, see Amy Erickson, *Women and Property in Early Modern England*, 24–26, 228–29.

154. Quoted in Leith-Ross, *The John Tradescants*, 131.

155. Quoted in ibid., 129.

156. Ashmole, *Elias Ashmole*, 3:853.

157. PRO: C 7/454/1.

158. PRO: C 33/221/744.

159. PRO: C 33/221/744.

160. PRO: C 33/221/744.

161. Ashmole, *Elias Ashmole*, 4:1393, 1397.

162. Leith-Ross, *The John Tradescants*, 137.

163. Quoted in Leith-Ross, *The John Tradescants*, 138. The marriage license of Hester and John Tradescant the younger indicates that Hester was 25 in 1638, the year she was married (Leith-Ross, *The John Tradescants*, 105).

164. Ashmole, *Elias Ashmole*, 4:1403.

165. Ibid., 4:1451.

166. Leith-Ross, *The John Tradescants*, 145–46.

167. Ashmole, *Elias Ashmole*, 4:1433.

168. Among the list of witnesses to the Submission are relatives of Hester Tradescant. As Leith-Ross observes of the document, while "it is surprising that Hester's relations persuaded her to sign it," presumably "Ashmole must have threatened her with further legal action if she refused" (*The John Tradescants*, 140–41).

169. Leith-Ross, *The John Tradescants*, 138–39.

170. Ashmole, *Elias Ashmole*, 4:1451.

171. Ibid., 4:1608.

172. Leith-Ross, *The John Tradescants*, 142.

173. PRO: C 7/541/2.

174. During the digging of the foundation of the new building, workers inadvertently caused a privy within the precincts of Exeter College to collapse, "& caused such an inundation that some of [them] had much ado to escape wth ye safety of their lifes, & were glad to leave their clothes swimming behind them" (quoted in Ovenell, *The Ashmolean Museum*, 16–17).

175. Ovenell, *The Ashmolean Museum*, 21–22. For a detailed contemporary account of the interior of the building, see ibid., 23–24.

176. Martin Welch, "The Foundation of the Ashmolean Museum," 49.

177. Ashmole, *Elias Ashmole*, 4:1714–15, 1719.

178. Edward Chamberlayne, *Angliae Notitia: Or the Present State of England*, part 2, 328; Ralph Thoresby, *The Diary of Ralph Thoresby*, 2:429.

179. Ashmole, *Elias Ashmole*, 4:1720.

180. Ovenell, *The Ashmolean Museum*, 20.

181. Martin Welch, "The Ashmolean as Described by Its Earliest Visitors," 61.

182. Quoted in Welch, "The Ashmolean as Described by Its Earliest Visitors," 62.

183. Ashmole, *Elias Ashmole*, 4:1707.

184. Ovenell, *The Ashmolean Museum*, 29.

185. Ashmole, *Elias Ashmole*, 4:1482–83, 1717–18.

186. Ibid., 4:1727.

187. Ibid., 4:1721. Welch suggests that the other "Society" to which Ashmole refers could have been either Cambridge University or the Royal Society ("Foundation of the Ashmolean Museum," 44).

188. Ovenell, *The Ashmolean Museum*, 37–38; Martin Welch, *The Tradescants and the Foundation of the Ashmolean Museum*, 10.

189. Ashmole, *Elias Ashmole*, 4:1821–22.

190. Ovenell, *The Ashmolean Museum*, 38. Plot's account of Ashmole's benefaction is headed by "an elaborate illumination of Ashmole's arms, impaling those

of his third wife," Elizabeth Dugdale, whose father had been enlisted to secure Ashmole's possession of the Tradescant rarities (Michael Hunter, *Ashmole*, 50).

191. Ashmole, *Elias Ashmole*, 4:1717 n.1.

192. Robert Plot, *The Natural History of Stafford-Shire*, 277.

193. Welch, "Foundation of the Ashmolean Museum," 58.

Chapter 2. Sons of Science: Natural History and Collecting

1. Quoted in Lisa Jardine and Alan Stewart, *Hostage to Fortune: The Troubled Life of Francis Bacon, 1561–1626*, 503. Thomas Hobbes was Bacon's assistant.

2. For a fascinating analysis of the apocryphal status of the legend presented by Aubrey, see Jardine and Stewart, *Hostage*, 503–11. Although they end up presenting much evidence to the contrary, Jardine and Stewart begin their fine biography of Bacon by asserting that Bacon would have preferred pursuing his scientific projects to engaging in politics, and that his career "constantly interfered with his beloved intellectual pursuits" (18).

3. William Rawley, Preface to Bacon's *Sylva Sylvarum*, in Sir Francis Bacon, *Works*, 2:335.

4. Paula Findlen, "Courting Nature," 57.

5. Paula Findlen, *Possessing Nature*, 5.

6. Lorraine Daston and Katharine Park, *Wonders and the Order of Nature, 1150–1750*, 237.

7. Harold J. Cook, "The Cutting Edge of a Revolution?: Medicine and Natural History Near the Shores of the North Sea," 60. Since the 1940s, as Cook observes, historians' preoccupation with tracing the origins of twentieth-century physics has fostered a lack of appreciation of the importance of natural history in the early modern period ("Cutting Edge," 45–48). On the "primacy of natural history" (p. 69) in the seventeenth century, see also Joseph M. Levine, "Natural History and the History of the Scientific Revolution."

8. Daston and Park, *Wonders*, 118. On the medieval denigration of "particulars," see J. G. A. Pocock, *The Machiavellian Moment: Florentine Political Thought and the Atlantic Republican Tradition*, 4–9.

9. Michel Foucault, *The Order of Things: An Archaeology of the Human Sciences*, 41.

10. Quoted in F. David Hoeniger and J. F. M. Hoeniger, *The Development of Natural History in Tudor England*, 13, 8.

11. William B. Ashworth, Jr., "Natural History and the Emblematic World View," 317.

12. Gesner's work was translated into English and plagiarized by Edward Topsell in the early seventeenth century. Ashworth notes that while Topsell essentially recycled Gesner, he also "frequently added new material to that he took from Gesner, and most of it consisted of references drawn from emblematic and hieroglyphic literature" ("Natural History and the Emblematic World View," 316).

13. F. David Hoeniger, "How Plants and Animals Were Studied in the Mid-Sixteenth Century," 145. On the evolution of the humanist interest in *materia medica*, see Findlen, *Possessing Nature*, 241–61.

14. Findlen, "Courting Nature," 58–73.

15. Andrew Cunningham, "The Culture of Gardens," 43; Roy Strong, *The Renaissance Garden in England*, 14–19.

16. Paula Findlen, "Francis Bacon and the Reform of Natural History in the Seventeenth Century," 245–46. On the English emulation of Italian gardens, see John Dixon Hunt, *Garden and Grove: The Italian Renaissance Garden in the English Imagination, 1600–1750*; and Strong, *Renaissance Garden in England*.

17. J. H. Elliott, *The Old World and the New, 1492–1650*, 40.

18. Ashworth, "Natural History and the Emblematic World View," 318; Hoeniger, "How Plants and Animals Were Studied," 141. On Gesner's innovative empiricism, see William B. Ashworth, Jr., "Emblematic Natural History of the Renaissance," 23–29.

19. Anthony Pagden, *European Encounters with the New World: From Renaissance to Romanticism*, 10.

20. Joseph Glanvill, *The Vanity of Dogmatizing: or Confidence in Opinions Manifested in a Discourse of the Shortness and Uncertainty of Our Knowledge*, 178.

21. Ashworth, "Natural History and the Emblematic World View," 324.

22. Sir Francis Bacon, *The Refutation of Philosophies*, 131.

23. Bacon, *Works*, 4:254.

24. Ibid., 4:93; William Rawley, *The Life of the Right Honourable Francis Bacon*, in Bacon, *Works*, 1:37.

25. Bacon, *Works*, 4:8.

26. Ibid., 4:12.

27. Quoted in Lorraine J. Daston, "Baconian Facts, Academic Civility, and the Prehistory of Objectivity," 40.

28. Bacon, *Advancement of Learning*, in *Works*, 3:356.

29. Daston, "Baconian Facts," 45. On the early modern concept of a "history" as a record of "facts," see Barbara Shapiro, "History and Natural History in Sixteenth- and Seventeenth-Century England," 3–12. On the relationship between Bacon's natural philosophy and civil history, see B. H. G. Wormald, *Francis Bacon: History, Politics and Science, 1561–1626*. In *A Culture of Fact*, Barbara Shapiro argues that Baconian natural history, like other early modern English "discourses of fact," was rooted in legal epistemology.

30. Bacon, *Works*, 4:93.

31. Daston and Park, *Wonders*, 230.

32. Bacon, *Works*, 3:331, 330.

33. Ibid., 4:269. On the place of "Heteroclites" and "prodigies" in Bacon's natural philosophy, see Daston and Park, *Wonders*, 220–31.

34. Sir Francis Bacon, *Gesta Grayorum*, in *Works*, 8:335.

35. On Bacon's inductive research method, see Lisa Jardine, *Francis Bacon: Discovery and the Art of Discourse*, 109–49; Michel Malherbe, "Bacon's Method of Science"; and Paolo Rossi, *Francis Bacon: From Magic to Science*, 201–19.

36. Bacon, *Works*, 7:254–55.

37. Julie Robin Solomon, "'To Know, To Fly, To Conjure': Situating Baconian Science at the Juncture of Early Modern Modes of Reading," 552–53.

38. Bacon, *Works*, 14:377n.1.

39. Ibid., 14:533n., 4:251.

40. Ibid., 4:102.

41. John E. Leary, Jr., *Francis Bacon and the Politics of Science*, 159.

42. Markku Peltonen, "Introduction," *Cambridge Companion to Bacon*, 16.

43. Bacon, *Works*, 4:255; Julian Martin, *Francis Bacon, the State, and the Reform of Natural Philosophy*, 164.

44. Bacon, *Works*, 4:251–52.

45. Harvey Wheeler, "Francis Bacon's *New Atlantis*: The 'Mould' of a Law-finding Commonwealth," 305.

46. Quoted in Jardine and Stewart, *Hostage*, 276.

47. Quoted in Jardine and Stewart, *Hostage*, 442–43. As Joel J. Epstein observes, a judge's acceptance of "gifts" to supplement his salary was considered normal practice in seventeenth-century England (*Francis Bacon: A Political Biography*, 154). Lisa Jardine and Alan Stewart note that Bacon's accusers "were annoyed, not that there was a Lord Chancellor who accepted bribes, but that there was a Lord Chancellor who failed to deliver the goods upon receipt of those bribes— Bacon had apparently taken the money and then ruled *against* the suits" (*Hostage*, 462). Thus Bacon was impeached for purely political reasons: "He fell because he stood as an ideal victim for a Parliament looking to vent hostility against the Crown" (Epstein, *Francis Bacon*, 154–55).

48. Bacon, *Works*, 4:21.

49. Ibid., 3:294. On *The Advancement of Learning* as Bacon's attempt to gain preferment from James I, see Jardine and Stewart, *Hostage*, 285–87; on the significance of Bacon's decision to publish the work, see Martin Elsky, *Authorizing Words: Speech, Writing, and Print in the English Renaissance*, 196–98.

50. Bacon, *Works*, 10:84–85. Timothy J. Reiss accepts such programmatic statements and argues that "Bacon seeks to lay the foundations of a new [analytico-referential] discourse" for the sake of "the betterment of human life and society" (*The Discourse of Modernism*, 207, 199).

51. Julian Martin, "Natural Philosophy and Its Public Concerns," 105. Martin goes on to argue, however, that rather than personal advancement, Bacon's "overriding ambition was the augmentation of the powers of the Crown in the state, and he believed his refashioned natural philosophy was but one (albeit novel) instrument by which to achieve this political aim."

52. Bacon, *Works*, 8:109.

53. Martin, "Natural Philosophy," 109.

54. Elsky, *Authorizing Words*, 189, 193. Leary similarly notes that "Bacon always justified his quest for political position on the grounds that power would enable him to do good, but in some respects his years in power were the least inspired and least productive period in his mature life" (*Francis Bacon*, 18).

55. Mario Biagioli, "Scientific Revolution, Social Bricolage, and Etiquette," 18.

56. Martin, *Francis Bacon*, 141. Martin argues that Bacon sought to control anti-authoritarian forms of knowledge, including "voluntary" tendencies among Puritans, independent thought among judges, and the individualism of practitioners of Paracelsian "chemical philosophy" (*Francis Bacon*, esp. 45–71, 105–29; "Natural Philosophy and its Public Concerns," 108–9). In a similar vein, Julie Robin Solomon argues that Bacon attempted to appropriate cognitive practices rooted in commercial culture and align them with the interests of the monarch (*Objectivity in the Making: Francis Bacon and the Politics of Inquiry*).

57. Mario Biagioli, "Etiquette, Interdependence, and Sociability in Seventeenth-Century Science," 237.

216   NOTES TO PAGES 65-67

58. Quoted in Jardine and Stewart, *Hostage*, 397.
59. Quoted in Jardine and Stewart, *Hostage*, 418. Jardine and Stewart enumerate the servants in Bacon's household on pp. 417–18.
60. Ibid., 24.
61. Lawrence Stone, *The Family, Sex and Marriage in England, 1500–1800*, 426. As Jardine and Stewart observe, Bacon's own father exemplified "the possibilities of social advancement brought about by the dual innovations of humanistic learning and Reformation land transactions in Tudor England" (*Hostage*, 23); however, as Mervyn James argues, "There could be no whole-hearted rejection of blood and lineage in a society for which this was still a central concept" (*Society, Politics, and Culture: Studies in Early Modern England*, 375). On the tenacity of the concept of lineage in the sixteenth and seventeenth centuries, see also Felicity Heal and Clive Holmes, *The Gentry in England and Wales, 1500–1700*, 20–47.
62. On Bacon's marriage, see Jardine and Stewart, *Hostage*, 288–91. Eleven days after Bacon died, Alice married his gentleman usher; in a codicil to his will, Bacon revoked the provisions he had previously made for Alice, "for just and great causes," leaving her only her marriage settlement (ibid., 512–13, 500).
63. Bacon, *Works*, 6:391.
64. Ibid., 6:390.
65. Ibid., 6:722.
66. Ibid., 11:63.
67. Ian Box, "Bacon's Moral Philosophy," 267–68.
68. Michel Foucault, *The History of Sexuality*, vol. 1, *An Introduction*, 147. My use of the term "homosociality" is informed by Eve Kosofsky Sedgwick's discussion of "male homosocial desire" in *Between Men: English Literature and Male Homosocial Desire*, 1–5.
69. Rawley, *Life of Bacon*, in Bacon, *Works*, 1:42–43. This image also appears in Thomas Randolph's elegy on Bacon, as he contrasts Bacon to the ancients: "Infantes illi Musas, hic gignit adultas; / Mortales illi, gignit at iste Deas" (They begat infant Muses, he adult; they brought forth mortals, but he gave birth to Goddesses), (Thomas Randolph, "In Obitum Francisci Verulamii," *Poetical and Dramatic Works of Thomas Randolph*, 2:650–51). Sarah Hutton notes that in *De Sapientia Veterum*, Bacon depicts the birth of Pallas Athena as "an allegory of counsel"— Jupiter is the king who swallows the advice of his councillor (as the mythical god devoured his pregnant wife, Metis) and proceeds to "give birth" to policies as if he had generated them independently ("The Riddle of the Sphinx: Francis Bacon and the Emblems of Science," 19). As the gravid Jupiter, Bacon thus assumes the role of king in the writings of Rawley and Randolph.
70. On the dating of this work, see Benjamin Farrington, *The Philosophy of Francis Bacon*, 18.
71. Sir Francis Bacon, *The Masculine Birth of Time*, 62. Bacon similarly addresses "sons" in *The Refutation of Philosophies*, and declares in the Preface to the *Novum Organum* that he invites all "true sons of knowledge" to join in his project (Bacon, *Works*, 4:42).
72. Bacon, *Masculine Birth*, 72.
73. Mark Breitenberg, *Anxious Masculinity in Early Modern England*, 89; Evelyn Fox Keller, *Reflections on Gender and Science*, 41. As Londa Schiebinger has

demonstrated, gendered images of the study of nature were common in works of early modern science ("Feminine Icons: The Face of Early Modern Science"); Bacon, I am suggesting, uses this traditional imagery in a potentially subversive way. As Graham Hammill points out, the eroticism and acts implied in much of Bacon's sexual imagery are not clearly heterosexual ("The Epistemology of Expurgation: Bacon and *The Masculine Birth of Time*," esp. 246–47).

74. Lisa Jardine, "Companionate Marriage Versus Male Friendship: Anxiety for the Lineal Family in Jacobean Drama," 236–37.

75. Alan Stewart, *Close Readers: Humanism and Sodomy in Early Modern England*, xxviii. As Stewart notes on the previous page, his formulation draws on Jonathan Goldberg, *Sodometries: Renaissance Texts, Modern Sexualities*, 19.

76. Many recent scholars conclude that the *New Atlantis* was written after Bacon was impeached, including Peltonen ("Introduction," *Cambridge Companion to Bacon*, 13) and Jardine and Stewart (*Hostage*, 500). J. C. Davis points out that we cannot be certain when the work was first composed, although he favors a date before 1621 (*Utopia and the Ideal Society: A Study of English Utopian Writing, 1516–1700*, 121–22).

77. In Bacon's text, the name of the institution is spelled "Salomon's House"; to avoid confusion, I have consistently amended the spelling to "Solomon's House."

78. Bacon, *Works*, 3:165.

79. Ibid., 3:164.

80. Ibid.

81. Ibid., 3:146–47.

82. Charles C. Whitney, "Merchants of Light: Science as Colonization in the *New Atlantis*," 256, 258. Denise Albanese (*New Science, New World*, 92–120) and Amy Boesky (*Founding Fictions: Utopias in Early Modern England*, 56–83) likewise argue that the activities of Solomon's House are rooted in imperialism. Boesky's chapter on Bacon is an expanded version of her essay "Bacon's *New Atlantis* and the Laboratory of Prose."

83. Bacon, *Works*, 3:165.

84. Ibid., 3:156–65.

85. Boesky, *Founding Fictions*, 80.

86. On the depiction of James I as King Solomon, see Jonathan Goldberg, *James I and the Politics of Literature: Jonson, Shakespeare, Donne, and Their Contemporaries*, 40–42.

87. Quoted in Goldberg, *James I*, 42.

88. Bacon, *Works*, 4:12.

89. Quoted in Jardine and Stewart, *Hostage*, 439. On the structure of the book, see Perez Zagorin, *Francis Bacon*, 74–75.

90. John Michael Archer, "Surveillance and Enlightenment in Bacon's *New Atlantis*," 118.

91. Robert K. Faulkner, *Francis Bacon and the Project of Progress*, 255.

92. Box, "Bacon's Moral Philosophy," 276; Wheeler, "Francis Bacon's *New Atlantis*," 293. Although he does not comment on the ideological implications of his observation, Zagorin similarly notes that rather than the king, "the true authority in Bensalem is Solomon's House" (*Francis Bacon*, 173–74).

93. Bacon, *Works*, 3:154–55, 156.

94. Ibid., 3:165.

95. Albanese, *New Science*, III. For opposing views, see Martin, who down-plays the subversive aspects of the *New Atlantis* to argue that Bacon's text unprob-lematically depicts a monarchy with imperial ambitions (*Francis Bacon*, 135–40), and Sharon Achinstein, who maintains that the *New Atlantis* "shows the workings of new knowledge in the service of traditional paternal authority" ("How To Be a Progressive Without Looking like One: History and Knowledge in Bacon's *New Atlantis*," 250). Although she observes that in Bacon's narrative, "politics was re-placed by scientific administration," Carolyn Merchant believes that "The pa-triarchal character of this utopian society was reinforced" in Bacon's depiction of Solomon's House (*The Death of Nature: Women, Ecology and the Scientific Revolu-tion*, 180).

96. On James I's representation of himself as a patriarch, see Jonathan Gold-berg, "Fatherly Authority: The Politics of Stuart Family Images," esp. 3–5.

97. Rosalys Coope, "The 'Long Gallery': Its Origins, Development, Use and Decoration," 62.

98. Bacon, *Works*, 3:165–66.

99. Ibid., 3:147.

100. Ibid., 3:148.

101. Ibid., 3:148–49.

102. Ibid., 3:149.

103. Ibid.

104. Ibid., 3:150.

105. Ibid., 3:151.

106. Arthur Johnston in *"The Advancement of Learning" and "New Atlantis,"* by Sir Francis Bacon, 290 n.231.

107. For a brief account of More's depiction of the patriarchal family, see Anthony F. C. Wallace, *The Social Context of Innovation*, 63.

108. I am using Raymond Williams's theory of the interplay of dominant and emergent ideologies (*Marxism and Literature*, 121–27). My analysis of Bacon's *New Atlantis* suggests that one needs to qualify Paula Findlen's assertion that in the sixteenth and seventeenth centuries, "Mastery of nature went hand in hand with the rhetoric of absolutism; museums were an eminently visible reminder of how political might, new forms of knowledge, and power over nature could be com-bined" (*Possessing Nature*, 407).

109. Bacon, *Works*, 3:127.

110. Ibid., 14:358.

111. On Bacon's shifting identity as a writer, see Elsky, *Authorizing Words*, 184–205, and "Shakespeare, Bacon, and the Construction of Authorship," 254–63.

112. Bacon, *Works*, 14:285.

113. Ibid., 14:351.

114. Jardine and Stewart, *Hostage*, 521, 524.

115. Bacon, *Works*, 14:539.

116. Adrian Johns, *The Nature of the Book: Print and Knowledge in the Making*, 1–40. Johns suggests that Bacon envisioned an elite, restricted audience for his works (50); his own practice, however, suggests that toward the end of his life Bacon embraced the indeterminate ability of print to reach an audience beyond a

hand-picked coterie (Elsky, *Authorizing Words*, 201–3). During an earlier period of frustrated political ambition, Bacon marveled that "By the Art of Printing, a thing unknown to antiquity, the discoveries and thoughts of individuals are now spread abroad like a flash of lightning" (*Thoughts and Conclusions*, in Farrington, 95; Bacon reiterates this image in *The Refutation of Philosophies*, 132).

117. Bacon, *Works*, 3:318.

118. Rawley reported that between 1621 and 1626, Bacon wrote "*The History of the Reign of King Henry the Seventh*; *Abecedarium Naturae*, or a Metaphysical piece which is lost; *Historia ventorum; Historia vitae et mortis*; *Historia densi et rari*, not yet printed; *Historia gravis et levis*, which is also lost; a *Discourse of a War with Spain*; a *Dialogue touching an Holy War*; the *Fable of the New Atlantis*; a *Preface to a Digest of the Laws of England*; the beginning of the History of the Reign of King Henry the Eighth*; *De Augmentis Scientiarum*, of the Advancement of Learning, put into Latin, with several enrichments and enlargements; *Counsels Civil and Moral*, or his book of *Essays*, likewise enriched and enlarged; the *Conversion of certain Psalms into English Verse*; the *Translation into Latin of the History of King Henry the Seventh*, of the *Counsels Civil and Moral*, of the *Dialogue of the Holy War*, of the *Fable of the New Atlantis*, for the benefit of other nations; his revising of his book *De sapientia veterum*; *Inquisitio de magnete*; *Topica inquisitionis de luce et lumine*; both these not yet printed; lastly, *Sylva sylvarum*, or the *Natural History*" (Rawley, "Life of Bacon," in Bacon, *Works*, 1:9–10).

119. Bacon, *Works*, 14:532n.2; Thomas Bushell, "Mr. Bushell's Minerall Overtures," in *Mr. Bushell's abridgement of the Lord Chancellor Bacon's philosophical theory*, 1. On Bacon's scientific works published after 1621, see Zagorin, *Francis Bacon*, 103–4, 106–7; for a fascinating account of Thomas Bushell's self-fashioned identity as the "heir of [Bacon's] knowledge in mineral philosophy" ("Minerall Overtures," 2), see Jardine and Stewart, *Hostage*, 523–24.

120. Rawley, "Life of Bacon," in Bacon, *Works*, 1:43.

121. On Rawley's activities, see Jardine and Stewart, *Hostage*, 521–23.

122. Quoted in Michael Hunter, *John Aubrey and the Realm of Learning*, 41–42.

123. Theodore M. Brown, "The Rise of Baconianism in Seventeenth Century England," 518.

124. Charles Webster, *The Great Instauration: Science, Medicine, and Reform, 1626–1660*, 515–16.

125. Hugh Trevor-Roper, *Religion, the Reformation and Social Change*, 225. On Hartlib and his circle, see William Eamon, *Science and the Secrets of Nature: Books of Secrets in Medieval and Early Modern Culture*, 324–29; Trevor-Roper, *Religion, the Reformation and Social Change*, 249–93; and Webster, *Great Instauration*. On utopian literature which emerged from this milieu, see Boesky, *Founding Fictions*, 84–100.

126. Theodore M. Brown, "The Rise of Baconianism," 505. On the spectrum of political affiliations held by "Baconians" during the Civil War and Interregnum, see also Michael Hunter, *Science and Society in Restoration England*, 24–29.

127. Steven Shapin, *The Scientific Revolution*, 95.

128. Alistair C. Crombie, "Science and the Arts in the Renaissance: The Search for Truth and Certainty, Old and New," 15; Eamon, *Science and the Secrets of Nature*, 301.

129. Katie Whitaker, "The Culture of Curiosity," 75; Whitaker's dissertation, "Curiosi and Virtuosi: Gentlemanly Culture, Experimental Philosophy, and Political Life in England, 1620–1685," provides a greatly expanded treatment of this subject. On the "curiosity" of the seventeenth-century virtuoso, see also Eamon, *Science and the Secrets of Nature*, 314–18; and Daston and Park, *Wonders*, 218–19, 305–10.

130. Quoted in Michael Hunter, *Science and the Shape of Orthodoxy: Intellectual Change in Late Seventeenth-Century Britain*, 84–87, 87n.78.

131. Daston and Park formulate this dynamic in *Wonders*, 158.

132. On princely encyclopedic collections, see above, Chapter 1.

133. Daston, "The Factual Sensibility," 458. Daston argues against viewing princely collections as microcosmic; Daston overstates her case, however, and I would suggest that while many of the subject positions constructed by early modern collections depend to some extent on the rarity of the objects amassed, nonetheless the symbolism of cosmic comprehensiveness typical of earlier princely collections distinguishes them from later cabinets of curiosities.

134. Walter E. Houghton, Jr., "The English Virtuoso in the Seventeenth Century," 53.

135. Eamon, *Science and the Secrets of Nature*, 302; as Eamon indicates, his analysis is indebted to Lawrence Stone's *The Crisis of the Aristocracy, 1558–1641*.

136. John Evelyn quoted in Michael Hunter, *Science and the Shape of Orthodoxy*, 83; on the idle, melancholic country gentleman, see Eamon, *Science and the Secrets of Nature*, 304.

137. Robert Burton, *The Anatomy of Melancholy*, Part 2, 86–87.

138. Henry Peacham, *Peacham's "Compleat Gentleman," 1634*, 160–61; Walker quoted in Houghton, "The English Virtuoso," 63.

139. Peacham, *"Compleat Gentleman,"* 39–40.

140. Bacon, *Masculine Birth of Time*, 72. On the Baconianism of Puritan reformers, see Webster, *Great Instauration*, passim.

141. Krysztof Pomian, *Collectors and Curiosities*, 5, 10.

142. Pomian, *Collectors and Curiosities*, 32.

143. Steven Shapin, *A Social History of Truth: Civility and Science in Seventeenth-Century England*, 48, 52.

144. Thomas Shadwell, *The Virtuoso*, 2.2.89. Shadwell's satiric depiction of Sir Nicholas explicitly lampoons the activities of the Royal Society: as Claude Lloyd has demonstrated, Shadwell draws on Thomas Sprat's *History of the Royal Society*, Robert Hooke's richly illustrated book about microscopy, *Micrographia*, and the Royal Society's *Philosophical Transactions* ("Shadwell and the Virtuosi"). Decades later, Jonathan Swift would similarly attack experimental science in the third book of *Gulliver's Travels*.

145. *The Tatler*, ed. Donald F. Bond, 3:134 (no. 216, 26 August 1710), 3:155 (no. 221, 7 September 1710).

146. Anon., *An Essay In Defence of the Female Sex*, 91. The essay is often attributed to Mary Astell; the original, a French work published in 1695, did not include the "Character of a Vertuoso" found in the English version of 1696. Transformed into "Dr. Fossile," Woodward was later ridiculed by John Gay, Alexander Pope, and John Arbuthnot in the play *Three Hours After Marriage* (1717). On satiric depictions of Woodward, see Joseph M. Levine, *Dr. Woodward's Shield: History*,

Science and Satire in Augustan England, 114–29. On the satirization of "curiosity" more generally, see Dennis Quinn, "Polypragmosyne in the Renaissance: Ben Jonson."

147. Anon., *An Essay In Defence of the Female Sex*, 94. On the Duchess of Beaufort as a plant collector, see Douglas Chambers, "'Storys of Plants': The Assembling of Mary Capel Somerset's Botanical Collection at Badminton." On virtuoso activities and gender ideology, see Lynette Hunter, "Sisters of the Royal Society: The Circle of Katherine Jones, Lady Ranelagh," and Frances Harris, "Living in the Neighbourhood of Science: Mary Evelyn, Margaret Cavendish and the Greshamites."

148. Quoted in Michael Hunter, *John Aubrey*, 93.

149. Eamon, *Science and the Secrets of Nature*, 306. Eamon discusses this genre on pp. 305–14.

150. Quoted in Eamon, *Science and the Secrets of Nature*, 306.

151. John Evelyn, *Evelyn's Sculptura With the Unpublished Second Part*, 147–48.

152. Evelyn to Boyle, quoted in Eamon, *Science and the Secrets of Nature*, 344.

153. Harold J. Cook, "Physicians and the New Philosophy: Henry Stubbe and the Virtuosi Physicians," in *The Medical Revolution of the Seventeenth Century*, 248.

154. Houghton, "The English Virtuoso," 72.

155. Michael Hunter, *Establishing the New Science: The Experience of the Early Royal Society*, 1.

156. Charles Webster, "The Origins of the Royal Society," 116. On the Royal Society's Baconianism as a form of ideological protective camouflage, see also Paul B. Wood, "Methodology and Apologetics: Thomas Sprat's *History of the Royal Society*"; and Michael Hunter, "Latitudinarianism and the 'Ideology' of the Early Royal Society: Thomas Sprat's *History of the Royal Society* (1667) Reconsidered," in his *Establishing the New Science*, 45–71.

157. Quoted in Alvin Snider, *Origin and Authority in Seventeenth-Century England*, 74.

158. Snider, *Origin and Authority*, 80. On the frontispiece, see also Boesky, *Founding Fictions*, 81–83; on the office of President in the early Royal Society, see Michael Hunter, *Establishing the New Science*, 18–19.

159. Michael Hunter, *Establishing the New Science*, 10; Antonio Pérez-Ramos, *Francis Bacon's Idea of Science and the Maker's Knowledge Tradition*, 12. On the construction of the Royal Society as a site of gentlemanly consensus, see also Steven Shapin and Simon Schaffer, *Leviathan and the Air-Pump: Hobbes, Boyle, and the Experimental Life*, 72–76, 283–331; and Shapin, "'A Scholar and a Gentleman': The Problematic Identity of the Scientific Practitioner in Early Modern England."

160. Webster, *Great Instauration*, 491–92.

161. Abraham Cowley, "Ode to the Royal Society," in Thomas Sprat, *History of the Royal Society*, B1v. For an insightful analysis of Cowley's depiction of Bacon in the "Ode," see Snider, *Origin and Authority*, 79–82.

162. Michael Hunter, *Establishing the New Science*, 11; Sprat, *History of the Royal Society*, 67. On the elite bias of the Royal Society's policies, see also Michael Hunter, *The Royal Society and Its Fellows 1660–1700: The Morphology of an Early Scientific Institution*, 8, 15; and Steven Shapin, "The House of Experiment in Seventeenth-Century England," 288.

163. Michael Hunter, *Science and the Shape of Orthodoxy*, 104. As Michael

Hunter and Paul B. Wood observe, this divergence reflected "a tension in the Baconian corpus" itself, for while the *Novum Organum* stressed "the value of systematic experimentation as opposed to casual observation," Bacon's own practice in the *Sylva Sylvarum* "sanctioned an alternative tradition comprising the random compilation of observations and the occasional rudimentary experiment" ("Towards Solomon's House: Rival Strategies for Reforming the Early Royal Society," 207–8). On the disparate outlooks of the early members of the Royal Society, see also K. Theodore Hoppen, "The Nature of the Early Royal Society."

164. Wood, "Methodology and Apologetics," 20.

165. Sprat, *History of the Royal Society*, 195.

166. Ibid., 403.

167. Ibid., 409.

168. Ibid., 405–6.

169. Quoted in Michael Hunter, *John Aubrey*, 64.

170. Michael Hunter, *Establishing the New Science*, 49. Henry Oldenburg sent copies of the printed lists to his correspondents, who appreciated the social cachet which the Society thus exhibited; as one foreign recipient of a membership list gushed, "like a second Apollo the King himself presides as supreme moderator and governor of this band of stars, among whom are to be found the sons of kings, princes, dukes, magnates, landowners, counts, barons, great patrons of learned men, and a host of men of all orders distinguished for their learning and wisdom" (quoted in Michael Hunter, *Royal Society and Its Fellows*, 10).

171. Michael Hunter, "Between Cabinet of Curiosities and Research Collection: The History of the Royal Society's 'Repository,'" in his *Establishing the New Science*, 125. My discussion of the Repository is greatly indebted to Hunter's analysis; as the author notes, this essay "largely supersedes" (xi) his earlier account of the Repository in "The Cabinet Institutionalized: The Royal Society's Repository and its Background," in *Origins of Museums*, ed. Oliver Impey and Arthur MacGregor, 156–68.

172. Thomas Birch, *The History of the Royal Society of London*, 1:393.

173. At the Annual Meeting in April 1666, it was revealed that Fellows of the Society were in arrears with their subscriptions to the tune of nearly £700 (Charles Richard Weld, *History of the Royal Society, with Memoirs of the Presidents*, 1:191).

174. Michael Hunter, *Establishing the New Science*, 127.

175. Nehemiah Grew, *Musaeum Regalis Societatis. Or a Catalogue & Description Of the Natural and Artificial Rarities Belonging to the Royal Society and Preserved at Gresham Colledge*, Epistle Dedicatory.

176. Michael Hunter, *Establishing the New Science*, 33; Sprat, *History of the Royal Society*, 72.

177. Quoted in Michael Hunter, *Establishing the New Science*, 128.

178. On Hubert's collection and catalogues, see above, Introduction.

179. Michael Hunter, *Establishing the New Science*, 123. The Society's operator (an employee involved in conducting experiments) was allowed to charge visitors to the Repository as a means of augmenting his salary (A. D. C. Simpson, "Newton's Telescope and the Cataloguing of the Royal Society's Repository," 191; on the duties of the operator, see Shapin, *Social History of Truth*, 363–64).

180. Grew, *Musaeum*, n.p.; Grew ominously notes that the list is incomplete, as there are "some Names which are lost."

181. Zacharias Conrad von Uffenbach, *London in 1710: From the Travels of Zacharias Conrad von Uffenbach*, 98. Writing in 1710, von Uffenbach goes on to lament that the high expectations raised by these printed representations of the Repository were shattered when he actually visited the collection, the objects displayed "not only in no sort of order or tidiness but covered with dust, filth and coal-smoke, and many of them broken and utterly ruined" (ibid.).

182. Johns, *Nature of the Book*, 476.

183. Ibid.

184. Ibid., 485, 499. Although the *Philosophical Transactions* were not an official publication of the Royal Society, being "formally" under the personal editorial and financial control of Henry Oldenburg, "few readers seem to have believed that this was really the case" (ibid., 499).

185. Paula Findlen, "The Economy of Scientific Exchange in Early Modern Italy," 6.

186. Birch, *History of the Royal Society*, 1:322, 344; 3:158.

187. Grew, *Musaeum*, 1, 8, 9, 31, 364, 368, 367.

188. Ibid., Epistle Dedicatory.

189. For a provocative analysis of the relationship between early modern miniatures and elite identity, see Patricia Fumerton, *Cultural Aesthetics: Renaissance Literature and the Practice of Social Ornament*, 67–110.

190. Grew, *Musaeum*, Tables 1, 2, 6.

191. *Philosophical Transactions* 1 (1665–66): 321. As the comments of von Uffenbach suggest, however (see above, n.191), the holdings of the Repository were not well cared for.

192. Levine, *Dr. Woodward's Shield*, 95; Stephen Bann, *Under the Sign: John Bargrave as Collector, Traveler, and Witness*, 124–26; Michael Hunter, *John Aubrey*, 86–87, 90.

193. Quoted in Margaret J. M. Ezell, "Richard Waller, S.R.S.: 'In the Pursuit of Nature,'" 219.

194. Bacon, *Works*, 8:335.

195. Ibid., 3:332; Sprat, *History of the Royal Society*, 251.

196. Henry Oldenburg, *The Correspondence of Henry Oldenburg*, 3:525.

197. Robert Hooke, *The Posthumous Works of Robert Hooke*, 338; Grew, *Musaeum*, Preface. For a Foucauldian analysis of the Repository and its relationship to the preoccupation with taxonomy characteristic of the "classical episteme," see Eilean Hooper-Greenhill, *Museums and the Shaping of Knowledge*, 133–66.

198. Michael Hunter, *Establishing the New Science*, 137.

199. Hooke, *Posthumous Works*, 338.

200. Quoted in Weld, *History of the Royal Society*, 1:190.

201. Grew, *Musaeum*, Table 2; "List of those who have Contributed."

202. Raymond Phineas Stearns, "James Petiver, Promoter of Natural Science, c. 1663–1718," 245–46. I am indebted to Stearns's article throughout my analysis of Petiver.

203. Stearns, "James Petiver," 244. Petiver labels the objects in his collection as "*Rariora Naturae*" in the title of one of his sets of published catalogues, the *Musei Petiveriani Centuria[e]*.

204. Richard Pulteney, *Historical and Biographical Sketches of the Progress of Botany in England*, 2:32.

205. Pulteney, *Historical and Biographical Sketches*, 2:32.

206. Quoted in Stearns, "James Petiver," 317.

207. On Petiver's trip to Leiden, where he acted as Sir Hans Sloane's emissary to purchase a collection, see ibid., 282.

208. Ibid., 253–54, 291.

209. Quoted in Stearns, "James Petiver," 266; on Bartar, see ibid., 258.

210. Quoted in ibid., 266. Petiver indeed published a series of papers in the *Philosophical Transactions* which were essentially catalogues of rarities he had acquired and the names of the people who had suppplied the specimens to him. The September 1701 issue of the *Transactions*, for example, featured "A Description of *some* Shells *found on the* Molucca Islands" which Petiver received from "my Ingenious Friends *Mr Sylvanus Landon* and *Mr Rowleston Jacobs*" (*Philosophical Transactions*, no. 274). For a list of the more than 20 papers Petiver thus published, see Pulteney, *Historical and Biographical Sketches*, 2:38–42.

211. Quoted in Stearns, "James Petiver," 322–23.

212. Quoted in ibid., 322.

213. Ibid., 261.

214. Quoted in ibid., 265; on Brown, see ibid., 258.

215. James Petiver, *Musei Petiveriani Centuria Prima [- Decima]*, 15.

216. Ibid., 43.

217. Oxford English Dictionary, s.v. "gazophylacium."

218. James Petiver, *Gazophylacii Naturae & Artis Decas Prima [- Decas Quinta]*, Table 6, Figure 5; Table 6, Figure 6; Table 3, Figure 8.

219. Pulteney, *Historical and Biographical Sketches*, 2:33.

220. Petiver, *Gazophylacii*, Table 7, Figure 4; Table 42, Figure 6; Table 44, Figure 13; Table 28, Figure 2.

221. Petiver, *Gazophylacii*, Tables 1, 3, 4, 11, 39. According to Stearns, Petiver also dedicates plates to different individuals in his *Pterigraphia Americana*, published in 1712 ("James Petiver," 315, 319).

222. James Petiver, *Gazophylacii Naturae & Artis: Decas Sexta*, Table 51, Figure 1, in *Jacobi Petiveri Opera*.

Chapter 3. The Countryside as Collection: Chorography, Antiquarianism, and the Politics of Landscape

1. Thomas Randolph, "On the Inestimable Content he enjoys in the Muses," *Works of Thomas Randolph*, 2:523

2. Mervyn James, *Family, Lineage, and Civil Society*, 27.

3. Steven Shapin, *A Social History of Truth: Civility and Science in Seventeenth-Century England*, 48.

4. Quoted in Shapin, *Social History of Truth*, 50.

5. Quoted in Keith Wrightson, "The Social Order of Early Modern England: Three Approaches,"181, emphasis added.

6. Felicity Heal and Clive Holmes, *The Gentry in England and Wales, 1500–1700*, 33.

7. Ibid., 22.

8. Lawrence Stone, *The Crisis of the Aristocracy, 1558–1641*, 22. On social mobility, see also G. E. Mingay, *The Gentry: The Rise and Fall of a Ruling Class*, 4–10.

9. Stone, *Crisis of the Aristocracy*, 94.

10. Ibid., 93.

11. Shapin, *Social History of Truth*, 63.

12. On the medieval property system, see Tom Williamson and Liz Bellamy, *Property and Landscape: A Social History of Land Ownership and the English Countryside*, 29–93.

13. C. B. Macpherson, "Capitalism and the Changing Concept of Property," 110–11.

14. On the sale and purchase of Crown lands in the sixteenth century, see Joyce Youings, *Sixteenth-Century England*, 158–63.

15. P. D. A. Harvey, "English Estate Maps: Their Early History and Their Use as Historical Evidence," 30. As Harvey observes, one could not construct a map from even the most detailed written survey: "The survey gives bounds and areas, but it does not give angles or shapes" (49).

16. I follow the definition of an estate map provided by Harvey, "English Estate Maps," 27.

17. Ibid., 31–32.

18. Andrew McRae, *God Speed the Plough: The Representation of Agrarian England, 1500–1660*, 18–19.

19. A. Sarah Bendall, *Maps, Land and Society: A History, With a Carto-bibliography of Cambridgeshire Estate Maps, c. 1600–1836*, 10; Norden quoted in ibid., 50. On enclosure and emparking, see Williamson and Bellamy, *Property and Landscape*, 94–115, 136–39; and Leonard Cantor, *The Changing English Countryside, 1400–1700*, 28–38.

20. McRae, *God Speed the Plough*, 190; Harvey, "English Estate Maps," 48; Bendall, *Maps*, 139.

21. McRae, *God Speed the Plough*, 190.

22. J. B. Harley, "Silences and Secrecy: The Hidden Agenda of Cartography in Early Modern Europe," 57.

23. Arthur Hopton, *Speculum Topographicum: Of the Topographicall Glasse* (London, 1611), quoted in Stan A. E. Mendyk, *"Speculum Britanniae": Regional Study, Antiquarianism, and Science in Britain to 1700*, 22.

24. Howard Marchitello, "Political Maps: The Production of Cartography in Early Modern England," in his *Narrative and Meaning in Early Modern England*, 85, 78. As Marchitello argues, although maps attempt to suppress their participation in historical process, they "are always narrational in nature" (63). Through annotation and amendment, however, maps can become more overtly diachronic in their representation of the landscape; for descriptions of amended early modern estate maps, see Harvey, "English Estate Maps," 43, 51–53.

25. Richard Helgerson, "The Land Speaks," in his *Forms of Nationhood: The Elizabethan Writing of England*, 133.

26. Lesley B. Cormack, "'Good Fences Make Good Neighbors': Geography as Self-Definition in Early Modern England," 81; Helgerson, *Forms of Nationhood*, 135, 133. On the continental humanist roots of English chorography, see

Cormack, "Good Fences," 81–82. Supposedly, to bear arms one needed to prove descent from three generations of gentry on both sides of one's family; however, "ways were frequently found to finesse that requirement" (Shapin, *Social History of Truth*, 53).

27. William Camden, "Mr Camdens Preface," in *Camden's Britannia, Newly Translated into English*. Gibson used the 1607 Latin edition of *Britannia* as the basis of his translation. On Gibson's 1695 edition, see Graham Parry, *"Britannia* Revised," in his *The Trophies of Time*, 332–33, and Stuart Piggott, "William Camden and The *Britannia*," in his *Ruins in a Landscape*, 44–48.

28. Camden, *Britannia*, 6.

29. As Bendall notes, "The right to heraldic devices symbolized the right to possess land" (*Maps*, 182).

30. Camden, *Britannia*, 142.

31. Ibid., 159.

32. Richard Carew, *The Survey of Cornwall*, 63–64.

33. Ibid., iiiir–v, 134r–v, 117r.

34. Ibid., 117r.

35. William Burton, *The Description of Leicester Shire*, 291.

36. Helgerson, *Forms of Nationhood*, 132.

37. Ibid., 136, 146–47, 326 n.61; Lesley B. Cormack, *Charting an Empire: Geography at the English Universities, 1580–1620*, 201; Heal and Holmes, *Gentry in England and Wales*, 434–35.

38. Helgerson, *Forms of Nationhood*, 122, 124.

39. Ibid., 136; Cormack, *Charting an Empire*, 164.

40. Carew, *Survey*, 100.

41. Ibid., 102–7.

42. William Burton, *Description*, "To the Reader."

43. Burton, *Description*, 174.

44. Piggott suggests that Camden's father, described as a *"pictor*," may have been involved in "heraldic draughtsmanship" (*Ruins*, 34).

45. Cormack, *Charting an Empire*, 195.

46. D. R. Woolf, *The Idea of History in Early Stuart England*, 21.

47. Thomas Blundeville, *The True Order and Methode of wryting and reading Hystories* (1574), quoted in F. J. Levy, "The Making of Camden's *Britannia*," 74.

48. Ibid.

49. Arthur B. Ferguson, *Clio Unbound: Perception of the Social and Cultural Past in Renaissance England*, xii.

50. Sir Francis Bacon, *Works*, 4:303.

51. Ibid.

52. Ibid., 4:304.

53. Ferguson, *Clio Unbound*, 55–56; Parry, *Trophies of Time*, 13.

54. Ferguson, *Clio Unbound*, 80–81; D. R. Woolf, "The Dawn of the Artifact: The Antiquarian Impulse in England, 1500–1730." We now regard this emphasis on physical artifacts as a hallmark of antiquarianism; for a provocative discussion of the primacy of sensory experience in the antiquarian's relationship to the past, see Stephen Bann, "Clio in Part: On Antiquarianism and the Historical Fragment," in his *The Inventions of History: Essays on the Representation of the Past*, 111–21.

55. Mendyk, *"Speculum Britanniae"*, 44–45; T. D. Kendrick, *British Antiquity*, 55. A cautionary figure for researchers, Leland apparently was driven mad by his inability to organize the vast "collections" he had so laboriously compiled.

56. Kendrick, *British Antiquity*, 162–64. Although Norden largely paraphrased Richard Carew's earlier work on Cornwall, his interest in and illustrations of archaeological sites were entirely original, and Mendyk links this difference in perception of the countryside to Norden's activities as a surveyor of the Duchy of Cornwall: "Since becoming surveyor Norden was obliged to illustrate his surveys with architectural drawings, bird's-eye views of the landscape, and the like" (*"Speculum Britanniae,"* 67–68).

57. Ken Arnold, "Cabinets for the Curious: Practicing Science in Early Modern English Museums," 78 n.69.

58. Kevin Sharpe, "Introduction: Rewriting Sir Robert Cotton," 6.

59. John Speed, "A Summary Conclusion of the Whole," in his *The Theatre of the Empire of Great Britaine*, n.p.

60. Parry, *Trophies of Time*, 75.

61. Speed explains that he has included coins of "such British princes as by their inscriptions are known to be theirs. And wheras some are not yet noted by that honor to the world; I haue vnto such added only blankes, if happily more be reueiled hereafter, and the bowels of the earth deliuer to others, her treasures hid, as formerly (and in these our searching daies) she hath already done" (*Theatre of the Empire*, 172; see Figure 7).

62. Camden, Preface, in *Britannia*.

63. Kendrick, *British Antiquity*, 151 n.1. On the development of Camden's *Britannia*, see also Levy, "The Making of Camden's *Britannia*."

64. On Cotton's acquisition of the stones and his display of his status through physical objects at Conington, see Glenys Davies, "Sir Robert Cotton's Collection of Roman Stones: A Catalogue with Commentary"; David Howarth, "Sir Robert Cotton and the Commemoration of Famous Men"; and David McKitterick, "From Camden to Cambridge: Sir Robert Cotton's Roman Inscriptions, and Their Subsequent Treatment." On Cotton's identity as a country gentleman, see Sharpe, "Introduction," 22–23.

65. *Britannia*, trans. 1610, quoted in McKitterick, "From Camden to Cambridge," 114–15. In his *Theatre of the Empire of Great Britaine*, Speed also included pictures of the inscribed stones "now preserved by Sir Robert Cotton of Connington" (222).

66. Woolf, "Dawn of the Artifact," 16–17.

67. Roger B. Manning, "Antiquarianism and the Seigneurial Reaction: Sir Robert and Sir Thomas Cotton and their Tenants," 277, 279–80.

68. Parry, *Trophies of Time*, 90; Kevin Sharpe, *Sir Robert Cotton, 1586–1631: History and Politics in Early Modern England*, 39–40. On Charles I's closing of Cotton's library, see also Sharpe, "Introduction," 21–22.

69. Before the eighteenth century, headstones were generally not erected in English churchyards; as David Cressy observes, "Families of the middling sort sometimes erected ephemeral memorials of perishable material, and tidy-minded bishops sought to have them removed" (*Birth, Marriage, and Death: Ritual, Religion, and the Life-Cycle in Tudor and Stuart England*, 470).

70. Nigel Llewellyn, *The Art of Death: Visual Culture in the English Death Ritual, c.1500–c.1800*, 104, 49.

71. Cressy, *Birth, Marriage, and Death*, 471, 462. John Phillips observes that the dynastic function of funerary monuments was heightened by post-Reformation iconoclasm: since previously acceptable images of the Virgin Mary and the saints were no longer condoned, rank and lineage became even more central to representations of deceased members of the elite (*The Reformation of Images: Destruction of Art in England, 1535–1660*, 118–19). As Phillips notes, although "funeral monuments constructed as family records predate the Reformation," the upsurge of iconoclasm "hastened the process" by which lineage became their primary concern (119 n.20).

72. Parry, *Trophies of Time*, 208.

73. On the function of heraldry in early modern English funerary art, see Nigel Llewellyn, "Claims to Status through Visual Codes: Heraldry on Post-Reformation Funeral Monuments."

74. John Weever, *Ancient Funerall Monuments With In The United Monarchie of Great Britaine, Ireland, and the Ilands Adiacent*, 10–11. For entertaining descriptions of pretentious early modern tombs encrusted with spurious genealogical claims, see Heal and Holmes, *Gentry in England and Wales*, 35.

75. McKitterick, "From Camden to Cambridge," 115.

76. William Burton, *Description*, "To the Reader."

77. Weever, *Ancient Funerall Monuments*, "The Author to the Reader."

78. On the Protestant ideology of iconoclasm and its clash with ceremonialism in early modern England, see Achsah Guibbory, *Ceremony and Community From Herbert to Milton*, 11–43. I follow Guibbory's use of the term "ceremonialist" to designate "those who embraced the English church's rituals and ceremonies" (*Ceremony*, 6).

79. Margaret Aston, *England's Iconoclasts*, 1:269. On iconoclasm during the reign of Henry VIII, see Phillips, *Reformation of Images*, 50–81, esp. 77.

80. Aston, *England's Iconoclasts*, 1:314–15, 317.

81. Ibid., 1:269.

82. Weever, *Ancient Funerall Monuments*, 18.

83. Guibbory, *Ceremony and Community*, 12.

84. Ibid., 13; Kevin Sharpe, *The Personal Rule of Charles I*, 317–45.

85. Quoted in Guibbory, *Ceremony and Community*, 13. Economic motives were also at work in the iconoclasm of the Civil War period, as in previous eras, for church brasses could be sold as scrap metal (Aston, *England's Iconoclasts*, 1:83).

86. Quoted in Mendyk, *"Speculum Britanniae"*, 174.

87. Quoted in Aston, *England's Iconoclasts*, 1:77.

88. Ibid., 1:64–65.

89. Quoted in ibid., 1:69.

90. John Evelyn, *The Diary of John Evelyn*, ed. E. S. de Beer, 3:132.

91. Nigel Llewellyn, "Cromwell and the Tombs: Historiography and Style in Post-Reformation English Funeral Monuments."

92. Ralph Thoresby, "Additions to the West-riding of Yorkshire," in Camden, *Camden's Britannia*, 736. On Fairfax's role in preserving the antiquities of York even as he led the troops which besieged the city, see Parry, *Trophies of Time*, 222; on Fair-

fax's financial support of the antiquarian Roger Dodsworth, see William Hamper in Sir William Dugdale, *The Life, Diary, and Correspondence of Sir William Dugdale*, 25n.

93. Parry, *Trophies of Time*, 364, 19.

94. Mendyk, *"Speculum Britanniae"*, 103.

95. Sir William Dugdale, *The Antiquities of Warwickshire*, Preface.

96. Dugdale, *Warwickshire*, 756. On Dugdale's use of the antiquarian research of Sir Simon Archer in compiling the chorography, see Ann Hughes, *Politics, Society and Civil War in Warwickshire, 1620–1660*, 300–301.

97. After he compounded for his estate in 1646, Dugdale "was confined sometimes to a mile, and sometimes to five miles, of his house" (Dugdale, *Life, Diary and Correspondence*, 22n).

98. Sir William Dugdale, *The History of St. Pauls Cathedral in London, From Its Foundation Untill These Times*, dedicatory epistle.

99. Dugdale, *St. Pauls Cathedral*, 172; *Dictionary of National Biography*, s.v. "Sir William Dugdale"; Dugdale, *Life, Diary and Correspondence*, 21.

100. *Dictionary of National Biography*, s.v. "Sir William Dugdale."

101. Dugdale, *Life, Diary and Correspondence*, 23.

102. Parry, *Trophies of Time*, 230.

103. J[ames] W[right], *Monasticon Anglicanum Epitomized in English* (1693), "To the Reader." In compiling the text, Dugdale drew heavily on the collections (research notes) of the Yorkshire antiquary Roger Dodsworth, although Dugdale tended to accept full credit for the work; on the authorship of the *Monasticon*, see David C. Douglas, *English Scholars, 1660–1730*, 32–38.

104. Dugdale, *Warwickshire*, Preface, Epistle Dedicatory.

105. Dugdale, *Life, Diary and Correspondence*, 26.

106. Dugdale, *Warwickshire*, Preface, "To my Honoured Friends the Gentrie of Warwickshire."

107. Hughes, *Politics, Society and Civil War in Warwickshire*, 300–301.

108. Dugdale, *Warwickshire*, Preface, b3.

109. Dugdale, *St. Pauls Cathedral*, dedicatory epistle, 192, 173.

110. Ibid., 192.

111. Dugdale, *Life, Diary and Correspondence*, 27.

112. Michael Wilding, *Dragons Teeth: Literature in the English Revolution*, 89. Wilding's viewpoint is shared by Guibbory, who argues that when Browne wrote *Religio Medici*, "the language of reasonable moderation and peace had become the rhetoric of Laudian repression" (*Ceremony and Community*, 127). Both Wilding and Guibbory thus contest Jonathan F. S. Post's assessment of Browne as a "moderate Protestant" (*Sir Thomas Browne*, 47).

113. Wilding, *Dragons Teeth*, 106.

114. Sir Thomas Browne, *Religio Medici*, in *The Works of Sir Thomas Browne*, ed. Geoffrey Keynes, 1:22. Unless otherwise indicated, all future references to Browne's works are to this edition, and volume and page numbers are included, in parentheses, in the text.

115. Post, *Sir Thomas Browne*, 49.

116. Geoffrey Keynes, Editor's Preface, in Browne, *Works of Sir Thomas Browne*, 3:xii.

117. As Post observes, Hall was dubbed the "Christian Seneca" and was com-

memorated "as a signal reminder of the unjust treatment of the righteous minister at the hands of the Puritan authorities"; Browne's religious affiliations are not strictly conservative, however, since he devotes even more time to praising his "Honord freind" Bishop Edward Reynolds (3:134), who was a tolerationist (Post, *Sir Thomas Browne*, 133, 52).

118. Quoted in Guibbory, *Ceremony and Community*, 132.

119. Ibid., 136.

120. Post, *Sir Thomas Browne*, 1–12; Browne, *Works of Sir Thomas Browne*, ed. Keynes, 4:vii–viii.

121. C. A. Patrides, "'Above Atlas His Shoulders': An Introduction to Sir Thomas Browne," in Sir Thomas Browne, *Sir Thomas Browne: The Major Works*, ed. Patrides, 21.

122. Quoted in Marie Boas Hall, "Thomas Browne, Naturalist," 184.

123. See the *Miscellany Tracts*, "Miscellaneous Observations and Notes," and "Notes on the Natural History of Norfolk" in the third volume of Browne's *Works*, ed. Keynes. On Browne as a typical virtuoso, see Arno Löffler, *Sir Thomas Browne als Virtuoso; die Bedeutung der Gelehrsamkeit für sein literarisches Alterswerk.*.

124. Post, *Sir Thomas Browne*, 133; Browne, *Sir Thomas Browne*, ed. Patrides, 263 n.1.

125. R. W. Ketton-Cremer, *A Norfolk Gallery*, 109–10. Likewise, near the conclusion of *Urne-Buriall*, Browne notes how the urns have survived tumult, "quietly rest[ing] under the drums and tramplings of three conquests" (*Works of Sir Thomas Browne*, ed. Keynes, 1:164); as Post comments, Browne thus "speak[s] to the disestablished" by suggesting the value of Anglican quietism in the face of war (*Sir Thomas Browne*, 143).

126. Sir Thomas Browne, "To my Worthy and Honoured Friend Nicholas Bacon of Gillingham Esquire," in his *Hydriotaphia, Urne-Buriall, or, A Discourse of the Sepulchrall Urnes lately found in Norfolk*.

127. Post, *Sir Thomas Browne*, 133.

128. Browne, *Works of Sir Thomas Browne*, ed. Keynes, 1:133; trans. from Browne, *Sir Thomas Browne*, ed. Patrides, 265 n.16. I am indebted to Richard F. Hardin for suggesting this reading to me. For an outline of Le Gros's lineage, see William Tylney Spurdens, "Particulars of the Hundred of Tunstead," 90–91. Browne's de-emphasis of Le Gros's lineage was ironically prescient: as Spurdens notes, Thomas Le Gros left only a female heir, "whose son Charles, took the name of Groos [sic]; but, having no issue male, he barr'd the entail, and sold this and the rest of the estates of this antient family to Lord Walpole" (91n.).

129. Robert Thoroton, *The Antiquities of Nottinghamshire*, Preface.

130. Woolf, "Dawn of the Artifact," 20.

131. Anthony Grafton, *The Footnote: A Curious History*, 179.

132. William W. E. Slights, "The Edifying Margins of Renaissance English Books," 682.

133. Evelyn B. Tribble, *Margins and Marginality: The Printed Page in Early Modern England*, 9; see also Tribble's second chapter, pp. 57–100, for elaboration of these ideas.

134. Parry, *Trophies of Time*, 256.

135. Bent Juel-Jensen, "*Musaeum Clausum, or Bibliotheca Abscondita*: Some Thoughts on Curiosity Cabinets and Imaginary Books," 135.

NOTES TO PAGES 133-145

136. C. A. Patrides, "'The Best Part of Nothing': Sir Thomas Browne and the Strategy of Indirection," 32–33.

137. Mendyk, *"Speculum Britanniae"*, 9.

138. Camden, *Brittania*, 158, 388.

139. Joshua Childrey, *Britannia Baconica: Or, the Natural Rarities of England, Scotland, & Wales*, Ba. On Childrey's background, see Mendyk, *"Speculum Britanniae"*, 166.

140. Childrey, *Britannia Baconica*, 21, 51, 30, 168.

141. Ibid., B2a.

142. Ibid., "Preface to the Reader."

143. Heal and Holmes, *Gentry in England and Wales*, 23, 39.

144. McRae, *God Speed the Plough*, 7.

145. Joan Thirsk, "Agricultural Innovations and Their Diffusion," 587. My analysis of the problems facing landlords after the 1640s is indebted to Christopher Clay, "Landlords and Estate Management in England."

146. R. F. Ovenell, *The Ashmolean Museum, 1683–1894*, 31–35.

147. Quoted in ibid., 31.

148. Robert Plot, *The Natural History of Oxford-shire, being an Essay towards the Natural History of England*, 308. All future references to the work are to this edition, and page numbers are included, in parentheses, in the text.

149. Ovenell, *Ashmolean Museum*, 32. On the seventeenth-century construction of the gentleman as a disinterested and thus trustworthy source of empirical evidence, see Shapin, *Social History of Truth*, 65–95.

150. Plot was also a linchpin of the Philosophical Society of Oxford and "encourage[d] the institution of a similar Society in Dublin" (Ovenell, *Ashmolean Museum*, 35).

151. Robert Plot, *The Natural History of Stafford-Shire*. All future references to the work are to this edition, and page numbers are included, in parentheses, in the text.

152. Mendyk, *"Speculum Britanniae"*, 204.

153. Ovenell, *Ashmolean Museum*, 32.

154. Garrett A. Sullivan, *The Drama of Landscape: Land, Property, and Social Relations on the Early Modern Stage*, 171.

155. McRae, *God Speed the Plough*, 238. There is an extensive literature on the pre-Restoration English country house poem and its attempt to idealize a vanishing feudal social order: see, for example, G. R. Hibbard, "The Country House Poem of the Seventeenth Century"; Hugh Jenkins, *Feigned Commonwealths: The Country-House Poem and the Fashioning of the Ideal Community*, 34–103; William McClung, *The Country House in English Renaissance Poetry*, 104–46; and Raymond Williams, *The Country and the City*, 27–34.

156. According to Jonson, pheasants and partridges lie "willing to be killed" in every field, while plump carp "run into thy net" and eels leap out of the water "Before the fisher, or into his hand" on the Penshurst estate; at Saxham, Carew insists, wildfowl willingly come to the house "as to the Ark," while oxen and lambs bring themselves "to be an offering"; fish similarly want to enjoy the spa experience offered within the house, taking "more pleasure . . . / Bathed in thy dish, than in the brook" (Ben Jonson, "To Penshurst," ll. 28–38, and Thomas Carew, "To Saxham," ll. 21–28, in *The Country House Poem*, ed. Alastair Fowler, 55, 86–87).

157. Sir John Beaumont, "My Lord of Buckingham's Welcome to the King at Burley," l. 5, in *The Country House Poem*, ed. Fowler, 96.

158. Thomas Carew, "To my Friend G.N. from Wrest," ll. 33–34, in *The Country House Poem*, ed. Fowler, 90.

159. Robert Herrick, "The Country Life, to the Honoured Master Endymion Porter," ll. 11–40, in *The Country House Poem*, ed. Fowler, 113–14. Richard Lovelace comes closer to celebrating Porter's art collection, describing "a stand / Of *Titian*, *Raphael*, [and] *Georgone* [Giorgione]" ("Amyntor's Grove," *The Poems of Richard Lovelace*, 72); but as the paintings appear within Amyntor's grove, they too become part of a natural landscape. On the identification of Lovelace's Amyntor as Porter, see Richard Lovelace, *The Poems of Richard Lovelace*, 274–75.

160. Jonson, "Penshurst," ll. 39–56, in *The Country House Poem*, ed. Fowler, 55.

161. Don E. Wayne, *Penshurst: The Semiotics of Place and the Poetics of History*, 67. Throughout his fine analysis of "To Penshurst," Wayne stresses that Jonson's poem is structured by the tension between a feudal ideal and the emergent socioeconomic relations of protocapitalism. On Robert Sidney's interest in his orchard and his use of the exotic fruit he grew as gifts for friends at court, see J. C. A. Rathmell, "Jonson, Lord Lisle, and Penshurst," 253.

162. Rowland Watkyns, "Upon the Golden Grove in the County of Carmarthin, the Habitation of the Right Honourable the Lord Vauhan, Earl of Carbery, Now Lord President of the Marches of Wales," ll. 27–28, in *The Country House Poem*, ed. Fowler, 157.

163. Fowler, ed., *The Country House Poem*, 157n.

164. Mildmay Fane, "Thorp Palace: A Miracle," ll. 1–2, 78, in *The Country House Poem*, ed. Fowler, 220, 222n.

165. Charles Cotton, from *The Wonders of the Peak*, ll. 1381–88, in *The Country House Poem*, ed. Fowler, 376.

166. Thomas Shipman, "Belvoir," ll. 197–202, in *The Country House Poem*, ed. Fowler, 359.

167. Anonymous, "Belvoir: Being a Pindaric Ode upon Belvoir Castle the Seat of the Earls of Rutland, Made in the Year 1679," ll. 1258, 500, 1270–74, in *The Country House Poem*, ed. Fowler, 363–64.

168. McRae, *God Speed the Plough*, 280.

Chapter 4. The Author as Collector: Jonson, Herrick, and Textual Self-Fashioning

1. Adrian Johns, *The Nature of the Book: Print and Knowledge in the Making*, xxi.

2. David Saunders and Ian Hunter, "Lessons from the 'Literary': How to Historicise Authorship," 492. My account of copyright and proprietary authorship is also indebted to Mark Rose, *Authors and Owners: The Invention of Copyright*, esp. 1–8.

3. In Adrian Johns's useful formulation, "A *text* is the content of any written or printed work, considered apart from its particular material manifestation" (*Nature of the Book*, xxi).

4. John Feather, "Rights in Copies to Copyright: The Recognition of Authors' Rights in English Law and Practice in the Sixteenth and Seventeenth Centuries," 206; Joseph Loewenstein, "The Script in the Marketplace," 270. On the Stationers' Company and its Register, see Johns, *Nature of the Book*, 213–30.

5. Lucien Febvre and Henri-Jean Martin, *The Coming of the Book: The Impact of Printing, 1450–1800*, 162.

6. Stephen Orgel, "What Is a Text?" 3.

7. Michel Foucault, "What Is an Author?" 148.

8. Foucault, "What Is an Author?" 141, 147, 159. For a useful summary of Foucault's argument, see Simon During, *Foucault and Literature: Towards a Genealogy of Writing*, 120–25.

9. Louis Montrose, "Spenser's Domestic Domain: Poetry, Property, and the Early Modern Subject," 92.

10. Michael Warner, *The Letters of the Republic: Publication and the Public Sphere in Eighteenth-Century America*, 6, 5. Works that similarly analyze print as being embedded in history include Johns, *Nature of the Book*; Jeffrey Masten, *Textual Intercourse: Collaboration, Authorship, and Sexualities in Renaissance Drama*; and Wendy Wall, *The Imprint of Gender: Authorship and Publication in the English Renaissance*. This body of scholarship questions the essentialist assumptions of earlier studies of print culture by, e.g., Elizabeth L. Eisenstein (*The Printing Press as an Agent of Change*) and Walter J. Ong (*The Presence of the Word*, and *Orality and Literacy: The Technologizing of the Word*).

11. Stephen Bann, *Under the Sign: John Bragrave as Collector, Traveler, and Witness*, 22.

12. Walter J. Ong, "Commonplace Rhapsody: Ravisius Textor, Swinger and Shakespeare," 108.

13. In using the term "saying" I follow Mary Thomas Crane, *Framing Authority*, 7.

14. Peter Mack, "Humanist Rhetoric and Dialectic," 90. On commonplace books, see also Peter Beal, "Notions in Garrison: The Seventeenth-Century Commonplace Book."

15. Rebecca Bushnell, *A Culture of Teaching: Early Modern Humanism in Theory and Practice*, 129.

16. Richard Halpern, *The Poetics of Primitive Accumulation: English Renaissance Culture and the Genealogy of Capital*, 49. On the theories and influence of Agricola and Erasmus, see Anthony Grafton and Lisa Jardine, *From Humanism to the Humanities*, 122–57.

17. Walter J. Ong, *Rhetoric, Romance, and Technology*, 48–49, 80.

18. Crane, *Framing Authority*, 39, 55, 62. On the classical depiction of rhetorical *copia* as a form of wealth, see Terence Cave, *The Cornucopian Text: Problems of Writing in the French Renaissance*, 3–6.

19. Desiderius Erasmus, *The Education of a Christian Prince*, 145.

20. Sir Thomas Elyot, *A Critical Edition of Sir Thomas Elyot's "The Boke named the Governour,"* 119–20.

21. Crane, *Framing Authority*, 74. As Crane notes, this sixteenth-century interest in the architectural inscription of texts is related to the Renaissance concept of the memory as a physical structure with ideas engraved on its walls and the concomitant belief that one could memorize something by envisioning it on the walls of a house.

22. Erasmus, *Education of a Christian Prince*, 144–45.

23. Crane, *Framing Authority*, 93.

24. Ibid., 94; Crane lists "hunting, singing, dancing, and romantic interchange" as the "aristocratic traditions" opposed by humanism (ibid., 78).

25. Paula Findlen, *Possessing Nature: Museums, Collecting, and Scientific Culture in Early Modern Italy*, 296.

26. Barbara M. Benedict, *Making the Modern Reader: Cultural Mediation in Early Modern Literary Anthologies*, 47. David Quint argues that humanism is thus allied with "bourgeois individualism," since "in his freedom to choose among literary models and his power to incorporate them into a new and autonomous self, the humanist resembles the self-made man of capitalist venture" ("Introduction," in *Literary Theory/Renaissance Texts*, 3).

27. Crane, *Framing Authority*, 6.

28. Citing Marcus Aurelius, William Baldwin maintained that "princes live more surely with the gathering to them men of good living and conversation, then with treasures of money stuffed in their chests" (quoted in Crane, *Framing Authority*, 98).

29. Mary Hobbs, *Early Seventeenth-Century Verse Miscellany Manuscripts*, 37; Arthur F. Marotti, *Manuscript, Print, and the English Renaissance Lyric*, 3.

30. Harold Love, *Scribal Publication in Seventeenth-Century England*, 80, 177.

31. On print and manuscript as class markers, see Ann Baynes Coiro, "Milton and Class Identity: The Publication of *Areopagitica* and the 1645 *Poems*," 265.

32. Richard S. Peterson, *Imitation and Praise in the Poems of Ben Jonson*. On Jonson's imitative classicism, see also, e.g., Robert C. Evans, *Habits of Mind: Evidence and Effects of Ben Jonson's Reading*.

33. Richard Dutton, *Ben Jonson, Authority, Criticism*, 29.

34. On Westminster School and its curriculum, see David Riggs, *Ben Jonson: A Life*, 11–14.

35. Ben Jonson, *Ben Jonson*, ed. Ian Donaldson, 521. All future references to *Timber* are to this edition; where appropriate, line numbers are included, in parentheses, in the text.

36. Beal, "Notions in Garrison," 146. As the text was published after Jonson's death, one cannot be sure to what extent its original editor, Sir Kenelm Digby, tampered with it before its publication in 1640; nonetheless, the substance of *Timber* provides valuable insight into Jonson's practice and theory of *imitatio*.

37. "*Tecum habita, ut noris quam sit tibi curta supellex*" (*Ben Jonson*, ed. Donaldson, 521; trans. 736).

38. The original Latin is found in *Ben Jonson*, ed. Donaldson, 521; trans. 736.

39. William Hodgson, "On his elaborated Art-contrived Playes. An Epigram" (1640), in *Ben Jonson*, ed. C.H. Herford, Percy Simpson, and Evelyn Simpson, 11:351.

40. On the depiction of the humanist reader as a book eater or a nectar-gathering bee, see Bushnell, *A Culture of Teaching*, 126–27, 135–36. For Jonson's concept of writing as eating and digestion, see Bruce Thomas Boehrer, *The Fury of Men's Gullets: Ben Jonson and the Digestive Canal*.

41. On Jonson's sources for these passages, see Peterson, *Imitation and Praise*, 7 n.7. This description of the notebook method as a process of feeding also informs Jonson's statement that the poet must demonstrate "an exactness of study and multiplicity of reading, which maketh a full man" (*Timber*, 2506–8).

42. Despite his valorization of labor, Jonson used the term "playwright," with its implication of manual craft, derogatorily: "Jonson always applies it to other people, never to himself, and it is always a term of abuse" (Dutton, *Ben Jonson, Authority*, 60).

43. Ibid, 59.

44. Richmond Barbour, "Jonson and the Motives of Print," 506.

45. Jesse Franklin Bradley and Joseph Quincy Adams, *The Jonson Allusion-Book*, 32.

46. Jonson was not unique in allying labor and ownership during the early seventeenth century, as legal arguments against monopolies propounded the conflation of skill and property; nonetheless, as Barbour notes, Jonson "was the first so visibly to apply the concept to a calculus of authorship" ("Jonson and the Motives of Print," 507).

47. Richard C. Newton, "Jonson and the (Re-)Invention of the Book," 44–45.

48. John Locke, *Two Treatises of Government*, 306.

49. Richard Handler, "On Having a Culture: Nationalism and the Preservation of Quebec's *Patrimoine*," 210.

50. Peterson, *Imitation and Praise*, 18.

51. Ben Jonson, *Ben Jonson: Poems*, ed. Ian Donaldson, 31, 55, 53, 43. (Hereafter, cited as *Poems*.)

52. Ben Jonson, *Conversations with William Drummond of Hawthornden*, in *Ben Jonson*, ed. Donaldson, 600.

53. Riggs, *Ben Jonson: A Life*, 52–53.

54. Jonson, *Conversations*, in *Ben Jonson*, ed. Donaldson, 602.

55. Jonson, *Poems*, 110; Lucius Cary, "An Eglogue on the Death of Ben Johnson, between Melybaeus and Hylas," in *Jonsonvs Virbivs: Or, The Memorie of Ben: Johnson Revived By The Friends Of The Muses*, 4.

56. Boehrer, *Fury of Men's Gullets*, 130. As Timothy Murray points out, *Timber* itself is an anomaly among commonplace books in part because it fails to identify Jonson's sources (*Theatrical Legitimation*, 48).

57. John Dryden, "Of Dramatic Poesy: An Essay" (1668), in *Literary Criticism of John Dryden*, 49.

58. William Cartwright, "In the memory of the most Worthy Beniamin Iohnson," in *Jonsonvs Virbivs*, 38.

59. In the Renaissance, "propriety" was bound up with notions of ownership and possession, rather than decorousness (Oxford English Dictionary, s.v. "propriety").

60. Newton, "(Re-)Invention," 36, 34.

61. Richard Helgerson, *Self-Crowned Laureates: Spenser, Jonson, Milton and the Literary System*, 151.

62. Peter Stallybrass and Allon White, *The Politics and Poetics of Transgression*, 75.

63. Riggs, *Ben Jonson: A Life*, 65.

64. Dutton, *Ben Jonson, Authority*, 43.

65. Quoted in ibid.

66. Riggs, *Ben Jonson: A Life*, 65; Gerald Eades Bentley, *The Profession of Dramatist in Shakespeare's Time, 1590–1642*, 290.

67. Dutton, *Ben Jonson, Authority*, 43; Joseph Loewenstein, *Responsive Readings: Versions of Pastoral, Epic, and the Jonsonian Masque*, 181 n.53, 119.

68. Bentley, *Profession of Dramatist*, 290; Dutton, *Ben Jonson, Authority*, 64. On Jonson's evolving use of classical conventions in the quartos, see *Ben Jonson*, ed. Herford, Simpson, and Simpson, 9:46–47.

69. Ben Jonson, *Sejanus*, "To the Readers," in *Ben Jonson*, ed. Herford, Simpson, and Simpson, 4:351.

70. Douglas Brooks, "'If He Be at His Book, Disturb Him Not': The Two Jonson Folios of 1616," 87.

71. Loewenstein, *Responsive Readings*, 181 n.53.

72. Joseph Loewenstein, "Printing and 'The Multitudinous Presse': The Contentious Texts of Jonson's Masques," 180. On the effect of Jonson's annotations of his masques, see also Murray, *Theatrical Legitimation*, 86–93.

73. John Jowett, "'Fall before this Booke': The 1605 Quarto of *Sejanus*," 281. On Jonson's use of marginalia, see also Evelyn B. Tribble, "Genius on the Rack: Authorities and the Margin in Ben Jonson's Glossed Works," in her *Margins and Marginality: The Printed Page in Early Modern England*, 130–57.

74. Orgel, "What is a Text?" 4. One might argue that Jonson constructs *Sejanus* as a nontheatrical text to compensate for the play's resounding failure on stage; however, as Loewenstein notes, Jonson similarly strips his other published plays of their theatrical contexts (*Responsive Readings*, 181 n.53). Since *Sejanus* was under suspicion by the Privy Council, however, Jonson's marginal notes, by emphasizing the erudition rather than the topicality of the text, may have served a protective function as well as asserting Jonson's authorial control over the work (Tribble, *Margins and Marginality*, 147).

75. David Lee Gants, "A Descriptive Bibliography of *The Workes of Beniamin Jonson*, London: William Stansby, 1616," 313, 325.

76. Riggs, *Ben Jonson: A Life*, 221. Pembroke became Lord Chamberlain in January 1616 (Martin Butler, "Jonson's Folio and the Politics of Patronage," 381).

77. D. F. McKenzie, *Bibliography and the Sociology of Texts*, 8.

78. When Sir Walter Ralegh testified at the trial of Essex in 1601, objections were raised when he was sworn in on a small decimo-sexto Bible, and so Ralegh had to be resworn on a folio edition of holy writ before the trial could proceed (Lisa Jardine and Alan Stewart, *Hostage to Fortune: The Troubled Life of Francis Bacon, 1561–1626*, 242).

79. Margreta de Grazia, citing the work of Stanley Wells and Gary Taylor, suggests that in 1623, quartos retailed at sixpence, and the newly published Shakespeare First Folio probably cost a pound—the equivalent of one-tenth of a London schoolmaster's annual salary (*Shakespeare Verbatim: The Reproduction of Authenticity and the 1790 Apparatus*, 33 n.65). David Lee Gants argues that an unbound copy of Jonson's folio probably sold for ten to fifteen shillings, with a plain calf binding costing about a third of that sum again ("Descriptive Bibliography," 3).

80. Febvre and Martin, *Coming of the Book*, 89.

81. Roger Chartier, "Texts, Printing, Reading," 167; Bentley, *Profession of Dramatist*, 56.

82. Bentley, *Profession of Dramatist*, 56.

83. T. A. Birrell, "The Influence of Seventeenth-Century Publishers on the Presentation of English Literature," 166.

84. De Grazia, *Shakespeare Verbatim*, 34.

85. Quoted in ibid., 32.

86. Ibid., 35. On the title page of Jonson's folio, see also Margery Corbett and Ronald Lightbown, *The Comely Frontispiece: The Emblematic Title-Page in England, 1550–1660*, 145–50; and Murray, *Theatrical Legitimation*, 65–68.

87. Quoted in Bradley and Adams, *Jonson Allusion Book*, 271.

88. Bentley, *Profession of Dramatist*, 55; Murray, *Theatrical Legitimation*, 96; Loewenstein, *Responsive Readings*, 120. The Statute of Anne, passed in 1710, gave legal recognition to English authors as "possible proprietors of their works" (Rose, *Authors and Owners*, 4).

89. Most of the nondramatic poems and some of the royal entertainments were printed for the first time in the folio.

90. Dutton, *Ben Jonson, Authority*, 64.

91. Loewenstein, "Printing," 182.

92. Richard C. Newton, "Making Books from Leaves: Poets Become Editors," 248.

93. Newton, "Making Books," 257, 263.

94. Jean Baudrillard, "The System of Collecting," 24.

95. Susan M. Pearce, *On Collecting*, 279.

96. Bann, *Under the Sign*, 78.

97. I am thus suggesting that we need to qualify Martin Butler's assertion that in reprinting his plays, Jonson "generally damped down the evidence of their specific historical embeddedness" ("Jonson's Folio," 379).

98. Murray, *Theatrical Legitimation*, 95; Loewenstein, "Script in the Marketplace," 273; Loewenstein, "Printing," 186; Butler, "Jonson's Folio," 377.

99. Countering W. H. Herendeen's suggestion that Jonson thus "proclaims his independence from any single company and presents himself as an employer of actors rather than as an employee" ("A New Way to Pay Old Debts: Pretexts to the 1616 Folio," 53), Barbour observes that Jonson did not need to mention the players at all ("Motives of Print," 528 n.38).

100. Jowett, " 'Fall before this Booke,' " 281.

101. Dutton, *Ben Jonson, Authority*, 63; Loewenstein, "Script," 267–68.

102. James K. Bracken, "Books from William Stansby's Printing House, and Jonson's Folio of 1616," 19–20. As Bracken outlines, it seems that the publisher of the folio, William Stansby, had to negotiate for the rights to reprint the texts owned by other stationers.

103. The inscription on the frieze is transcribed and translated in Corbett and Lightbown, *The Comely Frontispiece*, 145, 147.

104. Murray, *Theatrical Legitimation*, 70.

105. Ibid, 83.

106. Oxford English Dictionary, s.v. "catalogue."

107. Barbour, "Jonson and Print," 514.

108. Baudrillard, "System of Collecting," 24.

109. Jonson, *Every Man in his Humour*, Prologue, l. 14, in *Ben Jonson*, ed. Herford, Simpson, and Simpson, 3:303.

110. "To the Most Learned, and My Honor'd Friend, Mr. Cambden, Clarentiaux," in *Ben Jonson*, ed. Herford, Simpson, and Simpson, 3:301.

111. Riggs, *Ben Jonson: A Life*, 225.

112. Ibid.

113. Ibid, 224; W. David Kay, "The Shaping of Ben Jonson's Career: A Reexamination of Facts and Problems," 236.

114. Jonson, *Poems*, 5.

115. Richard Dutton, *Ben Jonson: To the First Folio*, 77.

116. The *Epigrammes* were entered in the Stationers' Register in 1612 (Marotti, *Manuscript*, 241 n.70).

117. See also, e.g., *Epigrammes* 49, 77, and 83.

118. Jonson, *Poems*, 6. George Puttenham's famous description of epigrams as verses inscribed on the fabric of a room, on dishes, or on jewelry is quoted in Marotti, *Manuscript*, 3–4. On Jonson's use of the equivocal term "piece," see Marjorie Swann, "Refashioning Society in Ben Jonson's *Epicoene*," 297–315, esp. 305–6.

119. Jonson, *Poems*, 5, 57. Stanley Fish observes that "a Jonson poem always has the problem of finding something to say, a problem that is solved characteristically when it becomes itself the subject of the poem, which is then enabled at once to have a mode of being (to get written) and to remain empty of representation" ("Authors-Readers: Jonson's Community of the Same," 239).

120. Jonson, *Poems*, 49, 54. On the artifactual physicality of Jonson's depiction of virtuous individuals, see Peterson, *Imitation and Praise*, 44–111.

121. Riggs, *Ben Jonson: A Life*, 232. On Jonson's shifting political affiliations and the ascendancy of Pembroke, see ibid., 215–20.

122. Herendeen, "A New Way to Pay Old Debts," 56.

123. Riggs, *Ben Jonson: A Life*, 234.

124. Loewenstein, "Printing," 186. Jonson also silently excises material referring to the Howards from the folio texts of *Hymenaei* and the *Barriers* (Riggs, *Ben Jonson: A Life*, 226).

125. Brooks, "'If He Be at His Book,'" 91, 93. Brooks, however, accepts an antitheatrical reading of the folio play texts, arguing that they "enlarge upon and refine Jonson's previous attempts to use publication as a strategy of individualization" (87).

126. On the political nature of *The Golden Age Restored*, see Butler, "Jonson's Folio," 381–82.

127. Ibid., 388.

128. Riggs, *Ben Jonson: A Life*, 221.

129. Some of Jonson's later Jacobean masques were privately published and distributed as presentation copies at court, but were not made publicly available (Dutton, *Ben Jonson, Authority*, 68).

130. At some point, though, Jonson seems to have assembled the collection of poems posthumously published in the 1640 folio as *The Under-wood*.

131. On Jonson's financial and political status during the late Jacobean and Caroline periods, see W. David Kay, *Ben Jonson: A Literary Life*, 160–68.

132. Dutton, *Ben Jonson, Authority*, 68.

133. Riggs, *Ben Jonson: A Life*, 86–97.

134. On the membership and meetings of the Tribe, see *Ben Jonson*, ed. Herford, Simpson, and Simpson, 1:107–113, 11:294–95, 11:435. The *Leges Conviviales* and Alexander Brome's translation of them may be found in *Ben Jonson*, ed. Donaldson, 510–11.

135. Baudrillard, "System of Collecting," 17.

136. Ibid., 13.

137. Marotti, *Manuscript*, 257.

138. Ian Donaldson, *Jonson's Magic Houses: Essays in Interpretation*, 198–216.

139. Jennifer Brady, " 'Noe fault, but Life': Jonson's Folio as Monument and Barrier," 194.

140. Nicholas Oldisworth, "A letter to Ben. Johnson. 1629," in *Ben Jonson*, ed. Herford, Simpson, and Simpson, 11:396–97.

141. *Ben Jonson*, ed. Herford, Simpson, and Simpson, 11:335–36. On the failure of *The New Inn* and Jonson's "Ode to Himself," see Riggs, *Ben Jonson: A Life*, 304–9.

142. R. Goodwin, *Vindiciae Jonsonianae*, in *Ben Jonson*, ed. Herford, Simpson, and Simpson, 11:343.

143. Henry Coventry, "Might but this slender offering of mine," in *Jonsonvs Virbivs*, 20.

144. [Sidney Godolphin,] "The Muses fairest light in no darke time," in *Jonsonvs Virbivs*, 27. The attribution to Godolphin is explained in *Ben Jonson*, ed. Herford, Simpson, and Simpson, 11:450.

145. John Ford, "On the best of English *Poets*, BEN: IONSON, *Deceased*," in *Jonsonvs Virbivs*, 50–51.

146. John Rutter, "An Elegy upon Ben : Iohnson," in *Jonsonvs Virbivs*, 40.

147. Henry King, "Vpon Ben. Iohnson," in *Jonsonvs Virbivs*, 17–18.

148. Alastair Fowler, "Robert Herrick," 243; L.C. Martin, Introduction, *The Poetical Works of Robert Herrick*, xvii.

149. On Herrick's career as a clergyman, see Martin, Introduction, *Poetical Works of Herrick*, xiv–xvi. Herrick was reportedly also absent from Devon and living in London in 1640, the same year that "*The seuerall Poems* written by Master Robert Herrick" was entered in the Stationers' Register; the book apparently was not published.

150. Ann Coiro, "Herrick's *Hesperides*: The Name and the Frame," 312.

151. Alastair Fowler, *Kinds of Literature: An Introduction to the Theory of Genres and Modes*, 197–98, 313 n.26.

152. Robert Herrick, *The Poetical Works of Robert Herrick*, ed. L.C. Martin, 72.1, 67.2. All future references to Herrick's poetry are to this edition. I have followed Martin's format for references to Herrick's poems: i.e., page number. number of poem on page. line number(s). The continuation of a poem is referred to by page and line number.

153. Leah S. Marcus, "Robert Herrick," 172.

154. T. S. Eliot, "What Is Minor Poetry?" 43. Eliot relegates *Hesperides* to the status of "minor poetry" on this basis.

155. John L. Kimmey, "Robert Herrick's Persona," 221; Kimmey, "Order and Form in Herrick's *Hesperides*," 256.

156. Ann Baynes Coiro, *Robert Herrick's "Hesperides" and the Epigram Book Tradition*, 109. Leah Marcus cites Coiro's narrative reading of the poems, although she suggests that the *Noble Numbers* are not easily reconciled with the "pattern of gradual decline and disillusionment" proposed by Coiro ("Robert Herrick," 178–79).

157. Randall Ingram, "Robert Herrick and the Makings of *Hesperides*," 144.

158. Fowler, "Robert Herrick," 244. Fowler reiterates this argument in *Kinds of Literature*, 134–35, and in "The Silva Tradition in Jonson's *The Forest*," 163–66. Roger B. Rollin similarly observes that "some of the time, Herrick's arrangement of his poems appears to be simply for the sake of variety," although he later cites Kimmey to suggest that the collection is also unified by a "loose narrative" ("Witty by Design: Robert Herrick's *Hesperides*," 147, 149).

159. Fowler, "The Silva Tradition," 163–64; *Kinds*, 134–35.

160. Robert B. Hinman, "The Apotheosis of Faust: Poetry and New Philosophy in the Seventeenth Century," 159, 163.

161. Eliot, "What Is Minor Poetry?" 43.

162. Patricia Fumerton, *Cultural Aesthetics: Renaissance Literature and the Practice of Social Ornament*, 172.

163. Marcus argues convincingly that despite the separate title page dated 1647, Herrick's sacred poems should be viewed as an integral part of his collection, as the *Noble Numbers* are presented both thematically and bibliographically as components of *Hesperides* as a whole ("Robert Herrick," 179). Regarding the anomalous date of the *Noble Numbers* title page, J. Max Patrick suggests that the printing of the entire collection began in 1647, "but that the setting up of the type for the main title page was left to the last, by which time 1648 had arrived or was near" (*The Complete Poetry of Robert Herrick*, 449).

164. Countering earlier views of Herrick as a jolly naif who frolicked about Devon oblivious to the turmoil of the 1640s, recent scholarship has demonstrated that many of Herrick's poems promote royalism and Laudian Anglicanism: see, e.g., Leah S. Marcus, *Childhood and Cultural Despair: A Theme and Variations in Seventeenth-Century Literature*; Claude J. Summers, "Herrick's Political Poetry: The Strategies of His Art"; Summers, "Herrick's Political Counterplots"; Marcus, *The Politics of Mirth: Jonson, Herrick, Milton, Marvell, and the Defense of Old Holiday Pastimes*; Peter Stallybrass, " 'Wee feaste in our Defense': Patrician Carnival in Early Modern England and Robert Herrick's *Hesperides*"; Achsah Guibbory, "The Temple of *Hesperides* and Anglican-Puritan Controversy"; Guibbory, "Enlarging the Limits of the 'Religious Lyric': The Case of Herrick's *Hesperides*"; and Guibbory, "Robert Herrick: Religious Experience in the '*Temple*' of *Hesperides*," in her *Ceremony and Community*, 79–118.

165. To appreciate the layout of the text, see the Scolar Press facsimile or an original copy of *Hesperides*. Throughout the volume, Herrick's poems praising the royal family are interrogated by other verses, often aphorisms, which seem critical of the King and his policies; I have argued elsewhere that Herrick's questioning of Laudian royalism also shapes his religious poetry ("Marriage, Celibacy, and Ritual in Robert Herrick's *Hesperides*"). Other assessments of Herrick's political ambivalence include Coiro, *Robert Herrick's "Hesperides,"* and Jonathan F. S. Post, "Robert Herrick: A Minority Report." Finally, however, a strictly political reading of the entire volume is limited, as Harold Toliver observes, by the fact that "the volume does not pursue the prominence Herrick assigns either the prince or the state, which as it turns out, is true of nearly everything: whatever holds the stage at a given moment may be flattered with thematic weight and dignity, but in the way of a variety show" ("Herrick's Book of Realms and Moments," in his *Lyric Provinces in the English Renaissance*, 149).

166. F.W. Moorman, Introduction, *The Poetical Works of Robert Herrick,* vii; Marcus, "Robert Herrick," 174.

167. Marcus, "Robert Herrick," 174.

168. On the iconography of the frontispiece, see Roger B. Rollin, *Robert Herrick,* 16–17. The poem and a translation may be found in Herrick, *The Complete Poetry,* ed. Patrick, 8.

169. Leah S. Marcus, *Unediting the Renaissance: Shakespeare, Marlowe, Milton,* 199. Marcus points out that the portraits of Jonson sometimes found in copies of the 1616 folio were inserted long after the book had been printed (ibid., 259 n.26).

170. Ibid., 201.

171. Thomas Moisan has noted this self-division in the speaker of Herrick's *"Argument"* and suggests that it "ever renders him at a given moment as but part of a disjunction" ("The 'Argument' and the Opening of Robert Herrick's 'Book,'" 138).

172. Fowler notes that "In Renaissance literary theory the epigram was a piece, a particle, of a larger kind such as tragedy or epic" ("Robert Herrick," 246). L. E. Semler argues that the lapidary form and subject matter of *Hesperides* emerge from Herrick's familiarity with contemporary visual arts and goldsmithing techniques ("Robert Herrick, the Human Figure, and the English Mannerist Aesthetic"; Semler includes an expanded version of this essay in *The English Mannerist Poets and the Visual Arts,* 95–134).

173. Robert Burton classified the fairies as "Terrestrial devils" (*The Anatomy of Melancholy,* Part 1, 192).

174. Hinman, "Apotheosis of Faust," 163. Harold Toliver similarly suggests that the *"Argument"* depicts Herrick as "a poet of isolated moments" (*Lyric Provinces,* 151). Herrick's *"Argument"* resembles the first poem of Thomas Bastard's *Chrestoleros. Seuen Bookes of Epigrames,* published in 1598; unlike Herrick, however, Bastard employs the quatrains and concluding couplet of the Shakespearean sonnet (*Chrestoleros,* Liber Primus, *"Epigr. I de subiecto operis sui,"* 9).

175. In early modern English folklore, the fairies parasitized human households to gain bath water and food, punished householders who did not maintain impeccable standards of hygiene, and substituted sickly fairy offspring for healthy human babies. On the relationship between Herrick's fairy poems and traditional fairy beliefs, see Marjorie Swann, "The Politics of Fairylore in Early Modern English Literature," esp. 464–69.

176. For a structuralist analysis of the decor of Herrick's Oberon poems, see Peter Schwenger, "Herrick's Fairy State." Daniel Woodward, arguing that an epithalamial structure underlies Herrick's fairy poems, suggests that the grotesque physicality of "Oberons *Palace*" bespeaks Herrick's vision of a "universal order" which encompasses even "things that from a limited perspective seem to deny or work against the beauty of creation" ("Herrick's Oberon Poems," 283).

177. Marcus, "Robert Herrick," 173.

178. Malcolm MacLeod, ed., *A Concordance to the Poems of Robert Herrick,* s.v. "Herrick" and "Herrick's."

179. For an outline of the circumstances of Nicholas Herrick's death and a provocative psychoanalytic reading of the poem, see Roger B. Rollin, "Robert Herrick's Fathers," 41–46.

180. Achsah Guibbory argues that the memorializing impulse in *Hesperides* is

rooted in Herrick's attempt to preserve ceremonialist religion (*Ceremony and Community*, 79–118). I would suggest that Herrick's Laudian emphasis on continuity exists in tension both with other religiopolitical outlooks expressed in Herrick's poems, and with the fragmentary structure of *Hesperides* itself.

181. On the significance of the title of Herrick's collection, see Coiro, "Herrick's *Hesperides*."

182. For a more detailed analysis of Herrick's fragmenting amatory poetics, see Marjorie Swann, "Cavalier Love: Fetishism and Its Discontents."

183. Martin, Introduction, *Poetical Works of Herrick*, xvii.

184. Ibid.

Epilogue

1. My account of Sloane's life draws upon E. St. John Brooks, *Sir Hans Sloane: The Great Collector and his Circle*; G. R. de Beer, *Sir Hans Sloane and the British Museum*; Arthur MacGregor, "The Life, Character and Career of Sir Hans Sloane"; and Edward Miller, *That Noble Cabinet: A History of the British Museum*, 36–41.

2. MacGregor, "Life of Sir Hans Sloane," 16.

3. John Evelyn, *The Diary of John Evelyn*, ed. E. S. de Beer, 5:48 (16 April 1691).

4. MacGregor, "Life of Sir Hans Sloane," 23. On Courten's collection, see Carol Gibson-Wood, "Classification and Value in a Seventeenth-Century Museum."

5. Zacharias Conrad von Uffenbach, *London in 1710 from the Travels of Zacharias Conrad von Uffenbach*, 185–86.

6. Marjorie Caygill, "Sloane's Will and the Establishment of the British Museum," 47.

7. William Stukeley, *The Family Memoirs of the Rev. William Stukeley, M.D.*, vol. 1, Publications of the Surtees Society 73 (1882): 126.

8. See above, Introduction.

9. MacGregor, "Life of Sir Hans Sloane," 20.

10. Von Uffenbach, *London in 1710*, 98.

11. Arthur MacGregor and A. J. Turner, "The Ashmolean Museum," 651.

12. MacGregor, "Life of Sir Hans Sloane," 35.

13. Miller, *That Noble Cabinet*, 36.

14. Robert Harley and his son Edward Harley, earls of Oxford, had accumulated a massive collection of printed books, pamphlets, and manuscripts. During the 1740s, Edward Harley's heirs found it financially necessary to sell off the printed material; the family's collection of manuscripts remained intact, however. While the House of Commons was debating the purchase of the Sloane collection, Edward Harley's daughter offered to sell the manuscripts to Parliament, on condition that "this great valuable Collection shall be kept together in a proper repository, as an addition to the Cotton Library, and be called by the name of Harleian Collection of Manuscripts" (Miller, *That Noble Cabinet*, 46). On the Harleian library, see also Richard Maxwell, "Robert Harley, First Earl of Oxford and Edward Harley, Second Earl of Oxford."

NOTES TO PAGE 199

15. Benedict Anderson, *Imagined Communities: Reflections on the Origin and Spread of Nationalism*, 1–46.

16. Jürgen Habermas, *The Structural Transformation of the Public Sphere: An Inquiry into a Category of Bourgeois Society*, 12.

17. Carol Duncan and Alan Wallach, "The Universal Survey Museum," 457, 456.

18. For similar accounts of the rise of the national museum, see also Tony Bennett, *The Birth of the Museum: History, Theory, Politics*, esp. 25–47; Carol Duncan, "Art Museums and the Ritual of Citizenship"; Duncan, *Civilizing Rituals: Inside Public Art Museums*, esp. 21–47; and Eilean Hooper-Greenhill, *Museums and the Shaping of Knowledge*, 167–90.

Bibliography

Primary Sources

Ashmole, Elias. *Elias Ashmole, 1617–1692*. Ed. C. H. Josten. 5 vols. Oxford: Oxford University Press, 1966.

Bacon, Sir Francis. *"The Advancement of Learning" and "New Atlantis."* Ed. Arthur Johnston. Oxford: Oxford University Press, 1986.

———. *The Essays*. Ed. John Pitcher. Harmondsworth: Penguin, 1985.

———. *The Masculine Birth of Time*. Trans. Benjamin Farrington. In Farrington, *The Philosophy of Francis Bacon*. Liverpool: Liverpool University Press, 1964. 59–72.

———. *The Refutation of Philosophies*. Trans. Benjamin Farrington. In Farrington, *The Philosophy of Francis Bacon*. Liverpool: Liverpool University Press, 1964. 103–33.

———. *The Works of Francis Bacon*. Ed. James Spedding, R. L. Ellis, and D. D. Heath. 14 vols. London: Longmans, 1857–74.

Bastard, Thomas. *Chrestoleros. Seuen Bookes of Epigrames*. 1598. Manchester: Spenser Society Publications 47, 1888.

Bradley, Jesse Franklin and Joseph Quincy Adams. *The Jonson Allusion-Book*. New Haven, Conn.: Yale University Press, 1922.

Browne, Sir Thomas. *Hydriotaphia, Urne-Buriall, or, A Discourse of the Sepulchrall Urnes lately found in Norfolk. Together with The Garden of Cyrus, of the Quincunciall, Lozenge, or Net-work Plantations of the Ancients, Artificially, Naturally, Mystically Considered*. London, 1658.

———. *Sir Thomas Browne: The Major Works*. Ed. C. A. Patrides. Harmondsworth: Penguin, 1977.

———. *The Works of Sir Thomas Browne*. Ed. Geoffrey Keynes. 4 vols. Chicago: University of Chicago Press, 1964.

Burton, Robert. *The Anatomy of Melancholy*. Ed. Holbrook Jackson. 1932. New York: Vintage, 1977.

Burton, William. *The Description of Leicester Shire*. London, 1622.

Bushell, Thomas. *Mr. Bushell's Abridgement of the Lord Chancellor Bacon's philosophical theory*. London, 1659.

Camden, William. *Camden's Britannia, Newly Translated into English.* Trans. and ed. Edmund Gibson. London, 1695.

Carew, Richard. *The Survey of Cornwall.* London, 1602.

Chamberlayne, Edward. *Angliae Notitia: Or the Present State of England.* London, 1684.

Childrey, Joshua. *Britannia Baconica: Or, the Natural Rarities of England, Scotland, & Wales.* London, 1661.

Cleveland, John. *The Poems of John Cleveland.* Ed. Brian Morris and Eleanor Withington. Oxford: Clarendon Press, 1967.

Dryden, John. *Literary Criticism of John Dryden.* Ed. Arthur C. Kirsch. Lincoln: University of Nebraska Press, 1967.

Dugdale, Sir William. *The Antiquities of Warwickshire.* London, 1656.

——. *The History of St. Pauls Cathedral in London, From its Foundation untill these Times.* London, 1658.

——. *The Life, Diary, and Correspondence of Sir William Dugdale.* Ed. William Hamper. London: Harding, Lepard, 1827.

Elyot, Sir Thomas. *A Critical Edition of Sir Thomas Elyot's "The Boke named the Governour."* Ed. Donald W. Rude. New York: Garland, 1992.

Erasmus, Desiderius. *The Education of a Christian Prince.* Trans. and ed. Lester K. Born. New York: Octagon, 1965.

An Essay In Defence of the Female Sex. London, 1696. Repr. New York: Source Book Press, 1970.

Evelyn, John. *Diary and Correspondence of John Evelyn.* Ed. William Bray. 4 vols. London: George Bell, 1879.

——. *The Diary of John Evelyn.* Ed. E. S. de Beer. 6 vols. Oxford: Clarendon Press, 1955.

——. *Evelyn's Sculptura With the Unpublished Second Part.* Ed. C. F. Bell. Oxford: Clarendon Press, 1906.

——. *Navigation and Commerce.* London, 1674.

——. *Numismata.* London, 1697.

Fowler, Alastair, ed. *The Country House Poem.* Edinburgh: Edinburgh University Press, 1994.

Gerard, John. *The Herball Or Generall Historie of Plantes.* Enlarged and amended by Thomas Johnson. London, 1636.

Glanvill, Joseph. *The Vanity of Dogmatizing: or Confidence in Opinions Manifested in a Discourse of the Shortness and Uncertainty of Our Knowledge.* London, 1661.

Grew, Nehemiah. *Musaeum Regalis Societatis. Or a Catalogue & Description Of the Natural and Artificial Rarities Belonging to the Royal Society and Preserved at Gresham Colledge.* London, 1681.

Hager, Herman. Transcription of Bodl. Add. B. 67, Appendix II to his review of

K.H. Schaible, *Geschichte der Deutschen in England. Englische Studien* 10 (1887): 445–53.

Herrick, Robert. *The Complete Poetry of Robert Herrick*. Ed. J. Max Patrick. Rev. ed. New York: Norton, 1968.

———. *"Hesperides": 1648*. Aldershot: Scolar Press, 1973.

———. *The Poetical Works of Robert Herrick*. Ed. L. C. Martin. Oxford: Clarendon Press, 1956.

Hooke, Robert. *The Posthumous Works of Robert Hooke*. 2nd ed. London: Frank Cass, 1971.

Hoole, Charles. *A New Discovery of the Old Art of Teaching Schoole, In Four Small Treatises*. London, 1660.

Hubert, Robert. *A Catalogue of Many Natural Rarities, With Great Industry, Cost, and thirty Years travel in Foraign Countries, Collected by Robert Hubert, alias Forges*. London, 1664.

———. *A Catalogue of part of those Rarities Collected in thirty years time with a great deal of Pains and Industry*. London: n.d. (1665?).

Imperato, Ferrante. *Dell'historia naturale di Ferrante Imperato napolitano*. 1599. Venice, 1672.

Jonson, Ben. *Ben Jonson*. Ed. Ian Donaldson. Oxford: Oxford University Press, 1985.

———. *Ben Jonson: Poems*. Ed. Ian Donaldson. Oxford: Oxford University Press, 1975.

———. *Ben Jonson*. Ed. C. H. Herford, Percy Simpson, and Evelyn Simpson. 11 vols. Oxford: Clarendon Press, 1925–63.

———. *Catiline*. Ed. W. F. Bolton and Jane F. Gardner. Lincoln: University of Nebraska Press, 1973.

Jonsonvs Virbivs: Or, The Memorie of Ben: Johnson Revived By The Friends Of The Muses. London, 1638.

Locke, John. *Two Treatises of Government*. Ed. Peter Laslett. Cambridge: Cambridge University Press, 1967.

Lovelace, Richard. *The Poems of Richard Lovelace*. Ed. C. H. Wilkinson. Oxford: Clarendon Press, 1925.

Marvell, Andrew. *The Complete Poems*. Ed. Elizabeth Story Donno. London: Penguin, 1987.

Moryson, Fynes. *An Itinerary*. 4 vols. Glasgow: MacLehose, 1907–8.

Mundy, Peter. *The Travels of Peter Mundy in Europe and Asia, 1608–1667*. Ed. R. C. Temple. 5 vols. Hakluyt Society ser. 2, no. 17, 35, 45–46, 55, 78. Cambridge: Hakluyt Society, 1907–36.

Oldenburg, Henry. *The Correspondence of Henry Oldenburg*. Ed. and trans. A. Rupert Hall and Marie Boas Hall. 10 vols. Madison: University of Wisconsin Press, 1966.

Parkinson, John. *Paradisi in Sole, Paradisus Terrestris.* London, 1629.

———. *Theatrum Botanicum, The Theater of Plantes.* London, 1640.

Peacham, Henry. *Peacham's "Compleat Gentleman," 1634.* Intro. G. S. Gordon. Oxford: Clarendon Press, 1906.

Pepys, Samuel. *The Diary of Samuel Pepys.* Ed. Robert Latham and William Matthews. 11 vols. Berkeley: University of California Press, 1970–83.

Petiver, James. "An Account of a BOOK. *Musei Petiveriani Centuria Prima.*" *Philosophical Transactions of the Royal Society,* no. 224 (January, 1697): 393–400.

———. *Gazophylacii Naturae & Artis Decas Prima [- Decas Quinta].* London, 1702–1706.

———. *Jacobi Petiveri Opera, Historiam Naturalem Spectantia.* Ed. James Empson and J. Millan. London, 1767.

———. *Musei Petiveriani Centuria Prima [- Decima].* London, 1695–1700.

Platter, Thomas. *Thomas Platter's Travels in England, 1599.* Trans. and intro. Clare Williams. London: Jonathan Cape, 1937.

Plot, Robert. *The Natural History of Oxford-shire, being an Essay towards the Natural History of England.* Oxford, 1677.

———. *The Natural History of Stafford-Shire.* Oxford, 1686.

Powell, Thomas. *Humane Industry: Or, A History of Most Manual Arts.* London, 1661.

Public Record Office (PRO): C 7/454/1; PRO: C 7/541/2; PRO: C 33/221/744.

Randolph, Thomas. *Poetical and Dramatic Works of Thomas Randolph.* Ed. W. Carew Hazlitt. 2 vols. London: Reeves and Turner, 1895.

Rawley, William. *The Life of the Right Honourable Francis Bacon.* In *The Works of Francis Bacon,* vol. 1. Ed. James Spedding, R. L. Ellis, and D. D. Heath. London: Longmans, 1857–74.

Shadwell, Thomas. *The Virtuoso.* Ed. Marjorie Hope Nicolson and David Stuart Rodes. Lincoln: University of Nebraska Press, 1966.

Speed, John. *The Theatre of the Empire of Great Britaine.* London, 1611.

Sprat, Thomas. *History of the Royal Society.* Ed. Jackson I. Cope and Harold Whitmore Jones. St. Louis: Washington University Studies; London: Routledge and Kegan Paul, 1959.

Stukeley, William. *The Family Memoirs of the Rev. William Stukeley, M.D.* 3 vols. Publications of the Surtees Society, vol. 73, 76, 80 (1882–87).

The Tatler. Ed. Donald F. Bond. 3 vols. Oxford: Clarendon Press, 1987.

Thoresby, Ralph. *The Diary of Ralph Thoresby.* Ed. Joseph Hunter. 2 vols. London: Colburn and Bentley, 1830.

———. *Musaeum Thoresbyanum.* In *Ducatus Leodiensis,* by Thoresby. London, 1715.

Thoroton, Robert. *The Antiquities of Nottinghamshire.* London, 1677.

Tradescant, John. *Musaeum Tradescantianum; or A Collection of Rarities Preserved at South-Lambeth neer London.* London, 1656.

——. *Musaeum Tradescantianum; or A Collection of Rarities Preserved at South-Lambeth neer London.* 2nd ed. London, 1660.

Uffenbach, Zacharias Conrad von. *London in 1710: From the Travels of Zacharias Conrad von Uffenbach.* Trans. and ed. W. H. Quarrell and Margaret Mare. London: Faber and Faber, 1934.

Weever, John. *Ancient Funerall Monuments With In The United Monarchie of Great Britaine, Ireland, and the Ilands adiacent.* London, 1631.

W[right], J[ames]. *Monasticon Anglicanum Epitomized in English.* London, 1693.

Secondary Sources

Achinstein, Sharon. "How To Be a Progressive Without Looking like One: History and Knowledge in Bacon's *New Atlantis.*" *Clio* 17 (1988): 249–64.

Agnew, Jean Christophe. "Coming Up for Air: Consumer Culture in Historical Perspective." In *Consumption and the World of Goods*, ed. John Brewer and Roy Porter. London: Routledge, 1993. 19–39.

Albanese, Denise. *New Science, New World.* Durham, N.C.: Duke University Press, 1996.

Allan, Mea. *The Tradescants: Their Plants, Gardens and Museum, 1570–1662.* London: Michael Joseph, 1964.

Anderson, Benedict. *Imagined Communities: Reflections on the Origin and Spread of Nationalism.* Rev. ed. London: Verso, 1991.

Andres, Glenn, John M. Hunisak, and A. Richard Turner. *The Art of Florence.* Vol. 2. New York: Abbeville, 1988.

Appadurai, Arjun. "Introduction: Commodities and the Politics of Value." In *The Social Life of Things: Commodities in Cultural Perspective*, ed. Appadurai. Cambridge: Cambridge University Press, 1986. 3–63.

Archer, John Michael. "Surveillance and Enlightenment in Bacon's *New Atlantis.*" *Assays* 6 (1991): 111–27.

Arnold, Ken. "Cabinets for the Curious: Practicing Science in Early Modern English Museums." Ph.D. dissertation, Princeton University, 1992.

Ashworth, William B., Jr. "Emblematic Natural History of the Renaissance." In *Cultures of Natural History*, ed. N. Jardine, J. A. Secord, and E. C. Spary. Cambridge: Cambridge University Press, 1996. 17–37.

——. "Natural History and the Emblematic World View." In *Reappraisals of the Scientific Revolution*, ed. David C. Lindberg and Robert S. Westman. Cambridge: Cambridge University Press, 1990. 303–32.

Aston, Margaret. *England's Iconoclasts.* Vol. 1, *Laws Against Images.* Oxford: Clarendon Press, 1988.

Bann, Stephen. *The Inventions of History: Essays on the Representation of the Past.* Manchester: Manchester University Press, 1990.

———. *Under the Sign: John Bargrave as Collector, Traveler, and Witness*. Ann Arbor: University of Michigan Press, 1994.

Barbour, Richmond. "Jonson and the Motives of Print." *Criticism* 40 (1998): 499–528.

Baudrillard, Jean. "The System of Collecting." In *The Cultures of Collecting*, ed. John Elsner and Roger Cardinal. Cambridge, Mass.: Harvard University Press, 1994. 7–24.

Bazin, Germain. *The Museum Age*. Trans. Jane van Nuis Cahill. Brussels: S.A. Publishers, 1967.

Beal, Peter. "Notions in Garrison: The Seventeenth-Century Commonplace Book." In *New Ways of Looking at Old Texts: Papers of the Renaissance English Text Society, 1985–1991*, ed. W. Speed Hill. Binghamton, N.Y.: Renaissance English Text Society, 1993. 131–47.

Bendall, A. Sarah. *Maps, Land and Society: A History, With a Carto-bibliography of Cambridgeshire Estate Maps, c. 1600–1836*. Cambridge: Cambridge University Press, 1992.

Benedict, Barbara M. *Making the Modern Reader: Cultural Mediation in Early Modern Literary Anthologies*. Princeton, N.J.: Princeton University Press, 1996.

Bennett, Tony. *The Birth of the Museum: History, Theory, Politics*. London: Routledge, 1995.

Bentley, Gerald Eades. *The Profession of Dramatist in Shakespeare's Time, 1590–1642*. Princeton, N.J.: Princeton University Press, 1971.

Biagioli, Mario. "Etiquette, Interdependence, and Sociability in Seventeenth-Century Science." *Critical Inquiry* 22 (1996): 193–238.

———. "Scientific Revolution, Social Bricolage, and Etiquette." In *The Scientific Revolution in National Context*, ed. Roy Porter and Mikuláš Teich. Cambridge: Cambridge University Press, 1992. 11–54.

Biester, James. *Lyric Wonder: Rhetoric and Wit in Renaissance English Poetry*. Ithaca, N.Y.: Cornell University Press, 1997.

Birch, Thomas. *The History of the Royal Society of London*. 1756. 4 vols. New York and London: Johnson Reprint Corp., 1968.

Birrell, T. A. "The Influence of Seventeenth-Century Publishers on the Presentation of English Literature." In *Historical and Editorial Studies in Medieval and Early Modern English: For Johan Gerritsen*, ed. Mary-Jo Arn and Hanneke Wirtjes, with Hans Jansen. Groningen: Wolters-Noordhoff, 1985. 163–73.

Boehrer, Bruce Thomas. *The Fury of Men's Gullets: Ben Jonson and the Digestive Canal*. Philadelphia: University of Pennsylvania Press, 1997.

Boesky, Amy. "Bacon's *New Atlantis* and the Laboratory of Prose." In *The Project of Prose in Early Modern Europe and the New World*, ed. Elizabeth Fowler and Roland Greene. Cambridge: Cambridge University Press, 1997. 138–53.

——. *Founding Fictions: Utopias in Early Modern England*. Athens: University of Georgia Press, 1996.

——. "'Outlandish-Fruits': Commissioning Nature for the Museum of Man." *ELH* 58 (1991): 305–30.

Bourdieu, Pierre. *Distinction: A Social Critique of the Judgement of Taste*. Trans. Richard Nice. Cambridge, Mass.: Harvard University Press, 1984.

Box, Ian. "Bacon's Moral Philosophy." In *The Cambridge Companion to Bacon*, ed. Markku Peltonen. Cambridge: Cambridge University Press, 1996. 260–82.

Bracken, James K. "Books from William Stansby's Printing House, and Jonson's Folio of 1616." *The Library* 6th ser. 10, 1 (1988): 18–29.

Brady, Jennifer. "'Noe fault, but Life': Jonson's Folio as Monument and Barrier." In *Ben Jonson's 1616 Folio*, ed. Jennifer Brady and W. H. Herendeen. Newark: University of Delaware Press, 1991. 192–216.

Brady, Jennifer and W. H. Herendeen, eds. *Ben Jonson's 1616 Folio*. Newark: University of Delaware Press, 1991.

Braunholtz, H. J. *Sir Hans Sloane and Ethnography*. London: British Museum, 1970.

Brears, P. C. D. "Ralph Thoresby, A Museum Visitor in Stuart England." *Journal of the History of Collections* 1 (1989): 213–24.

Bredekamp, Horst. *The Lure of Antiquity and the Cult of the Machine*. Trans. Allison Brown. Princeton, N.J.: Markus Wiener, 1995.

Breitenberg, Mark. *Anxious Masculinity in Early Modern England*. Cambridge: Cambridge University Press, 1996.

Brooks, Douglas. "'If He Be at His Book, Disturb Him Not': The Two Jonson Folios of 1616." *Ben Jonson Journal* 4 (1997): 81–101.

Brooks, E. St. John. *Sir Hans Sloane: The Great Collector and His Circle*. London: Batchworth, 1954.

Brown, Alexander, ed. *The Genesis of the United States*. 2 vols. New York: Houghton, Mifflin, 1890.

Brown, Jonathan. *Kings and Connoisseurs: Collecting Art in Seventeenth-Century Europe*. Princeton, N.J.: Princeton University Press, 1995.

Brown, Theodore M. "The Rise of Baconianism in Seventeenth Century England." In *Science and History: Studies in Honor of Edward Rosen*, Studia Copernicana 16. Wroclaw: Polish Academy of Sciences Press, 1978. 501–22.

Bushnell, Rebecca. *A Culture of Teaching: Early Modern Humanism in Theory and Practice*. Ithaca, N.Y.: Cornell University Press, 1996.

Butler, Martin. "Jonson's Folio and the Politics of Patronage." *Criticism* 35 (1993): 377–90.

Cantor, Leonard. *The Changing English Countryside, 1400–1700*. London: Routledge and Kegan Paul, 1987.

Cave, Terence. *The Cornucopian Text: Problems of Writing in the French Renaissance.* Oxford: Clarendon Press, 1979.

Caygill, Marjorie. "Sloane's Will and the Establishment of the British Museum." In *Sir Hans Sloane*, ed. Arthur MacGregor. London: British Museum Press, 1994. 45–68.

Chambers, Douglas. "'Storys of Plants': The Assembling of Mary Capel Somerset's Botanical Collection at Badminton." *Journal of the History of Collections* 9 (1997): 49–60.

Chartier, Roger. *The Cultural Uses of Print in Early Modern France.* Trans. Lydia G. Cochrane. Princeton, N.J.: Princeton University Press, 1987.

——. "Texts, Printing, Reading." In *The New Cultural History*, ed. Lynn Hunt. Berkeley: University of California Press, 1989. 154–75.

Clay, Christopher. "Landlords and Estate Management in England." In *The Agrarian History of England and Wales*, vol. 5.2, ed. Joan Thirsk. Cambridge: Cambridge University Press, 1985. 119–251.

Clifford, James. *The Predicament of Culture: Twentieth-Century Ethnography, Literature, and Art.* Cambridge, Mass.: Harvard University Press, 1988.

Coiro, Ann Baynes. "Herrick's *Hesperides*: The Name and the Frame." *ELH* 52 (1985): 311–36.

——. "Milton and Class Identity: The Publication of *Areopagitica* and the 1645 Poems." *Journal of Medieval and Renaissance Studies* 22 (1992): 261–89.

——. *Robert Herrick's "Hesperides" and the Epigram Book Tradition.* Baltimore: Johns Hopkins University Press, 1988.

Cook, Harold J. "The Cutting Edge of a Revolution?: Medicine and Natural History Near the Shores of the North Sea." In *Renaissance and Revolution: Humanists, Scholars, Craftsmen, and Natural Philosophers in Early Modern Europe*, ed. J. V. Field and Frank A. J. L. James. Cambridge: Cambridge University Press, 1994. 45–61.

——. "Physicians and the New Philosophy: Henry Stubbe and the Virtuosi Physicians." In *The Medical Revolution of the Seventeenth Century*, ed. Roger French and Andrew Wear. Cambridge: Cambridge University Press, 1989. 246–71.

Coope, Rosalys. "The 'Long Gallery': Its Origins, Development, Use and Decoration." *Architectural History* 29 (1986): 43–84.

Corbett, Margery and Ronald Lightbown. *The Comely Frontispiece: The Emblematic Title-Page in England, 1550–1660.* London: Routledge and Kegan Paul, 1979.

Cormack, Lesley B. *Charting an Empire: Geography at the English Universities, 1580–1620.* Chicago: University of Chicago Press, 1997.

——. "'Good Fences Make Good Neighbors': Geography as Self-Definition in Early Modern England." In *The Scientific Enterprise in Early Modern Europe:*

Readings from Isis, ed. Peter Dear. Chicago: University of Chicago Press, 1997. 64–85.

Crane, Mary Thomas. *Framing Authority: Sayings, Self, and Society in Sixteenth-Century England*. Princeton, N.J.: Princeton University Press, 1993.

Cressy, David. *Birth, Marriage, and Death: Ritual, Religion, and the Life-Cycle in Tudor and Stuart England*. Oxford: Oxford University Press, 1997.

Crombie, Alistair C. "Science and the Arts in the Renaissance: The Search for Truth and Certainty, Old and New." In *Science and the Arts in the Renaissance*, ed. John W. Shirley and F. David Hoeniger. Washington, D.C.: Folger Shakespeare Library, 1985. 15–26.

Cunningham, Andrew. "The Culture of Gardens." In *Cultures of Natural History*, ed. N. Jardine, J. A. Secord, and E. C. Spary. Cambridge: Cambridge University Press, 1996. 38–56.

Daston, Lorraine J. "Baconian Facts, Academic Civility, and the Prehistory of Objectivity." In *Rethinking Objectivity*, ed. Allan Megill. Durham, N.C.: Duke University Press, 1994. 37–63.

———. "The Factual Sensibility." *Isis* 79 (1988): 452–67.

Daston, Lorraine and Katharine Park. *Wonders and the Order of Nature, 1150–1750*. New York: Zone, 1998.

Davies, Glenys. "Sir Robert Cotton's Collection of Roman Stones: A Catalogue with Commentary." In *Sir Robert Cotton as Collector: Essays on an Early Stuart Courtier and His Legacy*, ed. C. J. Wright. London: British Library, 1997. 129–67.

Davis, J. C. *Utopia and the Ideal Society: A Study of English Utopian Writing, 1516–1700*. Cambridge: Cambridge University Press, 1981.

De Beer, G. R. *Sir Hans Sloane and the British Museum*. London: Oxford University Press, 1953.

De Grazia, Margreta. *Shakespeare Verbatim: The Reproduction of Authenticity and the 1790 Apparatus*. Oxford: Clarendon Press, 1991.

De Grazia, Margreta, Maureen Quilligan, and Peter Stallybrass, eds. *Subject and Object in Renaissance Culture*. Cambridge: Cambridge University Press, 1996.

De la Mare, A. C. "Manuscripts and Printed Books associated with the Tradescants in the Bodleian Library." In *Tradescant's Rarities*, ed. Arthur MacGregor. Oxford: Clarendon Press, 1983. 351–57.

Donaldson, Ian. *Jonson's Magic Houses: Essays in Interpretation*. Oxford: Clarendon Press, 1997.

Douglas, David C. *English Scholars, 1660–1730*. 2nd ed. London: Eyre and Spottiswoode, 1951.

Douglas, Mary and Baron Isherwood. *The World of Goods*. New York: Basic Books, 1979.

Duncan, Carol. "Art Museums and the Ritual of Citizenship." In *Interpreting Objects and Collections*, ed. Susan M. Pearce. London: Routledge, 1994. 279–86.

——. *Civilizing Rituals: Inside Public Art Museums*. London: Routledge, 1995.

Duncan, Carol and Alan Wallach. "The Universal Survey Museum." *Art History* 3 (1980): 448–69.

During, Simon. *Foucault and Literature: Towards a Genealogy of Writing*. London: Routledge, 1992.

Dutton, Richard. *Ben Jonson, Authority, Criticism*. Basingstoke: Macmillan; New York: St. Martin's, 1996.

——. *Ben Jonson: To the First Folio*. Cambridge: Cambridge University Press, 1983.

Eamon, William. *Science and the Secrets of Nature: Books of Secrets in Medieval and Early Modern Culture*. Princeton, N.J.: Princeton University Press, 1994.

Eisenstein, Elizabeth L. *The Printing Press as an Agent of Change*. 2 vols. Cambridge: Cambridge University Press, 1979.

Eliot, T. S. "What Is Minor Poetry?" In Eliot, *On Poetry and Poets*. London: Faber and Faber, 1957; repr 1969. 39–52.

Elliott, J. H. *The Old World and the New, 1492–1650*. Cambridge: Cambridge University Press, 1970.

Elsky, Martin. *Authorizing Words: Speech, Writing, and Print in the English Renaissance*. Ithaca, N.Y.: Cornell University Press, 1989.

——. "Shakespeare, Bacon, and the Construction of Authorship." In *Reading and Writing in Shakespeare*, ed. David M. Bergeron. Newark: University of Delaware Press, 1996. 254–63.

Epstein, Joel J. *Francis Bacon: A Political Biography*. Athens: Ohio University Press, 1977.

Erickson, Amy. *Women and Property in Early Modern England*. London: Routledge, 1993.

Evans, Robert C. *Habits of Mind: Evidence and Effects of Ben Jonson's Reading*. Lewisburg, Pa.: Bucknell University Press, 1995.

Ezell, Margaret J.M. "Richard Waller, S.R.S.: 'In the Pursuit of Nature.'" *Notes and Records of the Royal Society of London* 38 (1984): 215–33.

Farrington, Benjamin. *The Philosophy of Francis Bacon: An Essay on Its Development from 1603 to 1609 with New Translations of Fundamental Texts*. Liverpool: Liverpool University Press, 1964.

Faulkner, Robert K. *Francis Bacon and the Project of Progress*. Lanham, Md.: Rowman and Littlefield, 1993.

Feather, John. "Rights in Copies to Copyright: The Recognition of Authors' Rights in English Law and Practice in the Sixteenth and Seventeenth Centuries." In *The Construction of Authorship: Textual Appropriation in Law and Literature*, ed. Martha Woodmansee and Peter Jaszi. Durham, N.C.: Duke University Press, 1994. 191–209.

Febvre, Lucien and Henri-Jean Martin. *The Coming of the Book: The Impact of Printing, 1450–1800*. Trans. David Gerard, ed. Geoffrey Nowell-Smith and David Wootton. London: NLB; Atlantic Highlands, N.J.: Humanities Press, 1976.

Feest, Christian F. "The Collecting of American Indian Artifacts in Europe, 1493–1750." In *America in European Consciousness, 1493–1750*, ed. Karen Ordahl Kupperman. Chapel Hill: University of North Carolina Press, 1995. 324–60.

Ferguson, Arthur B. *Clio Unbound: Perception of the Social and Cultural Past in Renaissance England*. Durham, N.C.: Duke University Press, 1979.

Ferguson, Margaret W., Maureen Quilligan, and Nancy J. Vickers, eds. *Rewriting the Renaissance: The Discourses of Sexual Difference in Early Modern Europe*. Chicago: University of Chicago Press, 1986.

Findlen, Paula. "Courting Nature." In *Cultures of Natural History*, ed. N. Jardine, J. A. Secord, and E. C. Spary. Cambridge: Cambridge University Press, 1996. 57–74.

———. "The Economy of Scientific Exchange in Early Modern Italy." In *Patronage and Institutions: Science, Technology, and Medicine at the European Court, 1500–1750*, ed. Bruce T. Moran. Woodbridge, Suffolk: Boydell, 1991. 5–24.

———. "Francis Bacon and the Reform of Natural History in the Seventeenth Century." In *History and the Disciplines: The Reclassification of Knowledge in Early Modern Europe*, ed. Donald R. Kelley. Rochester, N.Y.: University of Rochester Press, 1997. 239–60.

———. "The Museum: Its Classical Etymology and Renaissance Genealogy." *Journal of the History of Collections* 1 (1989): 59–78.

———. *Possessing Nature: Museums, Collecting, and Scientific Culture in Early Modern Italy*. Berkeley: University of California Press, 1994.

Fish, Stanley. "Authors-Readers: Jonson's Community of the Same." In *Representing the English Renaissance*, ed. Stephen Greenblatt. Berkeley: University of California Press, 1988. 231–63.

Foucault, Michel. *The History of Sexuality*. Vol. 1, *An Introduction*. Trans. Robert Hurley. New York: Vintage, 1978; repr. 1990.

———. *The Order of Things: An Archaeology of the Human Sciences*. 1970; repr. London: Tavistock, 1986.

———. "What Is an Author?" In *Textual Strategies: Perspectives in Post-Structuralist Criticism*, ed. Josué V. Harari. Ithaca, N.Y.: Cornell University Press, 1979. 141–60.

Fowler, Alastair. *Kinds of Literature: An Introduction to the Theory of Genres and Modes*. Oxford: Clarendon Press, 1982.

——. "Robert Herrick." *Proceedings of the British Academy* 66 (1980): 243–64.

——. "The Silva Tradition in Jonson's *The Forest.*" In *Poetic Traditions of the English Renaissance*, ed. Maynard Mack and George deForest Lord. New Haven, Conn.: Yale University Press, 1982. 163–80.

Fox, Alistair. "Facts and Fallacies: Interpreting English Humanism." In *Reassessing the Henrician Age*, ed. Fox and John Guy. Oxford: Blackwell, 1986. 9–33.

Frye, Susan. "Sewing Connections: Elizabeth Tudor, Mary Stuart, Elizabeth Talbot, and Seventeenth-Century Anonymous Needleworkers." In *Maids and Mistresses, Cousins and Queens: Women's Alliances in Early Modern England*, ed. Frye and Karen Robertson. Oxford: Oxford University Press, 1999. 165–82.

Fumerton, Patricia. *Cultural Aesthetics: Renaissance Literature and the Practice of Social Ornament.* Chicago: University of Chicago Press, 1991.

——. "Introduction: A New New Historicism." In *Renaissance Culture and the Everyday*, ed. Fumerton and Simon Hunt. Philadelphia: University of Pennsylvania Press, 1999. 1–17.

Gants, David Lee. "A Descriptive Bibliography of *The Workes of Beniamin Jonson*, London: William Stansby, 1616." Ph.D. dissertation, University of Virginia, 1997.

Gibson-Wood, Carol. "Classification and Value in a Seventeenth-Century Museum." *Journal of the History of Collections* 9 (1997): 61–77.

Goldberg, Jonathan. "Fatherly Authority: The Politics of Stuart Family Images." In *Rewriting the Renaissance: The Discourses of Sexual Difference in Early Modern Europe*, ed. Margaret W. Ferguson, Maureen Quilligan, and Nancy J. Vickers. Chicago: University of Chicago Press, 1986. 3–32.

——. *James I and the Politics of Literature: Jonson, Shakespeare, Donne, and Their Contemporaries.* Stanford, Calif.: Stanford University Press, 1989 .

——. *Sodometries: Renaissance Texts, Modern Sexualities.* Stanford, Calif.: Stanford University Press, 1992.

Goldthwaite, Richard A. *Wealth and the Demand for Art in Italy 1300–1600.* Baltimore: Johns Hopkins University Press, 1993.

Grafton, Anthony. *The Footnote: A Curious History.* Cambridge, Mass: Harvard University Press, 1997.

Grafton, Anthony and Lisa Jardine. *From Humanism to the Humanities.* Cambridge, Mass: Harvard University Press, 1986.

Grassby, Richard. *The Business Community of Seventeenth-Century England.* Cambridge: Cambridge University Press, 1995.

Greenblatt, Stephen. *Marvelous Possessions: The Wonder of the New World.* Chicago: University of Chicago Press, 1991.

——, ed. *Representing the English Renaissance.* Berkeley: University of California Press, 1988. 265–78.

——. "Resonance and Wonder." In *Exhibiting Cultures: The Poetics and Politics of Museum Display*, ed. Ivan Karp and Steven D. Lavine. Washington, D.C.: Smithsonian Institution Press, 1991. 42–56.

Guibbory, Achsah. *Ceremony and Community From Herbert to Milton*. Cambridge: Cambridge University Press, 1998.

——. "Enlarging the Limits of the 'Religious Lyric': The Case of Herrick's *Hesperides*." In *New Perspectives on the Seventeenth-Century English Religious Lyric*, ed. John R. Roberts. Columbia: University of Missouri Press, 1994. 28–45.

——. "The Temple of *Hesperides* and Anglican-Puritan Controversy." In *The Muses Common-Weale: Poetry and Politics in the Seventeenth Century*, ed. Claude Summers and Ted-Larry Pebworth. Columbia: University of Missouri Press, 1988. 135–62.

Habermas, Jürgen. *The Structural Transformation of the Public Sphere: An Inquiry into a Category of Bourgeois Society*. Trans. Thomas Burger. Cambridge, Mass.: MIT Press, 1989.

Hall, Kim F. *Things of Darkness: Economies of Race and Gender in Early Modern England*. Ithaca, N.Y.: Cornell University Press, 1995.

Hall, Marie Boas. "Thomas Browne, Naturalist." In *Approaches to Sir Thomas Browne*, ed. C. A. Patrides. Columbia: University of Missouri Press, 1982. 178–87.

Halpern, Richard. *The Poetics of Primitive Accumulation: English Renaissance Culture and the Genealogy of Capital*. Ithaca, N.Y.: Cornell University Press, 1991.

Hammill, Graham. "The Epistemology of Expurgation: Bacon and *The Masculine Birth of Time*." In *Queering the Renaissance*, ed. Jonathan Goldberg. Durham, N.C.: Duke University Press, 1994. 236–52.

Handler, Richard. "On Having a Culture: Nationalism and the Preservation of Quebec's *Patrimoine*." In *Objects and Others: Essays on Museums and Material Culture*, ed. George W. Stocking, Jr. Madison: University of Wisconsin Press, 1985. 192–217.

Harley, J. B. "Silences and Secrecy: The Hidden Agenda of Cartography in Early Modern Europe." *Imago Mundi* 40 (1988): 57–76.

Harris, Frances. "Living in the Neighbourhood of Science: Mary Evelyn, Margaret Cavendish and the Greshamites." In *Women, Science and Medicine, 1500–1700*, ed. Lynette Hunter and Sarah Hutton. Stroud, Gloucestershire: Sutton, 1997. 198–217.

Harris, Jonathan Gil and Natasha Korda, eds. *Staged Properties: Props and Property in Early Modern English Drama*. Cambridge: Cambridge University Press, forthcoming.

Hartt, Frederick. *History of Italian Renaissance Art*. Revised David G. Wilkins. New York: Harry N. Abrams, 1994.

Harvey, P. D. A. "English Estate Maps: Their Early History and Their Use as Historical Evidence." In *Rural Images: Estate Maps in the Old and New Worlds*, ed. David Buisseret. Chicago: University of Chicago Press, 1996. 27–61.

Haskell, Francis. "Charles I's Collection of Pictures." In *The Late King's Goods*, ed. Arthur MacGregor. Oxford: Alistair McAlpine and Oxford University Press, 1989. 203–31.

Heal, Felicity. *Hospitality in Early Modern England*. Oxford: Clarendon Press, 1990.

Heal, Felicity and Clive Holmes. *The Gentry in England and Wales, 1500–1700*. Stanford, Calif.: Stanford University Press, 1994.

Helgerson, Richard. *Forms of Nationhood: The Elizabethan Writing of England*. Chicago: University of Chicago Press, 1992.

———. *Self-Crowned Laureates: Spenser, Jonson, Milton, and the Literary System*. Berkeley: University of California Press, 1983.

Herendeen, W. H. "A New Way to Pay Old Debts: Pretexts to the 1616 Folio." In *Ben Jonson's 1616 Folio*, ed. Jennifer Brady and Herendeen. Newark: University of Delaware Press, 1991. 38–63.

Hibbard, G. R. "The Country House Poem of the Seventeenth Century." *Journal of the Warburg and Courtauld Institutes* 19 (1956): 159–74.

Hinman, Robert B. "The Apotheosis of Faust: Poetry and New Philosophy in the Seventeenth Century." In *Metaphysical Poetry*, ed. D. J. Palmer and Malcolm Bradbury. Stratford-upon-Avon Studies 11. London: Edward Arnold, 1970. 149–79.

Hobbs, Mary. *Early Seventeenth-Century Verse Miscellany Manuscripts*. Aldershot: Scolar Press, 1992.

Hodgen, Margaret T. *Early Anthropology in the Sixteenth and Seventeenth Centuries*. Philadelphia: University of Pennsylvania Press, 1964.

Hoeniger, F. David. "How Plants and Animals Were Studied in the Mid-Sixteenth Century." In *Science and the Arts in the Renaissance*, ed. John W. Shirley and F. David Hoeniger. Washington, D. C.: Folger Shakespeare Library, 1985. 130–48.

Hoeniger, F. David and J. F. M. Hoeniger. *The Development of Natural History in Tudor England*. Charlottesville: University Press of Virginia for the Folger Shakespeare Library, 1969.

Holst, Niels von. *Creators, Collectors, and Connoisseurs: The Anatomy of Artistic Taste from Antiquity to the Present Day*. London: Thames and Hudson, 1967.

Hooper-Greenhill, Eilean. *Museums and the Shaping of Knowledge*. London: Routledge, 1992.

Hoppen, K. Theodore. "The Nature of the Early Royal Society." *British Journal for the History of Science* 9 (1976): 1–24, 243–73.

Houghton, Walter E., Jr. "The English Virtuoso in the Seventeenth Century."
    Journal of the History of Ideas 3 (1942): 51–73, 190–219.
Howarth, David. *Lord Arundel and His Circle.* New Haven, Conn.: Yale University
    Press, 1985.
———. "Sir Robert Cotton and the Commemoration of Famous Men." In *Sir Robert
    Cotton as Collector: Essays on an Early Stuart Courtier and His Legacy*, ed. C. J.
    Wright. London: British Library, 1997. 40–67.
Hudson, Roger. *The Grand Tour, 1592–1796.* London: Folio Society, 1993.
Hughes, Ann. *Politics, Society and Civil War in Warwickshire, 1620–1660.* Cam-
    bridge: Cambridge University Press, 1987.
Hunt, John Dixon. "Curiosities to Adorn Cabinets and Gardens." In *The Origins of
    Museums*, ed. Oliver Impey and Arthur MacGregor. Oxford: Clarendon
    Press, 1985. 193–203.
———. *Garden and Grove: The Italian Renaissance Garden in the English Imagination,
    1600–1750.* Philadelphia: University of Pennsylvania Press, 1996.
Hunter, Lynette. "Sisters of the Royal Society: The Circle of Katherine Jones, Lady
    Ranelagh." In *Women, Science and Medicine, 1500–1700*, ed. Hunter and Sarah
    Hutton. Stroud, Gloucestershire: Sutton, 1997. 178–98.
Hunter, Lynette and Sarah Hutton, eds. *Women, Science and Medicine, 1500–
    1700: Mothers and Sisters of the Royal Society.* Stroud, Gloucestershire: Sutton,
    1997.
Hunter, Michael. *Elias Ashmole, 1617–1692: The Founder of the Ashmolean Museum
    and His World.* Oxford: Ashmolean Museum, 1983.
———. *Establishing the New Science: The Experience of the Early Royal Society.* Wood-
    bridge, Suffolk: Boydell, 1989.
———. *John Aubrey and the Realm of Learning.* London: Duckworth, 1975.
———. *The Royal Society and Its Fellows 1660–1700: The Morphology of an Early
    Scientific Institution.* Chalfont St. Giles, Bucks.: British Society for the His-
    tory of Science, 1982.
———. *Science and Society in Restoration England.* Cambridge: Cambridge University
    Press, 1981.
———. *Science and the Shape of Orthodoxy: Intellectual Change in Late Seventeenth-
    Century Britain.* Woodbridge, Suffolk: Boydell, 1995.
Hunter, Michael and Paul B. Wood. "Towards Solomon's House: Rival Strategies
    for Reforming the Early Royal Society." In *Establishing the New Science: The
    Experience of the Early Royal Society*, ed. Michael Hunter. Woodbridge, Suf-
    folk: Boydell, 1989. 185–244
Hutton, Sarah. "The Riddle of the Sphinx: Francis Bacon and the Emblems of
    Science." In *Women, Science and Medicine, 1500–1700*, ed. Lynette Hunter and
    Hutton. Stroud, Gloucestershire: Sutton, 1997. 7–28.

Impey, Oliver and Arthur MacGregor, eds. *The Origins of Museums*. Oxford: Clarendon Press, 1985.

Ingram, Randall. "Robert Herrick and the Makings of *Hesperides*." *Studies in English Literature, 1500–1900* 38 (1998): 127–47.

James, Mervyn. *Family, Lineage, and Civil Society*. Oxford: Clarendon Press, 1974.

——. *Society, Politics, and Culture: Studies in Early Modern England*. Cambridge: Cambridge University Press, 1986.

Jardine, Lisa. "Companionate Marriage Versus Male Friendship: Anxiety for the Lineal Family in Jacobean Drama." In *Political Culture and Cultural Politics in Early Modern England: Essays Presented to David Underdown*, ed. Susan D. Amussen and Mark A. Kishlansky. Manchester: Manchester University Press, 1995. 234–54.

——. *Francis Bacon: Discovery and the Art of Discourse*. Cambridge: Cambridge University Press, 1974.

——. *Ingenious Pursuits: Building the Scientific Revolution*. New York: Doubleday, 1999.

——. *Worldly Goods: A New History of the Renaissance*. London: Macmillan, 1996.

Jardine, Lisa and Alan Stewart. *Hostage to Fortune: The Troubled Life of Francis Bacon, 1561–1626*. London: Victor Gollancz, 1998.

Jarvis, P. J. "The Introduced Trees and Shrubs Cultivated by the Tradescants at South Lambeth, 1629–1679." *Journal of the Society for the Bibliography of Natural History* 9 (1979): 223–50.

Jenkins, Hugh. *Feigned Commonwealths: The Country-House Poem and the Fashioning of the Ideal Community*. Pittsburgh: Duquesne University Press, 1998.

Johns, Adrian. *The Nature of the Book: Print and Knowledge in the Making*. Chicago: University of Chicago Press, 1998.

Jowett, John. "'Fall before this Booke': The 1605 Quarto of *Sejanus*." *TEXT: Transactions of the Society for Textual Scholarship* 4 (1988): 279–95.

Juel-Jensen, Bent. "*Musaeum Clausum, or Bibliotheca Abscondita*: Some Thoughts on Curiosity Cabinets and Imaginary Books." *Journal of the History of Collections* 4 (1992): 127–40.

Kaufmann, Thomas DaCosta. "From Treasury to Museum: The Collections of the Austrian Habsburgs." In *The Cultures of Collecting*, ed. John Elsner and Roger Cardinal. Cambridge, Mass.: Harvard University Press, 1994. 137–54.

——. "Remarks on the Collections of Rudolf II: The *Kunstkammer* as a Form of *Representatio*." *Art Journal* 38 (1978): 22–28.

Kay, W. David. *Ben Jonson: A Literary Life*. Houndmills, Basingstoke: Macmillan, 1995.

——. "The Shaping of Ben Jonson's Career: A Reexamination of Facts and Problems." *Modern Philology* 67 (1970): 224–37.

Keller, Evelyn Fox. *Reflections on Gender and Science*. New Haven, Conn.: Yale University Press, 1985.

Kemp, Martin. "'Wrought by No Artist's Hand': The Natural, the Artificial, the Exotic, and the Scientific in Some Artifacts from the Renaissance." In *Reframing the Renaissance: Visual Culture in Europe and Latin America, 1450–1650*, ed. Claire Farago. New Haven, Conn.: Yale University Press, 1995. 177–96.

Kendrick, T. D. *British Antiquity*. London: Methuen, 1950.

Kenseth, Joy. "The Age of the Marvelous: An Introduction." In *The Age of the Marvelous*, ed. Kenseth. Hanover, N.H.: Hood Museum of Art, Dartmouth College, 1991. 25–59.

Ketton-Cremer, R. W. *A Norfolk Gallery*. London: Faber and Faber, 1948.

Kimmey, John L. "Order and Form in Herrick's *Hesperides*." *Journal of English and Germanic Philology* 70 (1971): 255–68.

——. "Robert Herrick's Persona." *Studies in Philology* 67 (1970): 221–36.

Leary, John E., Jr. *Francis Bacon and the Politics of Science*. Ames: Iowa State University Press, 1994.

Leith-Ross, Prudence. *The John Tradescants: Gardeners to the Rose and Lily Queen*. London: Peter Owen, 1984.

Levine, Joseph M. *Dr. Woodward's Shield: History, Science, and Satire in Augustan England*. Berkeley: University of California Press, 1977.

——. "Natural History and the History of the Scientific Revolution." *Clio* 13 (1983): 57–73.

Levy, F. J. "The Making of Camden's *Britannia*." *Bibliothèque d'Humanisme et Renaissance* 26 (1964): 70–97.

Lightbown, Ronald. "Charles I and the Tradition of European Princely Collecting." In *The Late King's Goods: Collections, Possessions, and Patronage of Charles I in the Light of the Commonwealth Sale Inventories*, ed. Arthur MacGregor. Oxford: Alistair McAlpine/Oxford University Press, 1989. 53–72.

Llewellyn, Nigel. *The Art of Death: Visual Culture in the English Death Ritual, c.1500–c.1800*. London: Reaktion, 1991.

——. "Claims to Status Through Visual Codes: Heraldry on Post-Reformation Funeral Monuments." In *Chivalry in the Renaissance*, ed. Sydney Anglo. Woodbridge, Suffolk: Boydell, 1990. 145–60.

——. "Cromwell and the Tombs: Historiography and Style in Post-Reformation English Funeral Monuments." *L'Art et les révolutions*. Section 4, *Les iconoclasmes*. Strasbourg: Société alsacienne pour l'histoire de l'art, 1992. 193–204.

Lloyd, Claude. "Shadwell and the Virtuosi." *PMLA* 44 (1929): 472–94.

Loewenstein, Joseph. "Printing and 'The Multitudinous Presse': The Contentious Texts of Jonson's Masques." In *Ben Jonson's 1616 Folio*, ed. Jennifer Brady and W. H. Herendeen. Newark: University of Delaware Press, 1991. 168–91.

———. *Responsive Readings: Versions of Pastoral, Epic, and the Jonsonian Masque.* New Haven, Conn.: Yale University Press, 1984.

———. "The Script in the Marketplace." In *Representing the English Renaissance*, ed. Stephen Greenblatt. Berkeley: University of California Press, 1988. 265–78.

Löffler, Arno. *Sir Thomas Browne als Virtuoso; die Bedeutung der Gelehrsamkeit für sein literarisches Alterswerk.*. Nürnberg: H. Carl, 1972.

London, April. "*Musaeum Tradescantianum* and the Benefactors to the Tradescants' Museum." In *Tradescant's Rarities: Essays on the Foundation of the Ashmolean Museum*, ed. Arthur MacGregor. Oxford: Clarendon Press, 1983. 24–39.

Love, Harold. *Scribal Publication in Seventeenth-Century England.* Oxford: Clarendon Press, 1993.

MacGregor, Arthur. "The Cabinet of Curiosities in Seventeenth-Century Britain." In *The Origins of Museums*, ed. Oliver Impey and Arthur MacGregor. Oxford: Clarendon Press, 1985. 147–58.

———. "King Charles I: A Renaissance Collector?" *Seventeenth Century* 11 (1996): 141–60.

———. "The Life, Character and Career of Sir Hans Sloane." In *Sir Hans Sloane*, ed. MacGregor. London: British Museum Press, 1994. 11–44

———, ed. *Tradescant's Rarities: Essays on the Foundation of the Ashmolean Museum.* Oxford: Clarendon Press, 1983.

MacGregor, Arthur and A. J. Turner. "The Ashmolean Museum." In *The History of the University of Oxford*, gen. ed. T. H. Aston. Vol. 5, *The Eighteenth Century*, ed. L. S. Sutherland and L. G. Mitchell. Oxford: Clarendon Press, 1986. 639–58.

Mack, Peter. "Humanist Rhetoric and Dialectic." In *The Cambridge Companion to Renaissance Humanism*, ed. Jill Kraye. Cambridge: Cambridge University Press, 1996. 82–99.

MacLeod, Malcolm, ed. *A Concordance to the Poems of Robert Herrick.* Oxford: Oxford University Press, 1936.

Macpherson, C. B. "Capitalism and the Changing Concept of Property." In *Feudalism, Capitalism and Beyond*, ed. Eugene Kamenka and R. S. Neale. London: Edward Arnold, 1975. 104–24.

Malherbe, Michel. "Bacon's Method of Science." In *The Cambridge Companion to Bacon*, ed. Markku Peltonen. Cambridge: Cambridge University Press, 1996. 75–98.

Manning, Roger B. "Antiquarianism and the Seigneurial Reaction: Sir Robert and Sir Thomas Cotton and their Tenants." *Historical Research* 63, no. 152 (Oct. 1990): 277–88.

Marchitello, Howard. *Narrative and Meaning in Early Modern England.* Cambridge: Cambridge University Press, 1997.

Marcus, Leah S. *Childhood and Cultural Despair: A Theme and Variations in Seventeenth-Century Literature*. Pittsburgh: University of Pittsburgh Press, 1976.

——. *The Politics of Mirth: Jonson, Herrick, Milton, Marvell, and the Defense of Old Holiday Pastimes*. Chicago: University of Chicago Press, 1986.

——. "Robert Herrick." In *The Cambridge Companion to English Poetry, Donne to Marvell*, ed. Thomas N. Corns. Cambridge: Cambridge University Press, 1993. 171–82.

——. *Unediting the Renaissance: Shakespeare, Marlowe, Milton*. London: Routledge, 1996.

Marotti, Arthur F. *Manuscript, Print, and the English Renaissance Lyric*. Ithaca, N.Y.: Cornell University Press, 1995.

Martin, Julian. *Francis Bacon, the State, and the Reform of Natural Philosophy*. Cambridge: Cambridge University Press, 1992.

——. "Natural Philosophy and Its Public Concerns." In *Science, Culture, and Popular Belief in Renaissance Europe*, ed. Stephen Pumfrey, Paolo L. Rossi, and Maurice Slawinski. Manchester: Manchester University Press, 1991. 100–18.

Martin, L. C. Introduction. In *The Poetical Works of Robert Herrick*, ed. Martin. Oxford: Clarendon Press, 1956. xi–xl.

Mason, Peter. "From Presentation to Representation: *Americana* in Europe." *Journal of the History of Collections* 6 (1994): 1–20.

Masten, Jeffrey. *Textual Intercourse: Collaboration, Authorship, and Sexualities in Renaissance Drama*. Cambridge: Cambridge University Press, 1997.

Maxwell, Richard. "Robert Harley, First Earl of Oxford and Edward Harley, Second Earl of Oxford." In *Pre-Nineteenth-Century British Book Collectors*, ed. William Baker and Kenneth Womack. Dictionary of Literary Biography, 213. Detroit: Gale Group, 1999. 123–30.

McClung, William. *The Country House in English Renaissance Poetry*. Berkeley: University of California Press, 1977.

McCracken, Grant. *Culture and Consumption: New Approaches to the Symbolic Character of Consumer Goods and Activities*. Bloomington: Indiana University Press, 1988.

McKendrick, Neil, John Brewer, and J. H. Plumb. *The Birth of a Consumer Society: The Commercialization of Eighteenth-Century England*. Bloomington: Indiana University Press, 1982.

McKenzie, D. F. *Bibliography and the Sociology of Texts*. London: British Library, 1986.

McKitterick, David. "From Camden to Cambridge: Sir Robert Cotton's Roman Inscriptions, and Their Subsequent Treatment." In *Sir Robert Cotton as Collector: Essays on an Early Stuart Courtier and His Legacy*, ed. C. J. Wright. London: British Library, 1997. 105–28.

McRae, Andrew. *God Speed the Plough: The Representation of Agrarian England, 1500–1660*. Cambridge: Cambridge University Press, 1996.

Medici, Anthony G. "John Dee." In *Pre-Nineteenth-Century British Book Collectors and Bibliographers*, ed. William Baker and Kenneth Womack. Dictionary of Literary Biography 213. Detroit: Gale Group, 1999. 78–92.

Mendyk, Stan A. E. *"Speculum Britanniae": Regional Study, Antiquarianism, and Science in Britain to 1700*. Toronto: University of Toronto Press, 1989.

Merchant, Carolyn. *The Death of Nature: Women, Ecology, and the Scientific Revolution*. San Francisco: Harper and Row, 1980.

Miller, Daniel. *Material Culture and Mass Consumption*. Oxford: Blackwell, 1987.

Miller, Edward. *That Noble Cabinet: A History of the British Museum*. Athens: Ohio University Press, 1974.

Milner, Andrew. *Cultural Materialism*. Melbourne: Melbourne University Press, 1993.

Mingay, G. E. *The Gentry: The Rise and Fall of a Ruling Class*. London: Longman, 1976.

Moisan, Thomas. "The 'Argument' and the Opening of Robert Herrick's 'Book.'" *Explorations in Renaissance Culture* 16 (1990): 129–43.

Montrose, Louis. "Spenser's Domestic Domain: Poetry, Property, and the Early Modern Subject." In *Subject and Object in Renaissance Culture*, ed. Margreta de Grazia, Maureen Quilligan, and Peter Stallybrass. Cambridge: Cambridge University Press, 1996. 83–130.

Moorman, F. W. Introduction. In *The Poetical Works of Robert Herrick*, ed. Moorman. Oxford: Clarendon Press, 1915. v–xxiii.

Muensterberger, Werner. *Collecting, an Unruly Passion: Psychological Perspectives*. Princeton, N.J.: Princeton University Press, 1994.

Mukerji, Chandra. *From Graven Images: Patterns of Modern Materialism*. New York: Columbia University Press, 1983.

Mullaney, Steven. "Strange Things, Gross Terms, Curious Customs: The Rehearsal of Cultures in the Late Renaissance." In *Representing the English Renaissance*, ed. Stephen Greenblatt. Berkeley: University of California Press, 1988. 65–92.

Murray, David. *Museums: Their History and Their Use*. 3 vols. Glasgow: McLehose, 1904.

Murray, Timothy. *Theatrical Legitimation*. Oxford: Oxford University Press, 1987.

Newton, Richard C. "Jonson and the (Re-)Invention of the Book." In *Classic and Cavalier: Essays on Jonson and the Sons of Ben*, ed. Claude J. Summers and Ted-Larry Pebworth. Pittsburgh: University of Pittsburgh Press, 1982. 31–55.

——. "Making Books from Leaves: Poets Become Editors." In *Print and Culture in the Renaissance: Essays on the Advent of Printing in Europe*, ed. Gerald P.

Tyson and Sylvia S. Wagonheim. Newark: University of Delaware Press, 1986. 246–64.

Olmi, Giuseppe. "Science-Honour-Metaphor: Italian Cabinets of the Sixteenth and Seventeenth Centuries." In *The Origins of Museums*, ed. Oliver Impey and Arthur MacGregor. Oxford: Clarendon Press, 1985. 5–16.

Ong, Walter J. "Commonplace Rhapsody: Ravisius Textor, Swinger and Shakespeare." In *Classical Influences on European Culture, A.D. 1500–1700*, ed. R. R. Bolgar. Cambridge: Cambridge University Press, 1974. 91–126.

——. *Orality and Literacy: The Technologizing of the Word*. London: Methuen, 1982.

——. *The Presence of the Word*. New Haven, Conn.: Yale University Press, 1967.

——. *Rhetoric, Romance, and Technology*. Ithaca, N.Y.: Cornell University Press, 1971.

Orgel, Stephen. "What Is a Text?" *Research Opportunities in Renaissance Drama* 2 (1981): 3–6.

Orlin, Lena Cowen. "Three Ways to Be Invisible in the Renaissance: Sex, Reputation, and Stitchery." In *Renaissance Culture and the Everyday*, ed. Patricia Fumerton and Simon Hunt. Philadelphia: University of Pennsylvania Press, 1999. 183–203.

Ovenell, R. F. *The Ashmolean Museum, 1683–1894*. Oxford: Clarendon Press, 1986.

Pagden, Anthony. *European Encounters with the New World: From Renaissance to Romanticism*. New Haven, Conn.: Yale University Press, 1993.

Park, Katharine and Lorraine Daston. "Unnatural Conceptions: The Study of Monsters in Sixteenth- and Seventeenth-Century France and England." *Past and Present* 92 (1981): 20–54.

Parry, Graham. *The Trophies of Time*. Oxford: Oxford University Press, 1995.

Patrides, C. A. "'Above Atlas His Shoulders': An Introduction to Sir Thomas Browne." In *Sir Thomas Browne: The Major Works*, ed. Patrides. Harmondsworth: Penguin, 1977. 21–52.

——. "'The Best Part of Nothing': Sir Thomas Browne and the Strategy of Indirection." In *Approaches to Sir Thomas Browne*, ed. Patrides. Columbia: University of Missouri Press, 1982. 31–48.

Pearce, Susan M. *Museums, Objects and Collections: A Cultural Study*. Washington, D.C.: Smithsonian Institution Press, 1992.

——. *On Collecting: An Investigation into Collecting in the European Tradition*. London: Routledge, 1995.

Peck, Linda Levy. "Building, Buying, and Collecting in London, 1600–1625." In *Material London, ca. 1600*, ed. Lena Cowen Orlin. Philadelphia: University of Pennsylvania Press, 2000. 268–89.

Peltonen, Markku, ed. *The Cambridge Companion to Bacon*. Cambridge: Cambridge University Press, 1996.

Pérez-Ramos, Antonio. *Francis Bacon's Idea of Science and the Maker's Knowledge Tradition.* Oxford: Clarendon Press, 1988.

Peterson, Richard S. *Imitation and Praise in the Poems of Ben Jonson.* New Haven, Conn.: Yale University Press, 1981.

Phillips, John. *The Reformation of Images: Destruction of Art in England, 1535–1660.* Berkeley: University of California Press, 1973.

Piggott, Stuart. *Ruins in a Landscape.* Edinburgh: Edinburgh University Press, 1976.

Pocock, J. G. A. *The Machiavellian Moment: Florentine Political Thought and the Atlantic Republican Tradition.* Princeton, N.J.: Princeton University Press, 1975.

Pomian, Krysztof. *Collectors and Curiosities: Paris and Venice, 1500–1800.* Trans. Elizabeth Wiles-Portier. Cambridge: Polity Press, 1990.

Post, Jonathan F. S. "Robert Herrick: A Minority Report." *George Herbert Journal* 14 (1990–91): 72–96.

——. *Sir Thomas Browne.* Boston: Twayne, 1987.

Potter, Esther. " 'To Paul's Churchyard to Treat with a Bookbinder.' " In *Property of a Gentleman: The Formation, Organisation and Dispersal of the Private Library 1620–1920,* ed. Robin Myers and Michael Harris. Winchester: St. Paul's Bibliographies, 1991. 25–41.

Pulteney, Richard. *Historical and Biographical Sketches of the Progress of Botany in England.* 2 vols. London, 1790.

Quinn, Dennis. "Polypragmosyne in the Renaissance: Ben Jonson." *Ben Jonson Journal* 2 (1995): 157–69.

Quint, David. "Introduction." In *Literary Theory/Renaissance Texts,* ed. Patricia Parker and Quint. Baltimore: Johns Hopkins University Press, 1986. 1–19.

Rathmell, J. C. A. "Jonson, Lord Lisle, and Penshurst." *English Literary Renaissance* 1 (1971): 250–60.

Reiss, Timothy J. *The Discourse of Modernism.* Ithaca, N.Y.: Cornell University Press, 1982.

Riggs, David. *Ben Jonson: A Life.* Cambridge, Mass.: Harvard University Press, 1989.

Rinehart, Michael. "A Document for the Studiolo of Francesco I." In *Art, the Ape of Nature,* ed. Mosche Barasch and Lucy Freeman Sandler. New York: Harry N. Abrams, 1981. 275–89.

Rollin, Roger B. *Robert Herrick.* Rev. ed. New York: Twayne, 1992.

——. "Robert Herrick's Fathers." *Studies in English Literature, 1500–1900* 34 (1994): 41–60.

——. "Witty by Design: Robert Herrick's *Hesperides.*" In *The Wit of Seventeenth-Century Poetry,* ed. Claude J. Summers and Ted-Larry Pebworth. Columbia: University of Missouri Press, 1995. 135–50.

Rose, Mark. *Authors and Owners: The Invention of Copyright.* Cambridge, Mass.: Harvard University Press, 1993.

Rossi, Paolo. *Francis Bacon: From Magic to Science.* Trans. Sacha Rabinovitch. London: Routledge and Kegan Paul, 1968.

Saunders, David and Ian Hunter. "Lessons from the 'Literatory': How to Historicise Authorship." *Critical Inquiry* 17 (1991): 479–509.

Schiebinger, Londa. "Feminine Icons: The Face of Early Modern Science." *Critical Inquiry* 14 (1988): 661–91.

Schlosser, Julius von. *Die Kunst- und Wunderkammern der Spätrenaissance.* Liepzig: Klinkhardt and Biermann, 1908.

Schwenger, Peter. "Herrick's Fairy State." *ELH* 46 (1979): 35–55.

Sedgwick, Eve Kosofsky. *Between Men: English Literature and Male Homosocial Desire.* New York: Columbia University Press, 1985.

Seelig, Lorenz. "The Munich *Kunstkammer,* 1565–1807." In *The Origins of Museums,* ed. Oliver Impey and Arthur MacGregor. Oxford: Clarendon Press, 1985. 76–87.

Semler, L. E. *The English Mannerist Poets and the Visual Arts.* Madison and Teaneck: Fairleigh Dickinson University Press, 1998.

——. "Robert Herrick, the Human Figure, and the English Mannerist Aesthetic." *Studies in English Literature, 1500–1900* 35 (1995): 105–21.

Sessions, William, ed. *Francis Bacon's Legacy of Texts.* New York: AMS Press, 1990.

Shapin, Steven. "The House of Experiment in Seventeenth-Century England." In *The Scientific Enterprise in Early Modern Europe: Readings from Isis,* ed. Peter Dear. Chicago: University of Chicago Press, 1997. 273–304.

——. "'A Scholar and a Gentleman': The Problematic Identity of the Scientific Practitioner in Early Modern England." *History of Science* 29 (1991): 279–355.

——. *The Scientific Revolution.* Chicago: University of Chicago Press, 1996.

——. *A Social History of Truth: Civility and Science in Seventeenth-Century England.* Chicago: University of Chicago Press, 1994.

Shapin, Steven and Simon Schaffer. *Leviathan and the Air-Pump: Hobbes, Boyle, and the Experimental Life.* Princeton, N.J.: Princeton University Press, 1985.

Shapiro, Barbara. *A Culture of Fact.* Ithaca, N.Y.: Cornell University Press, 2000.

——. "History and Natural History in Sixteenth- and Seventeenth-Century England." In *English Scientific Virtuosi in the 16th and 17th Centuries,* ed. Shapiro and Robert G. Frank. Berkeley: University of California Press, 1979.

Sharpe, Kevin. "Introduction: Rewriting Sir Robert Cotton." In *Sir Robert Cotton as Collector: Essays on an Early Stuart Courtier and His Legacy,* ed. C. J. Wright. London: British Library, 1997. 1–39.

——. *The Personal Rule of Charles I.* New Haven, Conn.: Yale University Press, 1992.

——. *Sir Robert Cotton, 1586–1631: History and Politics in Early Modern England.* Oxford: Oxford University Press, 1979.

Shelton, Anthony Alan. "Cabinets of Transgression: Renaissance Collections and the Incorporation of the New World." In *The Cultures of Collecting*, ed. John Elsner and Roger Cardinal. Cambridge, Mass.: Harvard University Press, 1994. 177–203.

Simpson, A. D. C. "Newton's Telescope and the Cataloguing of the Royal Society's Repository." *Notes and Records of the Royal Society of London* 38 (1984): 187–214.

Slights, William W. E. "The Edifying Margins of Renaissance English Books." *Renaissance Quarterly* 42 (1989): 682–716.

Smuts, R. Malcolm. "Art and the Material Culture of Majesty in Early Stuart England." In *The Stuart Court and Europe*, ed. Smuts. Cambridge: Cambridge University Press, 1996. 86–112.

——. *Court Culture and the Origins of a Royalist Tradition in Early Stuart England.* Philadelphia: University of Pennsylvania Press, 1987.

Snider, Alvin. *Origin and Authority in Seventeenth-Century England.* Toronto: University of Toronto Press, 1994.

Solomon, Julie Robin. *Objectivity in the Making: Francis Bacon and the Politics of Inquiry.* Baltimore: Johns Hopkins University Press, 1998.

——. "'To Know, To Fly, To Conjure': Situating Baconian Science at the Juncture of Early Modern Modes of Reading." *Renaissance Quarterly* 44 (1991): 513–58.

Spurdens, William Tylney. "Particulars of the Hundred of Tunstead." *Norfolk Archaeology* 3 (1852): 90–91.

Stallybrass, Peter. "Patriarchal Territories: The Body Enclosed." In *Rewriting the Renaissance: The Discourses of Sexual Difference in Early Modern Europe*, ed. Margaret W. Ferguson, Maureen Quilligan, and Nancy J. Vickers. Chicago: University of Chicago Press, 1986. 123–42.

——. "'Wee feaste in our Defense': Patrician Carnival in Early Modern England and Robert Herrick's *Hesperides*." *English Literary Renaissance* 16 (1986): 234–52.

——. "Worn Worlds: Clothes and Identity on the Renaissance Stage." In *Subject and Object in Renaissance Culture*, ed. Margreta de Grazia, Maureen Quilligan, and Stallybrass. Cambridge: Cambridge University Press, 1996. 289–320.

Stallybrass, Peter and Allon White. *The Politics and Poetics of Transgression.* Ithaca, N.Y.: Cornell University Press, 1986.

Stearns, Raymond Phineas. "James Petiver, Promoter of Natural Science, c. 1663–1718." *Proceedings of the American Antiquarian Society* 62 (1952): 243–365.

Stewart, Alan. *Close Readers: Humanism and Sodomy in Early Modern England.* Princeton, N.J.: Princeton University Press, 1997.

Stewart, Susan. *On Longing: Narratives of the Miniature, the Gigantic, the Souvenir, the Collection*. Durham, N.C.: Duke University Press, 1993.

Stone, Lawrence. *The Crisis of the Aristocracy, 1558–1641*. Abridged ed. Oxford: Oxford University Press, 1967.

———. *The Family, Sex and Marriage in England, 1500–1800*. Abridged ed. Harmondsworth: Penguin, 1984.

Stoye, John. *English Travellers Abroad, 1604–1667*. Rev. ed. New Haven, Conn.: Yale University Press, 1989.

Strong, Roy. *The Renaissance Garden in England*. London: Thames and Hudson, 1979.

Sturdy, David. "The Tradescants at Lambeth." *Journal of Garden History* 2 (1982): 1–16.

Sturdy, David and Martin Henig. *The Gentle Traveller: John Bargrave, Canon of Canterbury and His Collection*. Abingdon: Abbey Press, 1983.

Sullivan, Garrett A. *The Drama of Landscape: Land, Property, and Social Relations on the Early Modern Stage*. Stanford, Calif.: Stanford University Press, 1998.

Summers, Claude J. "Herrick's Political Counterplots." *Studies in English Literature, 1500–1900* 25 (1985): 165–82.

———. "Herrick's Political Poetry: The Strategies of His Art." In *"Trust to Good Verses": Herrick Tercentenary Essays*, ed. Roger B. Rollin and J. Max Patrick. Pittsburgh: University of Pittsburgh Press, 1978. 171–83.

Swann, Marjorie. "Cavalier Love: Fetishism and Its Discontents." *Literature and Psychology* 42 (1996): 15–35.

———. "Marriage, Celibacy, and Ritual in Robert Herrick's *Hesperides*." *Philological Quarterly* 76 (1997): 19–45.

———. "The Politics of Fairylore in Early Modern English Literature." *Renaissance Quarterly* 53 (2000): 449–73.

———. "Refashioning Society in Ben Jonson's *Epicoene*." *Studies in English Literature, 1500–1900* 38 (1998): 297–315.

Thirsk, Joan. "Agricultural Innovations and Their Diffusion." In *The Agrarian History of England and Wales*, vol. 5.2, ed. Thirsk. Cambridge: Cambridge University Press, 1985. 533–89.

———. *Economic Policy and Projects: The Development of a Consumer Society in Early Modern England*. Oxford: Clarendon Press, 1978.

Thomas, Nicholas. *Entangled Objects: Exchange, Material Culture, and Colonialism in the Pacific*. Cambridge, Mass: Harvard University Press, 1991.

Tiersten, Lisa. "Redefining Consumer Culture: Recent Literature on Consumption and the Bourgeoisie in Western Europe." *Radical History Review* 57 (1993): 116–59.

Toliver, Harold. *Lyric Provinces in the English Renaissance.* Columbus: Ohio State University Press, 1985.

Trevor-Roper, Hugh. *Religion, the Reformation, and Social Change.* 3rd ed. London: Secker and Warburg, 1984.

Tribble, Evelyn B. *Margins and Marginality: The Printed Page in Early Modern England.* Charlottesville: University Press of Virginia, 1993.

Vickers, Michael. "Greek and Roman Antiquities in the Seventeenth Century." In *Origins of Museums,* ed. Oliver Impey and Arthur MacGregor. Oxford: Clarendon Press, 1985. 223–31.

Wagner, Anthony Richard. *English Genealogy.* 2nd ed. Oxford: Clarendon Press, 1972.

Wall, Wendy. *The Imprint of Gender: Authorship and Publication in the English Renaissance.* Ithaca, N.Y.: Cornell University Press, 1993.

Wallace, Anthony F. C. *The Social Context of Innovation.* Princeton, N.J.: Princeton University Press, 1982.

Warner, Michael. *The Letters of the Republic: Publication and the Public Sphere in Eighteenth-Century America.* Cambridge, Mass.: Harvard University Press, 1990.

Warwick, Genevieve. *The Arts of Collecting: Padre Sebastiano Resta and the Market for Drawings in Early Modern Europe.* Cambridge: Cambridge University Press, 2000.

Wayne, Don E. *Penshurst: The Semiotics of Place and the Poetics of History.* Madison: University of Wisconsin Press, 1984.

Webster, Charles. *The Great Instauration: Science, Medicine and Reform, 1626–1660.* London: Duckworth, 1975.

———. "The Origins of the Royal Society." *History of Science* 6 (1967): 106–28.

Welch, Martin. "The Ashmolean as Described by Its Earliest Visitors." In *Tradescant's Rarities,* ed. Arthur MacGregor. Oxford: Clarendon Press, 1983. 59–69.

———. "The Foundation of the Ashmolean Museum." In *Tradescant's Rarities,* ed. Arthur MacGregor. Oxford: Clarendon Press, 1983. 40–58.

———. *The Tradescants and the Foundation of the Ashmolean Museum.* Oxford: Ashmolean Museum, 1978.

Weld, Charles Richard. *History of the Royal Society, with Memoirs of the Presidents.* 2 vols. London: John W. Parker, 1848.

Wheeler, Harvey. "Francis Bacon's *New Atlantis*: The 'Mould' of a Lawfinding Commonwealth." In *Francis Bacon's Legacy of Texts,* ed. William Sessions. New York: AMS Press, 1990. 291–310.

Whigham, Frank. "Elizabethan Aristocratic Insignia." *Texas Studies in Language and Literature* 27 (1985): 325–53.

Whitaker, Katie. "The Culture of Curiosity." In *Cultures of Natural History,* ed.

N. Jardine, J. A. Secord, and E. C. Spary. Cambridge: Cambridge University Press, 1996. 75–90.

———. "Curiosi and Virtuosi: Gentlemanly Culture, Experimental Philosophy, and Political Life in England, 1620–1685." Ph.D. dissertation, Cambridge University, 1997.

Whitney, Charles C. "Merchants of Light: Science as Colonization in the *New Atlantis*." In *Francis Bacon's Legacy of Texts*, ed. William Sessions. New York: AMS Press, 1990. 255–68.

Wilding, Michael. *Dragons Teeth: Literature in the English Revolution*. Oxford: Oxford University Press, 1987.

Wilks, Timothy. "The Picture Collection of Robert Carr, Earl of Somerset (c. 1587–1645), Reconsidered." *Journal of the History of Collections* 1 (1989): 167–77.

Williams, Raymond. *The Country and the City*. London: Hogarth, 1973; repr. 1985.

———. *Marxism and Literature*. Oxford: Oxford University Press, 1977; repr. 1992.

Williamson, Tom and Liz Bellamy. *Property and Landscape: A Social History of Land Ownership and the English Countryside*. London: George Philip, 1987.

Wood, Paul B. "Methodology and Apologetics: Thomas Sprat's *History of the Royal Society*." *The British Journal for the History of Science* 15 (1980): 1–26.

Woodward, Daniel. "Herrick's Oberon Poems." *Journal of English and Germanic Philology* 64 (1965): 270–84.

Woolf, D. R. "The Dawn of the Artifact: The Antiquarian Impulse in England, 1500–1730." *Studies in Medievalism* 4 (1992): 5–35.

———. *The Idea of History in Early Stuart England*. Toronto: University of Toronto Press, 1990.

Wormald, B. H. G. *Francis Bacon: History, Politics, and Science, 1561–1626*. Cambridge: Cambridge University Press, 1993.

Wright, C. J., ed. *Sir Robert Cotton as Collector: Essays on an Early Stuart Courtier and His Legacy*. London: British Library, 1997.

Wrightson, Keith. "The Social Order of Early Modern England: Three Approaches." In *The World We Have Gained: Histories of Population and Social Structure*, ed. Lloyd Bonfield, Richard M. Smith and Wrightson. New York: Blackwell, 1986. 177–202.

Youings, Joyce. *Sixteenth-Century England*. Harmondsworth: Penguin, 1984.

Zagorin, Perez. *Francis Bacon*. Princeton, N.J.: Princeton University Press, 1998.

Index

Browne, Sir Thomas, 2, 13, 99, 121–34, 148,
188, 195, 229n.117; *Garden of Cyrus*, 127;
Musaeum Clausum, 132–33, 135; *Pseudo-
doxia Epidemica*, 122, 126, 127; *Religio
Medici*, 121, 122, 127, 134; *Repertorium*,
122–25, 126, 127; *Urne-Buriall*, 125–32, 135,
143
Buckingham, George Villiers, 1st Duke of,
2, 17, 31, 33, 39, 145
Burton, Robert, 77
Burton, William, 104, 105–7, 115, 118, 128,
138, 195
Bushell, Thomas, 75
Bysshe, Sir Edward, 48

Cabot, Sebastian, 23
Camden, William, 13, 99, 102–3, 104, 107,
110–11, 114–15, 130, 134, 148, 171, 173, 174,
195
Campbell, Thomas, 127
Canterbury Cathedral, 117
Carew, Richard, 13, 99, 103–4, 105, 118, 128,
138, 195
Carew, Thomas, 145–46, 177, 179, 181,
231n.156
Cartwright, William, 161–62, 177
Cary, Lucius, 161, 177
Castiglione, Baldassarre, 26
Catalogues. *See* Texts, catalogues of
collections
Cavendish, William, 177
Cecil, William, Lord Burghley, 62, 63, 97
Cecils, Earls of Salisbury, 29–31, 34
Ceremonialism, 115, 116, 126, 127, 228n.78
Charles I, 2, 11, 16–17, 18, 22, 31, 32, 39, 74,
113, 121, 146
Charles II, 39, 40, 44, 51, 126, 184
Charleton, Walter, 83, 132
Charleton, William. *See* Courten, William
Chartier, Roger, 28, 166
Chatsworth, 147
Childrey, Joshua, 134–35
Chorography, 13, 97, 98, 99–107, 108, 113,
114–15, 118, 119–20, 123, 134–43, 148, 195
Civil War, 32, 40, 81, 99, 113–21, 135–36, 150,
182
Cleveland, John, 208n.70

Clifford, James, 8
Coiro, Ann Baynes, 182
Cole, William, 86
Collecting: art, 2, 7, 16–19, 21–22; definition
of, 6; and elite display, 12, 16–22, 29, 31, 71,
78–79, 194; and identity of collector, 8, 14,
16, 35, 46, 78, 85, 96, 177, 178, 194–95, 200,
220n.133; theories of, 6–8, 203n.33; and
travel, 22–24, 26–27; and wonder, 24, 26.
See also Texts
Collection: arrangement of objects in, 29,
207n.57; concepts of, 11, 109–10, 195, 198,
200 definition of, 1; identity of visitors
to, 27, 37, 43, 85, 200. *See also* Curiosity
cabinets
Collector: definition of, 1; posthumous
identity of, 46, 53, 54, 86, 178, 179, 197–
98. *See also* Authorship; Collecting, and
identity of collector; Texts
College of Physicians, 39, 76, 81
Columbus, Christopher, 23, 71
Colwall, Daniel, 84–86, 87 fig.
Consumer culture, early modern, 5–6, 22–
23
Cook, Harold J., 57
Cope, Sir Walter, 2–3, 24, 30
Cormack, Lesley B., 107
Cosin, John, 116
Cotton, Charles, 147
Cotton, Sir Robert, 3, 110, 112, 113, 198, 199
Country house poems, 13, 99, 145–48
Country houses, 118, 138–40, 141, 142–43,
143–48
Courten, William, 196
Coventry, Henry, 180
Cowley, Abraham, 82
Crane, Mary Thomas, 154
Cressy, David, 114
Cultural materialism, 203n.45
Curiosity, 76–77, 78, 89; and curiosity
books, 79–80
Curiosity cabinets, 2, 23, 25, 26, 60, 76–77,
87, 89

Daston, Lorraine J., 23, 60, 77
De Critz, Sara, 50
Dee, John, 3

De Grazia, Margreta, 166
Dering, Sir Edward, 117
De Vic, Sir Henry, 40, 42
D'Ewes, Sir Simonds, 62, 117
Digby, Kenelm, 177
Dioscorides, 58
Dodsworth, Roger, 229n.103
Donne, John, 133, 184
Drayton, Michael, 181
Drummond, William, 160–61
Dryden, John, 161
Dugdale, Sir William, 13, 48, 99, 118–21,
   122, 123, 128, 130, 135, 138, 143, 148, 195,
   229n.103
Duncan, Carol, 7, 199
Dutton, Richard, 158, 163, 168, 176–77

Eamon, William, 77
Edward VI, 115
Eliot, T. S., 182, 183
Elizabeth I, 18, 62, 63, 115
Elliott, J. H., 58
Elsky, Martin, 64
Elyot, Sir Thomas, 153–54
Erasmus, Desiderius, 153, 154
Essay in Defence of the Female Sex, An, 79,
   220n.146
Estate maps, 100–101, 102
Euripides, 158
Evelyn, John, 1, 2, 4, 22, 23, 24, 30, 45, 46,
   49, 76–77, 80, 84, 117

Fairfax, Thomas, Lord, 117
Fairies, popular concepts of, 241n.175
Fane, Mildmay, 146
Faulkner, Robert K., 70
Feather, John, 151
Ferdinand II, Archduke, 19
Findlen, Paula, 24
Fish, Stanley, 174
Ford, John, 180
Foucault, Michel, 7, 57, 151–52
Fowler, Alastair, 146, 181, 183
Frobisher, Martin, 23
Fuller, Thomas, 42
Fumerton, Patricia, 9, 184
Funerary monuments, 109, 112, 113–17, 119,

120–21, 122–25, 129, 136, 190, 193, 227n.69,
   228n.71

Gardening, 29–31, 58
Gerard, John, 25, 209n.93
Gesner, Konrad, 57, 58, 213n.12
Godolphin, Sidney, 177, 180
Goldthwaite, Richard A., 6
Grafton, Anthony, 131
Grassby, Richard, 36
Gray, Henry, Earl of Kent, 145–46
Greenblatt, Stephen, 25, 207n.49
Grew, Nehemiah, 84, 85, 87 fig., 88 fig., 89,
   196
Guibbory, Achsah, 126

Habermas, Jürgen, 199
Hall, Joseph, 117, 123, 124, 183, 229n.117
Hamilton, James, 1st Viscount Clandeboye,
   195
Handel, George Frideric, 197
Handler, Richard, 159
Harleian manuscripts, 198, 199, 242n.14
Hartlib, Samuel, 76
Hatfield House, 29–30
Hatton, Christopher, Lord, 121
Heal, Felicity, 135
Helgerson, Richard, 8, 34, 105, 163
Henrietta Maria, Queen, 11, 31
Henry, Prince of Wales, 2
Henry VIII, 115, 154
Herbert, George, 184
Herendeen, W. H., 175
Herrick, Robert, 14, 146, 149, 150, 152, 181–
   93, 177, 195; "*The Argument of his Book,*"
   186–88; *Hesperides,* 14, 150, 181, 182–93;
   "*His Poetrie his Pillar,*" 190; "*To* Julia,"
   192; "*Upon Madam* Ursly," 188; *Noble
   Numbers,* 189, 240n.163; "Oberons *Pal-
   ace,*" 188–89
Hinman, Robert B., 183, 187
Hodgson, William, 157
Hollar, Wenceslaus, 39, 81
Holmes, Clive, 135
Hooke, Robert, 4, 49, 82, 86, 87, 89
Hooper-Greenhill, Eilean, 7, 20
Horace, 157, 158

Acknowledgments

Friends and colleagues have helped me immeasurably as I worked on this book. I have been privileged to join a department with great strengths in both early modern literature and the mentoring of junior faculty. Richard F. Hardin has made many acute suggestions about this project throughout its development, and during his term as Chair of the Department of English at the University of Kansas, he was unstintingly supportive of my research. David M. Bergeron took my prospectus—and its author—in hand at a critical time. Dennis Quinn shared his work on Ben Jonson and "curiosity" with me; Margaret Arnold has provided many thoughtful comments in our conversations together.

I have been grateful to receive assistance from outside my own department as well. Achsah Guibbory and Arthur F. Marotti painstakingly read the manuscript in its entirety and gave me invaluable suggestions for improvement. Geraldo de Sousa generously offered me much useful guidance, all the while buoying me up with his enthusiasm for my project. John Carey, Susan M. Pearce, and Valerie Wayne provided constructive feedback and encouragement. Dympna Callaghan, Luis Corteguera, and Jonathan Gil Harris kindly gave a first-time author good counsel. Matt Lindaman aided me with material in German. James Helyar assisted with obtaining illustrations. And Jerry Singerman, my editor at the University of Pennsylvania Press, has been a marvel of helpfulness and efficiency.

I would also like to express my gratitude to the organizations that have provided financial support for my research. The Rocky Mountain Modern Language Association (RMMLA) awarded me a Huntington Library/ RMMLA Fellowship, allowing me to spend a most productive month at the Huntington Library. The College of Liberal Arts and Sciences at the University of Kansas awarded me two summer stipends from the Humanities General Research Fund. And a Faculty Travel Grant from the Hall Center for the Humanities at the University of Kansas enabled me to spend time at the Public Record Office in London.

I must acknowledge more personal debts as well. Without the unceasing support of my husband, William M. Tsutsui, I could not have completed this book: he has read every draft of every chapter, helped me to clarify my arguments and prose, taken over all the household chores for months at a time, and, through everything, managed to keep us both laughing. Finally, I wish to thank the faculty members of the English Department at Queen's University, Kingston, Ontario, with whom I was fortunate enough to study as an undergraduate. Without them, I would never have embarked on the path that led to the writing of this book.